# ROOM FULL OF MIRRORS

ALSO BY
# CHARLES R. CROSS

*Heavier Than Heaven: A Biography of Kurt Cobain*

# ROOM FULL
# OF MIRRORS

A BIOGRAPHY OF **JIMI** HENDRIX

## CHARLES R. CROSS

NEW YORK

Library of Congress Cataloging-in-Publication Data

Cross, Charles R.
Room full of mirrors : a biography of Jimi Hendrix / Charles R. Cross.—1st ed.
p.    cm.
ISBN 1-4013-0028-6
1. Hendrix, Jimi. 2. Rock musicians—United States—Biography. I. Title.
ML410.H476C76    2005
787.87'166'092—dc22
[B]    2005046362

Hyperion books are available for special promotions and premiums.
For details, contact Michael Rentas, Assistant Director, Inventory
Operations, Hyperion, 77 West 66th Street, 11th floor,
New York, New York 10023, or call 212-456-0133.

FIRST EDITION

10  9  8  7  6  5  4  3  2  1

*For My Father*
*who during my boyhood*
*put an arm around my shoulder*
*and read me*
*"Prince Valiant" comics*

# CONTENTS

# AUTHOR'S NOTE

Biographers often spend time in graveyards copying down epitaphs, but rarely do they stand by watching a cemetery worker unearth a lost grave with a shovel, as was my providence in the course of writing this book. The rediscovery of the grave of Jimi Hendrix's mother was the most chilling moment in the four years it took to write *Room Full of Mirrors*: It was also unexpected. It occurred only because I simply couldn't believe that Greenwood Memorial Park had no exact location for Lucille Hendrix Mitchell's grave, and I pestered the cemetery's office until they finally sent a worker—armed with a shovel and an ancient map—to search the rows of decaying headstones. Biographers who choose deceased subjects are all gravediggers in a way, with a bit of Dr. Frankenstein thrown in; we seek to bring our subjects back to life, if only temporarily, in the pages of a book. Usually our goal is to animate our characters; rarely are we searching for final remains and ancient caskets. Nothing can prepare one for the moment of standing in a muddy graveyard, watching aghast as a groundskeeper pushes a shovel into the ground like a sloppy archaeologist.

If there was justice in that particular adventure, it springs from the fact that in some twisted way this biography began in that same graveyard, three decades before. It was in Greenwood Memorial cemetery, a few miles south of Seattle, that I first came as a teenage fan to pay my

respects to one of music's legends. Like any other pilgrim, I couldn't
visit Jimi Hendrix's grave without the lyrics to my favorite songs—
"Purple Haze," "Wind Cries Mary," Jimi's brilliant take of Dylan's "All
Along the Watchtower"—running through my memory. Dog-eared albums by the Jimi Hendrix Experience were the soundtrack for my
youth, as they were to a whole generation. My father heard enough of
*Electric Ladyland* through the walls of my childhood home that he knew
the exact moment to pound on my door—before Jimi hit the first fuzz-
box pedal.

   As a teenager standing by that grave, I knew only small details of
Jimi's history, but his was a life so outrageous, and lived to such an extreme, that it was ripe for mythologizing. Many of the 1970s press reports I read as a kid turned Hendrix into a god of the electric guitar,
and that icon status stripped away his humanity. He became, as he was
on a poster on my wall, an image in black light, sporting a larger-than-
life Afro, complete with halo. He seemed unknowable, so foreign that
he might as well have been from another planet. Some of that mystery
came from the genius of his playing—which, decades later, has never
been matched—and some was a haze of record company–created hype.

   This book is my four-year, 325-interview effort to crack that code
and to turn that black-light poster image into a portrait of a man. Although I began actual work on this book in 2001, it has been writing itself in the back of my mind ever since my first graveside visit in the
seventies. As a writer who specializes in Northwest music, I have always
sensed Hendrix looming as a subject to be faced one day, just as an aspiring actor knows that Shakespeare's canon awaits.

   My own first writing about Jimi came in the early 1980s, when an
effort began to construct a Seattle memorial. Though there were some
grand ideas for what might be appropriate—a public park was suggested, or renaming a street—the memorial became mired in the eighties "Just Say No" political furor over drugs. One television commentator
argued that to honor Jimi in any way was to glamorize "a drug addict."
Those hysterics derailed the initial effort, and the compromise memorial that resulted was a "heated rock" with Jimi's name attached, set in

the African savannah section of the Seattle zoo. That spurred me to write a magazine piece in which I called the heated rock racist, xenophobic, and evidence that musical heritage and African American culture were disregarded in predominantly white Seattle. The zoo rock—which remains today, the heating element broken last I checked—made Jimi Hendrix's grave even more important as a tour stop, since few thought a zoo was an appropriate place to mourn or honor Jimi.

I first met Jimi's father, Al Hendrix, in the late 1980s and interviewed him on several occasions about his son's legacy and history. One of my first questions to Al was about Jimi's grave: Why did rock's best-known left-handed guitarist have an etching of a right-handed guitar on his tombstone? Al said it was a mistake by the monument makers. Al was not a detail-oriented guy, particularly when it came to his late son's history.

Al was kind enough to invite me to his home, which itself was something of a roadside museum to Jimi. No parent wants to bury a child, and it was Al's unkind destiny to outlive his firstborn by three decades. The walls of his house were covered with gold record awards and photo enlargements of Jimi. There, among family photos of Jimi as a baby or in an army uniform, were several images that belong in any sixties photo collage: Jimi burning his guitar onstage at the Monterey Pop Festival; Jimi with the white-fringed jacket onstage at Woodstock; Jimi in his butterfly velvet suit onstage at the Isle of Wight. There were a few pictures of Jimi's brother, Leon, on the wall, and, bizarrely, a giant painting of Al's deceased German shepherd. On a basement wall was an image familiar to me—the same black-light poster of a godlike Jimi that I owned as an adolescent.

I never asked Al Hendrix why Jimi's mother's grave had been lost for almost fifty years, and Al died in 2002. In the several years *Room Full of Mirrors* took to complete, at least five of my interview subjects have passed away, including Experience bass player Noel Redding. I interviewed Noel on almost a dozen different occasions, but it was nonetheless sobering to realize after his sudden death in May 2003 that my conversation with him two weeks prior was his last telling of his own story before his passing. There were moments in writing this book when I sensed that the history of Jimi's era was slowly slipping away, and that fragility made the extensive research all the more delicate and imperative.

Still, there were conversations I had and places I visited where Jimi Hendrix seemed positively vibrant and almost breathing. On Seattle's Jackson Street, the historical center of Northwest African American nightlife—amid storefronts that five decades ago were clubs that hosted local talent like Ray Charles, Quincy Jones, and Jimi—one can find pieces of a life still freshly remembered. Just down the street from Twenty-third Avenue, sitting on blocks in an empty lot, is the house Jimi grew up in; it has been saved with an eye to future preservation. Stop by the flower shop on the corner, and the ladies behind the counter will remember Jimi from Leschi Elementary School. Across the street at a Starbucks, there's a gray-haired gentleman sipping coffee every morning who once danced the jitterbug with Jimi's mother, Lucille. And in the retirement home on the corner, eighty-eight-year-old Dorothy Harding sits in a wheelchair and tells stories of being Jimi's babysitter and of the stormy night he was born.

In Seattle's black community, most people knew, and know, Jimi Hendrix as "Buster," his family nickname. In the text herein, he is frequently called by that name, particularly by family. I've also taken the narrative liberty of using the spelling "Jimi" throughout Hendrix's life for consistency and to avoid confusion with Jimi's best childhood friend, Jimmy Williams, who shows up in this history often. Hendrix did not use the spelling "Jimi" until he was twenty-two, but even then he remained "Buster" to most of those who knew him in Seattle.

Searching for Buster led me to Jackson Street many times, and also to shadowy corners of London, San Francisco, Los Angeles, Harlem, Greenwich Village, and other points across the globe. It put me in beer-strewn dance halls in northern England where the Experience once played, and in dank Seattle basements where a teenage Jimi Hendrix practiced guitar with neighborhood boys. It led me to dusty census records, and to graveyards like Greenwood Memorial, where I watched when the shovel finally hit Lucille Hendrix's welfare grave marker—a brick really—which had been overgrown by a foot of soil. As that dirt slid off the shovel, the spot of Jimi's mother's grave was uncovered for the first time in several decades. When Jimi's brother, Leon, first saw the marker that indicated where his mother was buried, he wept. Leon had never known the exact location of his mother's remains.

In Al Hendrix's basement, there was another piece of Jimi Hendrix memorabilia that was buried in a way; it was stuck back in a corner and only pulled out for the faithful. It was a two-by-four-foot mirror that Jimi had created. Al was never very good on dates, but Jimi's brother, Leon, also attributed the piece to Jimi, created sometime in 1969. "It was in Jimi's apartment in New York," Leon recalled, "and it was shipped back to my dad after Jimi died." Inside the frame sit fifty-odd pieces of a shattered mirror, set in clay in the exact position they would have held upon the breaking of the mirror. The shards all point toward the center, where an unbroken plate-size circle rests. "This," Al Hendrix would say when he pulled the Salvador Dalí–esque art out of a cupboard, "was Jimi's 'Room Full of Mirrors.'"

"Room Full of Mirrors" was the title of a song Hendrix first began writing in 1968. He wrote several early lyric drafts of the tune and recorded a couple of takes of it. The song was never officially released during Jimi's lifetime, but Hendrix considered it for inclusion in what would have been his fourth studio album. As this particular song gives evidence, Jimi had an extraordinary sense of self-awareness and an uncanny ability to use music to express emotional truths. While audiences at Hendrix concerts clamored for his guitar theatrics on hits like "Purple Haze," Jimi, in private, was drawn more toward pensive and reflective songs such as "Room Full of Mirrors" or playing the blues standards he'd grown up on.

The song "Room Full of Mirrors" tells the story of a man trapped in a world of self-reflection so powerful it haunts him even in his dreams. He is liberated after smashing the mirrors, and wounded from the shattered glass, he seeks an "angel" who can give him freedom. Holding the physical manifestation of this concept—the broken mirror artwork that Jimi's father kept in his basement—one cannot help but think of the deep complexity of the man who created this song, and think of the day Jimi Hendrix stared at fifty slivers of his own reflection in this piece of art. "All I could see," he sang in the song, "was me."

*—Charles R. Cross*
*Seattle, Washington*
*April 2005*

# ROOM FULL
# OF MIRRORS

LIVERPOOL, ENGLAND
*April 9, 1967*

*"I used to live in a room full of mirrors,*
*All I could see was me."*

—JIMI HENDRIX, "Room Full of Mirrors"

"SORRY, MATES, WE can't serve your sort in here. We got rules, you know."

Those words from behind the bar came from the lips of a crusty-looking old salt whose hands shook with a palsy as he spoke. Upon issuing his warning, he turned away and began drawing another patron a pint. His initial look had been so quick—nothing more than a seasoned flick of an eye—that the two men standing before him had no idea why they were unable to get a drink. It was odd, as this was the kind of prototypical English pub that would serve anyone: children, men already too drunk to stand up, escaped convicts still in shackles if they had a pound note in their hand.

One of the men denied service was twenty-one-year-old Noel Redding, bass player in the Jimi Hendrix Experience. Noel had been born in Folkestone, a city in southeastern England, and he had already spent a lifetime in pubs and around cranky publicans. He had never been turned down when ordering a drink, except after closing time. But this wasn't closing time, and Redding couldn't imagine what might have made the bartender respond so. "I actually considered the thought," Noel recalled years later, "that this chap hated our single 'Hey Joe.'"

Both Noel and his companion, Jimi Hendrix, had purple scarves around their necks and sported huge translucent halos of frizzy hair. Noel wore bright violet bell-bottoms, while Jimi's tight trousers were made of wine red velvet. Jimi also had on a frilly pirate shirt that puffed out in the chest, and atop his jacket was a black cape. The only people who dressed like this were actors in an eighteenth-century drama, or rock stars. Still, both Noel and Jimi had looked plenty freaky in hundreds of other pubs and had never been turned down before. In London, it was usually the opposite: Once they were recognized, they were treated as royalty, as objects of adoration.

England was certainly falling in love with Jimi, who was twenty-four years old that year. During the six months he'd lived in Great Britain, he had been a guest of honor in many pubs, and even the beloved Paul McCartney had once bought him a pint. Jimi watched as legendary musicians he had long idolized—Eric Clapton, Pete Townshend, and the Rolling Stones' Brian Jones—had received him into their inner circle as a peer, and as a friend. The press trumpeted him as one of the rising stars of rock, calling him names like the "Wild Man of Borneo" and "The Black Elvis." Getting a pint between sets, as he and Noel were attempting to do, was only a problem when Jimi's numerous fans swarmed him. To avoid those very fans, many of whom found Jimi sexually irresistible, Noel and Jimi had chosen this off-the-beaten-track pub for a quick drink before their next set. They were in Liverpool, where the locals were partial to the hometown Beatles, of course, but not being served was unexpected for an ascending superstar anyplace in Britain. "It was your typical English pub," Noel noted. "It was filled with ship workers, shopkeepers, and the like."

Jimi's initial thought in the pub, according to what he later told Noel, was that he was being discriminated against because of his skin color. As an African American who had lived in the southern parts of the United States, Jimi knew what it was like to be denied service because of his race. He had often endured the prejudice of the "Jim Crow" South, the "white-only" drinking fountains, and other degradations. He once had the windows of his house in Nashville, Tennessee, shot out simply because he was black. He had spent three hardscrabble years performing on the Chitlin' Circuit—a route of juke joints, icehouses, and barrooms where rhythm-and-blues music was played primarily to African American audiences. Just to get to those gigs, traveling black musicians had to plan carefully in advance such things as finding food and using a toilet, simple services that were denied blacks in parts of white America. Soul legend Solomon Burke was on a Chitlin' Circuit bus tour with Jimi and recalled an incident when the band stopped at the only restaurant in a rural town. Knowing, as they did, the place would not serve African Americans, a white bass player in the entourage was enlisted to buy take-out food for the rest of the musicians. The white musician was just ten feet away from the bus when his to-go boxes began to slip, and Jimi scurried out to aid him. "The white guys who ran the place saw who the food was actually going to," Burke recalled. Hendrix and Burke watched in horror as the men came from behind the counter brandishing axes as weapons. "They took all the food and threw it on the ground," Burke said. "We didn't resist because we knew they would, and could, kill us and they'd probably have the sheriff on their side helping."

In England, Jimi had been free from most racial discrimination; he found that class and accent were the more obvious British social barometers. In the States, his ethnicity had been a career hindrance, particularly as he crossed genres and played outside the accepted color lines of rock and R&B. In England, though, his race and his American accent were novelties of sorts. As both a Yank and an African American, he was a unique outsider, and one who was revered for this status. "He was the first American black I'd ever met," Noel Redding recalled, "and that alone made him interesting." The musician Sting, who saw the 1967 Jimi Hendrix Experience tour as a teen, later wrote that the concert also represented "the first time I'd seen a black man."

Jimi's second impulse in the Liverpool pub that day was to wonder about his jacket. He was wearing an ancient military jacket that was a relic of the grand days of the British Empire. He had bought the cloak at a London flea market and it was fabulously ornate: There were sixty-three gold buttons on the breast; elaborate gold embroidery on the arms and center; and the coat had a collar that would have made anyone wearing it look a bit like a dandy. "That jacket had caused him problems before," recalled Kathy Etchingham, Jimi's girlfriend at the time. "These old pensioners would see this wild-looking black man walking down the street in this jacket, and they knew very well he hadn't been in the Hussars." English war vets of a certain age were quick to voice their disapproval of Jimi wearing the coat, and not having watched "Top of the Pops," they had no idea he was a rock star. Any conflicts the jacket caused, however, were usually quickly resolved when the eternally polite Jimi apologized, and mentioned that he was a recent vet of the 101st Airborne Division of the United States Army. This was enough to silence the old boys and to earn him a slap of gratitude on the back. Even in 1967 most in Britain recalled how the legendary 101st had parachuted into Normandy on D-day with the fearlessness of true heroes.

Hendrix did look heroic in the jacket. He was only five-foot-ten, but people frequently mistook him for being over six feet, at least in part because his gigantic Afro made him appear larger than life. His thin, angular frame, which was shaped like an inverted triangle, furthered this illusion; he had narrow hips, a small waist, but impossibly wide shoulders and arms. His fingers were abnormally long and sinuous, and like the rest of him, they were a rich caramel color. His bandmates jokingly called him "The Bat" because of his preference for covering his windows and sleeping during the day, but the nickname also fit his penchant for wearing capes, which furthered his superhero appearance. "When we walked down the streets in London," Kathy Etchingham recalled, "sometimes people would just stop and stare at him like he was some kind of apparition." He had wide, almond-shaped brown eyes that glistened when they caught the light. Jimi was immediately a favorite of British journalists, but the photographers positively adored him because he had the model-like ability of looking smashing from any angle, plus he had a softness of expression that helped every picture of him tell a story. Even in a medium as cool as a newspaper photograph, Jimi oozed a sexuality that seemed dangerous and exotic.

That glittering beauty meant nothing to the steely-eyed Liverpool barkeep and it did not earn Jimi a pint, despite repeated polite requests and several pound notes placed on the counter. Jimi might have considered informing the old gent about his blossoming fame, but his patience was waning. Though he was known for being quiet and well mannered, Jimi also had a fierce temper that would occasionally flare, particularly when fueled by alcohol, and heaven protect anyone in the way when it did. "When he got angry," Etchingham noted, "he blew up." At least in this pub, he'd yet to get a drink, which lessened the chance that he might throw the old man on the ground.

Finally, stuttering a bit, a tendency leftover from childhood that he still fell into when he was nervous, Jimi confronted the bartender. "Is it . . ." he said angrily, "is it because I'm black?"

The barkeep was quick and sure in his reply. "No, for God's sake, man! Didn't you read the sign on the door?" And with that the old man grabbed his bar towel and moved down to the other end of the bar, exasperated.

Once the possibility of racial prejudice was eliminated, an air of humor and levity returned to Jimi and Noel. They looked at each other with the grins of adolescent boys who had done something wrong and were waiting for it to be discovered. "We started to laugh," Noel recalled. "We had no idea what it was we'd done." Noel joked to Jimi that maybe in Liverpool you had to be a member of the Treegulls—Noel's nickname for the Beatles—to get a drink. Noel went outside to check the door; he saw two signs prominently thumbtacked. Above was a large poster for a circus, happening just up the road, and below was a handwritten sign that explained the reason Jimi and Noel had been barred from the pub. When Noel saw the second sign, he went into a laughing fit that momentarily brought him to the ground. This was one for the ages, Noel thought; this was one they'd be joking about aboard the band bus for months. "I thought," Noel recalled years later, "I couldn't wait until we could tell Mitch Mitchell this one—he'd never let us live it down." As he walked back into the pub to fill Jimi in, Noel found the barman and Jimi yelling at each other.

"I told you already, we can't serve you!" the barman insisted. "We've got rules." Noel moved to intervene, but the barkeep was heated up now and his lecture went on. "The sign on the door is very clear, and if we let one of you in, the whole goddamn place will be full of your sort, and that's no way to run a pub, no way at all. Having the circus here is bad enough for business. And the sign is very clear: 'No clowns allowed!'"

Noel recalled that it took Jimi several moments for the meaning of the words to sink in. Even after Noel whispered the explanation in Jimi's ear—"There's a circus up the street, and this chap doesn't want any clowns in here. He thinks we're *clowns*"—Jimi still seemed puzzled, almost stunned. Slowly this almost cosmic prank revealed itself to Jimi, and a huge, wide smile broke out over his face. He wasn't being kicked out of the pub because he was black, or wore a military jacket, or was too outrageous, or was dressed like a pirate, or wasn't a Beatle in Liverpool, though in some bent way it was all of that and more.

Jimi was the single most exciting rock star in Great Britain that spring; in just two months he would wear this same military jacket in his breakout American performance at the Monterey Pop Festival; following that show, he would be the hottest star in the world. Almost two months later to the day, Paul McCartney would hand Jimi a joint after a concert in London, slap him on the back, and say, "That was fucking great, man." But on this afternoon in a pub in McCartney's

Liverpool, Jimi couldn't get a pint of lager, no matter what he said. The barkeep was unconvinced that a pop star was sitting in front of him; he simply knew that this clown said he was with some kind of outfit called "The Experience." Clowns, particularly ones with Afros, the old man thought, were very, very bad for business.

# CHAPTER ONE

# BETTER THAN
# BEFORE

SEATTLE, WASHINGTON
*January 1875–November 1942*

*"Dear Al: Congratulations on your fine son. Mother and son are*
*well. Conditions lots better than before. Lucille sends love."*
—telegram from Delores Hall to Al Hendrix

JIMI HENDRIX WAS born the day after Thanksgiving, 1942. The healthy arrival of this eight-pound, eleven-ounce baby was seen by all as a true thanksgiving sign from God. When his aunt wired his father with the news, her short telegram included the line "Conditions lots better than before." That statement could serve as an epigraph for the larger history of the Hendrixes to that point, and, in an even wider context, as a wishful summation of the African American experience in the United States: Things had been bad for a long time, and perhaps this new generation could hope for an improvement and a more righteous world. Relatives on both sides of Jimi's family celebrated his birth as a new beginning. "He was the cutest baby you would ever want to see," recalled his aunt Delores Hall. "He was darling."

Jimi was born in the maternity ward of King County Hospital, later called Harborview, in Seattle, Washington. The hospital commanded a majestic view of the large natural harbor of Puget Sound. Seattle was slowly emerging as one of the major American port cities on the Pacific Coast and had a population of 375,000 in 1942. In the wartime years, it was a boomtown where shipyards cranked out navy vessels and the Boeing Airplane Company churned out the B-17 bombers that would win the war for the Allies. In 1942, the factories ran round-the-clock shifts, and a huge influx of laborers expanded the city and forever changed its racial demographics. In the 1900 census, there had been only 406 Seattle residents who reported themselves as black, about one half of 1 percent of the population. In the decade from 1940 to 1950, fueled by the war machine's need for labor and a large migration from the South, the city's population of African Americans ballooned to 15,666, and they became Seattle's largest racial minority.

Neither Jimi's mother nor father was part of the wartime migration, but World War II would nevertheless play a major role in the circumstances of their lives. At the time of Jimi's birth, his father, Al, was a twenty-three-year-old private in the U.S. Army, stationed at Fort Rucker, Alabama. Al had asked his commanding officer for paternity leave to visit Seattle, but he was denied furlough and jailed instead. His superiors told him he'd been imprisoned because they were convinced he would go AWOL to attend the birth. Al was in the stockade when the congratulatory telegram from his sister-in-law arrived. He later complained that white soldiers had been given leave in similar situations, but his complaints fell on deaf ears. Al would not meet his son until the boy was three years old.

Jimi's mother, Lucille Jeter Hendrix, was only seventeen when Jimi was born. Through an inopportune stroke of timing, Lucille found out she was pregnant the same week Al was drafted. They married on March 31, 1942, at the King County Courthouse in a ceremony performed by a justice of the peace, and they only lived together as man and wife for three days before Al was shipped out. The night before Al left, they partied at the Rocking Chair, a club where Ray Charles would later be discovered. Lucille was under the drinking age, but in

the wartime frenzy, that didn't matter to bartenders. The couple toasted
an uncertain future and Al's safe return from the service.

The circumstances of fate that gave the newly married couple their
first child when Al was three thousand miles away created a wound that
would forever fester in the marriage of Al and Lucille. Of course their
separation wasn't unusual in the turbulent time of World War II. Once
the Japanese attacked Pearl Harbor in December 1941, a harried madness developed in Seattle and other West Coast cities, where fear of a
Japanese assault was a backdrop to thousands of families being torn
apart. The day before Al and Lucille were married, Seattle became the
first city in the nation where Japanese Americans were gathered up and
sent to internment camps. Eventually, 12,892 persons of Japanese ancestry from Washington State were imprisoned, including friends and
neighbors of the couple.

Yet the relationship between Al and Lucille was strained by more
than just the turmoil of the war. Al was short but handsome, while Lucille had an extraordinary youthful beauty that turned heads when she
walked down the street. Other than their physical connection and a mutual love of dancing, they shared little to build a marriage on. Both had
come from backgrounds of extreme poverty, and Al left Seattle knowing that he would be able to do little to provide for his new wife and
child while overseas. Theirs had been a quick romance—a shotgun wedding, really—without the support of friends and family. As a teenage
mother-to-be, Lucille faced extreme challenges in the form of her age,
race, class, and economic situation. It was Lucille's very poverty that
helped breed a deep distrust in Al Hendrix that would cause him to
later raise questions of loyalty, fidelity, and paternity.

❦

PATERNITY AND BLOODLINE had been contentious issues in the
Hendrix family tree for centuries. The family history mirrored that of
many other slave descendants in that little of it was recorded in the an-

nals of history being written by whites. Jimi Hendrix would become one of the first black rock musicians to appeal to a largely white audience, but his own ethnic ancestry was multiracial and included a complex mix of Native Americans, African slaves, and white slave masters.

Jimi's maternal grandfather was Preston Jeter, born in Richmond, Virginia, on July 14, 1875. His mother had been a slave, and like many former slaves in Richmond, she continued in the same domestic position after the Civil War. Preston's father was his mother's former owner, though whether Preston was the result of rape or a consensual act—if such a thing can be possible in a slave–master relationship—is unknown. As a young man, Preston made the decision to leave the South after he witnessed a lynching. He headed for the Northwest, where he had heard conditions for blacks were better.

Preston was twenty-five when he arrived in Roslyn, Washington, a small mining town eighty miles east of Seattle in the Cascade Mountains. Unfortunately, he found riotous racial violence in Roslyn that mirrored the South, the result of mine management bringing in African Americans to break a strike by white miners. The county sheriff wrote the governor, warning, "There is a bitter feeling against the Negroes and . . . I fear there will be bloodshed." A number of racially motivated killings followed. "Murder is a regular thing," one town resident observed.

By 1908, African Americans had become a tolerated, if not an accepted, part of Roslyn's fabric. A photo from that year captures Preston among a group of black miners in front of the only saloon they were allowed to patronize, Big Jim E. Shepperson's Color Club. Still, racial intolerance remained high, and when a mine explosion killed forty-five men, including several African Americans, whites would not allow the black victims to be buried in the town graveyard. Eventually, twenty-four different cemeteries were designated in the town, each devoted to a single ethnicity or fraternal order.

After a decade in Roslyn, Preston left to work mines in Newcastle, Washington. By 1915, he was in Seattle, working as a landscaper. By then in his forties, he entertained hopes of finding a wife. Reading the *Seattle Republican,* he spotted an ad for a young woman looking for a husband.

❧

THE WOMAN IN the ad was Clarice Lawson, Jimi Hendrix's maternal grandmother. Clarice had been born in Little Rock, Arkansas, in 1894. Like many Arkansas African Americans, her ancestors included both slaves and Cherokees. Clarice would tell her children the U.S. government had hunted down her Cherokee forebears, until slaves hid them and, eventually, intermarried with them.

Clarice had four older sisters, and the quintet of Lawson daughters regularly traveled from their Arkansas home to the Louisiana Delta to pick cotton. On one of these trips, Clarice, who was twenty at the time, was raped. When Clarice later discovered she was pregnant, her sisters decided to take her west and quickly find her a husband. They picked Washington after hearing from railroad workers that the region offered greater opportunity for blacks.

In Seattle, they advertised for a husband, not mentioning Clarice's pregnancy. Preston Jeter responded, and though he was nineteen years older than Clarice, they began to date. When Clarice's sisters pressed him for marriage and gave him a sum of money as a dowry, he grew suspicious and broke off their relationship. Clarice had the child and it was put up for adoption. The sisters offered Preston more money if he would marry the now-grieving Clarice. He agreed, and they were wed in 1915. Though the marriage would last until Preston's death thirty years later, the unusual circumstances of their meeting would strain the relationship.

Both Preston and Clarice had come to the Northwest to start a life in a place where race was less an issue than it was elsewhere. To a degree, this was true in Seattle, which lacked the segregation of the white-only drinking fountains of the Jim Crow South. In the Northwest, however, African Americans encountered a less overt form of discrimination, but one that still limited opportunity. In Seattle, blacks lived almost exclusively in an area called the Central District, four square miles that contained some of the city's oldest, and most decrepit, homes. Outside of this neighborhood, landlords would rarely rent to African Americans, and many townships had laws banning real estate sales to nonwhites.

Although their housing options were limited, African Americans found some benefit in Seattle's de facto segregation. In the Central District, they developed a tight-knit community where ethnic pride was strong and neighborhood ties blossomed. "It was a small enough community that if you didn't know someone, you knew their family," recalled Betty Jean Morgan, a lifelong resident. The neighborhood was also home to Native Americans, as well as Chinese, Italian, German, Japanese, and Filipino immigrants; the local schools were filled with a patchwork of ethnicities. There were enough ethnic and religious minorities in the neighborhood—it was also the center of Jewish life in the city—that a multiculturalism developed that was unique at the time not only in Seattle but also in the entire United States. Historian Esther Hall Mumford titled her history of black Seattle *Calabash* in a nod to the African tradition of cooking in a pot big enough to feed the village, and that metaphor—a neighborhood inclusive and self-sufficient—was apt for Seattle's Central District in the first half of the twentieth century. Those strong social ties and a warm sense of inclusiveness would have a lasting impact on all who grew up within it.

Seattle's black community had its own newspapers, restaurants, shops, and most gloriously, its own entertainment district, centered on Jackson Street. There, nightclubs and gambling dens featured nationally known jazz and blues acts. So vibrant was the scene that one newspaper editor compared it to Chicago's State Street or Memphis's Beale Street. Though the Jackson Street clubs were not common stops for Preston and Clarice Jeter, this colorful and vibrant netherworld would be an important backdrop for their children's young adulthood and, eventually, for grandchild Jimi Hendrix.

∾〰∾

THE BIGGEST CHALLENGE to blacks in Seattle—and the one that threatened to supersede all others—was finding fair employment. African Americans were tolerated by white Seattle society in most situations, but the only professions open to blacks were service jobs as cooks, waiters, or railroad porters. In a pattern that was familiar, Preston Jeter found work as a longshoreman during a strike; it was a job normally held only by whites. Clarice found work as a domestic, a job that 84 percent of Seattle's African American women held in the 1910 census. Clarice, like most black mothers of the day, cared for white babies at the same time as she began to have children of her own.

Over the next ten years, Clarice would have eight children, two of whom would die in infancy and two who would be adopted out. Lucille, the youngest of the Jeter children, was born in 1925, eight weeks premature. Because of complications from a tumor, as well as postpartum depression, Clarice remained in the hospital for six months after Lucille's birth. Preston, then fifty years old and suffering from health problems of his own, couldn't care for the family, so Lucille's three sisters—Nancy, Gertrude, and Delores—initially raised the baby. The nurses brought her home on a day in December that featured a rare Seattle snowstorm. "They had to walk up the hill in front of our house very carefully with her," recalled Delores Hall, who was four at the time. "They put her in my arms and said, 'Be careful because this is your new sister.'"

The Jeters faced enormous challenges over the next few years. Clarice was in and out of the hospital, suffering from physical and mental health problems, and the children were sent to foster care with a big German family that lived on a small farm north of Greenlake. In this predominantly white area, they were frequently mistaken for Gypsies, another ethnic minority that was shunned by white Seattle.

When Lucille turned ten, the family was living together again in the Central District. As an adolescent, Lucille had remarkably beautiful eyes and a lithe frame. "She had long, thick, dark hair, which was straight, and a beautiful wide smile," said her best friend in junior high,

Loreen Lockett. Preston and Clarice were particularly protective of Lucille, who was fifteen before they allowed her to go to dances. Pretty and vivacious, Lucille drew attention even then. "She was a nice-looking girl and a very good dancer," recalled James Pryor. "She was very light-skinned with pretty hair. She could have passed." To "pass" was the African American vernacular for someone with a complexion light enough that they could pass in the world as white. To do so meant a con of sorts, but it opened up a world of employment options denied to most blacks. Even within the African American community at the time, lighter skin and straight hair were equated with beauty, and Lucille had both.

According to all accounts, fifteen-year-old Lucille was proper and a bit immature. She was also gifted with musical talent and could sing. Occasionally, she would enter amateur contests, and at one she won a five-dollar prize. Still, her greatest joy in life was to be on the dance floor with a good partner. One night in November 1941, Lucille stopped by a classmate's home on the way to a dance at Washington Hall. She had just turned sixteen and was in junior high. Like any schoolgirl, she was excited to be going to a concert, and the featured act that night was the legendary jazz pianist Fats Waller. A young man from Canada was visiting her friend. "Lucille," her classmate said, "meet Al Hendrix."

# CHAPTER TWO

# BUCKET OF BLOOD

VANCOUVER, BRITISH COLUMBIA
*1875–1941*

*"She worked at a place called the Bucket of Blood. There were
always cuttings down there, and fights. It was a tough place."*
—DOROTHY HARDING

WHEN JIMI HENDRIX first found fame in the late 1960s, his last
name was frequently misspelled in newspapers as "Hendricks." Hendrix
accepted this as part of show business, and it went along with numerous spellings of his first name. His family name had, in fact, been Hendricks until 1912, when his grandfather had shortened it to Hendrix.

Jimi's paternal family tree, like his maternal one, included ancestors who were slaves, slave owners, and Cherokees. Jimi's paternal
grandfather, Bertran Philander Ross Hendrix, was born in Urbana
City, Ohio, a year after the Civil War ended. He was born out of wed-
lock, and from a biracial coupling of his mother, a former slave, and a
white merchant who had once owned her. His mother named him after
the slave master, hoping the father would support the child, which
never occurred. When Bertran grew to adulthood, he took a job as a

stagehand with a Chicago vaudeville troupe. There, he met Nora Moore and the two married. Nora's great-grandmother was a full-blooded Cherokee. This bloodline, along with that of the Jeters, made Jimi Hendrix at least one-eighth Native American.

Nora and Bertran arrived in Seattle in 1909 when their all-black vaudeville troupe, the Great Dixieland Spectacle, came to perform at the Alaska–Yukon–Pacific Exposition at the University of Washington. They stayed for the summer, but eventually left for Vancouver, British Columbia, just north of the Washington border. Vancouver had even fewer minorities than Seattle, and with little demand for black vaudeville, Bertran found work as a laborer and servant. In Vancouver, the couple discovered a city that was so overwhelmingly white that they were oddities. They settled in Strathcona, the immigrant district that was also the center of bootlegging and prostitution and called the "square mile of sin" by locals.

Nora and Bertran had three children—Leon, Patricia, and Frank—in their first six years of marriage. In 1919, their fourth and last child was born, James Allen Hendrix, Jimi's father. Al, as he was always called, had six fingers on each hand at birth, which his mother considered a bad omen. She severed the extra digits by wrapping them with a tightened silk cord, though they grew back. As an adult, Al would sometimes scare Jimi's friends by showing them his extra miniature fingers, which sported tiny fingernails.

Like all black Canadian families, the Hendrixes struggled in an era when the best-paying jobs were reserved for whites. In 1922, Bertran lost a job as a bathroom attendant—considered one of the few jobs open to all races—after a local murder stirred up antiblack sentiment. He was finally hired as a steward at a golf course, a position he held until his death in 1934.

Bertran's death, and the early death of oldest son Leon, forced the family to survive on welfare payments from Canadian Relief, and eventually they lost their home. They moved in with Nora's new boyfriend in a ramshackle house on East Georgia Street. It was there, in a room he shared with his brother Frank and a boarder, where Al grew to adoles-

cence. One of his few luxuries was listening to "Midnight Prowl," a radio show that played the big-band hits of the day. When he was sixteen,
Al saw Duke Ellington perform and was photographed dancing at the
concert by a *Vancouver Sun* contributor. Seeing his picture in the paper
was one of the few thrills of Al's childhood.

As he grew into a man, Al regularly entered dance contests. He
would brag about how he could flip his partner in the air and, in a snazzy
move, slide her between his legs. Yet there were so few black women in
Canada—and dating a Caucasian woman in Vancouver was dangerous—
that Al felt adrift. He took a job at a neighborhood restaurant called the
Chicken Inn, which was a center of black culture in the city at the time.
There he would do dance routines between delivering meals, and he was
skilled enough that his dancing was regularly applauded.

When Al turned eighteen, he was offered an opportunity to box
for money. He was stocky and muscular, but even as an adult he was
only five-foot-six. The boxing promoter took him to Seattle's Crystal
Pool, where Al fought his first bout as a welterweight. He reached the
finals but lost in the championship, and found that the promise of a
paycheck had been a false lure. Worse than the defeat was his experience
at the Moore Hotel, where he and another black boxer were told that
the pool was "white only." He watched as the rest of the team swam.

Back in Vancouver, Al struck out everywhere he applied for a job.
He repeatedly sought work as a railroad porter but was told he was too
short, although there were no height requirements. He finally left
Canada for Seattle, hoping his chances would prove to be better there
and that the larger black population might offer him the opportunity of
finding a girlfriend.

He arrived in Seattle in 1940 with forty dollars in his pocket. His
first steady work was at the Ben Paris nightclub downtown, where he
bussed tables and shined shoes. Finally, he found work at an iron
foundry; it was hard physical labor but paid well. Al's only real joy at
the time came on the dance floor, where his worries would temporarily
lift. He had a brown zoot suit with white pinstripes, and over it he wore

a beige, knee-length, single-breasted coat. He was wearing that outfit on the night he first encountered sixteen-year-old Lucille Jeter.

∽᷈᷈᷈

LUCILLE WAS IN the ninth grade when she met Al, and though she was remarkably pretty, she was naive when it came to boys, and Al was her first boyfriend. His Canadian upbringing intrigued her, but it also alienated Al from some in Seattle's African American community. "People in Seattle were stuck-up about people from Canada," Delores Hall observed. Al's lack of acquaintances in Seattle would be an issue that would come up repeatedly for the couple: The fact that Lucille had many friends, and was so pretty, instilled a deep jealousy in Al. "Al was a very muscular guy," recalled James Pryor. "Everyone stayed away from Lucille because of him. He had a temper and he wasn't afraid to use it. If anyone did run around with her, they certainly didn't do it in public because Al would have killed them."

Al and Lucille had a few chaste dates, but it was an act of kindness and loyalty on Lucille's part that cemented their relationship. When Al suffered a hernia and was hospitalized, Lucille volunteered at the hospital as a candy striper. When Al was released, he began to formally court Lucille, visiting her parents regularly, as was the requirement of the day. Lucille's parents liked Al, but didn't take him seriously because they felt their daughter—at only sixteen—was too young to be deeply involved with a man.

Al lost his foundry job but found work at a pool hall. He was racking balls there when he heard that the Japanese had attacked Pearl Harbor. As a twenty-two-year-old, Al was certain to be drafted, and with war pressing, his relationship with Lucille accelerated. By late February, she was pregnant, something of a feat since Al was living in a boardinghouse where women visitors weren't allowed. When Lucille told her parents, they were furious. "She was the baby of the family and this is the last thing anyone expected," recalled Delores.

Al, somewhat sheepishly, told the Jeters he would marry their daughter, though this didn't appease Preston, who tried without success to talk Lucille out of marriage. The couple married at the King County Courthouse, and three days later Al was shipped out to the army. After his departure, Lucille, despite being pregnant and married, continued to attend school, hiding these two secrets from her classmates. She was so thin it would be months before her pregnancy would be obvious, and as for the marriage, Al had been too poor to buy her a ring. Finally, although Lucille had hoped to finish junior high, with a child on the way and no visible means of support, one afternoon she left her schoolbooks on her desk as the bell rang and never came back.

 споро

FOR A FEW months Lucille continued to live at home with her parents, though her relationship with them was strained by her situation. The Jeters were struggling financially and living on welfare; they were in no position to be supporting a jobless pregnant daughter. Eventually, Lucille found work as a waitress in the unruly Jackson Street club scene. She had to lie about her age, but in clubs like the infamous Bucket of Blood, legalities of all sorts were ignored. In between slinging drinks, Lucille would provide part of the entertainment. "She would sing," Delores Hall recalled, "and men would give her tips because she was such a good singer."

Working at the Bucket of Blood, Lucille became part of what hipsters called "the Main Stem." "That was the term used to describe where everything was happening," noted Bob Summerrise, one of Seattle's first black DJs, who owned a record store in the neighborhood. "You'd come into a new town and ask, 'Where's the Main Stem?' And it was a *wild* play there. Pimps, whores, gamblers, drug dealers, some drug addicts, but also all the other successful businesspeople of black life who went there to be entertained or have a drink." On the corner of Fourteenth and Jackson, a one-armed newspaper hawker nicknamed Neversleep bellowed out the day's headlines day and night. It was a neighborhood where something was always happening, and to simply announce that you were headed to Jackson Street was to make a statement about both your intentions and your morals. Certainly this was a very different side of black culture than the church-based community Lucille had grown up in. Lucille was quickly entranced by the exotic allure of Jackson Street's many clubs.

The Main Stem was also the center of rhythm and blues in the city. In clubs like the Black & Tan, the Rocking Chair, and the Little Harlem Nightclub, a colorful and rich alternative world existed, unseen by most of white Seattle. Jimmy Ogilvy, who would later front the Dynamics, visited Jackson Street as a teen and learned that being white was not as big an impediment as wearing the wrong clothes. "It was zoot suits, big hats, and patent leathers on up," he recalled. "You weren't admitted unless you were dressed right. The clubs didn't care if you were white; they just wanted you to be dancing and happening. You had to be suave."

To pretty, sixteen-year-old Lucille Jeter Hendrix, working on Jackson Street was a life-changing event. She wasn't initially savvy, but she quickly learned. Delores observed that the neighborhood "hardened" her sister, but it also enlarged Lucille's previously insular world. The district became her milieu—she knew people, they knew her, and she was never again completely comfortable up the hill in the more staid Central District world of her parents. Nor, for that matter, was she ever again completely comfortable in the traditional world Al Hendrix represented, which already seemed like a distant memory.

಄ಌ

LATE IN THE summer of 1942, Lucille's pregnancy began to show, and she could no longer work. By the fall she was living with family friend Dorothy Harding. Harding was only seven years older than Lucille but had already single-handedly raised three children (she would have six more). She was also one of the first African American women to work in a Seattle shipyard, a place that before the war had been off limits to both blacks and women. Perhaps more important, Harding straddled the worlds of the Main Stem and Main Street. Though she attended church every Sunday, Dorothy loved music and men—one of her children had been born of a brief relationship with singer Jackie Wilson. Lucille was very pregnant when she moved in with Harding. "She called me her auntie," Harding remembered. "I took care of her."

Lucille was at Dorothy's house on a stormy November night when labor began. They rushed to the hospital and it was a quick delivery. The baby was born at 10:15 AM on November 27, 1942. All were convinced the boy was the cutest child they had ever seen. That night Delores gave him the nickname "Buster," inspired by the character Buster Brown, from a comic strip by Richard Outcault, and also the name of a brand of children's shoes. Later on, it was said that Jimi acquired this nickname after Larry "Buster" Crabbe, the actor who played Flash Gordon in the movie serials Jimi adored. Jimi himself told this version of the story, but he was unaware that the name was used before he was able to sneak into a movie matinee. During his entire life, most of his relatives and neighbors in Seattle called him by the name inspired by a mischievous little boy in the funny papers.

At least part of the reason for the nickname was to avoid Lucille's choice of a legal name: Johnny Allen Hendrix. The name Johnny wasn't common in either her or Al's family, and this forever set off questions of paternity in the mind of Al, who was certain that the child had been named after John Page, a longshoreman who rented a room from Dorothy Harding. Harding denied that Page was involved with Lucille prior to her giving birth, but a relationship had clearly developed at some point. Lucille may indeed have named the baby after Page, but it could also have been a coincidence, since John was the most popular boy's name of 1942. In any case, no one called the baby Johnny, not even Lucille, and it would be the first of three legal names that Jimi Hendrix would have during the course of his life.

Al was informed of the birth by the telegram from Delores. When Lucille did finally send Al a picture with the child sitting on her lap, she captioned it, "This is the baby and I," not using the child's name. Another snapshot Delores took and sent to Al had a caption that read: "To my daddy with all my love, Baby Hendrix." On the reverse Delores wrote: "Dear Allen: Here, at last, is a picture of your little boy 'Allen Hendrix.' He is exactly two months and three weeks old. He looks twice as old, doesn't he? I hope you will receive it okay. Delores Hall."

These snapshots of Lucille and the baby are some of the only surviving pictures of Lucille. Wearing a suit coat and a modest skirt without stockings, she posed primly with her legs tightly crossed, but there was also a hint of sexiness to her wry smile. Her straight hair was pulled back in a ponytail, a style at the time more common for a schoolgirl than a housewife. She and her chubby-cheeked baby are both photogenic and share the same dark almond-shaped eyes. No soldier in the armed forces could have possibly looked at the photo without feeling a mix of pride, lust, and bittersweet longing.

Not long after the baby's birth, Al was sent to the South Pacific, and he was in Fiji when he received the first photo of his child. Al spent a good part of his tenure in the army away from combat, which gave him plenty of time to think about what might or might not be happening back in Seattle. In his autobiography, *My Son Jimi,* Al noted that when they first married, Lucille wrote often, but "after Jimi was born, she had a hard time." Some of her difficulties were financial, as Jimi would be a year old before any of Al's army pay was sent to her. But by mid-1943, other circumstances in Lucille's life conspired to complicate things. In June, her father, Preston, passed away, which sent her always-fragile mother, Clarice, into another mental breakdown. Clarice temporarily moved out of the family home, and while she was gone, their house burned to the ground. There was no insurance and the family lost everything they owned, including all their photographs.

✂ ✂ ✂

OVER THE NEXT year, Lucille and her baby lived a transitory life, moving from Dorothy Harding's, to her sister Delores's, and back again. In truth, no one really had space for Lucille or her child. She continued to work in restaurants and taverns and had Dorothy, Delores, or her mother Clarice watch Buster. "Lucille didn't even know how to change a diaper at first," Harding recalled.

Freddie Mae Gautier, a family friend, hinted at occasional neglect. In a court deposition, Gautier told a lengthy tale of how one winter day, Clarice showed up at the Gautier house with a bundle in her arms. "This is Lucille's baby," she announced. Gautier, who was twelve at the time, recalled the baby was "icy cold, his little legs were blue," and his diaper was frozen solid with urine. Gautier's mother cleaned the child, gave him a warm bath, and rubbed his skin with olive oil. When it came time for Clarice to leave, Mrs. Gautier announced that the child was staying with her until Lucille came to retrieve him. When Lucille arrived, she received a lecture on the proper care of an infant.

Eventually, the desperately poor Lucille found other men to support her, including, at least for a time, John Page. Whether this was callousness on her part toward Al, or the act of a teenage mother near starvation, or a combination of the two, is unknown. In the dark days of 1943, it was still undetermined how the war would go and whether any of the boys who had been shipped out would return. If Lucille Hendrix was unfaithful to her overseas husband, she was not the only war bride to stray. "I think she tried her best to wait for him," Delores observed. "He was gone quite awhile." Al, of course, had his opinions. "Lucille held out a good long while, I guess," he wrote in *My Son Jimi,* "before she started running around with her girlfriends and other men." Al complained that his letters to Lucille were frequently returned, and in the rare instances when she wrote him, her return addresses were seedy hotels.

Even Lucille's immediate family had concerns about the baby's welfare and about John Page. Family members were concerned enough that they consulted a lawyer, who told them that if Page took Lucille out of Washington, they might make a case for a charge of transporting a minor over state lines. Hearing that Page had taken Lucille and the baby to Portland, Oregon, her relatives traveled by train to Portland, where they found Lucille in the hospital after a beating. "She had Jimi with her," Delores recalled. "We got Jimi and her and took them home." Since Lucille was only seventeen at the time, Page was arrested, charged under the provisions of the Mann Act, and given a five-year prison sentence.

Lucille finally began to receive Al's wartime paychecks that spring, which helped her financial circumstances, but didn't seem to settle her down. The care of Buster fell—more and more—on Delores and Dorothy, and on Grandmother Clarice. When the boy was almost three, Lucille and Clarice took him to Berkeley, California, for a church convention. After the convention, Lucille returned home to work, but Clarice decided to visit relatives in Missouri. In an effort to spare the baby the long trip to the Midwest, a church friend, Mrs. Champ, offered to keep him temporarily. Mrs. Champ had one daughter of her own, a young girl named Celestine. Years later, Jimi Hendrix would often talk of the kindness Celestine had shown him as a toddler.

Mrs. Champ's care of the child was meant to be temporary, but it stretched on and an informal adoption appeared in the works. Delores corresponded with Mrs. Champ regularly and told her she needed to write to Al and tell him that the baby was in California. Thus, Al Hendrix, thousands of miles away in the Pacific, just weeks away from being released from the army, received a letter informing him that his child was under the care of a stranger.

# CHAPTER THREE

# OVER AVERAGE
# IN SMARTNESS

SEATTLE, WASHINGTON
*September 1945—June 1952*

*"He's over average in smartness for his age, and these people*
*are just crazy about him."*

—AL HENDRIX in a letter to his mother

AL HENDRIX RETURNED to Seattle on a troop transport ship in September 1945. As it sailed into Elliott Bay, he pointed at the city and remarked to a buddy, "I live right over there." In truth, Al didn't know where he was going to live, and whether he had a wife was equally uncertain. While overseas, he had begun divorce proceedings.

Once discharged, Al moved in with his sister-in-law Delores; Buster was still in California with Mrs. Champ. Next, Al traveled to Vancouver to see his family, and it was after spending several weeks there that he returned to Seattle and went to city hall to obtain a copy of his son's birth certificate, thinking it would aid him in transporting his child. He had been out of the army for two months before he headed to California to get the toddler.

Al's initial meeting with his firstborn child at the Champs' apartment was a strange one. He wrote in *My Son Jimi* that he was overwhelmed by the mixed emotions he felt upon seeing his child: "A new warm baby would have been different. Here he was, three years old, and he was able to look and judge for himself." At least part of the discomfort came from how much the child looked like his mother. Al was struck by the resemblance, especially the child's eyes. Even the boy's wide, flat smile recalled Lucille.

The Champs made an attempt to talk Al into leaving Buster with them. An adoption would have been easy to arrange, and considering the uncertainty ahead, few would have thought less of Al for agreeing to it. In a letter he wrote from Berkeley to his mother, Nora Hendrix, Al was conflicted over his situation, yet also overwhelmed with paternal love. He wrote that Buster was "a fine boy and he is sweet. He's over average in smartness for his age, and these people are just crazy about him—everybody is." Al wrote that Mrs. Champ was brokenhearted at the idea of losing the boy: "They are so attached to him, and love him so, and he's used to them too, it's a shame to take him away, but I love him too. But after all, he's my son, and I want him to know who his daddy is, though he calls me daddy all the time now." Al ended the letter by saying that if he were to leave California without the boy, "I'd never forgive myself for it, so when I leave here he'll be with me." He promised to see his mother by Christmas.

Jimi Hendrix never commented on what it felt like to meet his father for the first time, if, in fact, he remembered the occasion. Jimi had been to that point raised exclusively by women and had lacked any father figure. He was accustomed to Mrs. Champ and adored Celestine. When Al threatened to punish him on the train home, Jimi tearfully called for Celestine, his protector, who was no longer there. Al gave his son his first fatherly spanking on that train ride. "I guess he got a little homesick, and he misbehaved," Al later wrote.

In Seattle, Al and Jimi moved in with Delores, in the Yesler Terrace housing project. The project was the first racially integrated public housing in the United States, and despite the poverty of the residents, it was a tight-knit community where diverse cultures met on common ground. "Those were nice places in those days," Delores recalled. "There weren't many blacks, but everyone there got along." Buster fit in with the many other children, and it was the beginning of his multicultural upbringing.

In a turn of events that surprised all, Lucille showed up soon after Al and Buster. Her initial words to Al were "Here I am." For the first time, the three Hendrixes were in the same room. The reunion was bittersweet for them all: Lucille was unsure how she'd be greeted by her son—whom she hadn't seen in months—and by her husband; she hadn't seen him for over three years. Buster didn't know what to think seeing his two parents together for the first time. Al couldn't decide whether to voice his anger at Lucille or sweep her up in his arms. He was struck by how attractive his wife was: In the three years since he had seen her, she had transformed from a girl into a beautiful woman. By the end of the day, Al decided to abandon divorce proceedings. Lucille asked him, "Do you want to try to make it?" Al's response: "Maybe the best thing to do is to give it a bloody go again." The physical attraction between them was their strongest bond; it would keep them returning to each other's arms repeatedly, even during times of marital struggle.

By all accounts, the next several months were the smoothest ones the family would ever know. Living as they were with Delores, their expenses were minimal, and Al was still receiving small payments from the army, so he and Lucille were able go out almost every night. And Delores—who was more conservative than her sister—was a convenient babysitter. Lucille and Al would watch Delores's children while she worked days at Boeing; Delores would then care for Buster while they went out and renewed their romance. "They had their honeymoon then," Delores observed. "They'd go up and down Jackson Street."

The nascent family even took a road trip to Vancouver. Neither Lucille nor Buster had previously met Al's mother, Nora, and Al was pleased to show off his progeny. Buster took to his grandmother, and this would be the first of many trips he would make to visit her.

Eventually, Delores, who didn't drink, became fed up with Al and Lucille's drinking. "They would drink and party, and I was raising a family," she said. When Lucille was drunk, she was overly affectionate and emotional. Al was the opposite: Alcohol worsened his temper, and he became sour.

After Al found work at a slaughterhouse, his salary allowed them to move to a hotel that catered to transients in the Jackson Street area. Their modest room had only a single bed, which he, Lucille, and Buster shared. They had a one-burner hot plate to prepare meals; the room's only other furniture was a desk chair. They lived in this hotel room for months.

It was while the family lived at the hotel, and a full year after his return, that Al decided to change his son's name legally. He chose James as a first name because that was his own legal name, and Marshall as a middle name after the middle name of his deceased brother, Leon. Thereafter, some called the boy Jimi or James while the family called him Buster.

Living in the hotel put the family on turf that Lucille was familiar with—it was roughly the same neighborhood where she had worked as a waitress during the war. She knew many people, and a simple walk down the street meant she'd run into several acquaintances. Her popularity benefited Al by association, but it also fueled his jealousy. "Al only knew Lucille's friends," Delores said. "He didn't have friends of his own." Their neighborhood was one of the most diverse in the city, and their friendships included Chinese, Japanese, whites, and a number of Filipino families. Yet, in a sign that racial distrust in Seattle still ran deep, Al said he was later temporarily denied a seaman's license because the license board considered him a "threat to national security" because of the couple's nonwhite friends.

Al eventually received his merchant marine license and took a job on a ship headed for Japan. This assignment sent him thousands of miles away, and when he returned several weeks later, he found that Lucille had been evicted from their hotel. Al said the hotel manager told him this was because she'd been caught with another man in the room.

Delores disputed Al's version of events; whatever happened, it did not stop Al from taking Lucille back again immediately, and thus a pattern emerged: They would regularly break up and just as regularly get back together. "It was almost like a cycle," Al wrote in his autobiography. "Things would go along real nice for two or three months. After that I'd go, 'Uh-oh . . . something's going to happen.'" Even Jimi Hendrix observed the pattern, telling an interviewer years later that the relationship between his parents was fiery: "My mother and father used to fall out a lot," he said. "I always had to be ready to go tippy-toeing off to Canada." In Canada, he could stay with his grandmother Nora Hendrix; more often, he was shunted off to Grandmother Clarice, Delores, or Dorothy Harding in Seattle.

Dorothy Harding became the most frequent babysitting option after the reunited family moved to their first apartment in the spring of 1947 in the Rainier Vista project, where Dorothy resided. Rainier Vista was three miles south of the Central District in the Rainier Valley. The project itself was primarily populated by retired white families, but after the war it became home for increasing numbers of African Americans. The family's one-bedroom apartment at 3121 Oregon Street was so small that Buster slept in the closet. That closet became his retreat whenever his parents battled, as they did ever more frequently.

Most fights sprang from the family's financial problems and Lucille's complaints that Al didn't make enough to support them. She threatened to go out and find a job as a waitress, but to Al, such a possibility called his manhood into question. Most of the jobs he held during this period involved manual labor and none of them lasted long. He was also studying to be an electrician under the auspices of the GI Bill, with the hopes of better-paying work ahead. The couple was living on less than ninety dollars a month, with a rent of forty.

Lucille was used to life on the Main Stem, and the impoverished domestic life they experienced in Rainier Vista was in marked contrast to that. When Al came home from work, he'd be exhausted and he was rarely interested in going out. Al would tell her to go out without him. "When she came home," Delores recalled, "he'd be sitting out there drinking and he'd be mad. The next-door neighbor told me she'd hear fussing and fighting every night." Delores said Lucille would frequently have bruises when their fighting turned physical.

In early 1948, one of their fights was so bitter, according to Al, Lucille moved out and lived for a month with a Filipino man named Frank. If true, this apparently was not cause for divorce, and when Lucille returned, Al took her back. As Al wrote in his autobiography, "I'm not overly jealous, but with the things Lucille did, a lot of guys would say, 'Man, you sure can take it.' They'd tell me that they'd blow her away." Al did the opposite: When she left, he seemed to want her more. Delores Hall's story is that Al willfully misinterpreted Lucille's male friendships as love affairs, while Al contended she openly cheated on him—the truth is probably somewhere in between. Still, if half the incidents in Al's autobiography are true, he was a cuckold of the first order. Delores argued that Al's jealousies were a creation of his imagination, fueled by alcohol.

But not all of Al's worries were about phantoms. That year John Page was let out of prison and reappeared, seeking revenge. "He threatened to kill all of us," Delores said. Page came after Lucille with a gun, vowing that he was going to take her to Kansas City. He was driven off by a family friend with his own pistol. "John Page was determined he was going to use Lucille for prostitution," Delores explained. Page had apparently bragged to his friends that with Lucille's light skin, she would be a successful prostitute. Delores warned Lucille to avoid Page, but Lucille's response sounded naive and, to a degree, complicit. "I don't have much to do with him," she told Delores, "but he always gives me money and buys me fancy gifts." The situation was, as Dorothy Harding called it, "a terrible mess."

Page did not go easily. One night when Al, Lucille, Delores, and other relatives were leaving the Atlas Theater, Page appeared and grabbed Lucille.

"Get your hands off of her," Al yelled.

"She's my woman," Page replied. "I don't care nothing about you being her husband. You weren't around—you don't know nothing."

With that, the two men came to blows. Page was bigger than Al, though Al had boxing experience and landed the first punch, which briefly stunned Page. The fight continued down the street, and Al maintained his advantage. Eventually, the crowd separated the two men, and Page ran off. Lucille left with Al, and John Page did not bother them again.

A more constant demon than jealousy was alcohol, which was the fuel for most of the couple's bickering. "When they drank, they fought," observed Delores. Their house also became a frequent party pad: "When Lucille and I had alcohol at the house, we drank together and there'd be other people there too, so it was a party," Al wrote in *My Son Jimi*. Those parties were raucous enough that both Delores and Dorothy banned their children from visiting the Hendrix home; Jimi had to either leave or sit in his closet and overhear the racket. Both Delores and Dorothy noticed that Jimi became more withdrawn that year. When asked why he was so quiet, his response was frequently, "Mama and Daddy are always fighting. Always fighting. I don't like it. I wish they'd stop." When his parents' nightly bickering began, Jimi would often retreat to Dorothy Harding's house. He was so quiet, Harding wondered if he had a medical condition. "He barely said a word," she recalled.

When Jimi did talk, he had a slight stutter, which lasted until adolescence and reappeared even in adulthood when he was nervous. He couldn't pronounce Dorothy's name, so she became "Auntie Doortee." He began to attend preschool that fall and opened up a bit, but was frequently teased for his speech. Sometime in 1947, he was given his first musical toy, a harmonica, but he didn't show a strong interest, and it was soon abandoned. His favorite toy was a small dog made of rags that Delores had sewn for him. In the few photographs from this time, he is seen clutching the stuffed dog as if it were his most treasured possession.

During their good times, even Al admitted that Lucille was a good mother: "Lucille did really good with Jimi," he wrote in his book. "She'd be cuddling him and talking to him, and he'd be hugging on her." Jimi was a creative child and could play by himself for hours. From ages four to six, he had an imaginary friend, Sessa, who was a companion to all his doings.

⚮

IN THE SUMMER of 1947, Lucille became pregnant again. In Al's book, written fifty years after the fact, he contended that his wife conceived the child during a month they were separated, something Delores Hall disputed. In either case, Al and Lucille were certainly together that summer, and with her pregnancy, their relationship improved. Several of their friends report that Al was excited about another child in the family, in contrast to the less sanguine version in Al's book. "He kept saying again and again," said Dorothy Harding, "how happy he was because he wanted to see his baby born—he'd missed Jimi's birth because he was away."

The baby was born on January 13, 1948. Al named the child Leon, after his deceased beloved brother. Al was listed as the father on the birth certificate and was quick to show off the child to everyone in the hospital, as any new father would. Delores was also in Harborview Hospital, having had her third child just two days before Leon's birth. She and Lucille had beds next to each other in the maternity ward, and Delores recalled Al making a big deal over Leon: "He took his little wrappings off, and looked at him all over, and said, 'I'm so glad I got another son. Now I can see what the little toes look like, the little feet look like, the little hands.'" Perhaps because of his own birth defect, Al repeatedly counted Leon's toes and fingers.

Leon's birth marked the apex of the family's good times. Al was so enamored of his new son that everything in their lives seemed improved. "That was the time they got along beautifully," Delores said. "Al had a better job for a while, and the fighting seemed to slow down."

It was immediately clear to all—including Jimi—that Leon was Al's favorite. Jimi told his cousin Dee: "Daddy and Mommy are crazy about my little brother; they like him better than they like me."

Not long after Leon was born, the family moved to a two-bedroom unit in Rainier Vista. The apartment was still small, but at least Jimi and Leon had a room they could share. Jimi started kindergarten that September. At five years and ten months, he was slightly older than the other children, but not so much that he stood out. When school let out each afternoon, he headed into a large greenbelt just west of Rainier Vista. In these woods, he would fight daily battles with imaginary cowboys, pretending he was the Indian warrior he had heard about in his grandmother Nora Hendrix's stories.

Just eleven months after Leon was born, Lucille gave birth to another boy, whom Al named Joseph Allen Hendrix. Al was listed as the father on the birth certificate, though in his autobiography, he denied paternity of Joe. Yet while Jimi and Leon were both tall and lanky, Joe was short and stocky and looked enough like Al to be his twin.

Joe's birth was not a joyous occasion for the family. He had several serious birth defects, including the strange phenomenon of having two rows of teeth. He also had a club foot, a cleft palate, and one leg significantly shorter than the other. Jimi Hendrix had turned six the winter Joe was born, and the family now had three young children to feed when they had barely survived with one child. Far worse, though, was the fact that for the rest of their marriage, Al and Lucille would fight about which one of them caused Joe's medical problems. Lucille blamed Al for pushing her when she was pregnant; Al blamed her drinking.

As Joe grew older, it became apparent that he would need significant medical care. Al, afraid of the expense, began to distance himself emotionally from the child and the rest of the family. In contrast, Joe's neediness brought out Lucille's maternal instinct, and she investigated options for the operations he would need. She frequently took Joe by bus to Children's Hospital in northeast Seattle, in those days a two-hour bus ride each way. She discovered the state would pay for most of Joe's medical needs, but the family would have to shoulder some of the expense. Al refused. He had finished his electronics classes that year, but the only job he could find was as a night janitor at the Pike Place Market, sweeping up after the farmers.

By June 1949, the family reached the breaking point. The children had health issues related to malnutrition; in fact, Jimi and Leon survived only by eating with neighbors, a habit that would soon become an almost daily occurrence. Al made the decision that all three of his children would be sent to Canada to live for a time with his mother, Nora. Nearly seven, Jimi was the only child old enough to understand the emotional impact of yet another separation from his parents. Grandmother Nora was a more stable caregiver than Al or Lucille, but she had her own quirks. She was harsh with punishment—Joe said that when he wet his bed, she severely beat him—yet full of old-fashioned remedies for illnesses and knowledgeable about herbs. Jimi reveled in her tales of their Cherokee ancestors and of her life in early minstrel shows.

It was in Vancouver where Jimi began first grade in September 1949. He later told an interviewer that his grandmother would dress him up "in a little Mexican jacket with tassels" that she had made, and that other children teased him because of it. By October, Jimi and his brothers were sent back to Seattle to Lucille and Al, who were again on an upswing. The down cycle quickly followed, and by the fall of 1950, Jimi was temporarily living with Delores when he started second grade at Horace Mann Elementary. Jimi turned eight that fall, and the Hendrix family added another child: Kathy Ira, born sixteen weeks premature, and weighing just one pound ten ounces at birth. Worse yet, the family soon discovered that she was blind. For a time Kathy lived with the rest of the household, but eleven months after her birth, she was made a ward of the state and put into foster care. Al also denied paternity of Kathy, although she, like Joe before her, bore a remarkable resemblance to him.

A second daughter, Pamela, was born a year later in October 1951. She, too, had health complications, though nothing as severe as Kathy's. Al also denied paternity of Pamela, although he was listed as her father on her birth certificate. She, too, was given to foster care, though she stayed in the neighborhood and would occasionally see the rest of her family.

Jimi started third grade in September 1951 at Rainier Vista Elementary School. He was once again living with his parents, Leon, and Joe in their now-cramped two-bedroom apartment. Despite the family drama, Jimi found joy in the things that intrigued all boys: He read comic books, enjoyed going to the movies, and drew pictures of cars on his notepad. He wrote a postcard to his grandmother Nora that summer: "How have you been? I have been good. How is [my cousin] and them? Are they good too? We went to a picnic and I ate too much, but it was a good picnic. We had fun. Tweet, Tweet. Love, Buster."

Things were soon to get so complicated in the Hendrix household that even Jimi stopped his tweets. There were three children at that point (Jimi, Leon, and Joe; the two girls had already been given to foster care). Lucille was struggling with her drinking, as was Al, and Al was again unable to find steady work. Though there were a multitude of issues that seemed insurmountable, it was ultimately the questions involving Joe Hendrix that proved to be the undoing of the family. Lucille held out the hope that Joe, then three, could live normally with the help of an operation on his leg. But on this issue Al was steadfast: He repeatedly said he couldn't afford the operation. Lucille had already given away two daughters; the idea of giving away Joe, who had lived as part of their household for three years, was beyond her. She later said she felt Al had made the decision out of meanness and miserliness. "Al said he wasn't going to put that kind of money into a kid," Delores recalled, "even if he had it."

In the late fall of 1951, after Jimi turned nine, Lucille left Al. Al was heartbroken, and later told the story that he had been the one who left. It was not, however, the end of their relationship; not even divorce could kill the attraction they had to each other or the equally strong hate that followed it. They would be officially divorced on December 17, 1951, but they were back together again not long after, and just as quickly, they broke up again. In the official divorce proceedings, Al was awarded custody of Jimi, Leon, and Joe. This custody was really a paper formality: The Hendrix boys were thereafter raised by Grandma Clarice Jeter, Grandma Nora Hendrix in Vancouver, Aunt Delores Hall, friend Dorothy Harding, and others in the neighborhood, as they had been during most of their parents' marriage.

In the summer of 1952, Lucille and Al reunited long enough to go through one of the saddest rituals the family had ever endured. Al's refusal to help pay for Joe's medical expenses ensured that the only way to get Joe the care he needed was to make him a ward of the state. To accomplish this, Lucille and Al had to give up parental rights to three-year-old Joe. Lucille had pleaded with Al to reconsider, while Delores and Dorothy Harding both offered to adopt Joe. But Al vetoed these suggestions, perhaps worried that he'd still have a financial obligation.

Al borrowed a car for the heartbreaking occasion. Jimi and Leon knew something was up when they watched their father pack up their little brother's possessions and take him into the car. Delores had been recruited to watch Jimi and Leon, and she and the two of them waved good-bye to Joe. Leon remembered being confused; at almost ten, Jimi must have felt the deep sorrow of the occasion.

Joe certainly remembered the day. His mother held him in her arms on the car ride. "She smelled so good," Joe recalled, "like flowers." At the hospital, Lucille carried Joe out of the car and handed him to a waiting nurse. He then sat on the curb with the nurse, and as his mother climbed back in the car, he began to weep. "My dad," Joe recalled, "never even got out of the car. He kept it running the whole time." Joe climbed onto the nurse's lap and sat there as his parents drove away. In the years to follow, he would frequently run into his brothers Jimi and Leon in the Central District. They always felt fondness at seeing him, remembering the three years when they were all a family together. Joe even would run into Al Hendrix in the neighborhood from time to time, but Joe Hendrix never again saw Lucille. His last sight of his mother was a brief glimpse of her hand in the window as the car pulled away.

# CHAPTER FOUR

# THE BLACK KNIGHT

SEATTLE, WASHINGTON
*July 1952–March 1955*

*Sir Gawain: What knight?*
*Prince Valiant: The Black Knight. Who is he, sire?*
*Sir Gawain: A ghost.*

—from the film *Prince Valiant*

JIMI HENDRIX TURNED ten on Thanksgiving Day, 1952. Though Al and Lucille were officially divorced, his parents were briefly living together again, and in fact Lucille was six months pregnant. Al would later deny paternity of this child as well. Born on February 14, 1953, the baby was named Alfred Hendrix. Alfred was Al and Lucille's fourth child to be born with developmental disabilities, and he was immediately put up for adoption.

Lucille was living with Al when she had Alfred, but not long after the birth, she moved out again. "When Mom was home, we could smell bacon and pancakes cooking in the morning," Leon recalled, "and we would jump up yelling, 'Mama's home!' But that would only last a day, because they would be drinking and arguing, and Mama would leave."

Lucille roomed during this period with her mother, Clarice, who had an apartment above the Rainier Brewery. Leon and Jimi would sneak down to see her, and they came to associate the brewery smells with their mother. "Every time I smell hops, I think of my mama," Leon said.

Though their financial situation was dire, like countless children of divorce, the boys manipulated their parents to their advantage. "My dad used to punish us by sending us to our mother's house, so we would get in trouble on purpose," Leon said. Al's punishment was what he called "whippings," spankings done with a belt. When that failed to get the desired compliance, Al would send them to Lucille. "My dad would pack our little bags with our toothbrushes and things," Leon recalled. "Sometimes I think he just wanted to get rid of us for a little while. He worked really hard, but he never seemed to work out of the situation. He'd punish us by saying we had to spend a weekend with our mama, but we wanted that." Many times these planned exiles backfired when Al and Lucille would get into a row at the handoff, and Al would storm back home with the boys. Feeling cheated out of a visit with their mother, the boys would then sneak to her house, which would necessitate yet another whipping from Al when he found them. Al rarely beat them if he wasn't inebriated. "Sometimes he would get too loaded," Leon said, "and he'd forget what we were getting a whipping for." As Jimi grew larger, he began to resist these whippings by grabbing the belt and holding on to it so Al couldn't strike him. These attempts usually proved futile. "My dad was strong," Leon said. "He'd hold us with one hand and whip us with the other."

Al's job at the time was pumping gas on the swing shift for Seattle City Light. Raising his children by himself, Al had no one to watch them after school and he received frequent calls at work from concerned neighbors, jeopardizing his position. Jimi got into more trouble than Leon, but most of their misbehavior was minor, to be expected from unattended youths. "The neighbors started to take over watching us," Leon said, "because they knew what was going to happen—that welfare was going to take us away." The welfare department workers drove green cars, and Leon and Jimi learned to watch for those vehicles and beat a retreat if they saw one. They were careful not to skip school, to avoid the attention of the authorities there. "They weren't bad kids," recalled neighbor Melvin Harding. "They were just a little wild and lost."

Al wrote in his autobiography that he went hungry at times to feed the boys, but even with that sacrifice, there was little to eat. The house was also filthy, as Al was unable, or unwilling, to clean his residence or wash their clothes, which he said was women's work. For a brief while, Al got a new girlfriend, but she left after it became clear that Al wanted her mostly as a housekeeper. Leon and Jimi would usually end up at neighbors' around dinnertime. "Jimi and I used to be so hungry, we'd go to the grocery store and steal," Leon said. "Jimi would be smart: He'd open a loaf of bread, pull out two pieces, wrap it up, and put it back. Then he'd sneak into the meat department and steal a package of ham to make a sandwich out of it."

ぐるぐる

IN THE SPRING of 1953, the family's fortunes improved when Al got a job with the city engineering department as a laborer. With a more consistent income, he purchased a small two-bedroom home at 2603 South Washington Street, paying a ten-dollar down payment. The move put them back in the Central District, just a few blocks from Jackson Street. Most important to Jimi and Leon, the move gave them a yard and the first house of their own.

The house itself was just nine hundred square feet and already fifty years old, but it felt like a palace to the boys. Jimi and Leon shared a bedroom, and not long after they moved in, Al's niece Grace and her husband, Frank Hatcher, joined them. "Al asked us to come and live with him to take care of the children," recalled Frank. "He just couldn't do it himself. He was drinking a lot, and gambling, and a lot of times he didn't even come home." The Hatchers became the boys' de facto parents for a period, with Grace becoming one the boys' many mother figures. As for their real mother, Lucille visited only occasionally. She was

drifting from hotel to hotel and stopped by every few weeks, but was
no longer a routine presence.

Jimi switched schools at the end of April. He was now attending
Leschi, the most integrated elementary school in the city. Here, he met
up with the boys who would become his closest childhood friends:
Terry Johnson, Pernell Alexander, and Jimmy Williams. "It was like our
own separate family," recalled Pernell. Pernell's grandmother, Mrs.
Mae Jones, was raising him and she would play a large role in all the
boys' lives. "We used to eat breakfast there every day before school," remembered Jimmy Williams. "Mrs. Jones loved Jimi and me to death."

Terry Johnson came from the tightest family of the boys and had
grown up in the church. Jimi occasionally joined him at Grace
Methodist Church, and it was there that he had his first exposure to
gospel music. "Jimi came with me a few times," Johnson recalled, "and
I think it was one of the first times he'd been to church." Jimi found the
music intoxicating, and watching a powerful choir sing gave him an understanding of the power of live music.

Jimi's closest friend was Jimmy Williams, who came from a family
of thirteen children. Jimmy and Jimi became inseparable, perhaps because they were both introverts. To avoid the confusion of their identical names, they went by nicknames in their clique: Jimi was "Henry"
(shortened from Hendrix) or Buster; Terry Johnson was "Terrikins";
and Jimmy Williams was "Potato Chips," named for his favorite snack.
Pernell's own first name was different enough that he never needed a
nickname.

When school let out for summer, their entertainment came from a
swim in Lake Washington or a cheap matinee at the Atlas Theater,
where Jimi fell in love with the *Flash Gordon* serial and especially with
the movie *Prince Valiant*. The villain in *Prince Valiant* was called the
Black Knight, and Jimi and Leon would charge each other with brooms
in make-believe jousting matches, each arguing over who got to play
the role of the dastardly Black Knight. When the family adopted a dog,
the pet was named Prince, after Prince Valiant.

That same broom used for jousting was also fashioned into an imaginary guitar. Though Jimi had previously shown no particular interest in music, in 1953 he began to follow the popular charts and to play along to the radio, strumming a broom as if it were a guitar. "We'd always listen to 'The Hit Parade Top Ten,'" Jimmy Williams recalled. They preferred popular crooners like Frank Sinatra, Nat King Cole, and Perry Como. Dean Martin was Jimi's favorite at the time.

Almost every day after school, Jimi would listen to Al's radio and pretend to play along with the broom. Al, who thought a broom should be used only for sweeping, found this objectionable. "Jimi would be screwing around playing the broom," Leon recalled, "and my dad would come in, so Jimi would start sweeping again. Then my dad would see straw from the broom on the bed and get mad."

The boys also spent summers working in the fields south of Seattle, picking beans or strawberries. This job required rising early to catch a bus to the farm. Al would wake them up at 4 AM and they would walk to the Wonder Bread Bakery, where Jimi knew a worker who left out day-old doughnuts. They walked to Seattle's industrial district and took a bus to a farm twenty miles south of the city. At the farm, the pickers were paid a piece rate, so they'd work until they earned enough for lunch or ate as many strawberries as they could stand. Sometimes they'd swim in the Green River, and on one occasion Jimi saved Leon from drowning. "I fell in a canal, and Jimi swam in and saved me," Leon said. Many nights, on the way home from the fields, the boys would splurge on horsemeat hamburgers, which were ten cents apiece. "We'd get two, and that was the highlight of the day," Leon said. "Then we'd go home and wait for Dad, because, well, sometimes he didn't come home."

After a year, Grace and Frank Hatcher became fed up with Al's ways. When they had moved in together, Al had agreed to take cooking responsibilities every other week and the Hatchers felt he didn't keep up his end of the arrangement. "He'd just make rice, beans, and wieners," Frank Hatcher said. "He'd buy the cheapest meat: just necks, and horsemeat." Tired of this, the Hatchers moved out, and the boys were again left alone with their father. Al didn't trust either boy with his own key to the house, so Jimi, or one of his friends, would have to find which tavern Al was in and retrieve the key. "There were about five taverns he went to," recalled Pernell Alexander. "You just had to figure out which one he was in." Al favored the Shady Spot Tavern on Twenty-third or the Mt. Baker Tavern at Twenty-fifth and Jackson. At the Mt. Baker, Jimi could look in the window and see if his father was there without having to enter. Many times, Jimi and Leon gave up and spent the night with friends.

ᴄᴥᴧᴥ

MEANWHILE, THE FAMILY'S cat-and-mouse game with the welfare department continued. By 1954, acting on repeated complaints from neighbors, a social worker began stopping by the house every week. Child welfare was temporarily staved off because Delores Hall and Dorothy Harding made regular trips to the house to clean and to make sure the children's clothes were washed. Delores remembered going by one evening to find Al gone and the two boys attempting to cook dinner for themselves: "Jimi was frying eggs, and when he saw me, he had a huge smile on, and said, 'I'm making dinner!'" Many of the household duties fell to Jimi, not yet twelve, who cared for his brother. "Jimi was Leon's protector," recalled Pernell Alexander. "He did anything he could to make sure Leon was taken care of."

Eventually a welfare worker cornered Al Hendrix, and no attempt by the aunties to tidy up could hide the neglect that Leon and Jimi lived in. Al was given two choices: His sons could be sent to a foster home or be put up for adoption. Though the conditions they lived in were grim, it was the only world the boys knew, and both begged Al not to separate them. Al then made a decision that would briefly alter their lives: He argued that Jimi, almost a teenager, needed less caring for and thus should stay with Al. Leon, Al's favorite by every account, would go to foster care. The social worker approved the idea but told Al that Leon had to leave immediately. "Don't take him right now," Al begged. "I'll take him to the home tomorrow." It was one of the only times the boys had seen their father cry. The social worker relented, and Leon was given a one-night reprieve.

That night, on what they all thought would be their last together as a trio, Al was uncharacteristically affectionate. Normally the most physical contact the boys could expect from him was a pat on the back or a handshake; their favorite gesture, however, was when Al softly rubbed his knuckles on their scalps. Al's fingers were callused and rough from years of manual labor, and perhaps he felt his knuckles were kinder than a caress with his coarse palm. It was an odd way to show affection, but both Jimi and Leon grew to savor these moments of connection and tenderness. After the welfare worker left, Al spent much of the night rubbing their scalps, as if enough passes of his rough and broken knuckles could act as a salve for the pain his sons had been through and the further pain that lay ahead of them.

Both Leon and Jimi were crestfallen the next day when Al took Leon away, but the change proved far less dramatic than they expected. Leon was placed in a foster home six blocks away, and he and Jimi remained a daily pair. "I either would go play with Jimi at my dad's," Leon recalled, "or Jimi would come with me. We were never really apart." Arthur Wheeler, Leon's foster parent, confirms that story. "Jimi was over here all the time," Wheeler said. "He ate with us quite frequently."

Arthur and Urville Wheeler had six offspring of their own but opened up their house to needy children, sometimes housing as many as ten. They were church people and lived the teachings of the Bible by treating all their children, including the foster kids, as equals. Jimi became an informal foster child there. "Jimi was at our house more than he was at his dad's," recalled Doug Wheeler, one of the Wheeler sons. "A lot of times Jimi would spend the night so he could have breakfast before going to school. Otherwise, he might not have anything to eat." Jimi and Leon were astonished that the Wheeler kitchen always had food and that a bowl of fruit sat on the counter. Jimi would frequently lament, "I wish I could live here." He essentially did just that.

Surprisingly, despite the restlessness of his life, Jimi had a consistent attendance record at Leschi Elementary. He wasn't a stellar student, but his grades were fair and he showed promise in art. He made countless drawings in his notebook of the typical boy subjects of flying saucers and drag racers. Drawing automobiles interested him to such a degree that he sketched several designs for cars and sent them to the Ford Motor Company. That fall, at Al's urging, Jimi tried out for junior football. His coach was Booth Gardner, who decades later would become Washington's governor. "He was no athlete," Gardner recalled. "He wasn't good enough to start; to tell the truth, he really wasn't good enough to play." Jimi was also briefly a member of Boy Scout Troop 16.

In 1955, when he was twelve, Jimi's interest in music took another leap, after watching Jimmy Williams sing Perry Como's "Wanted" in a Leschi talent show. "There was a lot of applause," Williams recalled. "After the show Jimi came up to me and said, 'Wow, you are going to be famous. Will you still be my friend when you're famous?'" What Jimi had observed—perhaps for the first time in his life—was the power a stage had to transform someone, even a boy as shy as Jimmy Williams, into a performer. It was a lesson Jimi Hendrix would take to heart.

∾∾∾

THERE ARE MANY families from Seattle's Central District who assert that Jimi was a regular presence in their home for dinner and at bedtime. Jimi spent very little time during this period at his father's home and was, for all practical purposes, living off the kindness of others in the African American community. The contribution of the Wheelers and others like them to Jimi's well-being cannot be underestimated. These families, quite literally, kept him alive.

No family did more for Jimi Hendrix over the years than the Hardings. Auntie Doortee, as he called Dorothy Harding, had helped Lucille during labor, changed his diapers when he was an infant, and consistently maintained an interest in his well-being. Jimi called Dorothy Harding an auntie, but she was more of a mother to him than any other female in his life, including his own biological mother. If Auntie Doortee didn't see Jimi for a while, she would track Al down and berate him, something she did regularly, and she was the only woman from whom Al would take such criticism.

Harding was raising nine children of her own as a single mother and worked two jobs to accomplish this. By 1955, she worked the day shift at Boeing as a riveter and then hurried home to prepare food for her children before traveling to her second job as a domestic for a wealthy white family. The Harding family had a three-bedroom apartment in Rainier Vista, and during the twenty-five-year period they lived there, Dorothy slept on a sofa in the living room, giving the bedrooms to her children. Despite her struggles, Dorothy kept her children fed, clean, and took the lot to St. Edward's Catholic Church every Sunday. Many times Jimi accompanied them, and he seemed to revel in the ritual, if only because it made him feel part of an authentic family.

The older Harding boys played the role of Jimi's protector on numerous occasions. "There was a silent understanding that nobody would bother him, because of us," Melvin Harding recalled. "He wasn't a fighter. He was quiet, and he had a ready smile, the kind of smile that would break everybody down." Jimi was introverted, even downcast. "He was extremely sensitive," Ebony Harding noted. "He would never say he missed his mom or his dad, but you knew he did. He cried a lot."

It was during one of his many nights with the Hardings that Jimi uttered a statement that is so prescient each of the Hardings, who all tell the identical story, calls it otherworldly. "He told me," Dorothy Harding recalled, " 'I'm going to leave here, and I'm going to go far, far away. I'm going to be rich and famous, and everyone here will be jealous.' He said he was going to leave the country, and that he was never coming back. I told him that he couldn't do that, and leave me here. He said, 'No, Auntie Doortee, I'm going to take you with me.' " The Harding children all laughed at the bluster of Jimi's announcement.

Another prophetic truth came in the bedtime stories that the Harding children told one another. Though Jimi idolized the Harding boys, the family member who would have the most effect on his future career was Shirley. As one of the older girls, she had the responsibility of getting her young siblings to bed. She would tuck everyone in, dim the lights, and then sit in the hallway in the center of the bedrooms. From this perch, she would begin a nightly performance that was an enchanting elixir to Jimi. She would tell stories, "made-up stories," as Jimi used to call them, and he loved them.

The bedtime stories always involved three characters: Bonita, Audrey, and Roy. Their names never changed, though every night their identities would evolve. "They were like Aesop's fables," recalled Ebony Harding. "There was always a moral to them." If someone had done something particularly kind that day, Shirley would tell the story so that everyone knew it was about that person. And if someone had erred, that child would find himself characterized as Bonita, Audrey, or Roy, with his missteps chronicled and explained. Jimi frequently was the raw material for the character Roy in the nightly tale. Cleaning the Harding house was a never-ending chore, and Jimi took up the job of sweeping the kitchen so often that he stood out, thus becoming, in the stories, "Roy, the sweeping boy." Shirley would have Roy, Bonita, and Audrey experience many successes and failures, but none brought out more joy in the family—and in Jimi—than the tale of Roy making it big as a guitar player. "Roy became rich and famous because of his broom guitar," Shirley would tell the tale. "People would come from all over to hear him play. He became so rich that he drove around in a long black Cadillac. He was always happy. He had lots of money, but he still cleaned the kitchen, and swept the floor, and did the dishes." Here the tale had its moral punch: Even rich and famous boys had to remember to sweep the floor. "Roy was rich and famous, and he had this Cadillac," she continued. "He could go anywhere in the world. But Roy wasn't that kind of boy—he would go out in the world, but he would always come home in his Cadillac. He would drive to Rainier Vista, and honk his horn, and all the kids would come running, and give him love." By this point in the story, Jimi felt sure he was hearing his own distant future, coming to him like a delicious dream.

# CHAPTER FIVE

# JOHNNY GUITAR

SEATTLE, WASHINGTON
*March 1955–March 1958*

*Hero: The name is Johnny. Johnny Guitar.*
*First Bad Guy: That's no name.*
*Second Bad Guy: Heads, I'm going to kill you, mister; tails, you*
*can play her a tune.*

—from the film *Johnny Guitar*

IN THE SPRING of 1955, Jimi Hendrix was photographed with his sixth-grade class at Leschi Elementary. The class picture of forty-six children could be a postcard for the United Nations: There are equal numbers of African Americans, Caucasians, and Asian Americans in his class. "It was an idyllic time and place," recalled Jimmy Williams. "It was as if race didn't matter. We felt part of a larger whole." In the photograph, Jimi's expression is one of amusement at the adults making all these kids stay still. Jimi graduated from Leschi that spring and headed for middle school with a C average.

His family life, however, was anything but average. On March 30, 1955, at a hearing in the King County Courthouse—the same place where they married—Al and Lucille Hendrix signed away their parental rights to Joe, Kathy, Pamela, and Alfred Hendrix. The hearing was a formality, as these children had already been turned over, but nonetheless, in signing the court decree, Al and Lucille were in perpetuity giving away "any and all parental rights and interests in, and to, the children." Delores Hall said Lucille was "destroyed" by admitting in court her failure as a mother. The hearing was also significant in light of Al Hendrix's later claims that he was not the father of these children; in court, he admitted to fathering all four.

The hearing came at a time when Jimi's situation at home had reached a new low. Al had lost his job and had fallen behind on the mortgage payments. Conditions in the house deteriorated to the point that even visits from the various aunties couldn't keep up with the filth and disrepair. When football coach Booth Gardner stopped by one day, he found Jimi sitting alone in the dark. "The power had been turned off," Gardner recalled.

Jimi roamed the neighborhood at all hours of the day and night with little supervision. Many in the Central District came to know him as they would a stray dog who wanders from house to house. Yet there was also a child's sense of discovery in Jimi's waywardness, and he soon knew every musician in the neighborhood, simply by listening for the sounds of their rehearsals. He'd hear music coming from a house, and as a curious boy, he'd simply knock on the door. "My brother played keyboards," Sammy Drain recalled, "and Jimi heard, and one day just stopped by."

Yet there were dangers to the itinerant lifestyle for a teenage boy. One day Jimi was in the woods with a group of children. One of their neighbors, a developmentally disabled boy, kept lagging behind. Jimi and the other boys would yell at him to keep up, and after he fell out of sight, they went back to locate him. They found the boy about to be sexually assaulted by an older man, whom they scared off. A decade later, Jimi told a girlfriend that he himself had been sexually assaulted as a youth. He left out specific details, other than to say that a man in uniform had been the offender, but it was an incident that marked him.

That summer the welfare department again threatened to bring court action to force Jimi into foster care. As a compromise, Al agreed that Jimi could live with Al's brother Frank, who resided close by. At Frank's house, Jimi found another strong African American matriarchal figure in Frank's wife, Pearl. She ran her family like a drill sergeant, but also gave its members affection and homemade apple butter. "My mother explained to me that Jimi needed a place to stay because Al couldn't afford to take care of him," Diane Hendrix recalled. Frank Hendrix worked at Boeing and made a good income, so the extra plate at the table wasn't a burden. The most apparent negative for Jimi was that the move had taken him to a different middle school than his old pals were attending. When Jimi began seventh grade that fall, it was at Meany, while his friends were at Washington.

Al found landscape work, something he would continue to do for the rest of his life. But cutting grass didn't pay well, and he was forced to take in boarders. Cornell and Ernestine Benson moved in for a time, taking over what had been Jimi's room. Ernestine found that in addition to paying rent, Al expected her to do housework. Despite the fact that Al and Lucille had been divorced for several years, Al's ex was a frequent subject of his conversations. "He would call her a drunk," Ernestine recalled. "Sometimes he was calling her these names when *he* was drunk. But that was how men treated women in those days. It was accepted for men to drink, but a woman who drank was shunned." Al's own drinking, Ernestine recalled, was out of control, and at times he'd get lost coming home. "He'd come to a house with a gate, and since his house had a gate, he'd assume it was his," she said. "He'd walk right in, sit on the sofa, and say, 'Why are you all here?' And they'd say, 'We live here and you don't.' And then they'd call the police to get him out of there."

The appearance of Ernestine Benson did have one silver lining for Jimi: She was a blues-music fan and brought a large collection of 78 rpm records to the house. For the first time Jimi was exposed to Muddy Waters, Lightnin' Hopkins, Robert Johnson, Bessie Smith, and Howlin' Wolf. "I loved my blues," Ernestine recalled, "and Jimi loved the same down-home stuff." Jimi's only instrument was his broom, but as he listened to these blues sides, his air guitar became more animated. "He would play that broom so hard, he would lose all the straw," observed Cornell Benson.

⤳⤳⤳

IN FEBRUARY 1956, the never-ending shuffle of Jimi's life continued. Frank and Pearl broke up and sent him back to Al. The Bensons moved out, so for a time it was just Al and Jimi.

The move did allow Jimi to transfer to Washington Junior High, where he was reunited with his friends. In the past he'd been a fair student, but that year his grades declined dramatically. During the first half of the year he earned one B, seven C's, and one D. In the second half of the year, he had three C's, four D's, and two F's. Washington's principal, Frank Fidler, said Jimi was a frequent visitor to the school office, more for his poor grades than for discipline issues. "He was not a kid that got into a lot of trouble," Fidler recalled, "but he wasn't doing well academically."

Jimi finished the year at Washington and would have started eighth grade there in September 1956 had it not been for further problems at home. That month, the bank repossessed the house, and Jimi and Al were moved to a boardinghouse run by a Mrs. McKay. Jimi had to switch schools again and went back to Meany for eighth grade.

The McKay family had a paraplegic son who played a beat-up acoustic guitar with just one string. When the guitar was discarded, Jimi retrieved it and asked Mrs. McKay if he could buy it. "She said she'd sell it for five dollars," Leon recalled. Al was not willing to fork over the money, and eventually Ernestine Benson put up the money to buy Jimi his first guitar. To most, this instrument would have been a worthless piece of wood. Jimi, however, turned the guitar into a science project: He experimented with every fret, rattle, buzz, and sound-making property the guitar had. He wasn't exactly making music, but he was making noise. "He only had one string," Ernestine Benson observed, "but he could really make that string talk."

When he played air guitar now, at least he had a guitar to hold. At a matinee at the Atlas Theater, Jimi had seen the Nicholas Ray film *Johnny Guitar*. As Johnny Guitar, actor Sterling Hayden played only one song, and during most of the film, his acoustic was hung on his back with the neck pointing down. Still, that image had an indelible effect on Jimi. "He saw that movie," recalled Jimmy Williams, "and he loved the way that guy looked with that guitar on his back. He carried his guitar exactly like the guy in the movie." Like many teenagers, Jimi saw the guitar as a fashion accessory. Several of his classmates remember him taking the crippled guitar to school as a show-and-tell item. When asked if he could play, he replied, "It's broken." Still, he never let the guitar out of his sight. He even kept it on his chest while he slept.

Jimi was fourteen the summer of 1957. Two happenings within the next eighteen months would stick in his memory for all his years: He saw Elvis Presley perform and Little Richard preach.

The Elvis concert was the more predictable event. Elvis played at Seattle's Sick's Stadium on September 1. Jimi couldn't afford the dollar-fifty ticket, so he watched the show from a hill that overlooked the stadium. Though Elvis was just a speck, Jimi could still witness the madness of the sixteen thousand fans greeting the star's arrival onstage. Elvis played all his biggest hits and left the stage by diving into the backseat of a white Cadillac. When the Cadillac exited the field, it was Jimi's closest view of the King, who was outfitted in his gold lamé suit. Two months after the concert, Jimi drew a picture in his notebook of Elvis holding an acoustic guitar, surrounded by the titles of a dozen of his hit records.

Sometime the next year, Leon was running an errand for his foster mother when he spied a limousine and out stepped Little Richard. Richard shook Leon's hand and said he was preaching at a local church— this during a brief period when Richard renounced rock 'n' roll for the Lord. Leon ran to find Jimi and the two went that night to see

Richard preach. "We didn't really have any nice clothes," Leon said. "Jimi had on a white shirt but he had really ragged tennis shoes. People at the church looked at us." This incident was the basis of Jimi's later claim that he had been "kicked out" of church for improper clothing, which did not occur. Instead, despite the disapproving eyes of church elders, Jimi and Leon sat transfixed in a pew watching Little Richard's conk-styled hair bounce up and down as he preached of fire and brimstone. After the sermon, the boys waited around to meet Richard, but unlike others in attendance, they did not want to talk the Bible—they simply wanted to touch the first famous person they had ever been near.

❦

JIMI BEGAN NINTH grade in September 1957. The highlight of the year and perhaps of his life to that point was meeting Carmen Goudy, who would become his first girlfriend. At thirteen, she was younger than he but she did share his poverty. "If we had enough money between us for a Popsicle, that was a big deal," Carmen recalled. "We'd break the Popsicle in half." On the few occasions the teenagers had enough cash to see a matinee, it was only because Carmen had palmed her contribution to the Sunday-school collection plate. Most of their time was spent walking or hanging out in parks.

Carmen also lived in a boardinghouse, yet even to her, Jimi appeared poorer than poor. "He used to wear these little white buck loafers," she said. "He had a hole in the sole, so he'd cut these pieces of cardboard and put that in the bottom of his shoes. He'd walk so much that he'd wear out the cardboard. He came up with the idea that instead of just having one piece of cardboard in his shoe, he'd make up a supply of cardboard and keep it in his pocket. Then, if he was walking and his cardboard wore out, he could whip out this little piece and put it in his shoe." Jimi rarely had a lunch to bring to school, so Carmen would regularly split her sandwich with him.

What they each did have was an excess of desires, as both were dreamers. Carmen's fantasy was that she would be a famous dancer. Jimi's most immediate desire was to own a real guitar. After that, he announced, he was going to become a famous musician. These were the kind of teenage boasts that might have been mocked by schoolmates, but to Carmen and Jimi they were the glue of their romance. "We called it 'pretending,'" Carmen said. "We encouraged each other without suggesting that what the other said might be impossible."

Carmen had another asset that drew Jimi in; her sister was dating a man who played guitar. Jimi would frequently hang at the man's feet, as if by simply watching someone play he could acquire the ability. Jimi had learned to supplement his air guitar with noises he made with his mouth. "He made sounds that approximated notes," she said. "It was a bit like scat singing, but he actually could sing a guitar solo, not with words, but with sounds he made in his throat." As for actually singing, Jimi said his voice was inferior, and no matter how often Carmen urged him, he refused to croon to her. His childhood stutter had improved and it rarely came out except when he was nervous, which was often the case around Carmen.

Other boys in the neighborhood, who were Jimi's age, began to get their first instruments that year. Pernell Alexander was the first of his friends to own a guitar, though it was an acoustic with a neck that was as wide as a baseball bat, hardly a quality instrument. Later that year, Pernell acquired an electric guitar, and the instrument was such a popular neighborhood attraction that boys would stop by just to look at it.

When Jimi finally managed to acquire strings for his acoustic, being able to actually play his instrument was a relief—though the neck was warped and it wouldn't stay in tune. Nonetheless, he strummed it constantly, or at least until Al caught him. Jimi had been born left-handed, but his father insisted he write with his right hand. Al felt the same principle should apply to the guitar. "My dad thought everything left-handed was from the devil," Leon recalled. Jimi restrung the guitar so he could play leftie. This resulted in the almost comic routine that regularly occurred when Al arrived home and Jimi immediately flipped his guitar, keeping his song going all the while. "He learned to play left and right because every time my dad came into the room, he'd have to flip it and play upside down or my dad would yell at him," Leon said. "Dad was already unhappy that he was playing guitar all the time and not working." Al enlisted Jimi to help mow lawns whenever possible, an assignment the younger Hendrix tried to avoid as much as possible.

ᗡᗣᗢ

THAT FALL, LEON temporarily left foster care, and the three Hendrixes were together again in one tiny room of the boardinghouse. Jimi was in better spirits with his little brother around, and his grades showed some small improvement. That fall he had C's in English, music, science, and metal shop. He still flunked gym and received a D for general effort. Even those grades were remarkable considering that he now skipped school at least once a week. When he was truant, he walked the neighborhood, usually with his guitar strapped on his back like Johnny Guitar.

Though Jimi and Leon hadn't seen their mother in months, they heard from Delores that Lucille had remarried on January 3, 1958. After a very short romance, she had tied the knot with William Mitchell, a retired longshoreman who was three decades her elder. Despite the new marriage, it was Delores's assertion that Lucille was still occasionally seeing Al, at least when they would bump into each other at a tavern on Yesler they both frequented. "They'd run into each other there, and the whole thing would start again," Delores recalled.

It was health issues related to drinking that prompted Lucille's next visit with her sons. She had landed in Harborview Hospital twice in the fall of 1957, suffering from cirrhosis of the liver. In mid-January 1958, freshly married, she was back in the hospital with hepatitis. Delores took Jimi and Leon to visit her. The boys were shocked by their mother's pallid appearance in a wheelchair and by the deterioration she'd suffered since they'd last seen her. "She used to always look gorgeous and glamorous," Leon said. "She always wore jewelry and smelled nice. But this time there was none of that."

Lucille hugged and kissed the boys repeatedly, and after Jimi and Leon had left the room, she spoke to Delores alone. "You know, sister," Lucille said, "I'm not going to live long. I have all these kids, and I love them, and I want to take care of them and be a good mother, but I'm not going to be able to. I'm not going to make it." No matter how bad times had been in the past, Lucille had always maintained a sunny disposition; Delores was shocked to hear her younger sister so downcast. "You'll be fine," Delores told her. "You just take care of yourself." Lucille's condition improved, and she was out of the hospital the next week, giving hope that she was on the mend.

Years later, Jimi would write his most autobiographical song, "Castles Made of Sand," and refer to a woman in a wheelchair whose "heart was a frown." "That song is about our mother," Leon said. The song begins with a domestic spat, and the wife slams a door on her drunken husband. Another verse tells a tale of a young boy who plays in the woods, pretending he is an Indian chief. The crippled woman eventually decides to take her own life by jumping into the sea, pleading, "You won't hurt me no more," as she leaps. She lands on a "golden winged" ship. Jimi ends the song with a couplet about timelessness, using the image of "castles made of sand" washing into the sea.

❦

TWO WEEKS AFTER her last visit with Jimi and Leon, Lucille Jeter Hendrix Mitchell died.

Delores found out that her sister had been readmitted to the hospital on February 1, when she received a call from a friend of Lucille's who said she had been found unconscious in the alley next to a tavern on Yesler. Delores and Dorothy Harding immediately went to Harborview Hospital to see her. "The nurses said they didn't know what was wrong with her, but they said she'd be fine," Delores said. "They had so much going on that night that the hallways were full with shootings and knifings, and they hardly had looked at her." After the women complained, Lucille was finally taken to a room. They waited outside, but by the time a doctor arrived, Lucille had died of a ruptured spleen. "They might have saved her," Delores said, "but she had internal bleeding, and they never got to it."

Lucille's county death certificate listed her immediate cause of death as a "splenic rupture and hemorrhage." The certificate noted contributing conditions of "portal hypertension and portal cirrhosis." The portal vein carries blood to the liver; it can be compromised by cirrhosis, a liver disease usually caused by alcoholism. However, spleens, even in subjects with long-term cirrhosis, rarely rupture without trauma. Lucille must have either fallen or been struck for her spleen to rupture. There was much speculation in the family as to what happened to her outside that tavern, but the exact details were never discovered.

A friend came to the boardinghouse to tell Al the news. Jimi, who had turned fifteen the previous fall, overheard the conversation and began to weep; Leon was only ten and was more stunned than sad. Lucille had been taken to a funeral home in Chinatown, and Al borrowed a truck and took the children down there. Outside the funeral home, however, he had second thoughts about letting the boys see the body and made them stay in the truck while he paid his last visit to a woman with whom he had six children. "Al was the only man Lucille ever loved," Delores said. "She may have gotten in with other men, but she never loved anyone else."

Jimi cried while they waited in the truck, but Leon was stoic, thinking that if he showed no emotion, the pain would go away. When Al came back, he offered each boy a shot of Seagram's 7 from a flask of whiskey in his pocket. All three Hendrix males drank good long swigs, and Al drove them home.

The funeral was held four days later at a Pentecostal church. Al's mother, Nora, came down from Vancouver, and about two dozen of Lucille's friends attended. The funeral was scheduled for 2 PM on a Sunday. When it came time to begin, everyone was in attendance except Al, Jimi, and Leon. The preacher held the service up, hoping they were simply late. If Al wasn't going to come, Lucille's relatives thought, at least he'd have the decency to bring the boys. At 4 PM, two hours after it was scheduled, the funeral finally began. The boys never showed. "We kept waiting," Delores said, "and they just never came."

In his autobiography, Al explained that Jimi wanted to go to the funeral, but Al didn't have a car, so he gave Jimi bus fare and told him, "You got the fare, so you can catch the bus." Rather than take the bus to his mother's funeral by himself, Jimi stayed in his room weeping. "We both wanted to go," Leon recalled, "but my dad wouldn't let us."

When Dorothy Harding tracked Al down later that night, she smacked him upside the head. "I hated him for that," Harding recalled. "I told him that he would suffer for it in life." Perhaps more to the point, Delores told Al that Jimi and Leon would suffer for it. Al's response: "Well, there's no sense with them going up there now, it's all over with."

"No, Al," Delores replied, pointing at the boys, who were then in the next room, held in Dorothy's embrace. "That might be true for you, but it's never going to be over for them."

Jimi had always been shy, but after Lucille's death, he became more withdrawn and distant. During the rest of his adolescence, it was rare for him to initiate a conversation with anyone other than his closest friends. "He became extremely sensitive," Ebony Harding recalled. "He was very, very sad." There was also a sense of detachment that some noticed; it was almost as if having been through this, the deepest loss, he felt that nothing else really mattered. It also marked the beginning of a trait that many would notice in his adulthood: Instead of long-term planning, he lived every day as if it were his last. He continued to be a dreamer, but he also responded with resignation when things in his life went wrong.

Lucille's death permanently changed Jimi's relationship with Al. Even when Jimi hadn't known where his mother was, she remained an emotional presence in his life, an alternative that could at least be imagined. His father's choice not to let him attend the funeral stuck with Jimi as a bitter memory. "He never really forgave our dad for that," said Leon. As for the loss of his mother, Jimi rarely talked about it, even to his closest friends. Girlfriend Carmen Goudy found out from a classmate. Jimmy Williams heard from Leon. In his own internal world, Jimi began to idealize the mother he had lost, and Lucille increasingly became the subject of the poems and embryonic songs he'd begun writing that spring. Jimi had always been interested in science fiction and space, but to these boyish pursuits, he added a new fascination with angels. "Mama became an angel to him," Leon said. "He told me he was sure she was an angel, and she was following us around."

∽∽∽

ONE NIGHT LATER that spring, Delores Hall heard a noise on her front porch. She grabbed a flashlight and went to investigate. As she scanned the light over the porch, it illuminated Jimi's pie-shaped face. He was in a chair in the corner. "What are you doing out here so late at night, Buster?" she asked. "Nothing, Auntie," he replied.

"It was like he was lost," Delores Hall remembered years later. "He was so withdrawn that night. I'd hardly ever seen him like that."

Delores tried to lighten him up. "Why don't you come in?" she implored. "I'll get you something to eat."

"Oh, I'm just looking up at the stars," he said. "I'll come in later."

"You thinking about your mom?" she asked.

"How'd you know?" he answered. "I'm gonna see her someday. I'm going to see her again."

"I know you are," Delores replied. "We all are."

Jimi seemed to soften, as if this intensity could only be endured for so long. And then, as the spell lifted, he went back to sounding like a boy who'd read too many science-fiction comic books and seen too many *Flash Gordon* films at the Atlas Theater. "One of these days, I'm going to astral project myself up into the skies," he boasted. "I'll be going to the stars and the moon. I want to fly and see what's up there.

"I want to go up to the sky," he said, looking at his aunt, "from star to star."

# CHAPTER SIX

# TALL COOL ONE

*"The way he played 'Tall Cool One' was so smooth, you would have thought he was in the Fabulous Wailers."*

—CARMEN GOUDY

IN THE SPRING OF 1958, Jimi and Al left the boardinghouse and moved into a two-bedroom home on Beacon Hill with Cornell and Ernestine Benson. Leon had been sent back to foster care again, but there were still four people—Al, Jimi, Cornell, and Ernestine—living in a home that was less than five hundred square feet.

The move, to Jimi, nonetheless felt like a respite. Though residing on Beacon Hill put him farther away from the Central District and his friends, he was closer to the Hardings. He was also back with Ernestine, who made him meals and mothered him. And, of course, there was the important matter of her collection of blues records. Ernestine would occasionally even take Jimi down to Bob Summerrise's World of Music and let him pick out a record. Summerrise's legendary store carried a wide selection of records by blues and R&B artists; it also carried those of popular white artists, though, in a reversal of sorts, those were kept under the counter. Summerrise hosted a radio show that played cutting-edge black music, and Jimi was an avid listener.

Jimi turned fifteen that fall and his tastes in music began to mature. Now when he stopped by Pernell Alexander's house, they'd spin records by Elmore James and try to play along on their guitars. Through a friend, Pernell managed to get them tickets to see Little Richard, who was back on the rock 'n' roll circuit. They were able to sneak in early for a matinee performance and sit in the front row. During the concert, the two boys were so animated that when Pernell's friend got them back-stage after the show, Richard recognized them and slapped them on the backs. "You the boys who were dancing so much!" Richard exclaimed. The next day at school, Jimi told his entire class about his encounter with Little Richard, but few believed his good fortune. The pair also saw Bill Doggett that fall.

Jimi never took formal music lessons, but learned licks from neighborhood kids, most notably from Randy "Butch" Snipes. Butch could play guitar behind his back, imitating a T-Bone Walker move, and managed an admirable Chuck Berry duckwalk. Jimi sat at Butch's feet on many an afternoon, watching, and, if only in his head, trying to imagine how he could accomplish the same kind of showmanship.

Guitar moves were one of the few things Jimi was learning since his grades continued to decline. Their move to the house with the Ben-sons had meant yet another middle school transfer—his fourth school in three years. His report card for ninth grade showed him with three C's and five D's. If there was any good news, it was that he received only one F—ironically, in music. He occasionally brought his guitar to school, but apparently the results did little to impress his music teacher, who encouraged him to consider other career paths. The fact that he flunked music reflected more on the chasm between his interests— blues, R&B, rock 'n' roll—and the music theory that was taught by schools in the late fifties than it did on Jimi's nascent talent. He placed in the fortieth percentile in standardized tests that year, his poor marks a partial result of his woeful attendance record. That spring, he missed eleven days of school and was tardy almost every day. "I couldn't tell if it was because of his home life or just a lack of interest in regimented academics," observed Jimmy Williams. "Jimi was always a free spirit, and school just didn't really fit him."

His grades precipitated an event that would cause him the greatest shame of his youth: All the kids he had grown up with at Leschi Elementary were headed for high school. He, instead, was ordered to repeat ninth grade. He told almost no one of this development and lied when asked which high school he would be attending. Most adults in his life remembered Jimi as a bright kid. In fact, most of his problems with school came from not applying himself, or from missing class.

On the frequent occasions when Jimi skipped school, he made his rounds, like a cop on a beat. He inevitably stopped by Leon's foster home; he'd stop by Pernell's; he'd visit Jimmy Williams; and he'd stop in at Terry Johnson's. He'd walk Carmen home from school, even when he missed school himself. And his travels began to include the homes of a number of musicians, where he hoped he'd get some tips on playing. "In that era, guys were really open, and they would show you riffs and share stuff with you," recalled drummer Lester Exkano. "No one ever thought there would be any money to be made with music, so it was more a matter of personal pride to share these ideas with other players." Exkano remembered Jimi's favorite guitar players at the time were B.B. King and Chuck Berry.

A couple of musical families were significant, not just to Jimi, but to many aspiring players in the neighborhood. The Lewis family—with keyboardist son Dave Lewis and father Dave Lewis Sr.—inspired many. "They had this basement with a piano, and the door was always open," recalled Jimmy Ogilvy. "Dave Sr. could play guitar, but mostly he was always encouraging. He had showed Ray Charles and Quincy Jones some licks." The Lewis family provided a supportive environment where kids were told that being creative was a positive thing. The Holden family, with sons Ron and Dave and patriarch Oscar, also held court in this manner. In many ways, this informal school—the school

of rhythm and blues as practiced in the basements and back porches of
central Seattle—became Jimi's higher education.

ᴄᴧᴼᴠ

JIMI TURNED SIXTEEN that fall, and music became an increasingly
important part of his life. He had become proficient on his acoustic guitar, but what he most wanted was an electric model. "He was fascinated
with electronics," Leon recalled. "He had rewired a stereo and tried to
make it electrify his guitar." Ernestine Benson, seeing Jimi's interest in
music grow, hounded Al to buy the boy a proper instrument.

School continued to be a problem. Even retaking classes he had
failed the previous year, Jimi struggled. When he and Al moved again in
December to live for a few months with Grace and Frank Hatcher, it
necessitated yet another transfer to Washington Junior High. When the
spring term was over, Jimi had again failed math, English, and mechan-
ical drawing. He couldn't be held back a second time, so school officials
approved him for high school in the fall, hoping, no doubt, that the
new environment would improve his grades.

Father and son spent only a short time living with the Hatchers,
who quickly tired of Al's troubles. "Al was so inconsistent: drinking,
gambling, and coming home any old time," Frank Hatcher recalled. In
April 1959, they moved again, this time to an apartment on First Hill.
The building was so rodent-infested, Al never bothered to turn the gas
stove on or to use the kitchen. Prostitutes worked down the street. The
apartment was across from a juvenile detention center, which perhaps
served as a reminder to Jimi of where things could lead.

Despite the degradation around them, it was in that apartment
where Jimi found his greatest childhood joy when he received his first
electric guitar. Nagged constantly by Ernestine Benson to "get that boy
a guitar," Al finally relented and bought an instrument on time payments from Myer's Music. He purchased a saxophone at the same time,
thinking he would take the instrument up himself. For a brief while,

the two Hendrix males jammed together. When the next payment came due, however, Al returned the horn.

Jimi's guitar was a white Supro Ozark. It was right-handed, but Jimi immediately restrung it leftie; that still meant that the guitar's controls were reversed, which would have made it difficult to master. Jimi immediately called Carmen Goudy and yelled into the phone, "I've got a guitar!"

"You already have a guitar," she said.

"No, I mean a *real* guitar!" he exclaimed. He dashed over to her house. As they walked to Meany Park, Jimi was literally jumping for joy with the guitar in his hands. "Remember," Carmen said, "we were kids who were so poor, we didn't get stuff for Christmas. This was like having five Christmases all rolled up into one. You couldn't help but feel happy for him. I think it was the happiest day of his life."

In the park, Jimi tinkered with the guitar and tried a few of the licks he had learned on acoustic. He already had his moves down from his countless hours of playing air guitar, so he looked like a player even if his skills were raw. "I'm going to be your first fan," Carmen announced.

"Do you really think I'll have fans?" Jimi asked. She assured him that he would.

Their relationship had already advanced to kissing, though both were still learning the art. After they kissed, Jimi would explain what kind of kiss they'd just done. "That was a French kiss, where your tongue goes in the mouth," he'd say. She recalled that his kisses "were the juiciest." In the park that day, Carmen was frustrated that Jimi was more interested in the guitar than in kissing. This, of course, made him even more attractive to her, an advantage that Jimi would eventually sharpen into a fine-honed art.

∽∂∾

THE GUITAR BECAME his life, and his life became the guitar. With the instrument in hand, his next fixation became finding a band. Over the course of the following months, Jimi would play with virtually everyone who owned an instrument in the neighborhood. Mostly it was informal jamming, and much of it was unamplified, since Jimi didn't yet have an amplifier. If he was lucky, one of the older musicians would let him plug into his equipment, and he would wail away. He was able occasionally to check out an amp at a boys' club. He also didn't have a case for his guitar, so he carried it either unprotected or in a paper dry cleaner's sack, which made him look more like a hobo than a slick guitar man. Carrying his guitar in a sack, he mirrored Chuck Berry's "Johnnie B. Goode."

At the time, Jimi knew only a few riffs and no full songs. Carmen Goudy recalled that the first song he learned to play, start to finish, was "Tall Cool One" by the Fabulous Wailers. The Wailers were an R&B-influenced rock band from Tacoma, Washington, renowned locally for being the first group to perfect "Louie, Louie."

Initially, Jimi was drawn to the pop songs that were popular in the day. He often played with Jimmy Williams; Williams would sing while Jimi accompanied him with some crude guitar chords. "We'd do these standards," Williams recalled. "It was lots of Frank Sinatra and Dean Martin stuff. Jimi really worked on getting down the rhythm to those songs. And he loved Duane Eddy." Eddy, who specialized in upbeat rockabilly, became Jimi's first real guitar hero, and he quickly learned "Forty Miles of Bad Road," "Peter Gunn," and "Because They're Young." He picked up songs so fast, learning a new one every day, that Jimmy Williams used to joke that Jimi was "a human jukebox." When given a long solo, he'd play with flash, which wasn't always appropriate, even for Duane Eddy. Still, rock 'n' roll was only one of Jimi's many interests, and Williams recalled that Jimi's favorite song that summer was Dean Martin's "Memories Are Made of This."

On September 9, 1959, Jimi started tenth grade at Garfield High School. Though he was a year late, high school nonetheless marked an exciting transition for him. Garfield, located in the heart of the Central District, was the most integrated high school in Seattle, and one of the city's best. The student body was 50 percent white, 20 percent Asian, and 30 percent black. It was also huge: 1,688 students attended the year Jimi began.

During his first semester at Garfield, Jimi was tardy twenty days and his grades showed no significant improvement. He was so uninvolved in class that one of his teachers described him as "a nonstudent student." He came to school primarily because it allowed him to reconnect with Jimmy, Pernell, and his other friends from the neighborhood. Most of their daily discussions, sometimes in the back of the room during class, were about music. The school had a jukebox in the lunchroom and students were allowed to play it. Kids were forming bands, or talking about forming bands, all the time. Most neighborhood bands were informal, with revolving lineups depending on who was free on what night. In the back row of social studies, they would plan who would play bass and what song list their next band might tackle.

Jimi's very first gig was in the basement of the Temple De Hirsch Sinai, a Seattle synagogue. Jimi was playing with a group of older boys in what was billed as an audition for his permanent inclusion in the then-nameless band. "During the first set, Jimi did his *thing*," Carmen Goudy recalled. "He did all this wild playing, and when they introduced the band members and the spotlight was on him, he became even wilder." After the set break, the band returned to the stage without Jimi. Goudy began to worry that he had fallen ill; Jimi had been so nervous before the show, she feared he would throw up. After a search, she located him in an alley behind the building. Jimi looked despondent, as though he might start crying at any moment. He told Carmen that he had been fired after the first set—fired from his first band on the first night of his professional career. Rather than go home, he sat in the alley for an hour while he discussed the sorry state of his nascent career. Carmen quietly tried to suggest that maybe Jimi could play a bit more traditionally and with less flash. Hearing this, even from his girlfriend, offended Jimi. "That's not my style," he insisted. "I don't do that." Her main concern was Jimi's employability.

Not long after that, the relationship between Carmen and Jimi began to fade out, though not because of the disagreement. Other boys had begun to ask Carmen out, and she was drawn to them. "I really liked Jimi," she recalled, "but older guys had cars, and money to take me places." Carmen's dates with Jimi were almost always walks in the park: They frequently walked past a drive-in restaurant where they would witness other couples sipping Cokes, close together in the front seat of a car. "Older boys could buy me a hamburger, but Jimi had neither a car nor any money to go on a date." She remained friends with him throughout high school, but his juicy kisses were soon just a memory.

ᥒᥬ

JIMI'S FIRST SIGNIFICANT band would be the Velvetones, a group formed by piano player Robert Green and tenor sax player Luther Rabb. "We were really just a bunch of kids," recalled Luther. "We had a lineup that changed a lot, but included four guitar players, two piano players, a couple of horns, and a drummer. This was back in the era of 'the revue,' when each show had dance numbers. We had to dress up and glue glitter on our pants so they'd be shiny."

The Velvetones weren't a polished band. "Most of our songs were guitar/piano that mixed jazz, blues, and R&B," recalled Pernell Alexander, who played guitar with the group. A typical Velvetones set might include a jazz standard like "After Hours," followed by the Duane Eddy songs "Rebel Rouser" and "Peter Gunn." The band's one signature song was Bill Doggett's "Honky Tonk," an instrumental. "That became Jimi's standard," Terry Johnson observed. Initially, Jimi wasn't the best guitarist in the band, but he was getting better by the day. One of Jimi's physical gifts was longer than average fingers that allowed him to reach around the neck to hit high notes that were difficult for other players. He used this to its full advantage, playing individual notes that were not in the original compositions. Since he was a novice player, sometimes the result wasn't musically pleasing, but it drew the attention of a crowd. If nothing else, he was flashy.

One audition earned the Velvetones a steady weeknight gig at Birdland, the legendary club at Madison and Twenty-second Street. As a working musician, Jimi could now stop by and check out other bands for free, which was more of a benefit than the two dollars he might earn playing. On one of those visits, Jimi convinced Dave Lewis to allow him to solo while Lewis and his band were on break. These ten-minute spotlights gave Jimi a chance essentially to rehearse in front of a crowd and to try out some of his antics in a forum where nothing was at risk. As Lewis would later tell the story, Jimi frequently managed to shock the older, sophisticated audience that Lewis attracted: "He would play this wild stuff, but the people couldn't dance to it. They just stared at him."

One of the Velvetones' regular gigs was Friday nights at the Yesler Terrace Neighborhood House. Performing in the rec room of a housing project was hardly glamorous, and it didn't pay, but it gave Jimi and his bandmates a chance to experiment. "They were like sock hops, really, and some kids would dance, but mostly you were playing to other kids who were also musicians," recalled local musician John Horn. "They were playing R&B and some blues. Jimi was already something to watch—just the very fact that he was playing this right-handed guitar upside down was enough to keep you fascinated."

Jimi still didn't have an amp, and he knew not to ask his father for help in purchasing one. Though Al had bought the guitar, he regretted the decision, convinced that his son was spending entirely too much time on music. Al would later imply that he was supportive of Jimi's early bands, but the members of those groups, to a man, tell a different history. "Jimi would keep his guitar over at Pernell's house for fear that if it were kept at his house it would be destroyed," recalled the Velvetones' Anthony Atherton. "His father was pretty much against it, and music in the house, even practicing." Sneaking Jimi out of the house for practice or a gig became part of the band's daily duties. Several of the band members also witnessed Al hit his son when he was in a rage. "Al was like that," Pernell said. "He was a brutal man. Part of it was the times, and the way men were then. When the wife wasn't around to beat, they would beat the kids. It was a rough scene, man. It was straight-up ugly."

Al was infrequently home, but if he was, the band members knew to step lightly at the door. "Even as a teen, I knew Mr. Hendrix was noticeably a different kind of dad," recalled Atherton. "I was afraid of him because of the roar of his voice, and the way I'd seen him treat his own kids. Anyone who came around with an instrument was really in trouble. He'd say, 'Put that damn thing down; that's not going to get you a job.'"

One night after a gig at Birdland, Jimi left his guitar backstage at the club, thinking perhaps that it would be safer there than in his own home. When he returned the next day, the guitar had been stolen. "He was absolutely crushed," Leon recalled. "But I think he was even more upset that he knew he had to tell our dad, and he knew he was going to get a big whipping." It appeared, for the moment, that Jimi's career as a musician was over.

❦

IN THE FALL of 1959, Jimi began dating Betty Jean Morgan, whom he met at school. Betty had been raised in the South and had a thick accent—unusual for African Americans in Seattle. Their dates, given Jimi's lack of funds, were usually walks to Leschi Park. Betty's parents were traditional, and if Jimi was interested in taking their daughter out, he had to ask her father in person. Jimi enjoyed this formality. "He was a sweetheart," Betty Jean recalled. "My parents liked him because he was polite. My mother was a really good cook, and he adored her." When Jimi still had his guitar, he would play it on Betty Jean's porch in an effort to impress her.

Jimi turned seventeen that fall. Schoolmate Mike Tagawa recalled that he always dressed in styles that were two years out-of-date: "He dressed like what we called 'a rink.' He had black peg pants, a black-and-white-striped shirt with the collar up, and a belt that was one half inch wide and sat to the side. It was essentially the same look you saw in the movie *Grease*." When Jimi finally got a job as a paperboy for the *Seattle Post-Intelligencer*, he didn't keep it long: He quit after just three months, having had trouble collecting.

Jimi did frequently help his father mow lawns, and Al wanted him to go into the family business and work beside him. "If Jimi worked really hard all day," Leon recalled, "he'd get a dollar. But it was hard work and Jimi hated it." Jimmy Williams, in contrast, had a job at a grocery store making fifty dollars a week and tried to get Jimi on there. "That money would have made a world of difference in his life," Williams said, but Al refused to let his son take the position. "Al kept saying, 'I can't have him out working that late because he's got to study and go to school,'" Williams recalled. "But, of course, Jimi was rarely going to school and was never studying."

The friendships between the neighborhood boys began to shift as they grew older, got jobs, or left the area. Jimi seemed behind the others on many fronts, and even his relationship with Betty Jean had progressed only to kissing. He spent New Year's Eve of 1959 with Jimmy Williams playing Dean Martin's "Memories Are Made of This." He called Betty Jean on the phone at midnight, but considering she lived only a few blocks away, this would hardly have impressed her as romantic.

If Jimi slept with any other girl at the time, he never bragged or boasted of it to his friends. Jimmy Williams and Pernell Alexander recall a party they all attended where older, sexually experienced women were expected. On the face of it, the night seemed to offer Jimi a chance at losing his virginity. Pernell was always more streetwise, and prior to entering the house, he sat Jimi and Jimmy down on the front steps, as an older brother might do, and gave them the lowdown. "These girls' parents are gone, so they are going to want to be partying, maybe, all night. I hope you guys know what to do. Have either of you ever been laid?"

Neither Jimi nor Jimmy answered. It was obvious from their silence, and wide-eyed stares, that they were not experienced. "Well, all you gotta do is be cool," Pernell said as he entered the house.

Jimi and Jimmy did not follow. They remained on the porch looking at each other, searching for fortitude. To them, sexuality was closely associated with the lectures they'd been given about not getting girls pregnant. To add to their trepidation, they knew friends who had fathered children already. For a few moments they talked and considered what a problem a pregnancy would add to their already-difficult young lives. They were seventeen at the time, but they were still boys. "I can't afford to get a girl pregnant," Jimi fretted. Jimmy Williams echoed that sentiment. Eventually, Jimmy rose and started to walk away. Jimi stood up and followed his best friend home, never setting foot inside the house.

cాఅ

JIMI EVENTUALLY TOLD Al about losing his guitar, and he received the lecture of his life for it. For several weeks, Jimi came to school with the demeanor of a hound dog.

Prior to the loss, Jimi had begun to play in a band called the Rocking Kings. Like the Velvetones, this group was made up of high school kids, but they had managed several professional-level paying gigs. Though the band had an excellent guitar player in Junior Heath, Jimi made an impression at a "battle of the bands" concert earlier that fall that earned him a position in the band. "He seemed really straight," recalled drummer Lester Exkano. "He didn't smoke, and he didn't drink. He was a bit wilder than other guys." Jimi may have been a square offstage, but put him onstage, with an amplifier and spotlight, and he was transformed. The Rocking Kings had a manager, James Thomas, who tried to get them bookings and make them appear more professional. One of Thomas's managerial edicts was that everyone in the band had to wear suit coats. For one show Jimi had to rent a red jacket, and the rental ended up costing more than his take from the gig. It was a point Al did not quickly let Jimi forget.

After Jimi's guitar was stolen, he was useless to the Rocking Kings, and several members of the band finally pitched in to help buy him a new instrument. It was a white Danelectro Silvertone, bought at Sears Roebuck for $49.95, and it came with a matching amp. As he'd done with his previous instrument, Jimi usually left the guitar at someone else's house to avoid the wrath of his father. Jimi painted the guitar red and wrote the name "Betty Jean" in two-inch-high letters on the front. His aunt Delores remarked that he might have called the guitar "Lucille" after his mother had not B.B. King already taken the name.

B.B. King remained an influence, and songs like "Every Day I Have the Blues" and "Driving Wheel" were popular covers by the band. A Rocking Kings set might include "C.C. Rider," the original R&B version as done by Chuck Willis; Hank Ballard's version of "The Twist," which was slower than the Chubby Checker hit; popular numbers like "Rockin' Robin'" or "Do You Want to Dance"; covers of hits by the Coasters; Fats Domino's "Blueberry Hill"; and, almost always, songs by Duane Eddy and Chuck Berry. The band also played their own versions of the local favorites "David's Mood" and "Louie, Louie." "We mixed blues, jazz, and rock," recalled Exkano. "We'd play anything that would keep people dancing." The songs were driven by Exkano's unusual drum sound, which he called "a slop beat." "It was more of a shuffle," Exkano explained, "which made it easier to dance to. It was definitely a black sound, but our shows were mixed, and everybody came."

In June 1960, Al and Jimi moved yet again, this time to a small house at 2606 East Yesler Way, just a few blocks away from Garfield High. Jimi ended his sophomore year with a B in art, a D in typing, F's in drama, world history, and gym, and he had withdrawn from language arts, woodshop, and Spanish rather than fail. "He just wouldn't study," recalled Terry Johnson. "Then he'd get these failing grades, and that would further hurt his self esteem."

When school started again at Garfield the next September, Jimi went to classes for the first month, but it was soon obvious he was never going to graduate. Despite several warnings from school officials that he'd be expelled if he skipped class again, Jimi again failed to show up, and at the end of October 1960, he was officially taken off the ranks of Garfield students. His school files showed his reason for leaving was a "work referral," but he had no job other than as guitar player in the Rocking Kings. "He was so far away from graduating, it wasn't a matter of a few credits or classes," recalled principal Frank Hanawalt. "He had missed so much it was really impossible to make it all up. There were laws then that we couldn't keep a student on our books if they didn't attend class regularly." Around 10 percent of the student body at Garfield dropped out that year.

Years later, when Jimi became famous and began mythologizing his past to gullible reporters, he told a fantastic tale of how he had been "kicked out" of Garfield by racist teachers after he'd been discovered holding hands with a white girlfriend in study hall. The story was completely fabricated: Interracial dating was not unheard of at the school, though Jimi had no white girlfriend to hold hands with. No one who attended Garfield in that era can recall any high school girlfriend other than Betty Jean. Jimi did bond with Mary Willix, a white classmate who became a close friend—he often spoke to Mary about UFOs, the unconscious mind, and reincarnation. Jimi's friendship with Willix was platonic yet it was one of the few times in his youth he developed a relationship with a Caucasian female. "None of the other [white] women students hardly knew who Jimi was," Willix observed. Still, their camaraderie, along with many of the friendships Jimi made with musicians of all races at Garfield and in the Central District that fall, would leave a lasting impression. "The multiculturalism Jimi experienced at Garfield would stick with him for the rest of his life," Willix recalled. "It was truly a special place and everyone who went there was marked by it." These friendships, many formed around a mutual love of music, had more effect on Jimi than anything he learned in class.

As for Jimi's later fantastic tale of being kicked out of study hall for his imaginary white girlfriend, even the idea of Jimi sitting in study hall was enough to earn a chuckle from his friends and classmates. The truth was that on October 31, 1960, Halloween, seventeen-year-old Jimi Hendrix flunked out.

# CHAPTER SEVEN

# SPANISH CASTLE MAGIC

SEATTLE, WASHINGTON
*November 1960–May 1961*

*"The Spanish Castle was the Valhalla of the era of Northwest rock 'n' roll shows. If you made it there, you'd made it."*
—Seattle DJ PAT O'DAY

IT DIDN'T ACTUALLY take Jimi Hendrix "half a day" to get to the Spanish Castle, as he wrote in his 1968 song "Spanish Castle Magic" about the legendary dance hall. From the Central District it took just an hour by car. Yet the trip to the club, which was in Kent, Washington, was a career-defining journey as the Castle was the Northwest's premier dance hall, and to play there was the dream of any local musician. Hendrix first visited the club in 1959 to see the Fabulous Wailers, the most popular regional band of the era, and he returned whenever he had the chance. Constructed as a ballroom in 1931, the Castle had a capacity of two thousand. Complete with stylish neon lights and a stucco facade with turrets, the venue's place in Northwest history was cemented when the Fabulous Wailers released the 1961 live album *At the Castle*. DJ Pat O'Day booked most of the big shows at the hall. "The Spanish

Castle was the Valhalla of the era of Northwest rock-'n'-roll dance shows," he said. "It was *the* place, and every local band wanted to play on that stage."

Jimi's first time on the Castle stage came when the Rocking Kings opened for another band there in late 1960. The show itself wasn't particularly notable as the band was nervous but by late 1960, the Rocking Kings were getting decent bookings. They had played Seattle's Seafair Festival and had won second place in an amateur "All State Battle of the Bands."

Though most of the audiences at the Castle were white, the club was integrated and many of the white musicians in the region had embraced R&B and jazz music. "The Northwest scene was very influenced by African American culture," recalled Larry Coryell, who began his career in the Checkers, a popular Castle group. "There was an originality to Northwest music, part of which came out of the fact that Seattle was so geographically isolated. Because of that, the dirty R&B of the Wailers, the Frantics, and the Kingsmen became the homegrown sound."

"Louie, Louie" was the region's signature song, played at virtually every show by every band. The lyrics may have been indecipherable, but the song's powerful beat—which had been adapted from Richard Berry's almost calypso original—was decidedly danceable. The "dirty" sound Coryell referred to was partly the result of using low-fi equipment at high volume levels, but was also a result of intentional experimentation. "We would actually cut the cones of speakers, put towels on them, and stick toothpicks in the woofers, all to get crude feedback," recalled Jerry Miller, who later played with Moby Grape. Jimi's experiments with distortion began around this time when he dropped his amp once and discovered that the jostling deformed the sound of his guitar.

No band was better at "dirty but cool" than Tacoma's Fabulous Wailers. Though they were all white, the Wailers had perfected their own innovative R&B sound, and their guitar player, Rich Dangel, was a huge influence on Jimi. Dangel recalled Jimi coming up to him after a Castle gig and complimenting his playing. "He was a shy guy, but he was clearly trying to flatter me," Dangel said. "He offered to sit in if we ever needed another guitar player." That idea on its surface was absurd, but it showed that the once-shy Jimi was attempting to promote himself. Not many African American guitarists played at the Castle, and Jimi would surely have stood out in that context.

The story of Jimi milling around backstage at the Castle has become legend. Pat O'Day told the tale most often: "There was this black kid that used to hang around. He'd come up to me real polite and say, 'Mr. O'Day? If anyone's amp breaks, I've got an amp in the trunk of my car. It's a really good one. But if you need to use it, I get to play, too.'" It was common for amplifiers at the time to blow tubes. Jimi's suggestion was a minor form of blackmail: You need my amp, you get me with it. While the story is rooted in some truth—O'Day later promoted shows by the Jimi Hendrix Experience, and he and Jimi would wax nostalgic on the Spanish Castle—it is certainly exaggerated, since Jimi didn't own a car and his only amp at the time was his Silvertone, which no musician would have called "really good." Friend Sammy Drain recalled that one of the neighborhood fellows had an ancient Mercury that was occasionally employed to get to the Castle. "When Jimi wrote that line about 'half a day away,' he was talking about that car breaking down, because sometimes it did take half a day to get there," Drain said.

Unreliable cars became a troublesome part of the experience of being in the Rocking Kings. Once, for example, when the band was booked for a well-paying gig in Vancouver, their car broke down before the Canadian border. They ended up playing an impromptu show in Bellingham, Washington, until local police shut them down. For their effort, the band came away with only bus fare back to Seattle. The original group dissolved after this disastrous almost-tour, though manager James Thomas re-formed the band and put Jimi in a greater role by giving him backup vocal duty. Jimi rarely sang at this point, arguing that his voice was too weak. Thomas renamed the band Thomas and the Tomcats and took on the duties of front man himself. In this configuration, the band got a few gigs in rural towns far from Seattle, but car trouble continued to sabotage them. One show in eastern Washington

netted them thirty-five dollars, which meant that Jimi's take would have
been around six dollars for a weekend's work. Still, the rural audience
loved the band, particularly Jimi's solo on Earl King's "Come On,"
which had become the highlight of the Tomcats' show. The band was
ebullient on the ride home until they were caught in a snow flurry east
of Seattle. "It was about four in the morning," remembered Lester
Exkano, "and we were in James Thomas's 1949 Studebaker. Everyone
was tired, so we pulled over and slept for a while, hoping the snow
would stop." When they woke two hours later, the storm had turned
into a blizzard and they feared they might freeze to death if they didn't
keep driving. Exkano was at the wheel when the car went off the road,
hit a ditch, and rolled over. No one was hurt, but the young men were
all frightened.

Jimi, however, was more than scared. He announced he was sick
of late-night drives in beater cars. "I'm all done with this shit," he told
his stunned bandmates. And with that, he lay down in the snow and
started making snow angels. The rest of the band trudged up the road
to search for a tow truck. When they returned an hour later, Jimi was
still lying in the snow and appeared lifeless, with his coat up over his
head. "We honestly thought he had frozen to death," Exkano recalled.
When Lester went to check Jimi's vital signs, the guitarist leaped up and
yelled, "I fooled you! You can't kill me that easy!"

∽∝∾

MOST OF JIMI'S friends had graduated from high school by the
spring of 1961. Employment opportunities for young African American
males were few, usually limited to service positions. Even many service
jobs—being a clerk in a department store, for example—were off-limits
to blacks in this era. As late as the 1950s, blacks in Seattle could buy
clothes at downtown department stores but were not allowed to try
them on first. With limited prospects, several of Jimi's friends, including Terry Johnson and Jimmy Williams, joined the armed forces, the

most common post–high school choice for African American males in the neighborhood.

Having dropped out of school, Jimi's career options were even more limited than most. He had no work experience, except for helping his father with landscaping and playing in bands. When friends ran into him that spring and asked if he had a job, he always announced that his job was the Tomcats. He owned nothing but his guitar and his amp, but those precious things were enough for him to imagine a career as a guitarist. When Hank Ballard and the Midnighters came through town on a tour, Jimi got free tickets and attended the show with his guitar on his lap. Afterward, he hounded Ballard's guitar player to teach him licks, following the man around until he complied. Jimi had begun to promote himself in earnest; he might have been short on financial resources, but he had ambition and moxie. Still, even at the Tomcats' most successful stage, Jimi was earning less than twenty dollars a month, and most of his cut went to buy gear and stage clothes. Jimi was eighteen, and legally an adult, but he was still dependent on his father to survive.

Sometime that spring, Jimi came into proximity with the other rising local: Bruce Lee. "It was at the Imperial Lanes down on Rainier Avenue," recalled fellow Garfield alum Denny Rosencrantz. At the time Lee was known for his local karate demonstrations and his penchant for starting fights in the bowling alley's parking lot. Jimi was there to watch friends bowl—he didn't have enough money himself—and other than shaking Lee's hand, he probably had little to do with the man who would go on to become a martial arts legend.

Jimi's relationship with his father continued to be troubled that spring. Al felt his son was lazy, and now that Jimi was, for all intents and purposes, a man, Al was more vocal in his criticism. "My dad thought Jimi's idea of playing music was crap," Leon recalled. "He literally said that music was 'the devil's business.'" Al still wanted his oldest son to join with him in the landscaping business. Jimi hated the physical work of landscaping, and the idea of working as his father's assistant was anathema to him. During the times father and son did work together, their shared labor did not help to bond them, and Jimi complained that all Al ever paid him was one dollar. Jimi and Leon would both imitate their father's gravelly voice, saying, "Here's a dollar." During the spring of 1961, a gardening client of Al's observed Al punching Jimi. Jimi spoke of the incident in a 1967 interview: "He hit me in the face and I ran away." Leon remembered that even when Jimi was as old as eighteen, Al would give him a "whipping" with the belt.

Even to the other members of the Rocking Kings—none of whom came from privileged backgrounds—the poverty of Jimi's home stood out. Terry Johnson worked at a burger joint that was directly across from Garfield High, and Jimi would often stop by for free food. Jimi learned from Terry that the restaurant threw away unsold burgers or fries at closing time. Even when Terry wasn't on duty, Jimi visited before closing and asked if there was extra food that was going to be discarded. At first some of the stand's staff were taken aback by what was essentially begging from a boy they knew from school. But soon they realized how pitiful Jimi's situation was and began to collect a daily cache of unsold hamburgers. Sometimes Jimi would be lucky enough to get half a dozen burgers, which he would take home. But on many occasions, he quickly scarfed down whatever food he was given right there in the parking lot like a starving wild animal. As he ate he looked across the street at the high school he no longer attended.

Jimi continued to date Betty Jean Morgan, though it was rare when he could afford to take her anywhere other than the park. Nonetheless, that spring Jimi asked her to marry him. His move was impetuous, and both Betty Jean and her parents never considered it seriously. "My mother said I would have to wait until I graduated, which wasn't until 1963," she recalled. Though her parents liked Jimi, in all likelihood they also were holding out the hope that he'd get a job before aspiring to any union with their daughter.

Talk of marriage was derailed in early May, when Jimi came under the care and supervision of the Seattle Police Department. On May 2, 1961, he was arrested for riding in a stolen car. He was taken to the ju-

venile detention center directly across the street from the apartment he
had lived in just a year before. When Al came to bail him out, Jimi told
his father that he didn't know the car was stolen, and that it was parked
at the time he was arrested. Al wrote in his autobiography that the matter was quickly straightened out and that Jimi "didn't have to serve any
time." Police records tell a different story: Jimi spent one day in jail for
that first offense, was released, and then just four days later was arrested
for riding in another stolen car. The coincidence of the two arrests,
coming so close together, did not argue for leniency when Jimi was
brought in for the second offense; he spent the next eight days in juvenile jail. That week in jail was not the end of the matter, as Jimi still had
to deal with a court hearing where he would be formally sentenced and
faced a significant penalty.

The Seattle Police Department was routinely criticized during this
era for their overactive prosecution of black males. "The cops would
stop you even if you were just walking down the street," recalled Terry
Johnson. In 1955, Seattle's mayor created a panel to investigate police
brutality in the Central District. The panel's report concluded that common police beliefs included "All Negroes carry knives" and "Any Negro
driving a Cadillac is either a pimp or a dope-peddler." Jimi swore he
didn't steal either car, nor did he know they were stolen. Still, he was
facing up to five years in prison on each of his criminal charges.

Though Jimi was a dreamer, even his wild imagination couldn't
conjure up a scenario in which he'd be able to make a living as a musician in Seattle. He had already expressed an interest in joining the
armed forces, and with his court date looming, he considered the option more seriously since prosecutors often accepted a stint in the service as a plea bargain. Jimi had made one attempt to join the air force
earlier that spring along with Anthony Atherton. "At the office they
took one look at us," Atherton recalled, "and said we didn't have the
physical capacity to endure the g-forces of an aircraft." The more likely
reason was that the young men were black; there were few African
American pilots in the air force at the time.

Jimi's next choice was the army. He went down to a recruiting office and asked if enlisting would earn him a position with the 101st Airborne Division. He had read about the 101st in history books, and he'd drawn the famous "Screaming Eagle" patch in his notepad. "He kept saying how he was going to get himself one of those patches," Leon recalled. The patch itself became a fixation to Jimi as it conferred an identity to the wearer. For a boy who drifted through childhood without a stable home life, that insignia, and the manhood it stood for, was a powerful lure.

At a hearing in juvenile court on May 16, 1961, a public defender represented Jimi. The prosecutor agreed to a two-year sentence that would be suspended on the condition Jimi join the army. His conviction, however, remained in his permanent record. The next day, Jimi signed up for a three-year commitment in the Army. He was scheduled to take a train on May 29 to Fort Ord, California, to begin his basic training. If he was lucky, he would soon be a member of the storied 101st Airborne Division, the very company that parachuted behind enemy lines during D-day. Other than a few trips as an infant, Jimi had never been more than two hundred miles outside of Seattle. He had not yet even been on an airplane, much less jumped out of one.

On the night before he left for basic training, Jimi had one final gig with the Tomcats. It was at an outdoor festival on Madison Street, and the band played on a stage right across from Birdland, the club where Jimi had gotten his start with the Velvetones almost three years before. Leon attended, wanting to see his big brother's last show with the band, as did Betty Jean Morgan. After the concert, Jimi presented Betty Jean with a cheap rhinestone ring he had purchased, announcing it was an engagement ring. In a move that probably committed him to Betty Jean more than the ring, he asked if she would keep his beloved guitar at her house until he could send for it.

The street dance drew several hundred people, including a number of school friends and neighborhood buddies who had known Jimi in the eighteen years he had lived in Seattle. One was Carmen Goudy, who attended with a new boyfriend. There was no bad blood between Carmen and Jimi, nor did she feel bittersweet at seeing him onstage again. Yet as one of the only people who had seen his very first public concert—in the basement of a synagogue, at a show that got him fired—she couldn't help but notice how much his playing had improved in such a short time. He had confidence now, and though his solos were still overly flashy, he played with the kind of panache that forced audiences to watch him. "He was still a wild man when it came to playing," she recalled. "But he was good. He was *really* good."

The next day, he took the night train to California. Jimi had taken the same trip a decade and a half before with his grandmother Clarice and his mother, Lucille, heading to Berkeley. To a three-year-old, the train had been a glorious machine of wonder, but as an adult, he was lonesome before it even left the station. Jimi had spent all of his young life within walking distance of this station, but now the train was taking him south again, away from the only place he had ever called home.

# CHAPTER EIGHT

# BROTHER WILD

FORT ORD, CALIFORNIA
*May 1961–September 1962*

*"She's a real sweet woman, and I believe, a good mother, but as
you say, she is tempted a little by 'Brother Wild.'"*
—JIMI HENDRIX in a letter to his father

ON MAY 31, 1961, Jimi Hendrix arrived in Fort Ord, California, and
began basic training in the United States Army. When enlisting, he had
requested a position as a clerk and asked for an assignment with the
101st Airborne, though his final orders would come only after basic
training. Jimi had picked the Airborne, he said later, because the haz-
ards posed by jumping out of planes also came with a fifty-five-dollar-
a-month pay bonus, a significant amount of money to a kid who had
barely made that much in his entire life. He had also briefly considered
becoming an Army Ranger, another extremely tough duty. His military
records show that a month after he entered the service he weighed 155
pounds, and was five feet ten inches tall.

Years later, Jimi would tell an interviewer that he "hated the army
immediately," but that assertion is contradicted by some of his own let-

ters home. Initially at least, he reveled in the structure and formality of the service, which dictated when you ate, what you wore, and what you did every minute of the day. For one who had lived so independently as a teenager, and who was so neglected as a child, the army's order was a welcome change. At the very least, Jimi was getting three square meals a day, the most consistent nutrition of his life.

Jimi wrote Al dozens of letters during his first six months of duty. His initial reason for writing home was to borrow money—he complained that his army pay was late and didn't cover his basic needs. But the correspondence soon expanded to encompass his homesickness, and his future desires. There was a longing, and a wistfulness, in Jimi's letters to Al, which were frequent and lengthy. Jimi didn't need much of a reason to write—he wrote once simply to let his father know he'd lost a bus ticket. Al wrote back, though his missives were shorter and less regular. Yet the correspondence became important to both men, and it represented the deepest intimacy they would ever share as father and son. Despite his latchkey childhood, Jimi was a fragile boy who hadn't seen much of the world. Being so far away from his friends and family softened his feelings about home. Despite his father's many flaws, Jimi clearly loved Al, and felt loved in return. That affection was more apparent in their letters than it ever was in their interactions.

Jimi's first letter, written just five days after his arrival at Fort Ord, contained a plea for money ("please, if you can send a few dollars as soon as you can"), along with a lengthy list of his expenses ("shoe polish kit, $1.70; two locks, 80 cents each"). He also commented on his initial reaction to army cleanliness and grooming: "We have to clean the barracks up a little before we go to bed. I just wanted to let you know that I'm still alive, although not by very much. Oh, the army's not too bad, so far. It's so-so, although it does have its 'ups-and-downs' at times. All, I mean *all* my hair is cut off, and I have to shave." Jimi's facial hair had only recently started to grow, so shaving itself was new to the eighteen-year-old. He attempted to sound positive in the letter, but his homesickness was obvious. "Although I've been here for about a week, it seems like a month. Time passes pretty slow."

Jimi found time to write home at least once a week over the next two months, and some weeks more often. He initially had been told he would be sent to Fort Lee, Virginia, to typing school, but those orders never arrived, and he waited for his coveted assignment with the 101st Airborne. On August 4, he completed basic training and was given the rank of Private. He had been photographed in his army uniform a month before, and he sent that picture, along with the news of his promotion, to his father, Delores Hall, Dorothy Harding, and Betty Jean Morgan, with whom he'd also kept up a regular correspondence. His affection for his girl grew with distance. Her picture was on his bunk, and he continued to talk of marrying her. He even wrote letters to Betty Jean's mother and grandmother. In all likelihood, he wrote these letters to sweet-talk his future in-laws, but it was also because Jimi was lonely, and any letter he received in return buoyed his spirits.

He had been gone less than two months when he asked Al to collect his guitar from Betty Jean's mother and send it to him. It arrived on July 31, and that blessed occasion was reason enough to write another letter. This particular letter, which ran six pages on U.S. Army Training Center stationery, went beyond thanking his father for the all-important guitar. Jimi began by apologizing for not immediately answering Al's last letter: "We were out in the field for a week, and when you run out of stamps or paper there, you're out of luck—that's what happened to me." The guitar, Jimi wrote, "was a welcome sight. It made me think of you and home." He complained of being on an eight-week assignment, and that his superiors had threatened to add another year to his enlistment term.

Al had recently split with a girlfriend, Willeen, and Jimi used this occasion to speak of his thoughts on the character of his father's girlfriend. "She's a real sweet woman," he wrote of Willeen, "and I believe, a good mother, but as you say, she is tempted a little by 'Brother Wild.' If she would only understand that she had the best deal she *ever* had and probably *will* ever have [with you]. But I just know she still loves you because she used to tell me how she really cared for you a lot of times, enough times to convince me. And when it comes to that, it takes a lot to convince me, like with Betty, for instance."

Jimi wrote that army life hadn't changed his personality much, but he had learned how to clean up the barracks. He said he looked forward to seeing Al's new stereo, and that on his visit home he would plan on bringing photographs he'd taken on base. He promised to arrive on Saturday night if he was able to catch a plane. He ended with words about his father as sweet as he ever wrote: "As long as you're around, things are perfect for me, because you are my Dear Dad and I'll always love you . . . always. . . . So with all the love in the world, to Dear Old Dad, from your loving son, James."

Jimi ended this letter, as he ended most of his correspondence during the next few years, with a small illustration of his Danelectro guitar. In his letter he referred to an upcoming one-week leave he was due; he had hoped to be able to fly back to Seattle. The leave was delayed and a week later he wrote another letter to say he was still waiting for official orders. "Some people wait two, three, or four days," he observed, "others weeks or maybe even months. . . . It gives you a feeling of time being wasted although it *does* count." By "count," Jimi meant that each day that passed meant one less day of his three-year commitment. He'd been in the service for two months, and he was already tracking the days until he got out. He did end the letter with some good news: "I qualified as sharpshooter. That's the second highest to qualify with an M-1 rifle." How Jimi managed this feat is unknown; he was terribly nearsighted. An army physician had already singled out his bad vision on his record and had ordered him to get glasses, which Jimi refused to wear.

On September 1, Jimi finally got permission for his one-week leave. He took his guitar with him, wanting it in Seattle until he knew his next assignment. Jimi was unable, however, to afford a plane ticket, so he took a bus, which meant four of his seven days of leave would be taken up with travel. When he got off the bus in Seattle, he was freshly shaved and wearing his dress uniform, including, he was quick to point out, a blue cord around his sleeve for extra training. "He looked so handsome in that uniform," recalled his cousin Dee Hall. "He was proud to show it off to everyone."

His reunions with Al and Leon were both emotional. Al was proud of Jimi in his uniform, and he noticed that the time in the service had matured his son. The uniform dazzled Leon, who was also amazed that his older brother had five dollars to give him. Jimi visited Aunt Delores, Dorothy Harding, and a number of old friends from the neighborhood, but the reunion he had most looked forward to was with Betty Jean. He spent the bulk of his leave with her, or, put less romantically, with her and her parents. "He told my parents he was going to marry me as soon as I got out of school and that I'd be an army bride," Betty Jean recalled. On his last day in Seattle, Jimi gave Betty Jean a silk pillowcase he had brought her from California. He told her it was the pillowcase he slept on every night thinking of her, though it was unlikely any soldier with a silk pillowcase would have been allowed such an indulgence. He wrote on the pillowcase, "Love forever, always yours, James Hendrix, September 7, 1961."

During September, Jimi and Betty Jean exchanged letters almost every other day. When he missed a few letters in their regular cycle, she accused him of stepping out on her. "You're fooling with someone else down there. . . . You better write and leave those 'sapphires' alone, or you just better not come up here to see me." After a couple of fuming letters like this, Jimi wrote to Al to complain that his girlfriend's "emotions change about two or three, sometimes four, times as she writes." Jimi didn't help his case with Betty Jean when he wrote to tell her he was so poor her birthday gift would be coming late.

On Halloween, Jimi's long-delayed orders arrived: He had been assigned as a supply clerk for the 101st Airborne Division in Fort Campbell, Kentucky. He immediately broadcast this glorious news to all his correspondents. Al had his own good news: He wrote to say that Leon was back from foster care, and the two were together. Jimi's reply noted that he was "so glad" to hear that his brother and father were reunited and that he understood what it meant to be lonesome: "That's the way I feel when I start thinking about you, and the rest, and Betty." Jimi's letter ended with a pledge to "try my very best to make this Airborne for the sake of our name. . . . I'll fix it so the whole family of Hendrixes will have the right to wear the 'Screaming Eagle' patch."

He arrived at Fort Campbell on November 8 and immediately wrote his father. At the end of the letter, he included his guitar monogram illustration, but added a little parachutist, too. He wrote:

> Well, here I am, exactly where I wanted to go. I'm in the 101st Airborne. . . . It's pretty rough, but I can't complain, and I don't regret it . . . so far. We jumped out of the 34-foot tower the third day. It was almost fun. . . . When I was walking up the stairs to the top of the tower, I was walking nice and slow, just taking it easy. There were three guys that quit when they got to the top of the tower. You can quit anytime, and they took one look outside, and just quit. And that got me thinking as I was walking up those steps. But I have it made in my mind that whatever happens, I'm not quitting on my own.

Once he was at the top of the tower, the jump-master strapped Jimi into a harness and pushed him off the tower. Jimi wrote that the cable "snapped like a bullwhip," and he landed on a sand dune.

> It was a new "experience." There's nothing but physical training and harassment here for two weeks, then when you go to jump school, that's when you get hell. They work you to DEATH, fussing and fighting. . . . They really make the sparks fly, and half the people quit then too. That's how they separate the men from the boys. I pray that I will make it on the men's side this time.

❧

ONE RAINY NOVEMBER day, Jimi was in Service Club No. 1 at Fort Campbell practicing guitar when another serviceman happened by and heard him play. The club had instruments and amplifiers available for rental, and Jimi practiced there when he wasn't on active duty or writing letters.

When serviceman Billy Cox heard the music, he thought it a combination of "Beethoven and John Lee Hooker" and was intrigued. Cox had grown up in Pittsburgh and had played bass in a number of bands. "This was a sound I had never heard before," Cox recalled. "I went in and introduced myself to him. It was about that quick." Cox checked out a bass and began jamming with Jimi. With that bond, Cox and Hendrix immediately struck up a friendship that would be both personal and musical and would endure for nearly a decade.

With Cox as a bandmate, and his first real army buddy, Jimi's interests shifted. He was still fixated on the Screaming Eagle patch, and in fact he began jump school that next month, but he and Cox immediately formed a five-piece band with three other soldiers. They didn't have a name—and the lineup constantly shifted—but using a core of Billy and Jimi, they played base clubs on weekends. For a while they were a three-piece, with the two of them and a drummer. In this arrangement, Jimi and Billy shared vocal duties, and since Cox wasn't a strong singer, the short-lived group became Jimi's first venture into fronting a band. He still didn't like his own voice, but out of necessity he began to sing.

Fort Campbell sat on the border between Tennessee and Kentucky, sixty miles from Nashville. In nearby Clarksville, Tennessee, there were a number of clubs that catered to servicemen, including the Pink Poodle, which became Jimi's local haunt. The club served an almost exclusively black clientele; in the South, Jimi had first discovered true racial segregation. Though the army was officially integrated, soldiers socialized by race, and off base large portions of society were off-limits to blacks. Even music was defined by race, as Southern blacks were mostly interested in blues and R&B; Jimi's tasty "Louie, Louie" riffs were unwanted here. Cox remembered Jimi becoming deeply interested in Albert King, Slim Harpo, Muddy Waters, and Jimmy Reed, all blues legends who had gotten their start in the region.

That winter, Jimi finally got his chance to jump out of an airplane. In later interviews, he described the excitement he felt. "The first jump was really outta sight," he told *N.M.E.* "You're in the plane, and some cats had never been up in a plane before. Some people were throwing up." What Jimi didn't tell the interviewer was that his initial jump also represented his first time in an airplane. He did speak of his fascination with the sounds of the airplane ("the plane is going 'rrrrrrr'"), and of the jump itself ("the air is going 'ssssshhhh' past your ears"). He even borrowed a camera and photographed some jumps. On the back of one snapshot of another soldier he noted: "This is right before he touched; when he did, he hit with a *splat*."

The life of a parachutist had its risks, and Jimi feared his chute might fail. He also suffered, to a lesser degree, the dread of being called into actual combat. As Jimi wrote in a long letter he sent to his Aunt Delores in January, "I'm in the best division: the 101st Airborne. That's the sharpest outfit in the world. If any trouble starts anywhere, we will be one of the first to go." In 1962, when Jimi wrote to his aunt, increased tensions along the Korean border, in Eastern Europe, and in Cuba all loomed as possible sites of military action. The conflict in Southeast Asia was intensifying, and the Vietnam War was soon to include U.S. troops. With that as a backdrop, by early 1962, Jimi began to wonder whether the extra fifty-five dollars was worth it.

Jimi's army pay represented the first—and only—regular paycheck of his life. He had been promoted to Private First Class in January and completed the requirements to earn his 101st patch. Once he had purchased all the Screaming Eagle patches he needed to send to his family, he found himself with extra money for the first time in his life. With his letters to Betty, he began to include twenty-five-dollar savings bonds, which he thought would show her parents he was capable of supporting a family. He paid to have himself photographed at a photo studio and sent the picture to Betty Jean. One shot showed him posing in his fatigues in front of tropical backdrop. He also sent Betty Jean a poem he'd pasted to a card, titled "Sweetheart." He inscribed it, "From the one who will always love you, truly." And during the spring of 1962, he wrote her several times offering to pay her way out to him if she would agree to be married. "He wanted to fly me to Kentucky," she recalled. "He sent me a diamond ring as an engagement ring, and he had a wedding band he had already purchased."

Jimi's efforts to talk Betty Jean and her parents into an early wedding failed. Her parents insisted she graduate. These rejections of his marriage proposals only egged Jimi on more, however. Perhaps his actions represented a deep love for Betty Jean, or perhaps they were a desperate attempt to cure his loneliness.

∽∾∾

BY MARCH 1962, even Betty Jean noticed a shift in Jimi's correspondence, as the band became his primary subject. His father had sent his guitar early that winter, and with his instrument again, and the Screaming Eagle patch firmly adhered to his uniform, the original allure of the Airborne faded. As his interest in his band grew, his respect for the army, which had once been so high, dissipated. "They wouldn't let me have anything to do with music," Jimi told an interviewer a few years later. He had been trained in the use of several different weapons, but he felt safest with his guitar in his hands; he still slept with it resting on his chest. His squad mates found this odd, and it was yet another reason he stood out as a loner.

The one place he felt comfortable was with Billy Cox in their band. The group now had a name—the Kasuals—and they were slowly building a reputation in the area. They got weekend gigs in Nashville and at military bases as far away as North Carolina. Jimi quickly found that in the segregated South, African American bands could usually play only to black audiences. "He wrote and told me that he had a hard time down there being in a black band," said Betty Jean. "He said he saw prejudice in Tennessee that he'd never seen in Seattle, including a lot in the music business." The large Southern black population did support a number of clubs, however. Jimi also found himself meeting more available black women than he had ever known in Seattle. Handsome and flashy onstage, he found for the first time in his life that he was popular with women.

With his band continuing to play to crowds and their local fame on the upswing, touring possibilities for the Kasuals came up. The only snag was that Jimi and Billy were both full-time soldiers. Cox, at least, was near the end of his army commitment. Jimi couldn't quit the army; a prison term would await him if he went AWOL. By the first of April, he had served only ten of the thirty-six months in his enlistment, but to him the situation had become untenable. On April 2, he reported to the base hospital and said he had a serious, intimate problem that he needed to speak to the base psychiatrist about. Jimi told an outrageous tale about how he had developed homosexual tendencies and had begun fantasizing about his bunkmates. The doctor told him to get some rest.

His visits to the base psychiatrist became regular that April and May. He told the doctor that he could not stop masturbating and that it had become an addiction. In a move that was in all likelihood intentional, he was caught masturbating in the barracks. He claimed to the psychiatrist that he was in love with one of his squad mates. He said he couldn't sleep and was waking up with night terrors. He said he repeatedly wet himself. He claimed that he had lost fifteen pounds because of his lovesickness over his squad mate. These fabricated admissions represented a desperate gambit; if they failed to get him discharged, Jimi faced being ostracized by his peers. No soldier wanted to be known as a quitter, or as gay in the homophobic army. Even the perception of weakness in these matters could earn you a "blanket party," the nickname for a bunkhouse beating, or even a stray bullet. Perhaps in another attempt to prove that he was going mad, that month Jimi sold his guitar to another soldier in his unit.

Finally, on May 14, Captain John Halbert gave Jimi a complete medical exam. When Jimi had entered the army he had undergone a thorough physical and the only problem noted on his evaluation was that he "stuttered in the past." This time, filling out the same form, Jimi checked seven different maladies ranging from "chest pains" to "homosexual." In Jimi's medical records, Captain Halbert typed: "homosexual; masturbating; dizziness; pain and pressure in the left chest; loss of weight; frequent trouble sleeping; personal problems." Halbert missed the one giveaway on Jimi's own evaluation form: When he joined the army, Jimi had listed his profession as "student," though he'd been out of school for a year. After over a year of being in the army, he had a new profession: "musician."

The army gave in. Halbert recommended Jimi be discharged because of his "homosexual tendencies." Jimi never admitted his subterfuge, even to close friends. Instead, when he was asked why he got out of the army, he always told a story of how on his twenty-sixth leap out of an airplane, he broke an ankle. "I'd hurt my back too," he told one reporter. "Every time they examined me I groaned, so they finally believed me and I got out." He was pictured at a Kasuals gig in June with gauze around his ankle; whether this was a real injury, or an additional deception, can't be known, though his army medical files make no mention of an ankle break.

Jimi's final paycheck included a bonus for twenty-one days of unused leave. His initial plan was to travel to Seattle, marry Betty Jean, and find a job. "I found myself standing outside the gate of Fort Campbell on the Tennessee/Kentucky border with my little duffel bag and three or four hundred dollars in my pocket," he explained to *Rave* in 1967. "I was going back to Seattle, which was a long way away. . . . Then I thought I'd just look in Clarksville, which was near, stay there that night, and go home next morning. . . ."

In Clarksville, he walked into a jazz club and had a drink. He had another drink. "I felt real benevolent that day," he told *Rave*. "I must have been handing out bills to anyone who asked." He walked out of the bar several hours later and counted his money. He had sixteen dollars left, not enough to travel to Seattle. Jimi said his first thought was to call his father and ask for bus fare: "But I could guess what he'd say if

I told him I'd lost nearly $400 in just one day. Nope. That was out. All I can do, I thought, is get a guitar and try to find some work." Jimi remembered the guy he'd sold his guitar to in his outfit. He snuck back on the base, borrowed "Betty Jean" back, and after having spent almost three months trying to get out of the army, he ended up surreptitiously sleeping in his old bunk again.

Billy had three months left in his service commitment, and their plan was for Jimi to hang around Clarksville until Billy's discharge, then the two would make their mark. Their band had a few weekend gigs, but Jimi survived, as he would do on and off for the next four years of his life, by sleeping on friends' couches or shacking up with girls he'd met at clubs. That summer he began a relationship with a local woman named Joyce, in all likelihood his first sexual encounter. When Cox was finally released in September 1962, the three of them stayed for a time in a tiny apartment.

Jimi's relationship with Joyce put an end to his fantasies of marrying Betty Jean. He wrote Betty Jean that month and told her he wasn't planning on returning to Seattle, or to her; she immediately sent back his engagement ring. The idea of marrying had been a powerful daydream for Jimi, but once it passed and he began to discover the pleasures of the flesh, it would be years before he would ever again speak of settling down with one woman.

Even the guitar "Betty Jean" was banished. Billy Cox cosigned for a new Epiphone Wilshire guitar that Jimi purchased on time from a Clarksville music store. "Betty Jean," the cherished instrument Jimi had loved so much he'd slept with it every night, was sold to a local pawnshop.

# CHAPTER NINE

# HEADHUNTER

*"He was like a headhunter. Jimi was always looking to take
down the top man."*
—Guitarist JOHNNY JONES

WHEN BILLY COX was discharged from the army in September, he
and Jimi Hendrix went into music full-time. Their first opportunity
came when Jimi met a guy in a Clarksville bar who booked an Indianapolis club. "Jimi was always meeting people," Cox recalled. "I'd always have to be the one to tell him, 'This guy is not dealing with a full
deck.' Somebody had to be grounded." This one time, however, Cox
followed Jimi's lead. "We wound up driving up there in this 1955 Ply-
mouth that would not go in reverse," Cox said.

When they arrived, they found the club wouldn't book an all-black
band. Without enough money for gas home, they set out to find work
in venues that were more open. The afternoon they arrived, a "Battle of
the Bands" was scheduled at George's Bar on Indiana Avenue, in the
heart of Indianapolis's Main Stem. They entered the contest and did

well. Playing a version of "Soldier Boy" by the Shirelles, Jimi and Billy came in second. "We would have won if there wasn't another band, the Presidents, that the local girls liked better," Cox recalled.

The second-place finish didn't earn them a prize, but they were impressive enough that Presidents' guitarist Alphonso Young decided to quit his group and join up with Billy and Jimi. They formed a new band named the King Kasuals, with Hendrix as the centerpiece, Harry Batchelor as the group's singer, Cox on bass, and Young on rhythm guitar. Young could play with his teeth, and one spot in each set was reserved for his dental solo. It wasn't the first time Hendrix had seen this guitar trick—Butch Snipes back in Seattle could do it with aplomb—but it was the first time he was upstaged by a member of his own band. Jimi was a quick learner; he observed Young's stage antics and playing style and soon copied them.

The group moved to Clarksville and found work at Nashville's Del Morocco Club, where they played twice a week. On other nights they took jobs at any rib house, roadside juke joint, or pool hall that would have them. This was Jimi's first stab at being a professional musician, and he discovered that even with time to devote to his career— without the distractions of school or the army—he was making no more money than he had made with the Velvetones at high school sock hops. He was so poor for a time that he had to share a single bed with Alphonso Young in the apartment they rented. "Sometimes Jimi had a girl over, and we all three slept there, though it was just sleeping," Young recalled.

Girls were the main upside to Jimi's life that fall. Joyce was followed by Florence, who was followed by Verdell, who was followed by countless others. Joyce stuck around the longest and even went so far as to send Al a picture of her and Jimi taken in December 1962. In the photograph, Joyce is looking into the lens, while Jimi, his arm around her, is clearly ogling someone else. Wearing a skinny tie, white shirt, and suit coat, he looks debonair and urbane. His army hair had grown high and he fashioned it, as he would for the next several years, into a "conk," a version of the "marcel" hairstyle made famous by Little Richard.

Jimi was extraordinarily handsome, polite, soft-spoken, obviously talented, and of course quite penniless. He used this neediness to his full advantage. Jimi emphasized his destitution as part of a rescue scenario that many women found irresistible. His very shyness, which had been debilitating in high school, became an asset in R&B clubs, where adult sexuality was usually overt and rarely played softly. Jimi was tender, and tender was sexy. Seldom did he meet a woman who did not want to romance him, mother him, bed him, and, as usually was the case, feed and clothe him. These idylls played out for several weeks until the rescuers discovered their waif was, in truth, a Romeo, who in all likelihood had another Florence Nightingale already lined up.

Jimi's girlfriends during this era were exclusively black; it was a time and a place when even flirting with a white woman could get you killed. Nashville had been the very locale where records had first been segregated into "hillbilly" and "race" sections in record-store bins, and that division continued in all parts of life. Though racism in Tennessee was less prevalent than in Mississippi, where even in 1962 lynching was not unheard of, African Americans lived in a separate but unequal world. Schools and housing were still segregated, and lunch counters had only been recently integrated after a mammoth civil rights sit-in. The circle Jimi moved in was even more insular, as he spent much of his life inside the three or four area clubs that were open to blacks. When the band did tour, he was immediately reminded of his skin color since many gas stations in the South refused to allow blacks to use the restrooms. The previous year Medgar Evers had begun boycotts of such stations—Evers would be assassinated in June 1963 for his activism. Yet Jimi was neither an activist nor a black separatist, and his central focus, as always, was music, which he saw as being without color. Surf music had become popular that year with white audiences and Jimi loved to play surf runs on his guitar when he practiced. His bandmates, however, laughed when he suggested they include such heresy in their sets.

Practicing his guitar was the central activity in Jimi's life that year. He went to bed practicing, he slept with the guitar on his chest, and the first thing he did upon rising was to start practicing again. In an effort to find even more time to practice, he occasionally bought cheap amphetamines so he could stay up all night. This was Jimi's first regular use of illegal drugs; the amphetamine he was using was inexpensive and not much more powerful than No-Doz. Other than amphetamines, the only illicit drug he used was marijuana, also common among musicians in the era, but his poverty limited his access even to this.

Jimi's obsession with his guitar garnered him a nickname around Clarksville: Marbles. He was so named because people thought he had "lost his marbles" and was crazy as a result of his excessive practicing. The guitar had become an extension of his body and Billy Cox observed that Jimi managed to put twenty-five years into the guitar in a period of just five. Alphonso Young recalled that Jimi would practice on the way to a gig, play for up to five hours during one of their all-night shows, and then continue to practice on the car ride home. "He always had that guitar," Young said. In this singular obsession, Jimi bore a similarity to sax great John Coltrane, who frequently practiced during set breaks, which was also a regular routine for Jimi. Jimi was once observed going into a movie theater with his guitar, unable to put the instrument down long enough to watch a film.

This practicing slowly paid off. Jimi's development as a player came from his innate ability combined with his singular focus on learning every nuance of his instrument. His bandmates joked that it seemed like Jimi could play blindfolded, upside down, and behind his back. In fact, by 1962 he was capable of all three.

Making a living as a musician was another matter, however. Jimi imagined that studio work might help support him, and when Billy Cox was called for a studio job that November, he dragged Jimi along. The session was for a Frank Howard & the Commanders record at Nashville's King Records. Jimi was allowed to contribute but the producer thought his style so outrageous he killed Jimi's microphone. Jimi's style was, in fact, frantically wild at the time. His long practice sessions, along with his extraordinarily long fingers, had given him a virtuoso's ease at playing, but he still lacked the distinctive, individual tone that a great guitar player brings to the instrument.

The best guitar player in Nashville was Johnny Jones of the Imperials. Jimi had first met Jones back when he was in the army and the Imperials had a standing Tuesday-night gig in Clarksville. "He was just a kid," Jones recalled, "but he had a mission, it appeared. He'd sit right in front of the stage and watch me play." During one set break, Jimi came up and asked if he could hold Johnny's guitar during the intermission. He promised to sit in front of the stage with it and not break the instrument. When Jones agreed, the next week Jimi asked if Jones would keep his amp on during breaks. Jones left the amp on, mostly to appease Jimi and stop his nagging, and during set breaks Jimi quietly strummed the guitar, more in an attempt to discover the secrets of Jones's tone than to entertain the crowd.

After Jimi moved to Nashville, he attended every Imperials show he could, hoping to pick up something from Jones. Jimi had chosen an admirable mentor: At twenty-six, Jones was only six years older, but he had learned his playing from the successors of Robert Johnson. "My guitar was already *talking*," Jones said. "And when your guitar is talking, it's like you are writing a letter, and all you need is the punctuation marks." Jones had spent time in Chicago and had learned under Freddie King, Muddy Waters, T-Bone Walker, and Robert Lockwood Jr. Perhaps more important, he had grown up in rural Delta poverty and carried those troubled life experiences into his playing. "Jimi had been listening to records, but he hadn't rubbed elbows with someone who had mud on him, like me," Jones said. "That's what he needed to be a blues artist—you gotta be low-down *and* funky. Jimi couldn't get the big strings talking enough to be funky."

Jones liked Jimi and they became friends. Many nights after a show, the two men would sit in the front seat of Jones's car while Jimi asked questions about guitar playing. "Jimi was very analytical," Jones said, "but he simply needed to live more life if he was going to understand the blues." Through Jones, Jimi met two of his all-time heroes that fall: B.B. King and Albert King. "When B.B. came in, you should have seen Jimi's eyes light up," Jones recalled. "And to see him around Albert King, you would have thought Jimi was in heaven." Just as he had done with Jones, Jimi pestered Albert King with questions about his finger style and how he managed to bend the strings horizontally. Most young players would simply tell King how good he was; Jimi was impertinent enough to ask him how he became good. There was a strong sense of machismo among blues players and few were willing to ask such questions or show their own inexperience. Surprisingly, many of these established players felt so unthreatened by Jimi that they gladly shared their trade secrets, convinced that this skinny unkempt boy would never develop enough to challenge them.

Jimi, however, had both a deep streak of ambition and an inner belief in his own destiny. He became a musical cannibal, quickly assimilating different styles of playing and mastering techniques far quicker than his mentors thought possible. That fall he challenged his tutor Johnny Jones in a contest they jokingly called "head-hunting." Egged on by his friend Larry Lee, Jimi pushed a heavy amp into the club where Jones was appearing. As they entered, Lee taunted Jones: "We're coming at you tonight, old man. You better be good." Jimi, the challenger, was less boastful, threatening, "This is the night." Jones told them to "bring it on" and sent them to the bandstand.

As the showdown began, it quickly became clear that Jimi was outclassed. His amp wasn't as powerful as the one Jones used—a lesson Jimi would not soon forget—and his playing, while technically proficient, still lacked the deep tone that Jones had perfected. The audience actually laughed at some of Jimi's solos because they were such an obvious attempt to copy B.B. King. Jimi left the stage dejected, and Jones remained the headman. Afterward, Larry Lee berated Jimi for his poor showing: "What the hell was you doing? That man done just wiped you up." Jimi's speech pattern was always less colloquial than his peers and his response sounded like a scientist who had failed at proving a theory: "I was simply trying to get that B.B. King tone down and my experiment failed." Jimi played with Jones on several other occasions, but he was never able to best him. "He come looking for a shoot-out," Jones said, laughing, "but he was the one who got himself shot." These failures were essential to Jimi's emerging stage of development: A long line of guitar players could imitate B.B. King, but there was only one B.B.

In December, Jimi gave up. The bookings for the King Kasuals weren't improving, and he felt he was going nowhere. He borrowed enough money to manage a bus ticket to Vancouver, where he stayed with his grandmother Nora for a time. His choice of Vancouver, and not Seattle, said much about his strained relationship with his father and his desire to avoid Betty Jean. Though Vancouver was only a few hours away from Seattle, Jimi didn't visit during his stay. Instead, he hooked up with Bobby Taylor and the Vancouvers. "They played Motown-type stuff," recalled Terry Johnson, who would play with them a year later. "They also had a bit of surf, garage kind of rock to their sound." Hendrix's position was as rhythm player, while Tommy Chong, later of Cheech and Chong, played lead.

Jimi ended 1962 playing an extended residency with the group at a Vancouver nightclub called Dante's Inferno. The Vancouvers were a talented band, but Jimi was dismayed that their audiences were almost exclusively white. He soon felt some of the same yearning that his father had experienced in Vancouver some twenty-five years earlier: to be in a place where his ethnicity and music were embraced for their essence and not their oddity. After just over two months, Jimi took a southbound train and headed back to the Mississippi Delta. He was seeking some of the "mud" that Johnny Jones had talked about.

⌒⌒⌒

GROWING UP IN Seattle, Jimi had rarely been exposed to traditional Southern soul food. Yet whenever he'd visited his grandmother Nora, who had once worked as a cook at Vancouver's Chicken Inn, he ate the collard greens, grits, ham hocks, catfish, hog maws, corn bread, hush puppies, and sweet potato pie that were staples of Southern cooking. Nora ran a yearly church fund-raiser where she featured these traditional delicacies, and others. "We used to have chitterling dinners," Nora said once in an interview. "We'd sell it so fast; oh, it would make your head spin." The centerpiece of these dinners were chitterlings—pig intestines—commonly called chitlins. To properly cook this specialty took five hours or more, and when Nora had them on the stove, neighbors would hungrily gather.

In homage to the Southern-food delicacy, the name Chitlin' Circuit was coined to describe the procession of African American clubs in the Deep South. The route was considered to begin at New York's Apollo Theater, ran through Washington, D.C.'s Howard Theater, but then encompassed less-storied venues in rural areas. "The Chitlin' Circuit was basically anyplace where you were playing to black audiences," observed blues legend Bobby Rush. "It could be a roadhouse, barbecue joint, pool hall, or a bar."

For the years 1963 through 1965, the Chitlin' Circuit became Jimi Hendrix's milieu. Playing with the King Kasuals or, as was more often the case, in other bands as a hired backup musician, Hendrix soon felt as though he had seen the inside of every juke joint and tavern from Virginia to Florida to Texas. Yet even with a gig every night, it was difficult to make a living. The time did offer Jimi invaluable lessons on showmanship, audience interaction, and survival as a touring musician. It also forever engrained in him the notion that the job of a touring musician included being an entertainer: If the audience did not stay entranced, it mattered little how authentic the music was. With each passing gig, Jimi learned more of the Delta tradition, and his own playing matured.

That February, the King Kasuals were reconfigured to include a horn section. "We wanted to have the 'Show,'" said Alphonso Young. The "Show" was a term for the large, revue-style bands in vogue that decade. Many audiences on the Chitlin' Circuit expected more than music; a night's performance could include comedy, live theater, and pantomime. The Kasuals added an emcee, Raymond Belt, who opened their shows with his impersonation of comedian Moms Mabley. The band had to follow this farce, and to out-entertain a cross-dressing comic wasn't easy.

Hendrix was already a flashy player, but he perfected his first real "act" in the Chitlin' Circuit seedbed, where audiences required musicians to be entertainers. He began to play with the guitar behind his back, which he'd seen T-Bone Walker do, and he mimicked Alphonso Young's trick of playing with his teeth. Billy Cox bought Jimi a fifty-foot guitar cable, and Jimi was able to use this to play out on the dance floor and sometimes outside on the street. Jimi's onstage interactions with Alphonso Young began to take on more of the feel of dueling guitarists, which made their set more exciting. Jimi also took a cue from Young, who told Jimi he'd be wiser to stop practicing during set breaks and go out and meet the audience. "He was shy," Young recalled. "I told him to stay and mingle, get to know the crowd, and talk with them. That was the way to build fans who would come to see you night after night." Socializing with the audience, Jimi soon found, was also a good way to meet girls.

The Kasuals played all over Tennessee, Kentucky, Arkansas, and Indiana, but even as they found a wider fan base, it was clear their success would be limited. They were a dance band basically, playing hot R&B hits of the day to exclusively black audiences, and as such, there was a built-in ceiling to their fame.

Most band members took part-time jobs to survive. Jimi was the exception to this—he turned down all day-job possibilities in favor of spending more time with his guitar. It was an artistically admirable decision, but it also meant that he had to live off the generosity of others. When a club owner offered the Kasuals a free place to stay, they jumped at the chance, but soon found the offer came with a catch. On their first night in the house, for example, someone shot out their front window. They learned from the neighbors that the previous tenant had been an African American on trial for murdering a white man. Still, they stayed. "We didn't have anyplace else to go," said Young. Prior to this, Jimi had been squatting in a house that was under construction, rising before the workers arrived in the morning.

Though Jimi never had a day job, he did pursue many side musical projects. He toured during this time as backup for Carla Thomas, Tommy Tucker, Slim Harpo, Jerry Butler, Marion James, Chuck Jackson, and Solomon Burke. None of these tours was a long jaunt—most were just a few regional dates on the Chitlin' Circuit—but the experience was important. Jimi took any job in music, whether it paid well or not, and on every tour he learned something.

The tour with Solomon Burke was the most notable of 1963's various jobs. Already a legendary soul singer, preacher, and part-time undertaker, Burke weighed two hundred and fifty pounds and had a voice just as big. He had already scored two Top 40 hits, which made him the first bona fide star that Jimi backed. "I had a record out called 'Just Out of Reach (Of My Two Open Arms),' and Jimi could play that so well it would make you cry," Burke recalled. This particular tour was a five-act extravaganza that included Burke, Otis Redding, Joe Tex, Sugar Pie DeSantos, and comedian Pigmeat Markum. Even among this stellar lineup, Jimi stood out as one of the best guitarists, though his flashiness put him at odds with Burke. "Five dates would go beautifully," Burke said, "and then at the next show, he'd go into this wild stuff that wasn't part of the song. I just couldn't handle it anymore." One night on the tour bus, Burke traded Hendrix, the way one might trade a baseball player, to Otis Redding for two horn players. Jimi stayed with Redding's band for less than a week before he was fired for similar reasons. "We ended up leaving him by the side of the road," Burke remembered.

Similar dismissals followed. Jimi got a job backing the Marvelettes, a successful Motown group. The tour was a bill with Curtis Mayfield, whose smooth style became one of Jimi's greatest guitar influences. Yet when Jimi accidentally destroyed one of Mayfield's amplifiers, he was again fired. Many of Jimi's partings were traumatic: When a short stint with Bobby Womack fell apart, Womack's brother threw Jimi's guitar out a bus window while Jimi was sleeping. Jimi woke up horrified and had to borrow a guitar.

When he was stranded, Jimi turned to Billy Cox. Billy was always ready to rescue him from a lonely train station, or a roadhouse, and he acted the way a big brother might have. As for his own family, Jimi continued to stay in touch with them, though his correspondence home was short and usually confined to postcards as he moved from town to town. "Dear Dad," he wrote in March, "just a few words to let you know I made it to South Carolina." He sent Al a photo of the Kasuals that spring and wrote on the back, "We're one of the best rhythm and blues bands in Nashville." Considering that the Nashville music scene was one primarily associated with country-and-hillbilly music, it wasn't much of a boast.

By the fall of 1963, Jimi had toured on bills with some of the nation's best bands, and his interest in the King Kasuals waned. The Kasuals would eventually replace him. In the meantime, he took any tour he could get hired for. On one tour with Gorgeous George, Jimi found himself opening up for Sam Cooke and Jackie Wilson. On another, he was in a group that opened for Little Richard. After that show, Jimi jammed with Little Richard's band, the same group he had watched in awe as a teenager back in Seattle. With that session, he realized his own playing had come full circle: He could now respectfully play with the groups he'd grown up admiring. This awareness also helped cement his growing sense that playing in a Nashville cover band was not his fate.

When a New York promoter came through Nashville and offered work in New York, Jimi jumped at the opportunity. He attempted to convince his bandmates in the Kasuals to accompany him, but none would consider the move. Billy Cox was too practical and still held out hope that the Kasuals would make their mark in Tennessee. Bandmate Alphonso Young listened to Jimi's promises of fame and riches, but he had already become concerned about Jimi's increased use of amphetamines. "He was always taking these Red Devils, and other pills that they called speed," Young recalled. Young was a Jehovah's Witness and found all drugs abhorrent.

That November, on the day before President John F. Kennedy was shot, Jimi turned twenty-one. A month later, he headed for New York City on a Greyhound. Once again he carried his guitar on his back, in the style he'd learned from watching *Johnny Guitar* as a kid. At the bus station, one of his bandmates gave him a beige overcoat for the New York winter; at the time, the only coat he owned belonged with his army uniform, hardly fitting in sophisticated New York. As Jimi climbed on the bus, everything he owned was in a small duffel bag. It wasn't much, but as he moved to the back of the bus—as all African Americans were still required to do in the South—he pulled out his guitar for yet another public practice session. His fellow riders would have heard something to make any seasoned blues lover within earshot warm—there, beyond the fast playing and skillful technique, was the first hint of tone, smoothed out by almost three years of struggle in the South. This bluesman on the back of the bus had begun to sound like Jimi Hendrix, and no one else.

# CHAPTER TEN

# HARLEM WORLD

NEW YORK, NEW YORK
*January 1964–July 1965*

*"Harlem World was the name we used for what was happening
with the music scene—the black music scene. It was also this
larger concept we used to describe the girls, the community, the
sounds. Later, there was a 'Harlem World' club."*
—Friend TUNDE-RA ALEEM

JIMI ARRIVED IN New York City for the first time in early 1964. Having spent most of his life in Seattle, where the black population was small, he marveled at the vibrancy of Harlem, where upward of half a million African Americans lived. Both artistically and politically, the neighborhood was the true cultural capital of black America at the time. Jimi moved into a hotel on 125th Street where a room could be had for twenty dollars a week and set out to make his mark.

He soon found that the offer of work that had brought him to New York had disappeared. He knew no one in the city, so he began to haunt clubs like Small's Paradise and the Palm Café, looking for a gig as a sideman. During his first month in New York, he entered the

Wednesday-night amateur contest at the Apollo Theater and came in first, winning twenty-five dollars. The prize didn't immediately lead to other jobs, however, which was a deep disappointment. Jimi found that despite its huge scale, New York's music scene wasn't easy to break into. When he asked to sit in at clubs, he was frequently spurned. He had expected the city to be more open than Nashville, but he found the Harlem scene exceptionally narrow. Rhythm and blues, jazz, and blues were the only accepted genres and those styles were best played in strict accordance with how the masters had done them before. "Black people didn't want to hear any rock 'n' roll in Harlem," Taharqa Aleem recalled. "There was a dress code—if you didn't look, or sound, a certain way, you were shunned. Compared to the rest of the city, Harlem was like a whole other planet. We called the scene Harlem World, because our entire world was centered there."

Not long after arriving in New York, Jimi met Lithofayne Pridgeon, his first Harlem girlfriend. Fayne, as she was known, was a beautiful African American woman who had grown up on the streets and at nineteen was already a Harlem fixture. "Fayne was a supergroupie," said Taharqa, who would later marry her. "She had seen Otis Redding and James Brown; she knew all those guys." Some called her "Apollo Fayne" because she was often backstage at the famous theater. On their first real date, Fayne took Jimi home to her mother's house for a meal. Her mother loved to cook, and Jimi, who was nearly starving, needed to eat. Fayne would later write in an article for *Gallery* that she'd met Jimi at an orgy, though how he managed to get invited to something that exotic was never explained. Pridgeon found Jimi surprisingly old-fashioned: He frequently talked about his old high school girlfriend Betty Jean.

The two moved in together at the Hotel Seifer and later lived with Fayne's mother. In Pridgeon's *Gallery* article, she described her relationship with Jimi as one based on sex: "All our activity took place in bed," she wrote. "He came to bed with the same grace a Mississippi pulpwood driver attacks a plate of collard greens and corn bread after ten hours in the sun. He was creative in bed, too. There would be encore after encore." Jimi's sexual appetite was insatiable, according to Pridgeon: "There were times when he almost busted me in two." The only passion equal to his sexuality was his love of playing and she thought of her competition "not as a woman, but as a guitar." Jimi and Fayne had frequent disagreements about this and other things as well. In one letter that Jimi wrote when he was out of town on a rare touring gig, he begged her not to listen to others who were talking him down. "Don't listen to the niggers in the street," he wrote. Another argument ensued after Jimi refused to take Fayne out one night. His explanation: "You know how I hate to go out when my hair doesn't look right." Jimi was obsessed with his hair and spent hours making sure his curls looked right. This was his one point of vanity at the time: His clothes were ratty, his shoes ill-fitting, and his borrowed coat barely kept him warm, but his hair had to be perfect before he'd venture outside.

Though Jimi was infatuated with Pridgeon, there were others who also found him interesting, including one of Fayne's girlfriends. In an effort to fix that friend up elsewhere, Fayne invited Taharqa Aleem over for what was billed as a double date. Taharqa came with his identical twin, Tunde-Ra, and with a group now numbering five, the night took on a tone that was less than romantic. The Aleems, universally called "The Twins," had been born and raised in Harlem and had the street-smart toughness Jimi lacked. "We loved him immediately," Tunde-Ra recalled. "He was just really perceptive at a very young age." By the end of the night, Jimi was regaling Fayne, her female friend, and the Aleems with his stories of touring in the South and playing guitar. Within a month of arriving in New York, he had his first Harlem fan club.

The Aleems had been musicians themselves but had temporarily abandoned that avenue for drug dealing. They worked for "Fat Jack" Taylor, who ran a record company but made his money through narcotics. "He was one of the biggest drug czars in Harlem," Tunde-Ra said. Harlem's music clubs were awash in narcotics, prostitution, and gambling, all of which Jimi had observed to a lesser degree back on Seattle's Jackson Street. Yet in Harlem these pursuits were inextricably linked to the music scene and were big businesses. "Fat Jack was like a Charles Dickens character," Taharqa observed. "It was always these big parties, and pretty people, but of course it had a dark side. At the time we thought it was a way out of poverty."

No one on the scene was more impoverished than Jimi, and Fat Jack offered him a job hustling drugs. Jimi resisted that temptation and remained steadfast in his belief that music was to be his only calling in life. He later explained his position on nonmusic work to one interviewer: "People would say, 'If you don't get a job, you'll just starve to death.' But I didn't want to take a job outside music. I tried a few jobs, including car delivery, but I always quit after a week." Jimi's commitment to his musical dream made the Aleems reconsider their choice in work; the next year they abandoned hustling for music. Still, Jimi's stated musical ethics were contradictory at best: For a time he lived with the Aleems and had no problem about the fact that drug money paid the rent. Jimi's devotion to music was only possible because of patronage he enjoyed from others. Nor was Jimi a Puritan when it came to sexual morals. One of the first jobs he got in New York was touring behind a stripper named Pantera. "She was an exotic dancer with a snake," recalled Tunde-Ra Aleem. "We would travel up and down the state with her, and Jimi would sometimes join us and play in the background."

What Jimi most wanted was a touring gig with a big-time band. Through Fayne, he went to the Apollo Theater one night to see Sam Cooke, one of her former boyfriends, whom he asked for a job. Cooke already had a guitar player, but Jimi was emboldened by trying. His luck changed in February 1964 when he heard the Isley Brothers were looking for a new guitarist. His first meeting with them took place on February 9, 1964, at their New Jersey home. The Beatles were on "The Ed Sullivan Show" that night, and Jimi and the Isleys watched the historic appearance together, not knowing that this one event would transform America and make rock 'n' roll the dominant musical genre on the charts.

By March, Jimi was a member of the Isley band. His first studio session was for the song "Testify," which became a minor hit. A spring tour took him all over the East Coast, through the Chitlin' Circuit, and even to Bermuda. When the band returned to New York that summer,

Jimi went into the studio with them and cut several singles, including "The Last Girl," which featured a young Dionne Warwick on background vocals. The Isley Brothers were one of the biggest R&B bands of the era, yet Jimi later complained of the strict stylistic parameters he was held to, in both music and fashion. "I had to conform," he said in one 1967 interview. "We had white mohair suits, patent leather shoes, and patent leather hairdos. We weren't allowed to go onstage looking casual. If our shoelaces were two different types, we'd get fined five dollars. Oh man, did I get tired of that!" In the revue-style show favored by the Isleys, Jimi's place on the crowded bandstand was in the back row, and he would get only a twenty-second spotlight solo every set. He learned to savor these moments and take full advantage of them, but during most of the show, he was unseen if not unheard. When the tour landed in Nashville, Jimi quit and joined up with Gorgeous George Odell for a short tour.

On an off day in Memphis from the Gorgeous George tour, Jimi stopped by Stax Records. With equal parts naïveté and audacity, he went in the front door and announced that he was a visiting guitar player who hoped to meet guitar legend Steve Cropper. For once in his life, Jimi didn't have his guitar with him, perhaps thinking that to bring his instrument to visit Steve Cropper required more courage than even he could muster. The secretary told Jimi that Cropper was busy in the studio and he should come back later. "I won't be in town later" was Jimi's reply.

Cropper was in a studio lockdown when a secretary came and told him that there was a young guy there to see him; he told her to send him away. Cropper worked until six o'clock. As he walked out of the studio, the secretary came up to him and said, "That guy's still here." Jimi had waited all day. "I had no idea who he was," Cropper recalled, "but I met with him." He found Hendrix to be remarkably polite, and Jimi knew Cropper's entire discography. When asked about his own background, Jimi said modestly, "I play a little guitar, up in New York, and a few other places." Cropper asked if Jimi had done any session work, and Hendrix named off his Isley Brothers sides and "Mercy,

Mercy," a Don Covay record he had played on that was the first record featuring Jimi to break the Top 40. Cropper was impressed: "You played on that? That's one of my favorite songs. Pleased to meet you."

Cropper took Hendrix to dinner, content to have a young fan, and one with obvious talents. "I ended up inviting him back to the studio," Cropper recalled. "We talked for hours, and I showed him a few riffs." Jimi used Cropper's guitar to demonstrate the "Mercy, Mercy" lick.

Cropper was an ideal role model for any professional musician: He was a successful session player who played the blues with dignity and authenticity, and he had cowritten "Green Onions," a No. 1 hit for his band, Booker T. & the MG's. Hendrix was surprised to find he was white; like many listeners, he had imagined that Cropper's funky guitar could be played only by a black man. They were both, in a way, outsiders attempting to challenge conventional assumptions about white and black music.

When it came to making music and trading licks, the two men spoke the same language. Jimi had turned twenty-two that fall, and after a full year of gigging every night, his playing had matured. It was there on "Mercy, Mercy" in his introductory guitar riff, which wasn't a B.B. King rip-off, and in fact wasn't a rip-off of anything. "It was funky," Cropper recalled. "That riff had something special."

Jimi's guitar was starting to talk.

∽∼∾

IN TYPICAL FASHION, Jimi was stranded in Kansas City after missing the Gorgeous George tour bus. He waited for another tour to come through town, figuring he'd hook up with a revue almost the way one might catch a bus. And sure enough, within a week, another band hired him. "I didn't have any money so, you know, this group came up and brought me back to Atlanta, Georgia," Jimi explained in a later interview. This particular band is unknown, though Jimi would have only stayed with them for a few weeks—he played with so many groups, even he couldn't keep all the names straight.

In Atlanta that summer, Jimi was sitting in a restaurant with his guitar when another patron approached. "I asked if he played," recalled Glen Willings, who was with Little Richard's band the Upsetters. Jimi said he did play, and that he needed a gig. Willings took Jimi to audition for Little Richard, who hired him on the spot. Whether Jimi ever told Little Richard that as a child he had watched him preach, had met him backstage at Seattle's Eagles Auditorium, and had already jammed with an earlier version of his band is unknown. However, in a move that was odd considering Jimi was twenty-two, Richard had Bumps Blackwell, who was from Seattle, phone for Al Hendrix's approval before he was formally hired. "Bumps . . . rang Mr. Hendrix to see if it was okay for him to join us," Richard told author Charles White. "Al Hendrix told Bumps, 'Jimi just idolizes Richard. He would eat ten yards of shit to join his band.'" Little Richard's recollection was that Jimi was playing "B.B. King blues" at the time he joined the Upsetters, and Richard would later attempt to take sole credit for Jimi's interest in mixing rock and blues. Richard would also place himself as the inspiration for Jimi's stage moves, style of dress, and even his mustache; some of this was the kind of braggadocio Richard was infamous for, but the substance of his boast was true. Little Richard was such a matchless, groundbreaking performer that many musicians who came of age in this era owed him something.

Richard's Upsetters were the highest-profile backing band Jimi had ever played with and they were exceptionally tight. Still, the job was less than creatively satisfying, as Jimi found Richard to be a control freak of the first order who went as far as to dictate where his band members should stand. Though crowds went wild when Richard played hits like "Tutti Frutti" and "Good Golly, Miss Molly," there was little challenge for Jimi in repeating the same guitar chords night after night. By the time the tour hit Nashville a month later, Johnny Jones, Jimi's former mentor, observed that the position wasn't an ideal fit for Hendrix. "Jimi was getting better, and was more flashy, but I knew he wasn't going to be with Richard very long," Jones recalled. "Jimi was pretty, and Little Richard wasn't going to let anyone be prettier than he was."

Hendrix's tenure with Little Richard produced some of his favorite road stories, which years later he would revel in telling, imitating
Richard's shrill voice as he did so. One tale was of a night Jimi, tired of
the band's uniforms, wore a satin shirt. After the show, he was berated
for his insolence and fined by the bandleader. "I am Little Richard,"
Richard shouted, sounding like a preacher again. "I am the *only* Little
Richard! I am the *King* of Rock and Roll, and I am the only one allowed
to be pretty. Take that shirt off!"

৩৩৩৩

THE UPSETTERS GOT a rare night off in Los Angeles on New Year's
Eve, 1964. Jimi spent that evening at the Californian Club watching
the Ike and Tina Turner Revue. There he spied twenty-year-old Rosa
Lee Brooks, a singer in a girl group, and threw her a line that was un-
sexy, but was unquestionably true: "You look like my mother," he said.
Rosa Lee did bear a striking resemblance to Lucille. They kissed at midnight and went for burgers later at Tiny Naylor's. Brooks had an Impala
convertible, and Jimi sat in the rear seat playing his guitar as they drove,
looking like an honoree in a parade. Later they went back to his hotel.
"We celebrated New Year's *all* night long, until the early, early dawn,"
Brooks recalled.

For a good part of the evening Jimi complained about Little
Richard. He objected to the demeaning way Richard treated him, to
Richard's sexual advances, and to the formulaic music he had to play
night after night. "I prefer Curtis Mayfield myself," Jimi told Brooks.
He told her he was a novice songwriter and was working on material
for a future solo career. They joked about forming a duo. "We were going to become another Mickey and Sylvia, or Ike and Tina," Brooks
said. "Love Is Strange," a 1958 hit for Mickey and Sylvia, was one of
Jimi's favorite songs.

Jimi accompanied Brooks to a few of her gigs that week, and at
one he met Glen Campbell. Brooks was surprised that Jimi knew all of
Campbell's studio sessions and identified himself as a fan of Campbell's

work with the Beach Boys. Brooks's mother owned a restaurant, which kept Jimi interested for a time, as did their passionate sexual relationship. Brooks claimed her affair with Jimi prompted Little Richard to suggest the pair make love while he watched, an offer that Jimi declined.

On February 19, Jimi wrote to let his father know he was in Los Angeles. The postcard had one revealing bit of information: Jimi was now going by the name Maurice James. It would be the first of several pseudonyms he would use over the next three years. Where he got Maurice is unclear, but he told Rosa Lee he picked James in homage to guitar great Elmore James. The name change may have been indicative of Jimi's plan to leave Little Richard and become a solo act. If that was his intent, this strategy did not go far. When he quit the Upsetters that March, he immediately got another backing gig with Ike and Tina Turner. Ike Turner said Jimi joined for a short time until his flashy solos became "so elaborate they overstepped his bounds," and once again, he was promptly fired and rejoined Little Richard.

In early March, Rosa Lee Brooks cut a single called "My Diary" and brought Jimi along to play guitar. Arthur Lee was also involved in the session, and this marked the beginning of a long friendship between Jimi and Lee, who claimed to have been "the first black hippie." At the time of the session, Lee was most famous for being an oddball who would walk around Hollywood with one shoe and sunglasses he could not see through, but later, with his band, Love, he would produce several seminal psychedelic albums. The trio cut two songs that day that prominently featured Jimi's guitar work. The B-side, "Utee," is a throwaway, but "My Diary" proved Jimi was a worthy enough student of Curtis Mayfield that he could craft a guitar solo some mistook for Mayfield. The song received some airplay on Los Angeles radio but failed to become a hit.

Though Jimi was back with Little Richard, the two were still frequently clashing. Before an April show in Huntington Beach, California, Jimi had Rosa Lee Brooks curl his hair and—in what had to be considered a hostile act toward Richard—he wore a woman's blouse and a bolero hat onstage. Additionally, Jimi did every stage antic that

Richard had previously banned. "He played guitar with his teeth, behind his head, and he humped the guitar," Brooks recalled. "Everybody in the place went crazy." So, apparently, did Little Richard, who refused to pay him for the gig.

Jimi was making two hundred dollars a month with Richard, which was a fair backing-musician wage, but what with all the fines, his actual salary rarely hit that mark. After a show in Washington, D.C., he missed the bus, and when he caught up with the band he knew his position was in jeopardy. Jimi later insisted that he quit, but Richard's brother Robert Penniman, the tour manager, told a different story to author Charles White: "I fired Hendrix. . . . He was a damn good guitar player, but the guy was never on time. He was always late for the bus, and flirting with the girls, and stuff like that."

As for Rosa Lee Brooks, Jimi had promised her he would return to Los Angeles when he left Little Richard. But once he was ensconced back in Harlem, Los Angeles seemed far away. Brooks did get a letter from Jimi that fall asking if she could send him money to get his guitar out of the pawnshop. Jimi told this same story, of having his guitar in hock, several times that year, mostly to female benefactors—it was his one plea for money that was guaranteed to pull on the heartstrings of anyone who had witnessed how much he loved the instrument. Even an abandoned lover like Brooks, who had been left three thousand miles away, couldn't resist this appeal. Rosa Lee sent Jimi forty dollars, along with a picture of herself. "I just couldn't bear the thought of him without his guitar," she recalled. She never heard from him again.

# CHAPTER ELEVEN

# DREAM IN
# TECHNICOLOR

NEW YORK, NEW YORK

*July 1965–May 1966*

*"I used to dream in Technicolor that 1966 was the year that*
*something would happen to me."*

—JIMI HENDRIX in an interview with *Open City*

IN THE SUMMER of 1965, Jimi Hendrix was back in New York, staying for a time in Harlem with either Fayne Pridgeon or the Aleem twins
or renting cheap hotel rooms near Times Square. Having left Little
Richard's band, he rejoined the Isley Brothers for a month at a resort in
New Jersey. But the life of a backup musician had grown stale, and Jimi
began to reconsider his career. That summer marked his first attempt to
remake himself as a studio musician. How much meeting Steve Cropper had to do with this directional shift Jimi never commented on, but
it was likely considerable.

That July, Jimi offered himself to a number of record companies
as a session player. He had begun writing songs, and though his skills
were still unrefined, he took some rough ideas, including at least one
demo tape, to Juggy Murray at Sue Records. Sue had scored a 1962 hit

with Jimmy McGriff's "I've Got a Woman (Part 1)" and had a stable of R&B acts. Though Jimi's songs were of no interest to Murray, he was offered a position as guitar player. Murray suggested they first settle on a contract, and without even reading the piece of paper, Jimi signed a two-year agreement. He may, however, have had second thoughts because Murray didn't hear from him again for months. Like so many green musicians, Jimi had been seduced by the idea that having a producer interested in him was payment enough. In one of his few strokes of luck that year, the label developed financial problems and never held him to the contract. Jimi did find some studio work that summer with R&B bandleader Mr. Wiggles. Wiggles hired Jimi to play on a series of singles for the Golden Triangle label. "He was just a hurricane on the guitar," Wiggles recalled. Like many of Jimi's studio sessions from this era, his work was uncredited—45 rpm singles rarely listed anything other than the name of the recording artist.

In a letter to Al on August 8, 1965, Jimi mentioned his career shift. "I'm starting all over again," he wrote. "When you're playing behind other people, you're still not making as big a name for yourself as you would if you were working for yourself. But I went on the road with other people to get exposed to the public and see how business is taken care of, and mainly, just to see what's what. And after I put a record out, there'll be a few people who know me already and who can help with the sale of the record." He boasted that Al might soon be hearing him on the radio: "Just in case about three to four months from now, you might hear a record by me which sounds terrible, don't feel ashamed, just wait until the money rolls in." Jimi signed the letter Maurice James, but he had also begun to use the stage names Jimmy James and Jimmy Jim. These shiftings of name caused great confusion, and if his goal was to establish a solid reputation, they did not help his cause. Still, the name changes reflected a trait that was a core part of Jimi's character: He was constantly reinventing himself whenever his interest in music, fashion, or culture changed. This chameleon-like nature would later make Jimi— as a star—appear mysterious and enigmatic. Yet early in his career, when there were no fans to wow, it hurt his ability to develop a following.

By October 1965, "Maurice James" was residing in the Hotel America, a cheap midtown hotel. In the lobby early that month, he met Curtis Knight, who led a group called the Squires. Though Knight was a guitar player and bandleader, he made the bulk of his money running prostitutes. "He was a pimp with a band," recalled Lonnie Youngblood, another musician on the scene. Knight asked Jimi to join the Squires, and Jimi agreed. According to Knight, Jimi considered quitting music that month and had once again pawned his guitar to pay his rent. Knight loaned Jimi a guitar, and realized that as long as Jimi was borrowing the instrument, he had some control over him. Knight would use Jimi as the main facet of his band over the next eight months. Though the Squires were vastly inferior to the other bands Jimi had played with, there was one major benefit to the group: Knight put Jimi front and center and promised to make him a star. Knight had cut a number of singles by 1965, but none had charted. The first session he did with Jimi—a cover of Bob Dylan's "Like a Rolling Stone" recrafted as "How Would You Feel"—would not change that streak even with Jimi's spirited solo.

"How Would You Feel" had the sound of a cover song because it had been cut for producer Ed Chalpin, who ran PPX Productions. Chalpin had become a successful label owner by marketing quick cover versions of U.S. hits in overseas markets. Chalpin would scour the U.S. charts, and when a song began to take off, he would hastily record a cover for overseas markets. Chalpin initially found little notable about Jimi because Jimi couldn't read music. Still, after Chalpin heard him play, he realized he had talent and signed him to a recording and producing contract on October 15, 1965.

The contract—which Jimi did not read before signing—stated that Jimi would "produce and play and/or sing exclusively for PPX Enterprises Inc., for three years." It also specified that Hendrix would "produce . . . a minimum of three sessions per year." As compensation, Jimi was to receive 1 percent of the retail price of all records he produced. With the contract, PPX would have "exclusive rights to assign all masters produced" by Jimi. As cash compensation, Jimi would get "one dollar," which was a standard contract clause in many music-industry deals at the time when no money was being exchanged up front. Essentially, Jimi received no advance for the chance of future payments, though the offer of 1 percent of retail was a higher royalty rate than most contracts offered in the day.

The contract was signed in a coffee shop down the street from PPX's studios. "The man was happy to sign it," Chalpin recalled. "He knew that no backup musician ever gets a royalty. I was giving him a good royalty, with no deductions. And he knew he was going to be an artist. If it was a hit, and his name was on label, he would get a royalty." Chalpin had been prescient enough to know the magic word to lure Jimi: *artist*. The suggestion that he was an artist and not a backup musician was enough to put Jimi into a somnambulistic trance. "He was so happy to be an artist on his own right," Chalpin observed, "he would have signed anything."

Over the next eight months Jimi played on two dozen studio sessions for Chalpin, participating in what a court would later determine to be thirty-three total songs. Most of the tracks they cut were notable only for Jimi's guitar solos, as Curtis Knight was an inferior singer. Perhaps the best thing that can be said about Jimi's studio work with Knight was that Jimi learned the basics of how to record and overdub in Chalpin's studio. "No Such Animal" is one of the only standout tracks Jimi contributed to, in part because of Jimi's upbeat solo, but also because the song did not feature Knight's vocals.

Chalpin also arranged what had to be the strangest recording date of Jimi's entire career: a session for B-movie actress Jayne Mansfield. Mansfield was best known for her extraordinarily large bust. One can only imagine what Jimi thought finding that his career as a studio musician had come down to putting a little atmosphere on a tape of Mansfield butchering a song called "As the Clouds Drift By."

Curtis Knight and the Squires played regularly in New York in clubs like the Purple Onion and Ondine's, but never drew much of a following, and Jimi made very little money from the band. On the plus side, the Squires didn't go on tour and played only around New York.

Jimi even sang on a few songs. However, any creative freedom that was offered was diminished by the fact that the Squires strictly played covers. One of Jimi's specialties at the time was to play a hit like Wilson Pickett's "In the Midnight Hour" but to add enough new guitar work so that an audience member who saw the band night after night would get something unique at each performance. He did this strictly for his own satisfaction—at the time the Squires had no fans avid enough to be repeat customers.

∽∾∾

WHEN JIMI FOUND he couldn't make enough with the Squires to survive, he went on the road with Joey Dee and the Starliters, playing fifty-eight shows in sixty days. The job represented a coup for Jimi, as the Starliters were a successful band and their "Peppermint Twist" had been a No. 1 hit. "Jimi auditioned in my garage in Lodi, New Jersey," recalled Joey Dee, "and we hired him immediately. He was a great guitar player." The Starliters were the first racially integrated band Jimi had joined since Seattle, and their sound was more rock 'n' roll than his other early bands. Their tour concentrated on the Northeast, but they did make some appearances in the South, where Jimi found that being in an integrated band was even more difficult than playing in an all-black group. They slept in black-owned hotels, sometimes as far as fifty miles from the venue, and ate sitting on flour sacks in the kitchen since the three black band members were not welcome in most restaurants. Though Jimi would later complain that he wasn't paid enough, his tenure with the Starliters offered firsthand evidence that white musicians existed who were willing to stand up for civil rights. "There were many times I was offered more money to tour without the black players, but I refused," Joey Dee recalled. On the tour, the Starliters played to crowds as large as ten thousand, the biggest Jimi had yet seen. Still, because of the racial tension caused by the mixed band, in many venues the musicians were not allowed to leave the backstage area during set breaks.

Perhaps because of their shared burden of prejudice, the Starliters were a close band, and Jimi quickly ingratiated himself. "He was really shy at first," recalled member David Brigati, "but he opened up and told wild stories of being on the road with the Isleys and Little Richard." Jimi also told a tale about touring with James Brown and how on one occasion when he interrupted the Godfather of Soul, Brown punched him and fired him.

As a dance band, the Starliters had little choice but to play their hits note for note. Still, Jimi was given a solo every night during which he played with his guitar behind his head. The tour also represented the first time since Garfield High School and a few shows on military bases when Jimi was playing to white audiences. "In certain towns it was an all-white crowd," Brigati said. To his amazement, Jimi found that he was the subject of the ardent stares of young girls who pressed against the stage. This surprised Jimi, who at the time didn't feel particularly handsome. "Jimi had a lot of acne," friend Tunde-Ra Aleem recalled. "That added to his withdrawn nature." These young white fans helped boost Jimi's self-confidence, and he began to brag to his bandmates about his female fan club. "He was a magnet for them," Brigati observed. "There was something he had that just seemed to draw girls in."

One night in Buffalo, three East Indian women slept with Jimi after declaring that he had the face of a Hindu god—they had met him in the hotel and weren't even fans of the band. At one tour stop, a particularly adventurous white woman slept with Brigati, but after their liaison talked about her fantasies of an interracial affair. She suggested he phone the other band members. Brigati called them. "Before I could even get out of the bed," Brigati said, "one guy was on top of her." Jimi, however, stopped and asked, very politely, if he could take off his cowboy boots. Brigati left the room, and when he returned two hours later, the woman was by herself. She told Brigati it had been "the greatest day" of her life.

Road sex had become a routine part of Jimi's life as a touring musician, but even these opportunities were not enough to keep him interested in the Starliters. He later told the *N.M.E.* that "after sucking on a peppermint twist salary I had to quit," but he must have realized he was no closer to his dream of releasing his own records. While on tour with the Starliters, he had celebrated his twenty-third birthday. As 1965 became 1966, he confessed to a number of friends that he'd dreamed the coming year would change his life. "I used to dream in Technicolor that 1966 was the year that something would happen to me," he told one reporter. "It sounds a bit silly, but it's the honest-to-God's truth."

That magnificent destiny would have to wait, however, because as 1966 began, Jimi was back to the same grind. He was playing with Curtis Knight and the Squires, trying to pick up the occasional studio gig, and wondering how he was going to eat. His romantic life wasn't much smoother, as his main Harlem girlfriend, Fayne Pridgeon, had married Taharqa Aleem. Jimi was still staying with the couple in their apartment, but Fayne was uncomfortable with the situation. "Fayne couldn't understand how I would allow him to stay there after we got married," Taharqa recalled. One night Taharqa and Fayne, thinking they were alone, had a quarrel. "She wanted me to get rid of him," Taharqa said, "but I said 'let him stay.'" They later found out Jimi had overheard them.

Hearing that he might soon be on the street, Jimi moved to a cheap hotel. On January 13, he sent Al a postcard of the Empire State Building: "Everything's so-so in this big raggedy city of New York," he wrote. "Everything's happening bad here." He was facing eviction because of overdue rent, and often he went without eating. If there was any solace to his situation it came in the line he used to close his postcard to his father: "Tell Ben and Ernie that I play the blues like they NEVER heard." His boast was meant for Ernestine Benson, who had first exposed Jimi to blues artists through her extensive record collection. His line "Everything's happening bad here" could have been a lyric from one of those classic songs, but was also evidence of a shift that was internal and artistic. The miserable conditions that Jimi endured through 1965—the poverty, the segregation he'd experienced during his trips south, the loneliness—had made it one of the most difficult years he had known since the death of his mother. Yet the turmoil also matured him as an artist; it gave him some of the "mud," the pathos, that Johnny Jones said was essential for every great blues player. Jimi was not just playing the blues, he was living them as well.

そꙮ

HIS IMMEDIATE SALVATION came when King Curtis and the All-Stars needed a fill-in guitarist for a show at Small's Paradise in Harlem. Small's had launched the career of organist Jimmy Smith and had hosted every important African American musician of the age. Malcolm X had once worked there as a waiter. "Jimi had a fearlessness then, because I don't care how bad you were in Harlem, you had to meet the prerequisite," observed Taharqa Aleem. "You can be bad all you want, but you better dress like everybody else, you better look like everybody else, you better walk like everybody else, and you better talk like everybody else." For most of the night, Jimi lay back in the band, as part of the rhythm section. The moment of truth came during his first solo, which he nailed. It didn't hurt that the All-Stars included soon-to-be-legends Bernard "Pretty" Purdie on drums and Cornell Dupree on guitar. Playing with Dupree, who was a notable guitarist himself, Jimi learned interplay and how to play "more greased," as Dupree put it, adding more feeling and more soul. Jimi quickly learned the band's material. "In all my years, I've never seen another guitar player pick up the material like that," Bernard Purdie recalled.

Jimi played and recorded with King Curtis for the next several months, but also picked up occasional gigs with the Squires. Yet he still struggled to pay for food and rent. That winter Diana Carpenter met Jimi at the Ham and Eggs coffee shop at Broadway and Fifty-second. She noticed him because it was a cold day and he was wearing a thin jacket, without lining. "He was positioned in a way that I could see he had a hole in the bottom of his shoes," she recalled. The restaurant charged a fifty-cent minimum seating charge for a glass of water, which was all Jimi had in front of him.

Carpenter was a sixteen-year-old runaway working as a street prostitute at the time. She was in the restaurant with her pimp, and as she went to leave, Jimi said to her, "You are so cute!" She was shocked he possessed the insolence to speak to her in front of the pimp. The pimp took offense, told Jimi to "shut his mouth," and yanked Carpenter out of the restaurant. A few weeks later, Jimi ran into Diana again, with no pimp in tow, and they began a relationship.

Her profession was at first an asset rather than a problem to Jimi, and maybe even a bit of a fetish. She was making far more money than he, and even after a day's work she was still equal to his sex drive. "He was very active," she recalled. "Two or three times a night." Carpenter was a light-skinned African American and Jimi told her she also looked like his mother; either this was one of his favorite lines or he found himself most attracted to women who resembled Lucille. Carpenter only worked during the day—she had found this the easiest way to avoid arrest—so she had nights free and attended many of his shows. "He was always complaining that Curtis Knight owed him money," Carpenter said. "But even if Curtis paid him, Jimi wasn't making enough to cover rent." Some thought Jimi was Carpenter's pimp, but though he lived off her, he didn't pimp for her.

Even with her income, they had little to waste. One evening, as they were walking along Fifth Avenue, Jimi asked her to pick out the jewelry she would want when he was rich. She pointed to an outrageous gem. "One day I'll buy you that," he boasted. One of their frequent topics of conversation was how rich and famous he was going to be. "How rich?" he'd ask. "Really rich, and really famous," she'd answer. On some occasions, this conversation took a darker tone. "If I don't get rich and famous in a year, I'll go crazy," he told her once. There was an increasing desperation to Jimi's fantasies, as if they would evaporate if not quickly fulfilled. He spent hours a day practicing, dragging a borrowed amp four blocks from a nearby club to their hotel since he couldn't afford cab fare.

Once Jimi came home to find a john choking Carpenter. He grabbed the man and threw him out of the room, but the incident soured him on her job. That same week, Diana was arrested, jailed, and put on a bus to the Midwest. She escaped and returned to Jimi, who was in tears, saying he'd feared a trick had killed her. He also broke down in tears once when she described her childhood sexual abuse; he told her he had been the victim of similar abuse though he didn't give many specifics except to say it occurred during his childhood.

In early May, Carpenter discovered she was pregnant, and at Jimi's insistence she stopped working the streets. Jimi's only income was from occasional gigs, and by late spring, they were stealing to survive. On one occasion, when Jimi and Carpenter both were shoplifting, a store owner observed them and chased them with a baseball bat. It took several blocks for them to outrun the owner, and they barely escaped. Jimi frequently raged, "I gotta change this bullshit. I can't stand this any longer. I don't want to die the death of a dog." Secretly, Carpenter went back to working the streets to earn some money. When Jimi discovered her deception, he hit her with a belt. "We both knew I was pregnant at the time," she said. "It was the only time he was like that." As he hit her, he began a screed that was unlike anything she had ever heard come out of his mouth. "When I tell you to do something, you do it!" he bellowed. "You like to be hardheaded, I'll show you. I'll show you that fat meat is greasy." It was not the way Jimi normally talked or acted. Carpenter was shocked at the meanness that was unleashed.

Their relationship deteriorated from there. When Carpenter suggested they splurge on a matinee of a Lana Turner film called *Madame X*, Jimi flew into a rage, thinking it was a movie about prostitution. She stormed out, picked up a john who was an undercover cop, and was promptly arrested. The police discovered she was underage and gave her a choice of three years in jail or a bus ticket home to her parents. Pregnant, hungry, and worried for the health of her unborn child, she took the bus ticket. In February 1967, she gave birth to a daughter, Tamika, who weighed less than five pounds. Because of the timing of her pregnancy, and the fact that she took only white johns on the street, Carpenter was convinced that the child was Jimi's. She had no idea where to write him; they had stayed at so many cheap hotels she gave up on the idea of ever locating him again.

꩜

JIMI'S AFFAIR WITH Carpenter might have turned him off to the idea of a prostitute as a girlfriend, but there was one undeniable link between these women and his past: the cheap hotels, fast lifestyle, and hard living were all reminiscent of his youth. It may not have been what Jimi wanted in life, but it was what he knew, and in that way it was comfortable.

Immediately after Carpenter's departure, and perhaps before, Jimi began seeing his first white girlfriend, Carol Shiroky. She was also a prostitute, though a call girl rather than a streetwalker. It was a short and tumultuous relationship. Shiroky bought Jimi a new guitar to help free him from Curtis Knight and Jimi spent hours filing down the frets—it was a right-handed guitar and he had restrung it lefty, necessitating some doctoring to retool the hardware.

Through Shiroky, Jimi met Mike Quashie, an entertainer at the African Room on West Forty-fourth Street who was known as "The Spider King." Quashie had been pictured on the cover of *Life* magazine in 1961 and introduced the limbo to America. He was six-foot-two but could shimmy under a bar seven inches off the ground. Quashie met Jimi in Shiroky's hotel room, and seeing the guitarist wearing pink and yellow curlers in his hair, Quashie assumed Jimi was a pimp. Quashie regaled Jimi with stories of voodoo but found Jimi so quiet and withdrawn that it was off-putting. "He was very down," Quashie said. "He would talk about his depression, frustration, and anxiety. It was not easy for him." Some of the act that Jimi would later shock the world with—wearing scarves, playing on his knees, and the use of pyrotechnics—he copied from Quashie. Jimi tried out some of this outrageousness with the Squires, but drew little reaction.

After one particularly exasperating Squires gig, Jimi wrote a poem about his dissatisfaction. It detailed how his so-called friends were interested only in his outrageous fashion sense and didn't "dig the way I'm thinking." He had so few friends at the time that his true subject must have been his bandmates in the Squires. He never finished the poem or set it to music. Like many of his writings from the era, it was simply an idea jotted on a scrap of paper and stuck into a guitar case. The title of this particular poem could have summed up Jimi's inner demons, both past and future. He called it, "My Friends of Fashion Turned Out to be My Enemies of Thought."

# CHAPTER TWELVE

# MY PROBLEM CHILD

NEW YORK, NEW YORK
*May 1966–July 1966*

*"Kaleidoscopic, fantastic images surged in on me, alternating, variegated, opening and then closing themselves in circles and spirals, exploding in colored fountains, rearranging and hybridizing themselves in constant flux. It was particularly remarkable how every acoustic perception, such as the sound of a door handle or a passing automobile, became transformed into optical perceptions. . . . There was to my knowledge no other known substance that evoked such profound psychic effects in such extremely low doses, that caused such dramatic changes in human consciousness and our experience of the inner and outer world."*

—DR. ALBERT HOFFMAN, *LSD: My Problem Child*

A BROWN-EYED GIRL, a Minnesota-born folksinger, and a psychedelic drug came into Jimi Hendrix's life on a night late in May of 1966 and each would have an indelible effect on his career. This trio of forces would help open an inner world for Jimi that had been previously untapped and forever change what had seemed, up until then, his sideman fate. Once these changes took hold, his previous life—playing fetch-and-get-it for Little Richard, or dancing in a costume in an R&B revue—would be just distant, and unpleasant, memories. It would be the next phase of his frequent reinvention of himself, and this persona would prove to be a powerful and lasting one.

He met the girl first. She was twenty-year-old Linda Keith, a strikingly beautiful model, who was everything Jimi was not: She was British, Jewish, well-off, highly educated, and an integral part of swinging London's in crowd. Perhaps most impressive to Jimi, her then boyfriend was Keith Richards of the Rolling Stones. Linda had begun dating Richards in 1963 and had witnessed the genesis of the Stones, which made her, by proxy, something akin to British music royalty. The Stones were due to arrive in the U.S. in a month for their highly anticipated 1966 tour; Linda had come over early to get a bigger taste of New York's club scene. As a music freak, she loved the blues and traveled with a case of her favorite 45s. Beautiful, smart, and music savvy, her presence was enough to make young men swoon.

They swooned when she walked into the Cheetah Club in late May, where Jimi was playing another woeful gig with Curtis Knight and the Squires. Throughout that spring, Jimi had sworn he was going to quit Knight's band for good, and he finally kept that promise—this particular stand would represent his last Squires booking. And no wonder he wanted to leave: The club was almost vacant.

The Cheetah was in a building that had once housed one of New York's grand turn-of-the-century ballrooms. It had reopened in April 1966 as a sophisticated nightspot with spotted fur wallpaper, but it had yet to catch on. A bar lined one side of the room, and the performers played on a fifty-foot-wide stage. Linda recalled that there were fewer than forty people in a room that could hold two thousand. She initially paid scant attention to the band, until she noticed the guitar player. "The way his hands moved up and down on the neck of the guitar was something to watch," she recalled. "He had these amazing hands. I found myself simply mesmerized by watching him play."

Linda was the girlfriend of a famous guitar player, not a talent scout, but she recognized in Jimi an extraordinary ability. Seeing him play to a tiny and unappreciative crowd also ignited her sense of justice. "He was just a brilliant player, and a brilliant blues guitar player," she remembered. "He was clearly a star, though he was such an odd-looking star, and it was such an odd place, it didn't seem right." When the set ended and Jimi was nursing a drink at the bar, Linda and her friends invited him to their table and lavished him with compliments. Attention from beautiful models was something Jimi knew little of; one can only imagine the look on his face when Linda told him she was Keith Richards's girlfriend and that Richards was due in town soon.

Linda and her friends remained for the last set. When it ended, they invited Jimi back to an apartment on Sixty-third Street. There they talked of music, politics, and, inevitably, of drugs. One of Linda's friends was among the drug cognoscenti. Jimi was asked if he'd be interested in taking some acid. His answer showed both his naïveté and his complete inexperience with psychedelics. "No, I don't want any of that," he said, "but I'd love to try some of that LSD stuff." He said this straight-faced, not knowing that acid was the street name for LSD.

Prior to 1966, Jimi's drug experimentation had been limited, partially by economic circumstances, to marijuana, hashish, cheap speed, and, on some rare occasions, cocaine. "In Manhattan, the drugs of choice were cocaine and marijuana," Taharqa Aleem observed. "Nobody in Harlem was doing acid then." Some African Americans perceived LSD as a "white" drug. Later that summer, Jimi tried to talk his uptown friend Lonnie Youngblood into tripping with him. "Jimi was saying all that crap you have in your mind, the spiderwebs, this clears and focuses it," Youngblood recalled. Lonnie gave Jimi a lecture about the dangers of LSD and how the drug could make you think like a white person. "That was white kids' drugs," Youngblood said. "I didn't want hallucinations. I had a wife, a kid, a car, and an apartment."

Dr. Albert Hoffman had discovered lysergic acid diethylamide in 1938 while researching the ergot fungus. Hoffman had accidentally dosed himself and immediately noticed the hallucinogenic effect. He later described that first trip in his memoir, *LSD: My Problem Child:* "In a dreamlike state, with eyes closed (I found the daylight to be unpleasantly glaring), I perceived an uninterrupted stream of fantastic pictures, extraordinary shapes with intense, kaleidoscopic play of colors." By the forties, Sandoz Pharmaceutical was commercially marketing LSD, billing it as a cure for everything from alcoholism to schizophrenia. Official distribution of the drug stopped in August 1965 after it became controversial, and nonprescription use became widespread. The drug was legal when Hendrix first took it (it became illegal in the United States in 1967).

Dr. Timothy Leary, one of the first scientists to do extensive testing with LSD, much of it on himself, proclaimed that the "set" and "setting" of an LSD experience were as important as the dosage. The "set" was the mind-set of the user; the "setting" referred to the environment where the drug was used. For Jimi Hendrix, the set and setting for his first acid trip could not have been more ideal: He was being lavished with praise by a brainy British model who knew who Robert Johnson was, he was in a trendy apartment with the walls painted red with leopard spots, and he was listening to Keith's collection of blues singles—it would have been intoxicating without drugs. Needless to say, the trip went rather well.

Jimi later described to a friend that on his first acid trip he "looked into the mirror and thought I was Marilyn Monroe." After May 1966, he chose to look in that mirror often. Lysergic acid diethylamide became a lens that filtered much of the music he would create during the rest of his life. That is not to say that he created all of his work stoned; however, once he had entered the world of acid, psychedelic thinking informed what he played, the songs he wrote, and the lyrics he penned. Jimi insisted to close intimates that he played colors, not notes, and that he "saw" the music in his head as he played it. His description of his creative process has an eerie similarity to what Dr. Hoffman wrote about his own first acid trip: "Every acoustic perception . . . became transformed into optical perceptions."

Drugs weren't the only thing Jimi found transforming that evening. Bob Dylan's *Blonde on Blonde* had come out two weeks before and Linda Keith had a copy. In addition to being an acid virgin, Jimi had not yet listened to Dylan's latest record. He was probably already tripping when Dylan belted out, "Everybody must get stoned" on the album's opener, "Rainy Day Women #12 & 35." Jimi would later cite *Blonde on Blonde* as his favorite Dylan album; listening to "I Want You," "Stuck Inside of Mobile with the Memphis Blues Again," and the mournful "Sad Eyed Lady of Lowlands" for the first time—while tripping on acid—would have made a lasting impression on anyone.

Linda would later describe the evening as a "night of magic," but reports over the years that suggest her relationship with Jimi that evening was sexual are in error. "I was going out with Keith [Richards]," she said. "And I was a middle class girl with middle class values." Yet the evening *was* intimate for Jimi in a way that was new for him. Their discussion that night—on the subjects Jimi was most passionate about, music and the guitar—was not the kind he usually had with a woman. Eventually, Linda's friends became exhausted by the talk about whether Delta or Chicago blues were preferable, and they went to bed in the other room. Jimi and Linda stayed up all night in the living room, chastely, she insisted.

Linda was surprised at how open and, in a way, naive, Jimi was when he discussed his career. He was clearly frustrated by his position in life, but not ashamed to talk about that disappointment, a trait uncommon among macho guitar players. When Jimi inserted pink plastic curlers into his hair at one point—he carried them in his guitar case—she was shocked that he would curl his hair in front of people he considered sophisticated.

When it came to the blues, they shared a rabid love for the genre. Linda was well versed in American roots music, and as if to prove her point, she produced a number of obscure 45s from her traveling case. She played "Little Bluebird" by Johnny Taylor, "Yours Truly" by Snooks Eaglin, and a selection of other rare blues sides, many of them from Keith Richards's personal collection. When the singles were exhausted, they kept going back to *Blonde on Blonde* as if it were something that couldn't be left alone. Jimi told Linda he was an admirer of Dylan and they both agreed the album was a work of genius. Jimi played along with his guitar all night. "It was the most special concert you could imagine," Linda said. "I would play him a record, and he would either play along, or play me back his own version. It was like a private recital."

Their conversation also included the topic of songwriting and a discussion of what makes a song powerful. Jimi told her he had written a number of tunes and he played her an embryonic version of "Red House" and several songs that later would end up on *Are You Experienced*. Linda was impressed and pestered her new protégé about why he had spent so much time touring behind others. She asked the obvious question: "Why are you playing with Curtis Knight?" To this, Jimi had a simple, straightforward reply: "I don't have my own guitar." Whether or not Carol Shiroky had purchased Jimi a guitar by this point is unclear. "It was possible," Linda recalled later, "that he was using me to get a guitar. But I don't think so."

She told him she'd get him a guitar. At that point she was already a believer and willing to do whatever she could to help him. Sometime during that night he told her his real name was Jimi Hendrix, not Jimmy James, his stage name of the moment. She asked why he didn't sing. "Well, you know, I'm not that great a singer," he said. Jimi had felt his singing voice was weak since junior high when he had unfavorably compared himself to friends like Jimmy Williams, but he had begun to reevaluate this in light of popular singers like Dylan. "Now days, people don't want you to sing good," he wrote in a letter to Al that year. "They want you to sing sloppy and have a good beat to your song. So that's what angle I'm going to shoot at. That's where the money is." Still, he remained unsure of himself and sang only a few songs with Curtis Knight.

"Sure, you are a good singer," Linda Keith replied that night, having heard his living-room concert for the better part of several hours. And as if she needed more ammunition, there it was on the turntable: Bob Dylan. Nothing else needed to be said. On the blurred cover of *Blonde on Blonde,* staring out at Jimi was a skinny fellow with a wild mane of hair in a long coat who, for every reason other than skin color, could have been Jimi himself. And he had a voice that Jimi simply could not let go of.

∽∾∾

THOUGH *BLONDE ON BLONDE* accelerated Jimi's own ambition and his belief that he could sing, his interest in Dylan predated his night with Linda Keith by a couple of years. This admiration—some called it an obsession—put him at odds with his friends in Harlem. Fayne Pridgeon remembered Jimi spending his last few dollars in 1965 on Dylan's *Highway 61 Revisited,* much to her chagrin. An earlier time, Jimi brought a copy of "Blowin' in the Wind" to the DJ booth in a Harlem club. The DJ, unfamiliar with Dylan, unwisely agreed to spin it. Jimi was run out of the club by an angry mob yelling, "Get out, and take your hillbilly music with you!"

Not long after hearing *Blonde on Blonde,* Jimi bought a Bob Dylan songbook. Since he couldn't read music, it must have been Dylan's lyrics that attracted Jimi. He kept the songbook with him always, and frequently it was the only item in his travel bag. When musician Paul Caruso met Jimi in early 1966, Jimi's first question was "How'd you get that Bob Dylan haircut? You know, the white Afro?" Jimi may have had to use curlers, but he had the Dylan hairdo down.

Hendrix would later claim that he met Dylan in 1966 at a club called the Kettle of Fish on MacDougal Street. Dylan's only comment on their relationship came in notes for a 1988 museum exhibit. "I knew Jimi slightly before he became a big star," Dylan wrote, "[but] never saw him much after that."

Part of Linda Keith's appeal for Jimi was that she was the first woman he had ever met who also appreciated Dylan, and on their first night together he exhausted the subject. She was more interested in knowing about Jimi's personal life, and at one point asked if he had a girlfriend. "Many," he replied, though the only one he named was "Auntie Fayne," whom he said he ate with once a week uptown. He failed to bring up Carol Shiroky, with whom he was in all likelihood living at the time, or Diana Carpenter, who was pregnant with his child.

Dylan was still on Jimi's mind two weeks later when he ran into musician Richie Havens at the Cheetah. Jimi was playing that night with Carl Holmes and the Commandeers, another B-grade R&B band. Havens was so impressed with Jimi's playing that he asked him where he had learned it. Their conversation eventually turned to Dylan, and Havens said his own set included a cover of "Just Like a Woman." Jimi wanted to witness this and asked Richie where he played. Havens began to describe the coffeehouse scene in Greenwich Village. Though Jimi had been living in New York on and off for two years, he gave the impression to Havens of having just arrived. "You've got to go down to the Village," Havens replied. "That's where it's happening." Before they parted, Havens wrote down the names of some Greenwich Village clubs including the Café Wha?

இல்லை

THE CAFÉ WHA? was located downstairs at the corner of MacDougal and Minetta Streets in the heart of Greenwich Village. The Wha was literally a cave: a dark basement with earthen walls in one alcove. The club was known more for the fact that Mary Travers had worked there as a waitress before her Peter, Paul and Mary days, and that Dylan had played there a few years before, than as a launching pad for new talent. It didn't have a liquor license and consequently attracted a crowd of teenagers, who were almost exclusively white, as were the bands. During summers, the Wha opened at ten in the morning and closed at 2 AM. There was no cover charge during the week, though patrons were expected to buy one drink per set, and they usually bought a "Green Tiger," a seventy-cent glass of carbonated water with lime. Musical acts played five sets for which they were paid a total of six dollars. It was in this unlikely venue that Jimi began his effort to transform his career, and his life.

Hendrix had first begun to explore Greenwich Village that spring, taking several "expeditions" in April and May. Paul Caruso recalled with clarity the first time he ever saw Jimi walking down MacDougal Street: "He looked ridiculous. He had on striped pants, a calypso shirt with huge puffy sleeves, and those Little Richard sausage curls." It was as if a pirate from Harlem had been set loose among the beatniks, bohemians, and radicals that populated the Village. The countercultural movement had just begun to blossom in 1966, and Greenwich Village had been one of its incubators. Long hair was in vogue, beads on men became popular, drug experimentation increased, and societal norms about sex and marriage were being challenged. Jimi hadn't fit in up in Harlem, but in Greenwich Village he found his outrageousness was embraced and encouraged.

It is unknown what day Hendrix first walked into the Wha, but he almost certainly returned on a Monday, which was the club's open-mic audition night. Janice Hargrove was in the audience the day he auditioned, as she was on most days—her boyfriend worked as the club's dishwasher and she would later become hostess. "Anybody could get up and try out," she recalled. "Most people were so-so. Jimi played, and everyone in the club was totally blown away, all fifteen people." Jimi didn't have a body of material yet, so he performed several covers, but he made his guitar solos the centerpiece of the act. The club's manager offered him work. In the excitement of the evening, or perhaps thinking it was safe, Jimi left his guitar at the club overnight. In yet another repetition on the theme, the guitar was stolen.

Jimi returned the next night and, finding his guitar missing, flew into a rage. The club owners questioned all the employees but to no avail. For the occasion of his first gig at the Wha, Jimi had to borrow an instrument. "Someone gave him a right-handed guitar," Hargrove said, "and without hesitation, he turned it upside down and started playing it. That fact alone blew us away. He did it without so much as a pause;

he just flipped it and started playing. He was as good playing someone else's guitar upside down as he was playing his own lefty guitar." At the end of the evening, Jimi was invited back the next night.

That same week, while shopping for guitars at Manny's Music, Jimi ran into a fifteen-year-old runaway named Randy Wolfe. Hendrix bragged to Wolfe that he had a solo gig that night at the Wha and invited him to join his band. Jeff "Skunk" Baxter, later of the Doobie Brothers, worked at Manny's and was invited to play bass for the show. Jimi had walked into a music store, met two strangers, and formed a band on the spot.

For a name, he decided to call the motley crew Jimmy James and the Blue Flames. He had picked the name because Junior Parker had a group called the Blue Flames, but he also called the group the Rain Flowers, based on his mood. Not long after starting to play the Wha, Hendrix decided to change the spelling of his first name to "Jimi" because he thought it looked more exotic. The only marquee the Wha had was a chalk sandwich board, so changing names took no effort. The lineup of the Blue Flames was fluid—and since two of the players were named Randy, Jimi called Wolfe "Randy California," which later became his stage name, and the other Randy became "Randy Texas." Jimi was so clearly the focal point that many in the audience hardly noticed the rest of the group. "Jimi didn't really have much 'Jimi Hendrix music' at the time," observed Tunde-Ra Aleem. "He ended up playing covers, but he would make them Jimi songs." Randy California said the band developed just four different original songs that summer, and the only one that remained in Jimi's repertoire was "Mr. Bad Luck," which later became "Look Over Yonder." Some witnesses argue that Jimi played early versions of "Foxy Lady" and "Third Stone from the Sun," but if so, they were rarities rather than the core of the set.

Instead of Hendrix music, Jimi played covers such as Howlin' Wolf's "Killin' Floor" or Dylan's "Like a Rolling Stone," putting his own unique stamp on them. "We would play songs that were popular at the time," recalled Blue Flames drummer Danny Taylor, "but Jimi always did extended versions. We'd do 'House of the Rising Sun,' 'Hang

On Sloopy,' 'Midnight Hour,' 'Knock on Wood,' and 'Mercy, Mercy.'" For evening shows, the sets would include more R&B and less rock. To stretch out their sets, the group had a version of "Summertime" that went on for almost twenty minutes. Another set highlight was a re-working of "Wild Thing," which had been a huge No. 1 hit for the Troggs that summer. The Troggs version had been a concise two min-utes and forty-two seconds, but Jimi could stretch the tune into a twelve-minute opus, and he might play it every set but do it differently each time. Free from the confining sets of the Chitlin' Circuit, Jimi wasn't against applying blues harmony to rock progressions or inserting wild rock solos into the middle of blues classics. Many blues guitar players could bend the strings for an added tone—Jimi applied the same principle to an entire song. He *bent* the music, and in doing so made whatever he played his own.

By June 1966, Jimi was also experimenting with a crude version of a fuzz box crafted for him by a member of the Fugs. This effects box sat between the guitar and the amplifier and would distort the note and thicken the sound—it made a light string sound heavy and a heavy string sound like a sledgehammer. This psychedelic sound, when com-bined with bending the strings and with feedback created by overdriv-ing the amplifier, sounded a lot like the "dirty" Northwest sound Jimi had heard back at the Spanish Castle. By 1966, Jimi's technical prowess was so advanced he was able to quickly master new effects and make them musical. His command of these crude electronic devices was so great he could attract a crowd of guitar players who simply marveled at his use of the new technology. "It was amazing," recalled drummer Danny Taylor. "The squealing that he could do with that guitar was a piece of art."

But even to those not interested in the electric guitar, a Blue Flames show was still something to watch. Freed for the first time to lead a group, Jimi took every move he had ever watched Little Richard, Solomon Burke, Jackie Wilson, or Johnny Jones do and brought a black stage show to a white audience. Borrowing scarves and jewelry from Mike Quashie's limbo act, Jimi dressed exotically. And once the show began, he pulled out every trick he knew: He played the guitar with his teeth; he played behind his back; he played under his legs; he humped the guitar with his leg in a manner that was clearly sexual; and he did this all while keeping the tempo of the song going. He brought "the show" he'd seen on the Chitlin' Circuit and in Mike Quashie's "Spider King" act, and filtered it for the white audience at the Wha. If Jimi had attempted the same kind of performance at the Del Morocco in Nashville, or at Small's Paradise in Harlem, he would have been laughed off the stage because his act was so over-the-top. But in the summer of 1966, the white kids from Long Island who hung around the Wha found it magical. Inspired by Dylan, acid, the limbo Spider King, the encouragement of Linda Keith, and new friends he was meeting in the Village, the "Jimi Hendrix" whom the world would soon come to know was created that summer in a dim, basement New York club. By the first of July, the Wha rewarded Jimi with a pay raise—he was now making ten dollars a night.

# CHAPTER THIRTEEN

# DYLAN BLACK

NEW YORK, NEW YORK

*July 1966–September 1966*

*"We all called him 'Dylan Black' because of his hair. Once you saw him, you didn't forget him. It was like he was hot-combing it; it looked exactly like Dylan's."*

—ELLEN MCILWAINE

THE BLUE FLAMES played for several weeks at the Wha, and while it would be an exaggeration to say they built a large following, they did attract a few loyal fans and drew the attention of a number of the many musicians in Greenwich Village. Richie Havens sent Mike Bloomfield, considered the best guitarist in New York; Bloomfield emerged from the show announcing he wasn't going to pick up the guitar again. "Hendrix knew who I was and that day, in front of my eyes, he burned me to death," Bloomfield told one interviewer. "H-bombs were going off, guided missiles were flying—I can't tell you the sounds he was get-ting out of his instrument. He was getting every sound I was ever to hear him get, right there in that room with a Stratocaster. . . . How he did this, I wish I understood." Bloomfield, true to his word, failed to appear for his next scheduled show, and Richie Havens had to fill in.

Bloomfield's reaction mirrored that of many guitarists upon first viewing Jimi: It was as if Jimi's talent negated their own, as if his playing was something he did to *them*. They took his rising star personally, which led to admiration but also to jealousy. Even Jimi's rehearsals began to attract aficionados. Guitarist Buzzy Linhart caught a rehearsal where Jimi essentially played an entire show to a handful of guitar players. "He was performing even though the only audience was a few musicians," Linhart recalled. "He could throw the guitar out of his hands and play it as it came back by him." For the first time in Jimi's life, he had others in awe of him and he reveled in the attention.

Linda Keith was still trying to find a producer as impressed with Jimi as the local guitarists were. She took Andrew Loog Oldham, the Rolling Stones' manager, to a show at the Wha, hoping he'd be interested in signing Jimi. Linda tried to soft-sell Jimi, but found Oldham unimpressed. "I was more concerned about her interactions with Jimi than I was in signing him," Oldham remembered. "It was obvious that she knew him, and clear that she knew him well. And she was the girlfriend of my lead guitarist, so that's what I was worried about. The part of me that did like the music could see that he was trouble, and I had enough trouble already with the Stones." Oldham recalled that Jimi spoke to Linda from the stage several times, something the manager found disconcerting, if only because of what might have occurred had Keith Richards been in the club. "Keith was the kind of guy who might actually kill someone involved with his girlfriend," Oldham said.

Linda remembered the night differently and argued that Oldham simply didn't appreciate Hendrix and couldn't see past his thrift-store clothes. "Andrew thought Jimi was crap," she said. "Yes, Jimi had a terrible image, and Andrew was all image. Andrew's whole thing was that he was into strings, and the wall of sound. Andrew just didn't see it. Jimi wasn't everyone's cup of tea." It probably did not help Jimi's case that he had a bad outbreak of acne that week.

Undaunted, Linda tried again, this time contacting Seymour Stein of Sire Records. Stein was impressed with what he saw—particularly by the fact that Hendrix had a few original songs—yet the evening deteriorated when Jimi began smashing his guitar in frustration. Linda panicked, perhaps because she had pilfered this guitar from Keith Richards, though it was easily repaired. Stein went with Linda on a second occasion to see Jimi only to witness a row between Linda and the guitarist, forestalling any discussion of business.

Linda Keith's relationship with Keith Richards was falling apart that summer for a variety of reasons, including Richards's jealousy of Jimi. For her part, Linda argued that she and Jimi never began a serious romantic relationship, and that a love affair didn't develop because Jimi refused to settle down. "I told him that he wouldn't be able to carry on with all the women he had if he were involved with me," she said. "I gave him something of an ultimatum, and he chose the other women. I suppose I was one of the few women who wouldn't accept that. All his girlfriends had to have a secondary role, they were providing him with something: money, food, or more women."

Linda Keith was amazed at how Jimi managed to juggle his many girlfriends, and how he conned every one into thinking she was his sole focus. "He had this depth with women," she observed. "All the women who say they were the great love of his life, they probably *were* in that moment. Or at least that's what he told them." She recalled being in Jimi's Lennox Hotel room once when there were seven women sleeping in his bed—they were in all likelihood prostitutes rather than Jimi's girlfriends, yet the display still made an impression. Jimi argued that his wandering ways were part of his "nature." Linda felt hurt that Jimi couldn't be monogamous, and oddly, Jimi was hurt that she had higher standards. In fact, he felt snubbed. Jimi avoided direct conflict as much as possible, preferring instead to wander away from a disagreement or an uncomfortable situation, and that's how he dealt with their erstwhile relationship—he continued to pine for her, but was unable to forgo the other women he met and bedded.

Despite Jimi's philandering, Linda worked tirelessly to bring him to the attention of the world, and few musicians have had the luck of winning such a determined champion. Linda even brought the Rolling Stones to one of Jimi's shows at Ondine's, a midtown ballroom. The Stones could create gossip-column items simply by appearing at someone else's show, yet their appearance at Jimi's went unreported and the band was unimpressed. They spent most of the night dancing or fending off admirers; the only Stone who paid attention to Jimi was Keith Richards, who couldn't help but notice how much his girlfriend was talking about this Jimi cat.

In fairness, the Ondine's appearance may not have been the Blues Flames at their finest, as the club was in midtown and most of the facility was a disco. The Blues Flames always had a greater appeal to the more forgiving audiences in Greenwich Village. Jimi never attempted to play his band in Harlem, figuring that his hybrid of rock and blues wouldn't fly there. He did repeatedly invite his friend Lonnie Youngblood down to the Wha to see a Blues Flames show, but appreciating Jimi's music was too large a leap for Youngblood. "Jimi began to hang around with these white kids, these freaks," Youngblood recalled. "He kept playing me these songs he'd written, and he wanted me to record them with him, but when I heard them, they were weird." Hendrix repeatedly bragged to Youngblood that with the right group the two of them could "own the Café Wha." "I didn't have any interest in that," Youngblood said. "I went back to my briar patch at Small's Paradise."

For some months, Jimi remained a man torn between two musical cultures: the strict, regimented tradition of uptown Harlem R&B and the loose amalgam of folk and rock that was developing in the Village. His exceptional musicianship made him comfortable in both worlds, yet he knew not to bring downtown back uptown. "If he would have taken that to Harlem, he would have been laughed at," observed Taharqa Aleem. The Aleems were some of Jimi's only black friends who went to the Village to see him play. "The revelation took place then," Tunde-Ra said. "It was the epiphany for him artistically." This cross-pollination of genres happened, as did most of the major events in Jimi's career, without a master plan. Jimi did not set out to mix blues, rock 'n' roll, and R&B; his musical imagination was simply so wide that combining genres was inevitable. The unique sound he forged that summer in the basement of Greenwich Village clubs was an accident, in a way, but it was also a visionary, brilliant accident.

⌒⌒⌒

HAVING STRUCK OUT with Andrew Loog Oldham, Seymour Stein, and the Rolling Stones, Linda Keith felt she had failed. "I was truly grasping at straws," she said. "I was starting to doubt myself, and thinking I was mad." Her savior, and Jimi's, came in the form of Bryan "Chas" Chandler, who was the bass player in the Animals. The Animals were a successful U.K. band with eight Top 40 hits; their 1964 hit "House of the Rising Sun" had topped the charts on both sides of the Atlantic. Chandler had planned to leave the Animals when their 1966 U.S. tour ended and he was looking for producing opportunities. Though Chandler was only twenty-eight at the time, he had a decade of experience in one of the biggest rock bands in the world, and he knew a hit when he heard it. That summer he heard a version of Tim Rose's "Hey Joe" and became convinced that if he found the right artist to cover this song in England, he'd have a smash.

On the night of August 2, Linda ran into Chandler outside a club. "I had never really talked to Chas before, though I knew who he was," she recalled. Chandler was hard to miss: He was six-foot-four, and had the barrel-chested build of a Newcastle coal miner—which was the fate that had awaited him before he discovered music. Linda told Chas there was a guitar player down in the Village he should check out. They made arrangements to attend the next afternoon.

When Chandler and Linda showed up at the Wha for the Wednesday-afternoon show, there were two dozen teenagers inside sipping Green Tigers. Chandler, who was dressed in a suit, stood out. "He was better dressed than anyone in there, so you could tell he was a manager type," recalled Danny Taylor from Jimi's band. Hendrix had been tipped off that Chandler was coming and put on his A-game performance. As fate would have it, Jimi also had recently discovered Tim Rose's "Hey Joe," and when he played this song, Chandler became so excited he spilled a milk shake on himself. "I thought immediately he was the best guitarist I'd ever seen," Chandler recalled in *A Film About Jimi Hendrix*.

After the set, Jimi, Chas, and Linda retreated to a table and Chandler introduced himself. Chandler asked Jimi about "Hey Joe" and how he had figured out his unique guitar parts for the song. This bit of serendipity—their mutual love affair with "Hey Joe"—was the beginning of their working relationship. As they talked, and Chandler heard about Jimi's years on the road backing up Little Richard and the Isley Brothers, he became convinced that Jimi had the makings of a star. "I just sat there and thought to myself, 'There's got to be a catch here somewhere, somebody must have signed him up years ago,'" Chandler recalled in an interview years later. "I just couldn't believe that this guy was standing around and nobody was doing anything for him." Jimi told Chandler about Juggy Murray and the Sue Records contract, and Chandler said he would try to straighten that out. When asked if he had any other contracts, Jimi failed to mention—or forgot—the contract he'd signed with Ed Chalpin and PPX.

Chandler asked if Jimi would consider coming to England, where Chandler was certain he'd succeed. In future tellings of the story, Jimi always stated that he immediately said yes, but many on the Village scene remember it differently: The idea of going to England scared Jimi at first. He knew so little about Britain that he asked whether his electric guitar would still work with their electricity. Still, when the meeting ended, a gentleman's handshake was exchanged. Chandler had another month of touring the U.S. with the Animals; he assured Jimi he'd return to straighten out all the details.

If Jimi took Chandler seriously, he gave no indication in what he said to his friends or in how he conducted his career over the next month. He continued to play in the Village with the idea that he might get signed Stateside and put out a record. It would be another five weeks—back when Chandler returned—before Jimi would even apply for a passport. In the meantime, he went back to winning his own fans in Greenwich Village one by one.

Converting more musicians to his cause was not difficult. John Hammond Jr. was in the middle of a gig when a friend rushed in to tell him that a guy across the street was playing songs off of Hammond's recent album. Hammond had recorded the influential *So Many Roads* the previous year using a lineup of soon-to-be superstars: Robbie Robertson, Levon Helm, and Garth Hudson, all later of the Band; Charlie Musselwhite; and Mike Bloomfield. Hammond went to the Wha, where he was amazed to find Jimi playing the same licks Robertson had done on *So Many Roads,* but playing them better. After the set, Hammond introduced himself. "Jimi told me he was from Seattle," Hammond recalled. "He was very open, friendly, and talented. Anybody that heard him, or saw him play, knew he was going to be a star—it was obvious." The two struck up a friendship and Hammond agreed to add Jimi to his band for a two-week stint at the Café Au Go Go. That same week Hammond arranged for his famous father, John Hammond Sr., to see Jimi. Hammond Sr.—whose signings had already included Billie Holiday and Bob Dylan, and would later include Bruce Springsteen—became yet another industry legend who passed on Jimi Hendrix.

Though the Café Au Go Go held only two hundred people, it was the Village's showcase club and a place where many musicians were discovered. As part of Hammond's band, Jimi returned to his position as backup guitar player, but he was given a solo spot during the set. Musician Kiernan Kane was among the audience of twenty who witnessed Jimi's first Au Go Go show. "What he could do with that Strat was mind-bending," Kane recalled. "There was a lot of flash, but there was also substance, and it was twisted in this way that drew you in." Kane returned the next night, and the hall was empty enough for him to sit in the same seat he'd had the night before, directly in front of Jimi.

Ellen McIlwaine was the headlining act at the club that first week and she befriended Jimi during the run. He was already the highlight of the opening act, but he had the audacity to ask if he could sit in with McIlwaine's band during her set; she was so flabbergasted she said yes.

On paper, Jimi was supposed to be the backup guitarist, but he had managed to make the entire evening "the Jimi Show," and that night he won many fans. "He just blew everybody away," observed Bill Donovan, who worked at the club. "He played behind his back, all that stuff he had stolen from T-Bone Walker. We thought he invented it. No one there realized there was a black tradition that went back to the 1920s." The crowds slowly began to grow, along with Jimi's reputation.

Yet when a real blues artist was booked at the Au Go Go the next week, Jimi suffered a humiliation on the level of his Nashville showdown loss. Trying the same technique he had used to muscle his way into Hammond's and McIlwaine's groups, Jimi asked if he could sit in with legendary harmonica player Junior Wells. Halfway through his set, Wells announced to the crowd, "I hear we got a real wild man in the audience who needs to play." As Jimi climbed onstage, Wells departed to the dressing room. Puzzled, Jimi led the band through three songs, expecting Wells to come back in. When Wells did return, he was screaming obscenities at Jimi: "You dirty little muthafucker! Don't ever try to steal my band again!" Wells nudged Jimi off the stage. At first Jimi looked confused, as if he expected Wells to announce this was a prank. But when it was apparent it was no joke, Jimi's face turned ashen. "He was crestfallen," Bill Donovan said. "I thought he might cry. We didn't see him for a couple of days after that."

McIlwaine was one of the few musicians in the Village who had seen Jimi back when he was with an all-black band. "I saw him in Atlanta with King Curtis," she recalled, "and we all called him 'Dylan Black' because of his hair." McIlwaine asked her manager if he'd consider handling Jimi. The manager's reply: "You don't want him in your group—he's black." Though the Village was one of the most progressive scenes in all of the U.S., racial equality had yet to arrive to the music business. One night, the Au Go Go booked a traditional all-black soul revue and Jimi and McIlwaine watched the act together. The all-white audience of Village hipsters was unimpressed. Jimi turned to McIlwaine and said, "They've never seen a soul group before." It was an important piece of knowledge for Jimi: To succeed with white audiences he had to achieve a balance—too much "show" and he'd lose them. The patterned dance steps of the Isley Brothers' band would look too formal when performed in front of a white audience that was sitting down. At the same time, Jimi needed a select few of those moves to establish himself as a showman because just being a talented guitar player—black or white—was not a ticket to stardom. He needed to be flashy but not cartoonish. Even Jimi's level of onstage sexuality had to be tempered and not comic. During one gig with McIlwaine, another band member shot a tube of toothpaste between Jimi's legs during a solo, making a mockery of him.

By August, Jimi managed to arrange a two-week booking for the Blue Flames at the Café Au Go Go. Now he didn't have to shine behind Hammond or McIlwaine; he had the stage to himself. When he heard from Buzzy Linhart that Dylan occasionally stopped by the Au Go Go, Jimi would scan the audience each night hoping to see his idol's famed face. One night in the club's tiny dressing room, he asked Bill Donovan a question that to those who lived and worked in the Village sounded almost infantile. "This songwriter knocks me out, Bob Dylan. You ever heard of him?" Jimi inquired. "Uh, *yeah,* I've heard of him," Donovan replied. Jimi then followed with a twenty-minute discourse on the majesty of *Blonde on Blonde.*

Linda Keith was still attending Jimi's shows regularly, and by late August she and Keith Richards had broken up. Richards was angry, and to exact his vengeance, he rang up Linda's parents and told them that their very proper daughter was involved with a "black junkie" in New York. The absurdity of Keith Richards, of all people, suggesting that Jimi was a "junkie" was apparently lost on Linda Keith's father, who panicked. Richards gave Mr. Keith explicit instructions on where they could find Linda and her alleged paramour. Mr. Keith hired a barrister and immediately made Linda a ward of the court. He then flew to New York to drag her back.

Mr. Keith went to look for his daughter at the Café Au Go Go on an evening Jimi was playing. It was probably not the first time a concerned father had faced Jimi down over an errant daughter, but it was certainly the first time the father was a proper British gentleman. A confidante ran back and warned Jimi and Linda that Mr. Keith was about to storm into the dressing room. Jimi turned to the mirror and patted down his hair. "Oh, do I look all right?" he asked. As Linda later recalled, it was an instance of levity in an otherwise incendiary situation: "As if this wild man, by patting his wild hair down, would have made himself in any sense look acceptable to my father, this elderly Jewish British gentleman," she said. Her father spirited Linda from the club and back to England. She wouldn't see Jimi for two months, though she did write him care of the Wha.

By the first week of September, Chas Chandler had arrived back in New York. Jimi didn't have any club dates that week, so even locating him became a sleuthing job for Chandler, who later said he spent four days scouring fleabag midtown hotels. Once he found Jimi, the two men had a series of meetings wherein they planned their strategy for launching the artist then known as Jimi James on the world.

Though Chandler would initially be described as Jimi's manager, from the beginning he worked in partnership with Michael Jeffrey, who managed the Animals, and soon was Jimi's comanager. Whereas Chas was outgoing and gregarious, and did most of his business in pubs over a pint, Jeffrey was a private and intellectual man, whom many found hard to know. Though at five-six, Jeffrey was almost a foot shorter than Chandler, he suggested a sinister power behind the dark glasses that he wore at all times. He had worked for the British intelligence services in a clandestine role he only vaguely hinted to, and there were suggestions that he'd killed people. These rumors were likely exaggerations, though Jeffrey did little to defuse them. Like many powerful rock managers—from Led Zeppelin's Peter Grant to Bob Dylan's Albert Grossman—Jeffrey used fear and intimidation to his advantage in his business dealings.

Immigration laws in Britain were strict and even getting Jimi into the country required passport papers that vouched for his past. Since Jimi was a touring musician who had no paperwork-verified past, these documents had to be created out of thin air. Correspondence was forged that made it look like Jimi was being asked to come to the U.K. by a promoter. Jeffrey put up the few hundred dollars it cost Chandler to buy back Jimi's contract from Juggy Murray at Sue Records. They also had to obtain Jimi's birth certificate from Seattle and get him up-to-date on his vaccinations. All of these matters Jeffrey handled; with a phone call, he had the ability to bypass regulations.

Jimi's main concern continued to be the musical direction toward which his career might head, a subject Chandler tried to avoid. Jimi had also wrongly assumed that Chas wanted Jimi's entire band, a touchy point Chas said they'd deal with later. Jimi wanted Randy California to accompany him and went so far as to contact Randy's stepfather asking for permission, but it was clear that Randy, a fifteen-year-old runaway, was not going to get a passport. Jimi asked the other members of the Blue Flames to join him as well. "Jimi asked if I wanted to go along," said drummer Danny Taylor, "but I didn't want to get stranded there." This was Jimi's major worry as well. Jimi also asked Billy Cox to come. Billy politely declined but wished Jimi luck.

As decision time loomed, Jimi still had doubts, but there was so little holding him in New York that the move wasn't much of a risk. He later said his thoughts were, "Well, I'll starve my way over there," just as he had starved his way in America. Jimi and Chandler had one last meeting at which Jimi expressed his final reservations. "What's the point in me coming to England as a guitar player?" he asked Chandler. "You've got Eric Clapton and Jeff Beck over there. You don't need one more guitar player." Then Jimi himself gave Chandler the answer to his question: "If you can guarantee that you'll introduce me to Clapton, I'll come to London." That was one thing, Chandler replied, that could be promised; he would make sure Jimi got to meet Eric Clapton. With that, a departure date of September 23 was set.

Jimi was never big on farewells. He made the rounds and visited Fayne Pridgeon, Carol Shiroky, the Aleems, and Lonnie Youngblood. He also asked to borrow money. He told everyone he was going to England for a short time to put a record out, and he'd be back in the States soon. "To someone who had grown up in Harlem, or even Seattle,"

Tunde-Ra Aleem noted, "England was like another planet." Jimi didn't phone or write to tell his father he was leaving the country. By 1966, his correspondence with Al had slowed to a trickle, and the idea of going to a foreign country for a career in music was hardly something Al would have supported.

On the evening of September 23, 1966, Jimi boarded a Pam Am flight at John F. Kennedy International Airport. He was sitting in first class for the first time in his life—Michael Jeffrey, of course, was paying for the ticket. All Jimi had for luggage was his guitar and a small bag that contained a change of clothes, his pink plastic hair curlers, and a jar of Valderma face cream for his acne. The only other items he owned were a few pieces of clothing he had left with a friend. He had been so broke that before he left for the airport, he had stopped by the Café Au Go Go to see if he could borrow money from anyone in John Hammond's band. Drummer Charles Otis gave him forty dollars, which was the only money he had in his pocket when he got on the plane.

# CHAPTER FOURTEEN

# WILD MAN OF
# BORNEO

LONDON, ENGLAND

*September 1966–November 1966*

*"You've got to come downstairs and see this guy Chas has
brought back. He looks like the Wild Man of Borneo."*

—RONNIE MONEY, wife of bandleader ZOOT MONEY, describing Jimi

JIMI HENDRIX TOOK his first step on British soil on Saturday, September 24, arriving at Heathrow at nine in the morning. A member of the Animals' road crew carried his guitar through customs because of laws restricting foreigners from emigrating to England for employment, an appearance Jimi didn't want to create. Despite that bit of subterfuge, Tony Garland, the press officer in Michael Jeffrey's office, met them at the airport and had to spend two hours sorting out Jimi's work permit. "I had to invent a story that Jimi was this famous singer who'd come to England to collect his royalties," Garland recalled. "Otherwise, they weren't going to let him in." Finally, he was given a one-week visa and cleared to enter.

On the way from the airport, they stopped by the house of Zoot and Ronnie Money in Fulham. Zoot was a successful bandleader, while his wife was ever present on the club scene, and Chas was interested in showing off his new act as soon as possible. Jimi pulled out his Strat and attempted to play a few songs through the Moneys' stereo. When that failed, he grabbed an acoustic guitar and began to play. Andy Summers, who a dozen years later would help form the Police, lived in the basement of Money's house and heard the commotion. When he came upstairs to join the informal party, he witnessed Hendrix's technical skills and became the first of legions of Great Britain's guitar players to be awed and dazed by Jimi.

Rooming upstairs was twenty-year-old Kathy Etchingham, who was sleeping late. Etchingham was an attractive brown-eyed girl who worked as a hairdresser and part-time DJ. She had previously dated Brian Jones of the Rolling Stones, Keith Moon of the Who, and a few other rock stars. Ronnie Money tried to wake her up to tell about the new sensation in the living room. "I vaguely remember the bed shaking from the commotion downstairs," Etchingham recalled. "Ronnie said, 'Wake up, Kathy. You've got to come downstairs and see this guy Chas has brought back. He looks like the Wild Man of Borneo.'" The tag Wild Man of Borneo would later end up as one of Jimi's nicknames in the London tabloids, a consequence of Jimi's unkempt physical appearance and his race, both of which were so unusual on London's music scene that he might as well have been a new anthropological discovery. With Chandler escorting him around and showing him off, in a way Jimi was. The name was racist, of course, and the description would never have been used for a white musician. Still, Jimi enjoyed the nickname: It made him sound interesting and foreign, qualities he hoped to cultivate. The papers also called him "Mau Mau," and that too generated controversy, always an important ingredient for getting a new artist attention in the media.

Etchingham was too tired from the previous night's party to take a peek at the so-called wild man, but later that evening, she went out for a drink at the Scotch of St. James and Jimi was onstage. The Scotch was a club that attracted a clientele of musicians and industry people. Jimi had asked to jam, and unlike his initial foray into the clubs of

Harlem, he was immediately welcomed. Rather than a liability, his race offered him a huge advantage in London: There were so few musicians who were black on the scene, and so many fans of American blues, that he was afforded instant credibility.

As Jimi started to play—mostly blues tunes, attendees would recall—the club went silent and the crowd watched in a sort of shared rapture. "He was just amazing," Etchingham recalled. "People had never seen anything like it." Eric Burdon of the Animals was one of the many musicians at the club that night. "It was haunting how good he was," Burdon said. "You just stopped and watched." Playing blues standards with his gimmickry included, Jimi immediately managed to wow the crowd.

Chas called Etchingham over to a booth where he was sitting with a few young women, including Ronnie Money and Linda Keith. Though he was buoyed by the strong response Jimi was getting, the manager was concerned about violating Jimi's temporary visa. "I'm going to get him off," Chandler announced. "He's not supposed to work, even without pay." Jimi was yanked from the stage and eventually settled in the booth next to Linda Keith.

When Linda left for a moment, Jimi called Kathy Etchingham over. Linda returned and Etchingham's version of the next few events is dramatic: "Linda said something to Ronnie that was nasty about me. And a fight broke out. The tables had a slate top and there was a bottle of whiskey on our table. Ronnie picked up the bottle of whiskey and broke it on the slate. She put the jagged edge underneath Linda's chin. This all happened in seconds." Etchingham recalled that Chas panicked, not wanting Jimi in the middle of a bar fight, and insisted Kathy take him by taxi to their hotel. Linda Keith called this story "ludicrous" and denied it occurred. If it did, the idea of two English "birds" fighting over him would have been something Jimi would have found delicious.

The veracity of the evening's next drama was uncontestable, however: Walking out of the club, Jimi—unaware that traffic patterns in Britain were the reverse of the U.S.—immediately stepped in front of a taxi. "I managed to grab him by the collar and pull him back, and the taxi just brushed him," Etchingham recalled. At the hotel, Jimi and Kathy went to the bar, where Jimi threw out the question "Would you like to come to my room?" Etchingham, who found Jimi charming and handsome, consented. They would stay together for the next two years, on and off, and Etchingham would be one of his longest-term girl-friends. Perhaps more important at the time, Kathy knew everyone on the scene, and she became Jimi's entrée into a new social world. Her friends, who included members of the Who, the Rolling Stones, and many other bands, soon became the friends of her new boyfriend.

Jimi had been in England less than twenty-four hours and he'd al-ready wowed a key segment of London's music scene and found him-self a girlfriend. He had always been a master of reinvention, but how quickly his life transformed after only one day in England must have caused even him to marvel. The happenings of the day were also illus-trative of how much Jimi's personal life—and his career—were shaped by seemingly random events: He met a girl; she became his girlfriend. If his first day in London was filled with serendipity, his life over the next two years would follow a similar pattern. Everything that had once been so hard—getting attention for his music, trying to make enough money to live—suddenly was so easy it felt preordained. Jimi had spent twenty-three years of his life struggling with identity and seeking a place in a world where he felt like an outcast. In one single day in Lon-don, it felt like his entire life had permanently been recast.

∾∾∾

IN THE TIME line of rock-'n'-roll history, Jimi Hendrix could not have arrived in London at a better moment. While rock 'n' roll had been invented in America—and arguably the first rock 'n' roll record was Ike Turner's "Rocket 88," a song Jimi learned during his brief tenure with Ike and Tina—London was the capital of the entire cultural world in 1966. Hendrix's arrival came during the height of a sixties explosion of fashion, photography, film, art, theater, and music. *Time* magazine had done a "Swinging London" cover story in April 1966, broadcasting to the rest of the world that London was the cultural trendsetter. To Jimi's eyes, the most obvious sign of London's "youthquake miracle," as author Shawn Levy called it, would have been the fashions. In London, hair was long, skirts were short, and Mods and Rockers had turned the simple act of dressing for a concert into a political statement.

By 1966, the height of the British Invasion had subsided in America, yet British bands continued to dominate sales charts worldwide and the Beatles remained the most popular group on both sides of the Atlantic. "Before the Beatles," observed Vic Briggs, "no one thought rock 'n' roll had any future. You imagined that you'd play rock music for two years, and then find a real job. But the Beatles changed everything, and people began to have actual careers in music." London was filled with nightclubs, concert venues, and pubs, and simply watching the movements of the Beatles, whom Mick Jagger called "the four-headed monster," became a nightly sport.

In his first week in London, Jimi had two main goals: to form a band and get a proper work permit so he could stay in the country. Chandler's initial plan was to sell Hendrix to the British public as an authentic imported American bluesman. To accomplish this, Chandler needed to get Jimi onstage in London's showcase clubs, which made the work permit a necessity. "The only way Chas could do that was through Michael Jeffrey," Eric Burdon observed. Jeffrey knew the right strings to pull and the correct government officials to bribe, as he had ties to the bookers who ran the club circuit in England; there were vague hints of his connections to organized crime. "England was knee-deep in that kind of manipulation in that era," Eric Burdon noted. "It was like the whole thing was run by Frank Sinatra."

In truth, Jeffrey was more James Bond than Sinatra; he spoke in a whisper and always wore a camel-hair coat. Jeffrey had gotten his start in the music business running the Club A Go Go in Newcastle. "He showed quite a skill at bullshitting people," Burdon recalled. When the club suspiciously burned down, the insurance money helped him sign Newcastle's Animals as his first act, which was where he met Chas.

Newcastle had a unique working-class culture, and a distinctive accent to boot—Chas talked like a Newcastle "Geordie," while Jeffrey, originally a Cockney from London, could speak several languages including Russian. Though class distinctions were slowly breaking down in London in the sixties—a big part of the social revolution—Chas's roots were working class, while Jeffrey was of the public school upper class. Despite Jeffrey's cultured background, he was not against challenging convention: To foil an audit by Inland Revenue, he kept his books in Russian, hoping to confuse any auditors.

The office of Jeffrey-Chandler management was in a low-rent district at 39 Gerrard Street, up a flight of stairs in a warren-like building. The neighborhood was filled with photographers, artists, and others who worked on the fringes, including a pornographer three doors away. Jeffrey preferred doing business in the office, while Chandler was usually at the pub around the corner.

The first member of Jimi's new band came in the form of Noel Redding, a twenty-year-old guitar player, formerly of the Loving Kind and the Lonely Ones, obscure groups but useful learning stops. Spying a "musicians wanted" ad in *Melody Maker,* Noel came to audition for the job of guitarist in the Animals. He was asked if he'd have any interest in joining a band with Jimi. "Chas asked if I could play bass," Noel recalled. "I said no, but I'd try." Redding picked up a bass for one of the first times in his life and jammed with Hendrix. They played "Hey Joe" and "Mercy, Mercy." Afterward, Jimi asked if they could chat and Noel suggested a pub. There Jimi tasted English bitter for the first time and said Noel's frizzy hair reminded him of Bob Dylan. Anyone who looked like Bob Dylan was okay with Jimi, and with that, Noel was offered the job of bass player. Like many of Jimi's musical choices, this one was impulsive, but in all things, Jimi reacted on his first impulses. Noel accepted on the condition he receive ten shillings for train fare home. Noel became an excellent bassist, but he continued to harbor the desire to play guitar, which forever created a competition between him and Jimi, one that was not only musical but also, occasionally, personal when they both sought to bed the same groupies.

Sometime that week the band was named. According to Noel, Michael Jeffrey came up with the idea for the name "The Jimi Hendrix Experience." "We all thought it was wild, but then we really were 'an experience,'" Noel said.

As they continued with auditions to fill out the band, Chandler's vision and Jimi's diverged: Hendrix, having spent most of his history in large, revue-style bands, was convinced he needed a nine-piece group, complete with horns, traditional for R&B. Chandler wanted a smaller group, both because it would be cheaper and because he wanted the band centered on Jimi. Jimi went so far as to contact his old neighborhood friend Terry Johnson to ask him to join the large band he was planning. "I was in the service," Johnson recalled, "and he managed to track me down. He wanted an organ player." When Terry said he'd just reenlisted and had another four years in the air force, Jimi's answer said much about his own military service choices: "They got ways of getting out of that," Jimi told him. "Just go say you're gay." Johnson told Jimi that a gamble like that could result in getting killed by your squad mates. Terry declined the risk and Jimi went back to the auditions of English musicians.

Perhaps to satisfy Jimi's desire for a keyboard player, Chandler phoned Brian Auger, who led the Brian Auger Trinity, a blues-based rock band with heavy jazz influences, and proposed a rather radical idea. "I've got this really amazing guitar player from America," Chandler told Auger. "I think it would be perfect if he fronted your band." Chandler was expecting Auger to fire his own guitar player, Vic Briggs, and, in essence, turn his band over so Jimi could lead it. Offended by the suggestion, Auger declined, knowing nothing about Jimi Hendrix at that point. As a fallback, Chandler asked if Jimi could at least jam with the Trinity at a show they had that evening. To this, Auger agreed.

Trinity guitarist Vic Briggs was setting up his gear for that show when Chandler came into the club and asked if Jimi could join in. Briggs, with a British sense of politeness that would have been completely out of place in America, agreed, and even offered Jimi a guitar, though Jimi said he had his own. Briggs was using one of the first Marshall amplifiers, an experimental model that had four six-inch speakers—smaller than the later Marshall stacks, but still capable of yielding tremendous power. When Jimi plugged his guitar into the amp, he turned the amplifier volume knobs to their maximum, much to Briggs's amazement. "I had never had the controls up past five," he recalled. Jimi noticed Briggs's look of horror and said, "Don't worry, man, I turned it down on the guitar." Jimi shouted out four chords to Brian Auger and began.

The sound that came out was a wall of feedback and distortion, which itself was enough to turn every head in the club—the moment also marked the beginning of Jimi's love affair with powerful Marshall amplifiers. Jimi's apparent ease in playing complicated parts stunned those in attendance. "Everyone's jaw dropped to the floor," Auger recalled. "The difference between him and a lot of the English guitar players like Clapton, Jeff Beck, and Alvin Lee, was that you could still tell what the influences were in Clapton's and Beck's playing. There were a lot of B.B. King, Albert King, and Freddie King followers around in England. But Jimi wasn't following anyone—he was playing something new." In a role reversal of sorts, Jimi was now in the position that Johnny Jones had once held on the Nashville club scene: He was immediately considered the headman, the victor in every showdown.

On Saturday, October 1, Eric Clapton and his band Cream were playing a show at Polytechnic in central London. Chas had bumped into Clapton a few days before and told him he'd like to introduce him to Jimi. Meeting Clapton, of course, was the one promise Chandler had made to Jimi before they left New York. Clapton mentioned the Polytechnic gig and suggested Chandler bring his protégé. In all likelihood, Clapton meant he would be glad simply to meet Jimi, but nonetheless Jimi came with his guitar. Chandler, Jimi, and their girlfriends stood in the audience during the first half of the show, and as the set break began, Chandler called up to the stage and summoned Clapton over, asking him if Jimi might jam. The request was so preposterous that no one in Cream—Clapton, Jack Bruce, or Ginger Baker—knew quite what to say: No one had ever asked to jam with them before; most would have been too intimidated by their reputation as the best band in Britain. Jack Bruce finally said, "Sure, he can plug into my bass amp." Jimi plugged his guitar into a spare channel. "He got up there and played a killer version of Howlin' Wolf's 'Killin' Floor,'" recalled Tony Garland, who was in the audience. "I'd grown up around Eric, and I knew what a fan he was of Albert King, who had a slow version of that song. When Jimi started his take, though, it was about three times as fast as Albert King's version, and you could see Eric's jaw drop—he didn't know what was going to come next." When Clapton recalled the show in an interview with *Uncut*, he noted, "I thought, 'My god, this is like Buddy Guy on acid.'"

When Jack Bruce later told his version of the fabled event, he focused on Clapton's reaction and alluded to graffiti in London at the time that proclaimed, "Clapton is God." "It must have been difficult for Eric to handle," Bruce said, "because [Eric] was *'God,'* and this unknown person comes along, and *burns*." Jeff Beck, another of London's hot guitarists, was in the audience that night, and he, too, took warning from Jimi's performance. "Even if it was crap—and it wasn't—it got to the press," Beck later observed. Jimi had been in London for only eight days and he had already met God, and burned him.

∽∾∽

AS IF JIMI'S luck needed to get any better that fall, French singer Johnny Hallyday was in the audience at one of his club jams. Hallyday was thoroughly impressed and offered Jimi two weeks of supporting dates on an October tour of France, which was exactly the kind of debut Chandler was seeking. They did, however, have to find a drummer, if only a temporary one. Chandler phoned John "Mitch" Mitchell, who had just left Georgie Fame's band, and asked him to audition. Mitchell was only twenty, but he had considerable experience touring and doing studio sessions. Mitch was a diminutive five-foot-seven, but he was a powerhouse drummer, and after two auditions, he was given the job.

From their first rehearsals as a trio, the Jimi Hendrix Experience was surprisingly loud. At one of those rehearsals, a familiar figure appeared at the studio door and asked them to keep it down—it was composer Henry Mancini.

Before heading to France, all three members of the band signed production contracts with Chandler and Jeffrey. These contracts gave Chandler and Jeffrey 20 percent of all income earned; on record sales, the band would split 2.5 percent of all royalties. Jimi separately signed a publishing agreement with Chandler that gave Chandler a 50 percent interest in Jimi's songwriting for a period of six years. The band was put on salary, starting at fifteen pounds a week, as an advance against future earnings. If those contracts seemed to substantially benefit management, and would later make management far richer than the band, at the time no one knew if the group would ever earn a shilling, and most unknown bands would have been happy to collect any salary. To pay for the band's gear and travel expenses, Jeffrey borrowed money from his parents and Chandler sold his bass guitars. If the band ever made any serious money, the members had agreed to have it funneled through a shell company called Yameta that had been set up in the Bahamas to avoid Inland Revenue. Jeffrey had successfully used this method to avoid paying taxes on much of the Animals' income, but even Chas Chandler would quietly complain that the numerous shell companies benefited Jeffrey most of all; they certainly made accurate accounting an impossibility.

For his part, Jimi was more than happy with his fifteen pounds a week. As was typical, he signed his contracts with Jeffrey and Chandler without reading them and was concerned only with the cash he was getting up front. He used a salary advance to help update his wardrobe at some of London's unusually named fashion boutiques, stores such as "Granny Takes a Trip" or "I Was Lord Kitchener's Valet," both of which specialized in vintage clothing. At Granny's, customers walked in under a fifteen-foot-high painting of Sitting Bull and a sign above the entrance warned ONE SHOULD EITHER BE A WORK OF ART OR WEAR A

WORK OF ART. They were words that Jimi took to heart. For outerwear, he replaced his ragged New York overcoat with an ornate antique military jacket from the glory days of the British Empire. He bought a number of pairs of velvet pants in bright colors. Though Chandler had urged him to buy mohair suits, Jimi declared that he was done with that style and was moving on. His choices in clothes, which were all outrageous, put him ahead of the fashion curve for the first time in his life. Singer Terry Reid recalled that Jimi's clothes were a hot topic among other musicians: "Even before we knew his name, we called him 'that guy walking around who looks like he walked into a girl's closet and put everything on.'" The boy who had grown up wearing hand-me-downs had suddenly blossomed into a fashion trendsetter as one of the first men to explore "vintage chic."

With crushed velvet pants, his military coat, a gigantic black Western hat, and his windblown hairstyle, Jimi turned heads just walking down the street. "People would just stop and stare at him," Etchingham recalled. "It wasn't because they knew his music; it was just because he looked so strange." Etchingham herself was a smart dresser who kept up with current styles. Paired with the handsome Jimi in his antique military clothes they cut quite a sight. Occasionally, Jimi and Kathy shopped at Selfridges department store, and their very presence in public was enough to elicit snickers from fellow shoppers. Some of that was because their interracial relationship was still ahead of the times, but mostly it was because of Jimi's outlandish appearance.

Jimi and Kathy had immediately moved in together, but they were staying in a hotel, an expense Jimi could ill afford. When Etchingham ran into Ringo Starr at a club and complained about their cramped hotel room, Ringo offered a two-bedroom flat he wasn't using, and Jimi and Etchingham moved to 34 Montagu Square along with Chas and his girlfriend. It was an unusual relationship for a musician and his manager to be roommates, but it suggested the fatherly role that Chandler played at the time. As for his own father, Jimi hadn't written Al for months, and when he tried to phone, he discovered that Al had moved.

Jimi next called Ernestine Benson back in Seattle. Ernestine told him that Al had remarried and that his new stepmother was Ayako "June" Jinka, a mother of five, who was Japanese.

Jimi called Al next. In his autobiography, Al wrote that Jimi used the phone call to talk about the band and life in England. Al, in turn, told Jimi how he'd married and had planned to adopt one of June's children. But both Jimi and Kathy Etchingham spoke of the phone call in a very different way. "Jimi called collect," Etchingham recalled, "and Al was furious at that kind of waste of money. Jimi kept telling him about England, but Al didn't believe it." Jimi himself later said the first thing Al asked when he heard Jimi was in London was "Who had I stolen the money from to pay for the crossing." Finally, Jimi handed the phone to Kathy, hoping her accent might convince his father of his whereabouts. "Mr. Hendrix, it's true, Jimi's here in England," Etchingham said. Al's response was such a surprise to her that she remembered it decades later. "You tell my boy," Al told her, "to write me. I ain't paying for no collect calls." And with that, Al hung up. After putting down the receiver, Jimi said to Kathy, "What's he doing adopting other people's children when he couldn't even look after his own?"

∽◌∾

ON THURSDAY, OCTOBER 13, the Jimi Hendrix Experience played their debut show in Evreux, France, at the Novelty Theatre. As an opening act for Johnny Hallyday, their set lasted only fifteen minutes. It was an odd pairing: Hallyday was frequently called the "Elvis of France," and his style was, in fact, far closer to Presley's than it was to the sophisticated blues rock the Experience was attempting. Yet the Experience's set was so short they didn't have much time to make any impression, good or bad. They played "Hey Joe," "Killin' Floor," and a few covers. A French newspaper called Jimi "a bad mixture of James Brown and Chuck Berry, who pulled a wry face onstage for a quarter of an hour and also played with his teeth." Noel remembered the band as underrehearsed and ragged. "Jimi was still getting comfortable singing," Noel said. "We hardly knew each other."

A few days later, the short tour hit Paris for a show at the Olympia. This date was sold out, because of Hallyday's popularity, and twenty-five hundred fans packed the hall. Brian Auger's Trinity had been added to the lineup. "If the French audience didn't like you," Auger recalled, "watch out, because you might even get a few tomatoes thrown at you. But if they loved you, they went crazy." Playing roughly the same set as they'd played at their debut, but sounding more confident and adding Jimi's showstopping cover of "Wild Thing," the band put on their first truly great show and the French fell in love with them. "Jimi just wiped the floor with the crowd," Vic Briggs remembered. Chandler's plan was starting to work: In France at least, there was an audience for Jimi's mixture of blues and rock.

A week after Paris, and a month to the day after Jimi's arrival in England, Chandler took the band into the studio to cut "Hey Joe" as their first single. For the B-side, Jimi had suggested "Mercy, Mercy," but Chandler told him he'd have to write material of his own if he ever wanted to make money from music publishing. Though Jimi still felt unsure of himself as a songwriter, with Chandler's encouragement he sat down and wrote "Stone Free" in one evening, his first complete song. Chandler would later recall that he simply suggested Jimi put down his feelings, and that was enough to help him in his nascent songwriting. The song was a rather simple construction with true-to-life lyrics about how Jimi didn't want to be tied down by any one woman, consequently he was "stone free to ride the breeze."

Jimi's first U.K. press mention came in the October 29 *Record Mirror:* "Chas Chandler has signed and brought to this country a 20-year-old Negro called Jim [sic] Hendrix who—among other things—plays the guitar with his teeth and is being hailed in some quarters as a main contender for the title of 'the next big thing.'" This first press report had gotten Jimi's age wrong, described him as a Negro, misspelled his name, and remarked mostly on his gimmickry. Though the piece was error-filled, the news item elated Jimi. He cut the clipping out and saved it like a prized treasure in his wallet. As journalist Keith Altham observed, "It seems ridiculous in retrospect, but the gimmicks were necessary early on for publicity. You first have to grab the attention of the media before anyone will notice you." Jimi reveled in showing off his arsenal of flashy moves: He liked the attention they brought but quickly tired of having to perform them night after night on cue.

The Experience next traveled to Munich, Germany, where Jeffrey had arranged a four-night stand at the Big Apple club. From Munich, Jimi sent his father a postcard. "Dear Dad: Although I lost the address, I feel I must write before I get too far away. We're in Munich now; we just left Paris, and Nancy, France. We're playing around London now. That's where I'm staying these days. I have my own group and will have a record out in about two months named 'Hey Joe' by the Jimi Hendrix EXPERIENCE. I hope you get this card. I'll write a decent letter. I think things are getting a little better."

The Big Apple gig required the band to play two shows a night, common for their bookings over the next year. Jimi did his entire routine twice each evening, and with each show the crowds got larger and were more enthusiastic. "That was really the first time we all knew something big was going to happen," Noel Redding recalled. "You could feel that we were just on the cusp of success." Making use of a long guitar cord, Jimi walked in the audience as he played. When he went to get back onstage, he threw his guitar before him, and in doing so cracked the neck. Upset about the damage, and knowing that it would cost him two months' pay to buy a new instrument, Jimi grabbed the neck of the guitar, raised it above his head, and brought it down on the stage with a violent fury. It may have been one of the only moves he made all night that wasn't rehearsed or done as a crowd pleaser. Nonetheless, the audience applauded madly and dragged Jimi offstage at the end of the show. Seeing that response, Chandler determined then and there to have Jimi smash more guitars over the next few shows. The destruction of a guitar—many times the same guitar patched up night after night—became an occasional part of Jimi's set, done when all the other gimmicks had failed to excite a crowd. It became Jimi's great exclamation point, and a way for him to exorcise years of anger and frustration. The boy who had waited so long for his first guitar was now onstage destroying them.

# FREE FEELING

*"We don't want to be classed in any category. If it must have a tag, I'd like it to be called 'Free Feeling.' It's a mixture of rock, freak-out, blues, and rave music."*

—JIMI HENDRIX to *Record Mirror*

JIMI HENDRIX TURNED twenty-four that November and it was the first birthday he celebrated as a rising star. Yet despite his growing fame, he still carried a wadded-up dollar bill in the sole of his boot, a remnant of his years of poverty. He had originally used a silver dollar, back in the Chitlin' Circuit days, but had spent it and switched to a paper bill. Many times he'd used that last dollar to get out of a jam and later replaced it. In England, he substituted a pound note and decided to move the cache to the inside brim of his hat. He told Kathy Etchingham, "When you've been penniless, you never forget it."

By November, press agent Tony Garland had begun writing Jimi's first official press bio and found himself incredulous when Jimi named off all the legendary R&B bands he'd played with. Garland recalled that

at one point they were listening to a King Curtis record on the stereo
and Garland asked Jimi if he knew who the guitar player was. "I played
that, muthafucker," Jimi said with a big grin on his face. Garland feared
that if the bio listed every one of the dozens of bands Jimi had played
with, journalists might think it was bogus.

But press bio or not, the very boots on his feet told the story of
Jimi's years of struggle. "When you saw the soles on those things," Garland observed, "they were completely worn through." Not only were
his shoes old, they were decidedly out of fashion. "He had these
winker-pinker black boots with zippers on the sides," Noel Redding
said. Some thought that the worn-out soles were what caused Jimi's curious gait, but even after he bought a pair of stylish size-eleven Cuban
boots with square toes, the unusual pigeon-toed walk remained. "You
could tell by the way he walked that he had had the wrong-sized shoes
on as a kid, and that his gait was all screwed up," observed Eric Burdon.
"It was like his toes made a triangle as he moved."

In fact, much about Jimi seemed angular: He walked in a shuffle
with both toes pointing inward; his body was V-shaped, with wide
shoulders that sloped down to an impossibly small waist; and if he was
walking down the street with the other two members of the Experience
in tow, they would invariably be in a triangle formation with Jimi in
front and Noel and Mitch trailing. Though Noel and Mitch couldn't
have been whiter in complexion—their skin was so pale it seemed
translucent—the appearance of all three members began to merge at
one point: They dressed the same, all three wore a similar hairstyle, and
other than skin color, they could have been brothers. They had a distinctive look, part of which Jimi had copied from trendy British design-
ers, but much of it was a happy accident caused by whatever influences
Jimi happened to encounter on a given day. Mitch and Noel were his
followers, both in the band and in terms of fashion: When Jimi
switched to bell-bottoms, so did they. For Noel, the curly Afro came
naturally, and he grew one even larger than Jimi's; Mitch had to get a
permanent to achieve the same result. Their hair, however, was the one
feature that truly stood out, and as their Afros all grew, the three men

began to resemble top-heavy bobble-head dolls. "With all that hair," Eric Burdon recalled, "their heads were as wide as their torso." This wall of hair was a remarkable sight when it was backlit and pho-tographed, and rarely did the photographers fail to emphasize their Afros. They were more than photogenic—they were angelic.

A press reception and concert at the Bag O' Nails club had earned Jimi's first interview with the *Record Mirror*. "Britain is really groovy," Jimi remarked in a piece headlined MR. PHENOMENON. He said he pre-ferred no genre labels be applied to the band's sound, but if one must categorize, "I'd like it to be called 'Free Feeling.' It's a mixture of rock, freak-out, blues, and rave music." Jimi did most of the talking when the band conducted interviews, but Noel and Mitch frequently interjected comedic remarks. Noel was the biggest jokester of the three, but they all took a lighthearted approach to being rock stars. Jimi would urge Noel to do his Peter Sellers imitation, while Jimi frequently mimicked Little Richard. Their friendships were forged out of their shared expe-riences on the road and in the studio, but as with any relationship formed in work circumstances, it was Jimi's band and that shaded everything. Noel and Jimi had the closest friendship in the group, though Noel frequently felt Jimi overstepped his bounds by telling the band what to play in the studio. Since their management took care of all business, and the job of being in a band was itself not unlike an ex-tended adolescence, what bonded them most was humor and boyish pranks, plus, of course, a shared pride in the music they were creating. "It felt for a time," Noel recalled, "like it was us against the world."

While checking out a recording studio, Jimi met the Who for the first time. "He looked scruffy," Pete Townshend recalled. "I was very unimpressed." Jimi tried to ignore drummer Keith Moon, who was in a foul mood and kept yelling, "Who let that savage in here?" Townshend gave Jimi a few hints on where to buy amplifiers but also wondered whether this Yank really needed top-rated equipment.

A few days later Townshend saw Jimi perform for the first time and finally understood what the fuss was about. "I became an immedi-ate fan," Townshend recalled. "I saw all of Jimi's first London shows.

There were about six." Those dates included club gigs at Blaises, the Upper Cut, the Ram Jam Club, the Speakeasy, the 7½, and the Bag O' Nails. Though all of these were smallish venues and none of the gigs paid more than twenty-five pounds, there was a buzz around the band and Jimi was being touted as the hottest guitar player in London. Members of bands far more famous than the Experience—including the Rolling Stones and the Beatles—began to come to his shows to chat him up. Jimi had met Brian Jones of the Rolling Stones back in New York, but now Jones became Jimi's biggest booster, dragging other stars to come see him play. Jimi, who had initially marveled at all the legends he was meeting, now watched as his own heroes acted starstruck around him.

After one show, Eric Clapton invited Jimi back to his flat. Jimi came with Kathy Etchingham, and though the mood was friendly, neither Eric nor Jimi was particularly talkative, and their girlfriends ended up doing most of the conversing. Despite the reverence each guitarist had for the other, the two men had such different backgrounds that their only mutual reference point was a love of the blues. "It was a very strained meeting," Kathy Etchingham recalled. "They were both in awe of each other. We had to center all the discussion around music." As Jimi left several hours later, he remarked to Etchingham, "That was hard work."

When Little Richard came through London in December, Jimi told Etchingham they were going to visit the legendary singer. Kathy put on a dress and Jimi donned his finest clothes, including his antique military jacket. When they got to Richard's hotel, they were welcomed in and Richard was delighted to see Jimi. The lightheartedness of the night only lessened when Jimi asked for fifty dollars still owed him from his tenure in Richard's band. Richard refused to pay, arguing that Jimi had forfeited the salary by missing the band's bus. Jimi needed the money, but being able to appear before Richard as a bandleader himself was more important, and that alone felt like revenge.

Though Jimi left without the fifty dollars, his mood was light on the walk home until he and Etchingham found themselves surrounded by seven policemen. At first, the couple had no idea what they'd done

wrong and wondered if the police were offended by an interracial couple alone. Then one police officer shouted at Jimi, "Do you realize that
our soldiers died in that uniform?"—referring to Jimi's antique jacket.
Jimi remained polite and said he meant no offense. He'd been harassed
about the jacket before by pensioners and he regularly calmed them
down by saying he was a vet of the 101st Airborne. Though Jimi was
later perceived as a counterculture revolutionary, he forever held great
respect for the military. He'd even researched the history of his cloak
and discovered it wasn't a style worn by front-line troops, but instead
was used by those "who tended the donkeys." He tried to explain this
to the police officers. When one cop kept insisting that it was treason-
ous to wear a jacket a soldier might have died in, Jimi replied, "People
died in a Royal Veterinary Corps dress jacket?" The policeman thought
Jimi was sassing him and he forced Jimi to remove the jacket. The officers told him if they caught him wearing the jacket again he'd be arrested. As they left, Jimi stood there shamed, holding the jacket folded
in his hands. The instant the police were out of sight, he put the jacket
on and walked home.

◌◌◌

THOUGH JIMI HAD a growing musical reputation and was famous
among guitar players, the matter of whether he could actually make any
money had yet to be settled. That answer depended completely on how
well "Hey Joe" did as the Experience's first single. The band had begun
recording an album even before they had a record deal; if "Hey Joe"
failed, chances of that album coming out were nil. Decca Records had
rejected a demo of "Hey Joe," as did at least two other labels. Eventually, Chandler convinced Kit Lambert and Chris Stamp, the managers
of the Who, to put Jimi on their new Track Records imprint. Track
booked the band on television for "Ready, Steady, Go!," one of the few
media outlets where a band could get penetration across Britain. The
Experience's appearance aired on December 16, 1966, the day the single
was released, and the song became an immediate hit.

The success wasn't entirely organic. Though the single placed as high as number four on the charts, Jimi's management played a significant role in artificially inflating its ranking. "They were going around to record shops and buying them all up just to push it up the charts," Etchingham said. "It's called payola, and I know it happened because I bought several of them myself." Etchingham recalled the day the single hit No. 6 as one of the only times she ever witnessed Jimi jump for joy. "It was like, 'Fantastic! Let's go to the pub and celebrate!'" Chandler also took the occasion to make a joke that was typical of the inner circle of the Experience's humor: "The reward for you, Jimi, is two weeks with Kathy in South Africa." In South Africa at the time, their relationship would have gotten them arrested, or worse.

To celebrate, Jimi had a pint at the pub. He'd rarely drunk alcohol when he was in America, but in Britain he developed a taste for the social life of the pubs and began to drink more. He also began chain smoking, many times starting the second cigarette before the first was finished. Drugs were also omnipresent on the U.K. music scene, particularly hashish. One of Jimi's favorite tricks, which he learned from Michael Jeffrey, was to empty the tobacco out of a cigarette, insert hash, and then repack the tobacco around it. With these cigarettes, Jimi could get stoned in public places without raising an alarm. Once, backstage at a gig, he smoked a hash cigarette while talking to a policeman.

LSD was only then making its way through London, and initially it wasn't a common drug in the Experience tour van. Instead, the band favored cheap speed, which provided no euphoria but helped them stay up all night to play or record. That winter the band played numerous dates all over England, trying to raise money to pay for studio time. It was not uncommon for them to play a show in a town several hours north of London, then rush back to the city and do a session in the middle of the night when studio time was less expensive. "We'd be playing in Manchester, and then we'd drive from Manchester back to London," Redding said. "We'd get back at three in the morning and put down the tracks. And then we'd go to bed at five and get up the next morning only to have to go back up north again for another show. And we'd be back in London that next night doing more recording. That was how we made the first album."

During the evening of the day the Experience taped "Hey Joe" for "Ready, Steady, Go!" they went into CBS Studios and cut "Red House," "Foxy Lady," and "Third Stone from the Sun." Studio engineer Mike Ross was dumbstruck when their roadie brought in four twin Marshall amplifier stacks, which meant a total of eight speakers. He asked Jimi if he should mic every one, but Jimi suggested putting a single mic twelve feet away. Once the band began to play, Ross was forced to retreat to the control room because of the deafening volume of the band's sound. "It was the loudest thing I ever heard in that studio," Ross recalled. "It was painful on your ears."

"Red House" was one of many songs that Jimi had been working on for a year or more, and like much of the material that ultimately was used for his debut album, he had performed snippets of it in New York. During January 1967, driven by a desperate need to finish an album quickly, Jimi was writing a song every other day. He felt that winter as if the songs simply came to him, almost unconsciously. "Red House," however, had specific roots in Jimi's past. Though the basic theme of the twelve-bar blues is as old as the blues itself — the singer's woman doesn't love him anymore and has moved — Jimi told Noel the song was written about his old high school girlfriend Betty Jean Morgan. Betty Jean had been Jimi's first love, and she did have a sister, like the woman in the lyric. Betty Jean's home, however, was brown and not red. Jimi was already enough of a songwriter to know that "Brown House" would not have had the same ring to it. Still, the words or title hardly mattered; it was Jimi's brilliant guitar solo that did the talking and made the song his first classic blues.

No better example existed of Jimi's mysterious muse — and the way the music was moving through him — than the song "The Wind Cries Mary." On the afternoon of January 10, Jimi did an interview with *Melody Maker* in his apartment. That evening, Etchingham was attempting to make a meal and Jimi insulted her cooking. Usually she joked with him over this topic and snapped back, "Eat it or starve." Her cooking was a common cause of their fights, but on this occasion, the scene turned ugly. "I got very angry and started throwing pots, and I stormed out," Kathy said. When she returned the next day, Jimi had written "The Wind Cries Mary." Mary was Etchingham's middle name.

The recording of this song was equally easy for Jimi. They had twenty minutes left in a session and Chandler almost jokingly asked Hendrix, "You got anything else?" Jimi produced the freshly written song and the band learned it on the spot. "We simply didn't rehearse," Noel noted. "For 'The Wind Cries Mary,' Jimi just basically played the chords, and being an ex–guitar player, I could pick up the stuff really fast, and we got the feel, and we put it down. We weren't rushing it, but we sort of knew that we had to throw it down quickly." That twenty minutes of recording time even included Hendrix's guitar overdubs. The version they cut that night became their third single.

⤞⤝⤟

NO DAY IN the entire history of the Experience was as productive as January 11, 1967, which saw the band work in the studio all day and then play two shows in the evening at the Bag O' Nails. The day session at De Lane Lea Studio produced several tunes, among them "Purple Haze," "51st Anniversary," and another take of "Third Stone from the Sun." Jimi had drafted the lyrics to "Purple Haze" backstage at a concert two weeks before. Though the song would forever be linked in the popular imagination with LSD, Jimi said it was inspired by a dream he had that mirrored the novel *Night of Light: Day of Dreams* by Philip José Farmer, of which he had read an excerpt. In an early lyric draft, Jimi wrote "Jesus saves" underneath the title, a line not from the Farmer novel, and perhaps something he was considering as a chorus. He later complained that the version of the song that was released—and became the Experience's second successful single—had been shortened. "The [original] song had about a thousand words," he told an interviewer. "It just gets me so mad, because that isn't even 'Purple Haze.'"

After that long studio session, which had been more difficult than usual—they'd spent four hours on "Purple Haze" alone—Jimi and the band still had two shows to do at the Bag O' Nails. A legendary nightclub that looked like something out of a Charles Dickens novel, the Bag was at the bottom of a long stairway in a dank basement on a narrow street in Soho. The crowd that had gathered that night to watch the Experience was the ultimate who's who of London's rock elite—if the proverbial bomb had been dropped on the Bag that evening, the British music scene might have ceased to exist. Though there are several versions of who exactly was in the audience, most accounts include Eric Clapton, Pete Townshend, John Lennon, Paul McCartney, Ringo Starr, Mick Jagger, Brian Jones, Beatles' manager Brian Epstein, John Entwistle, Donovan, Georgie Fame, Denny Laine, Terry Reid, Jeff Beck, Jimmy Page, Lulu, the Hollies, the Small Faces, the Animals, and Roger Mayer, perhaps the most important person in the crowd. Mayer wasn't famous but he was an electronics whiz who in his spare time developed effects boxes for guitar players. Mayer was so impressed by what he heard that he would later make devices strictly for Jimi.

Singer Terry Reid had not yet seen the Experience and recalled, "It was as if all the guitar players in the world had shown up." When Reid sat down in the Bag, he was surprised to find Paul McCartney sitting next to him. "Have you seen this guy yet? He's amazing," McCartney said. What Jimi did to start the show shocked Reid even more. "Thanks for coming," Jimi said as he walked onstage. "I'd like to do this little song that I know is very close to your heart. It's number one on the charts." That alone was enough to surprise the audience of musicians. "We were thinking," Terry Reid said, "if it's number one on the charts, it's not close to our hearts because if it was over number ten, we hated it." Jimi then introduced "Wild Thing." "'Wild Thing' was a pop throwaway and it was what everybody stood against!" Reid observed. "And he played it, and banged the shit out of this bloody thing, and takes off into outer space. Imagine the most horrible song in the world turned into the most beautiful." Reid went to the bathroom at one point and, coming back, bumped into Brian Jones. "It's all wet down in the front," Jones warned. Reid replied: "What are you talking about? I can't see any water." To which Jones said, "It's wet from all the guitar players crying."

A week residency at the 7½ Club followed the Experience's extraordinary night at the Bag. Clapton, Townshend, and Jagger all returned. At one show, Townshend found himself standing directly next to Clapton. Each had been dumbfounded by Jimi's sudden appearance on the scene, and each had become immediate fans, but both men were also concerned by what Jimi might mean to their own careers. The two developed a friendship that winter based almost solely on discussing Hendrix and what they might do in response to him. During this particular show, as they watched Jimi play an intense version of "Red House," their fingers accidentally brushed. Clapton grabbed Townshend's hand, and they clasped together the way two schoolgirls might while watching a particularly gripping film.

Though Mick Jagger had been unimpressed with Hendrix back in New York, he had to revise his opinion now that Jimi was a London smash. Jagger brought Anita Pallenberg and Marianne Faithfull to one club date. "Mick told me he'd seen Hendrix in New York," Faithfull recalled. "I think his line to me was, 'He's gonna tear the whole world apart.'" When Jimi played the Speakeasy near the end of January, Mick returned with Faithfull. During a set break, Jimi came to their table and flagrantly flirted with Faithfull in front of Jagger. Perhaps because of Jimi's friendship with Keith Richards's girlfriend Linda Keith, Jagger treated Jimi as a competitor; when they were both in the same room, Mick strutted around like a peacock trying to outshine Hendrix's plumage. Jimi reacted with outright hostility toward Mick, and his display with Faithfull was brazen. "He asked me why I was with Mick," she recalled, a question few men at the time would dare pose. In an attempt to bed her, Jimi told Marianne he'd written "The Wind Cries Mary" for her. Faithfull, however, stayed true to her name. "It's one of the greatest regrets in my life," she said. "I should have just gotten up, and said, 'Okay, mate, let's go.'" Jimi, she was convinced, would have dropped anything to go off with her, if only to make Jagger jealous.

Jimi was still involved with Etchingham, but he seemed incapable of fidelity. Matters weren't helped by the fact that Chandler thought it better to present Jimi as a bachelor in the press, so whenever an interviewer showed up at their flat, Kathy was hustled off. Sometimes the journalists would be females, and there were more than a few times when Etchingham returned to chase half-disrobed girls out of the flat. Meanwhile, like his father before him, Jimi suffered from tremendous jealousy, which was ignited when he drank. Etchingham was very attractive and Jimi imagined every man was after her. One night at the Bag O' Nails, Kathy was on the phone and Jimi thought she was talking to another man. Jimi grabbed the receiver and began hitting her with it; his sudden violence was as shocking as it was hurtful, because it was so out of character. She screamed. At that moment John Lennon and Paul McCartney walked into the club and calmly took the phone away from Jimi.

It was rare for Jimi to be violent, and any aggression he displayed was usually linked with excessive drinking. The Bag O' Nails incident was also indicative of his quick temper, which seemed in such contrast to his normally polite manner. The same trait that made him such a talented musician—the ability to be lost in the moment of performance— also caused Jimi to act on his immediate desires or urges, with a recklessness at times. This allowed him to be a great improviser in the context of music, but his mercurial, almost childlike nature could be painful for anyone who cared for him. One night after a show in Manchester, Etchingham caught Jimi having sex in a women's restroom with a girl he'd just met. Kathy had already become hardened to such betrayals. Her only response was resignation: "Hurry up or we'll miss the train back to London." Jimi's excuse: "She wanted my autograph." Though Kathy was closer to Jimi than anyone else, they began to fight so often that Chas Chandler took Etchingham aside and urged her not to battle with Jimi in public: Chas felt that a public spectacle might hurt Jimi's image. Etchingham told Chas this was ridiculous, and she and Jimi went back to their quarrels, sometimes in London's pubs.

The Experience ended January with two shows at the famous Saville Theatre on a bill with the Who. These shows were attended by Lennon,

McCartney, George Harrison, and the members of Cream. At the end of one show, Jack Bruce left the theater, went home, and wrote the riff for "Sunshine of Your Love," inspired by Jimi.

∾∾∾

IN THE LONG and storied history of British rock 'n' roll, no single performer had ever enjoyed such a rapid rise to London fame as Jimi Hendrix, a man who had spent the first two-thirds of his life in Seattle and had come to England knowing nothing about the nation's history except what he'd absorbed through "Prince Valiant" comics. But by early spring 1967, it still remained to be seen whether Jimi's act would work outside of London, since tastes in the rest of England were not as avant-garde. The Experience finished their debut album that spring, and decided to title the LP *Are You Experienced*. The album had been recorded in several different studios, whenever the band could cobble together time. When Chandler added up all the bills for the sessions that had stretched over months, he discovered that they totaled only seventy-two hours. Several times he and Jeffrey had been unable to keep current with their bills, and studio tapes were held as blackmail until the account was settled. To speed up sessions, Chandler would trick the band into thinking they were rehearsing when he was actually recording. "Chas would always say, 'Okay, lads, let's run through it,'" recalled Noel. "And we'd run through the track and then Chas would say, 'Okay, do it again.' But he'd actually already taken the first take without us knowing. And then after the second take, we'd walk out, have a smoke, and he'd say, 'We got it.' And we'd say, 'What do you mean, we haven't even started it yet?' And he'd taken the first take." Chandler had risked everything on making the record, including much of his own money and all of his personal reputation. Early reviews, like one written by Keith Altham in the *N.M.E.,* proved it had been worth the effort: "The LP is a brave effort by Hendrix to produce a musical form which is original and exciting." When the record finally came out, it would go as high as No. 2 on the British charts, kept out of the top slot only by the Beatles.

Jimi was satisfied with his debut album, though he wasn't completely pleased with the production. When he received his first advance acetate of the disc he immediately took it home and rang up Brian Jones to come over for a listen. Brian arrived with friend Stanislas De Rola. "We stayed up all night and listened to the acetate nonstop," De Rola recalled. "Jimi was so proud of his record." Brian Jones was also impressed, and expressed his desire to produce Jimi in the future, an idea that Jimi said he would entertain. All of Jimi's London friends were, like Jones and De Rola, associated with the music business, and the boundaries between personal and professional relationships were few. Yet at the time, all of Jimi's life *was* the music business and he had no world separate from his work.

Before the release of the album, the Experience had a tour of English cinema houses, their first venture into the hinterlands. The British dates were part of a package that resembled the revue shows Jimi used to play back on the Chitlin' Circuit. The headliners were the Walker Brothers, but also on the bill were Engelbert Humperdinck and Cat Stevens, with the Experience as the opening act in this odd spectacle. Backstage on the first date of the tour, Jimi, Chas Chandler, and journalist Keith Altham were discussing what Jimi could do to stand out on the bizarre bill. They discussed smashing a guitar, but Altham argued that Townshend now had a corner on that trick. "Maybe I should smash an elephant," Jimi joked. Altham then came up with a suggestion that seemed equally impossible: "It is a pity," he said, "that you can't set your guitar on fire." Jimi's eyes lit up at the idea and he sent a roadie for lighter fluid. After a few test runs in the dressing room, he announced it was possible to at least make your guitar look like it was aflame. When showtime came around and the Experience ended their short five-song set with the song "Fire," Jimi poured lighter fluid on the instrument and threw a match at it. It took three attempts, but eventually the guitar burst into flames. Jimi twirled it around like a windmill before a stagehand rushed onstage and doused it with water. A city fire marshal was backstage, and he lectured Jimi for several minutes; Jimi protested that he had swung his guitar in an attempt to put the flames out. Only a couple thousand people had witnessed the flaming guitar stunt, which lasted all of thirty seconds, but once it was in the papers, it became legendary. Few rock performers had such an uncanny knack for generating press; Jimi seemed a natural at it. By the middle of 1967, everything he did in England drew a headline in the papers. On one date of the Walker Brothers tour a crazed fan chased Jimi with a pair of scissors and managed to cut a lock of his hair—even that later made the news. Advertisements for his shows now touted, "Don't miss this man who is Dylan, Clapton and James Brown all in one."

Though this package tour was bringing Jimi to a whole new set of fans—mostly Walker Brothers' fans—Jimi tired of the circus-like atmosphere backstage. When the tour hit Liverpool for two shows at the Empire, he and Noel snuck away to a local pub during the break between shows, but were denied service because the bartender mistook their clothes for clown costumes: This misfortune certainly wouldn't have happened to tour mate Engelbert Humperdinck, who always wore a tuxedo. Later that same night, road manager Neville Chesters agreed to give a Liverpool friend a ride back to London. The band liked the fellow and decided to let him roadie for the next two weeks. His name: Lemmy Kilmister. He would later start the band Motörhead.

One of the more insightful newspaper articles on the Experience appeared that March in the *Express,* where Jimi filled out a "Life Line" survey in which he was asked his likes and dislikes. He disliked "marmalade and cold sheets" and liked "music, hair, mountains, and fields." His favorite foods were strawberry shortcake and spaghetti. His hobbies were "reading science fiction, painting landscapes, daydreaming, and music." He listed his favorite composers as Dylan, Muddy Waters, and Mozart. But more revealing were his answers to questions about his past. He lied about his age, cutting three years off his true age because his handlers told him youth would impress more girls. For parents, he listed only his father, and for siblings, only his brother Leon.

His professional ambition, he listed, was "to be in a movie and caress the screen with my shining light." Most of the survey he answered with flirty, sarcastic remarks, but under the category "Personal Ambition," Jimi wrote that his desire was "to have my own style of music," a goal already fulfilled in his first year in Britain. And then he added a line that only a few people back in Seattle would have understood. His real ambition, he wrote, was "to see my mother and family again."

Few in England had heard Jimi ever talk about his mother. Tony Garland, who had written Jimi's press bio and put the *Express* piece together for him, didn't know whether she was alive or dead. Kathy Etchingham, at least, knew she was dead. "He told me she drank herself to death," she recalled, "but he also said she was a goddess in the sky and an angel." Though Jimi's mother had been dead for almost ten years, Jimi still dreamed about her and had brief snippets of memory that passed like a quick shadow. He told Etchingham his most vivid memory was of a day when he and Leon were in the backseat of a car his mother was driving. It was a summer day, the windows were down, and he could smell her perfume in the air. It was rare for Jimi to talk about such deep feelings or memories. "He was usually not a touchy-feely guy," Kathy observed. Etchingham had also had a difficult childhood, one of the few things she had in common with Jimi.

Most of Jimi's free time was spent practicing guitar, but he also enjoyed watching the madcap comedy "The Goon Show" on television and playing a British version of Monopoly. He rarely had time off, but when he did, he read science-fiction books. His favorite board game was Risk, the game of world domination. "He was very good at it, and he played to win," remembered Etchingham.

By late spring, on the eve of the release of *Are You Experienced* in the United Kingdom and Europe, another kind of world domination came into Jimi's focus: Chandler and Jeffrey were beginning to plan how to take the Experience worldwide. They had made Jimi a star in Europe, almost solely by touring his dynamic live show, but whether they could translate that to the States was unknown. In March, Jeffrey had signed a deal with Warner Bros. to release Jimi's upcoming album in America, and the label had paid a record-high $150,000 for the rights. A press release for Warner Bros. touted, "We shall introduce a completely new conception in promotion which should put Jimi right at the top in a very short time."

The true brilliant stroke of promotion happened again because of opportune timing. Producer Lou Adler and musician John Phillips were organizing a music festival in Monterey, California, that June. Andrew Loog Oldham and Paul McCartney were made the British advisers to the event. McCartney had been an early booster of Hendrix: Paul had written a review of "Purple Haze" for *Melody Maker* and called Jimi "Fingers Hendrix; an absolute ace on the guitar." Both Oldham and McCartney picked the Who and Hendrix as the most important U.K. acts for the festival. There was hardly any money in the gig, but the exposure would be important in breaking Jimi in America. Import copies of Jimi's debut had begun to make their way though the hipster community in America, and a few songs were being played on U.S. underground radio stations, yet Jimi was still unknown in his home country.

Jimi had rarely talked about playing in America—he had been so warmly embraced by Britain that it was hard for him to imagine going back to a nation where he had struggled so long for recognition. At a show in May at the Saville Theatre, he had introduced one song by saying, "When I played in my backyard at home, kids used to gather round and hear me, and said it was cool. I want to thank you now for making this my home." When Chandler came by the flat to announce that the Experience would soon be headed to California, Etchingham recalled that Jimi only had one thing to say. "I'm going home," he said. "Home to America again."

# CHAPTER SIXTEEN

# RUMOR TO LEGEND

LONDON, ENGLAND
*June 1967–July 1967*

*"The Jimi Hendrix Experience owned the future, and the
audience knew it in an instant. When Jimi left the stage he
graduated from rumor to legend."*

—PETE JOHNSON in the *Los Angeles Times* on the Monterey Pop Festival

BEFORE HEADING TO America for the Monterey Pop Festival, Jimi
Hendrix had a few more concert commitments to fulfill in the United
Kingdom and more recording to complete. Though *Are You Experienced* had just come out in England, the band had immediately begun
work on a sophomore effort, and the sessions between albums seemed
to merge together. "We never stopped," recalled engineer Eddie
Kramer. "Chas came from the old school of 'We've got four hours, let's
make the most of it.'" Jimi had the same strong work ethic: There was
little he enjoyed more than playing, so an all-day studio session to him
was just another opportunity to be with his guitar.

The sessions for the album that would be known as *Axis: Bold as
Love* also went quickly, though they were complicated by the band's

experiments with phasing, guitar effects, feedback, and some of the devices Roger Mayer had created. Mayer's day job was as an acoustical analyst for the government, but in his off hours he built effects for Jimmy Page and Jeff Beck, including early versions of a fuzz box. When he saw Hendrix play at the Bag O' Nails, it was like Dr. Frankenstein finding his monster, and thereafter Mayer made effects for him, too. Mayer had constructed an "Octavia," and Jimi used the device on "Purple Haze"— it could change guitar notes an entire octave, creating an otherworldly effect. "Jimi was always asking me, 'Roger, what can we do?'" Mayer recalled. "We were trying to use sounds to create emotions and paint pictures. We had only crude technology at the time, but if we didn't have something we'd build it." Jimi nicknamed Mayer "The Valve," and he called him their secret weapon. Using Mayer's inventions, along with commercially available products like the Vox Wah-Wah and the Fuzz Face, Jimi was able to create sounds that no other guitarist could immediately mimic.

Technology could also come back to haunt Jimi, particularly on the concert stage when a venue's sound system was inferior. When his gear broke or went out of tune, he'd invariably become frustrated and his performance suffered. At a show on May 29 in Spaulding, a crowd of four thousand watched one of Jimi's onstage temper tantrums. When the spectators jeered after the performer took several breaks to get his guitar in tune, he yelled, "Fuck you. I'm gonna get my guitar in tune if it takes all fucking night." His reputation for being a showman was already causing him problems; the crowds wanted to watch a spectacle and were impatient when they didn't get the display they had read about in the papers. Feminist scholar Germaine Greer was at the Spaulding show and later wrote about it for *Oz:* "They . . . didn't even care whether 'Hey Joe' was in tune or not. They just wanted to hear something and adulate. They wanted him to give head to his guitar and rub his cock over it. They didn't want to hear him play. But Jimi wanted, like he always wanted, to play it sweet and high. So he did it, and he fucked with the guitar, and they moaned and swayed about, and he looked at them heavily and knew that they couldn't hear what he was trying to do and never would."

If the audience was dismayed and confused by Jimi's jumbled performance that day, equally befuddling was Pink Floyd, the opening group. Three days later Jimi attended Floyd's London show and found it almost as star-packed as his own concerts. With their heavy psychedelic sound, Floyd were pushing the limits even more than Jimi, and their fearlessness inspired him. That same week, the Beatles' *Sgt. Pepper's Lonely Hearts Club Band* had been released in England—it was the only thing that stopped *Are You Experienced* from reaching the No. 1 slot on the charts. Jimi loved *Sgt. Pepper's* and felt there was a certain kismet in the fact that the Beatles were exploring the same psychedelic terrain as he.

The Beatles' album played a role in two of the most legendary shows Jimi would ever perform: the Experience's "farewell England" concerts on June 4. The two shows (early and late) were at the Saville Theatre, which was owned by Brian Epstein, the Beatles' manager. Because of Epstein, there was a possibility the Beatles would be in attendance, which would mark their first public outing since the release of their landmark album three days before. Paul McCartney had gone out on a limb in recommending Jimi for the upcoming Monterey Pop Festival—if Jimi had a bad show in London, like the one Germaine Greer witnessed in Spaulding, it would be a catastrophe.

Thirty minutes before the Experience were set to go on—and not long after Procol Harum had wowed the crowd with the debut of "A Whiter Shade of Pale"—Jimi stormed into the dressing room and announced to Noel and Mitch that he had a new song to open their set. He was holding a copy of *Sgt. Pepper's* in his hand. He put the album on a portable record player he'd brought, and as his band sat dumbfounded, he played the title track. "We'll open with this," Jimi announced. Mitch and Noel looked at each other in disbelief. "We thought he'd gone daft," Noel recalled. Jimi played the song a few times as they learned the chords.

The Experience came onstage to thunderous applause. Obvious to many in the hall, and probably to Jimi, Paul McCartney and George Harrison were sitting in Epstein's box. Also in the audience were the usual Hendrix superstar fans: Eric Clapton, Spencer Davis, Jack Bruce, and pop singer Lulu. Jimi began by thanking the opening bands and thanking the audience for coming to what would be his last shows in England "for a long, long time." And with that, he started into "Sgt. Pepper's Lonely Hearts Club Band."

To cover a song like "Sgt. Pepper's" just three days after the album had been released, with the Beatles in the audience, was one of the gutsiest moves Jimi ever made in his life. If he had played an inferior version of the song, or done a take that was derivative rather than inspired, it would have been an embarrassment that might not have been overcome. Anything less than a brilliant performance would have been an insult both to Brian Epstein, who ran the hall, and to the Beatles. The very gall of the choice was unbelievable, and it required complete and total confidence to pull it off—and Jimi had that. He was no longer the B.B. King clone who four years earlier had been laughed off the stage at Nashville's Del Morocco Club. The combination of his technical skill and his supreme confidence was unstoppable. "The Beatles couldn't believe it," Eddie Kramer recalled. "Here was Hendrix playing a song off their album that had just come out, and he'd taken the song and figured out a completely new arrangement, which was killer. It took *balls,* and straight-ahead testosterone." Jimi even added a feedback-laden solo that made the song his own. It was recognizable as a cover, but he'd found a new way of structuring the melody based around his guitar parts rather than the horns the Beatles had used. "It was basically done just off the cuff," Noel recalled, "but that's how we did everything. We were fearless."

The "Sgt. Pepper's" cover was only the start of the Saville Theatre show; the Experience went on to play for another hour and do such numbers as "Foxy Lady," "Purple Haze," "Hey Joe," and Jimi's interpretation of Bob Dylan's "Like a Rolling Stone." Jimi did have technical problems that night, and though they temporarily dampened the show, they didn't destroy it. The only destruction came when Jimi smashed what he called "my darling guitar," which was more of a topic of conversation in London pubs the next day than the "Sgt. Pepper's" cover, though in actuality this kind of showboating was less risky than the cover choice. The guitar demolition occurred during "Are You Experienced?" after Jimi switched guitars and grabbed a Strat he had hand-painted. A poem was on the back, which he dedicated to Britain. It read: "May this be love or just confusion, born out of frustration, wracked feelings of not being able to make true physical love to the Universal Gypsy Queen of true, free expressed music. My darling guitar, please rest in peace. Amen." As his set ended, Jimi smashed the guitar in pieces and kicked the shards out into the audience.

Critic Hugh Nolan wrote that the Experience had stolen the heart of London and "hit town with all the impact of a 50-megaton H-Bomb." Nolan said that if Jimi ever returned to England after his Monterey trip—there was some worry that once back in America, he'd stay there—"Jimi Hendrix can be sure that things will never be the same again here." A more important endorsement came from Paul McCartney, who called the "Sgt. Pepper's" cover "one of the greatest honors of my career."

After the show, the Experience were invited to Brian Epstein's for a private party. To their amazement, McCartney opened the door holding a huge joint in his mouth. He passed it to Jimi and said, "That was fucking great, man." A year earlier, Jimi was playing R&B covers with Curtis Knight and the Squires. In what had seemed like the blink of an eye, he was the toast of London and, better yet, he was smoking the Beatles' marijuana.

～⌢～

TWO WEEKS LATER, the Experience, along with Brian Jones and Eric Burdon, flew from Heathrow to New York City for a short layover before heading to California for the Monterey show. In New York, Jimi was immediately reminded that regardless of his status in the London music scene, in America he was still an African American in a nation where race was a divisive issue. The band checked into the Chelsea Hotel but left after a woman in the lobby mistook Jimi for a bellhop and insisted he carry her bags. Later that same day, Jimi couldn't get a cab to stop for him. He was dressed outrageously—in a floral jacket with a bright green scarf—but the reminder of the racial divide was chilling. After a five-hour flight, he'd gone from Beatle confidant to bellhop.

Once Jimi began to explore the clubs in the Village, things went better. At a restaurant, he ran into the Mothers of Invention, who were aware of his fame in England and bought him a beer. He caught Richie Havens at the Café Au Go Go, and Havens was excited to hear of his success. Later, Jimi went and watched the Doors at the Scene Club and from that show got a better idea of where rock in America was headed.

The next day the Experience flew to San Francisco for an overnight. The last time Jimi had spent time in the Bay Area was when he was stationed at Fort Ord. In that six-year span, San Francisco had undergone a sea change: The youth movement was in full force, and thousands of young adults had moved to the Haight district during what would later be termed the "Summer of Love." In London, even the most avant-garde musicians dressed sharply in fine suits, but in San Francisco Jimi looked like Little Lord Fauntleroy in his Carnaby Street clothes. In America, youth fashion was all about long hair, jeans, and beads. And unlike England, the youth movement in America had already become highly politicized by the Vietnam War, which by 1967 was producing several hundred U.S. casualties every week. Dr. Martin Luther King Jr. had called for antiwar and civil rights protesters to unite, and demonstrations had become frequent all over the U.S. Within the larger youth movement, there were also numerous anarchist elements that involved themselves in events and the Monterey Pop Festival was not immune: The festival was plagued by groups like the Yippies and the Diggers who demanded it be free.

"The First International Festival of Music," later to be known by all as Monterey Pop, had grown out of a desire to raise the cultural respect granted to rock 'n' roll. "A conversation had taken place between

John Phillips [of the Mamas and the Papas], Paul McCartney, myself, and a few other people about how rock wasn't considered an art form the way jazz was," recalled coproducer Lou Adler. ABC TV provided financing with an idea of showing footage from the three-day concert as a movie of the week. D. A. Pennebaker was hired to film the event, which took place at the Marin County Fairgrounds.

The Experience arrived on the Friday the festival started. Organizers had brought in a hundred thousand orchids, and everyone in Monterey appeared to have flowers in their hair. The festival promoters had planned for ten thousand fans, but at least ninety thousand came, and "alternative" stages were set up outside the festival gates for jam sessions. And perhaps most central to the Zeitgeist, infamous chemist Augustus Owsley Stanley III was freely handing out LSD to musicians backstage. Owsley's favorite color for his self-produced LSD was purple, and Jimi was amazed to discover that the drug had been nicknamed "purple haze" by some who had heard his English singles.

The Experience were not due to perform until Sunday night, so Saturday Jimi made his way among the crowd, hanging with Buddy Miles of the Electric Flag, Eric Burdon, and Brian Jones. Jimi was wearing his antique military jacket with an "I'm a virgin" button on it, while Jones had on an antique wizard's coat. "They couldn't have looked more freakish," Eric Burdon observed. "Brian was dressed like a rich old lady with furs, and Jimi was just outrageous." That Saturday Jimi watched the Electric Flag, and then Big Brother and the Holding Company, getting to see Janis Joplin give one of the defining performances of the festival. But the highlight of Saturday was Otis Redding, who awed the crowd with his showmanship and talent. Steve Cropper was playing behind Otis, and Jimi briefly spoke with the guitarist backstage. It had been only three short years since the then-unknown Jimi had visited Cropper at Stax.

Backstage, Jimi was particularly excited to talk to Jerry Miller of Moby Grape, whom he'd first met back at the Spanish Castle in Seattle. They joked about the bust size of Gail Harris, a teenager who used to sing with the Fabulous Wailers. Later that night, at one of many impromptu jams, Jimi asked to borrow Miller's Gibson L5 guitar to give it a workout. Jimi took the guitar to an alternative stage surrounded by sleeping people. "People in the crowd actually groaned when they saw him because no one knew who he was, and they wanted to get some sleep," Eric Burdon recalled. "He started playing this beautiful, sad, melodic stuff, and it developed into a happy jam." There are differing accounts about which musicians were involved, but at some time during the night the drowsy audience would have witnessed Jimi onstage with Ron "Pigpen" McKernan of the Grateful Dead, Jorma Kaukonen and Jack Casady from Jefferson Airplane, and possibly Jerry Garcia of the Grateful Dead, playing "Walking the Dog" and "Good Morning Little Schoolgirl." "Nobody was a legend then," recalled Jack Casady. "The most unique part of Monterey was that all these musicians got to meet each other." On Sunday, Jimi led another jam backstage—during the Grateful Dead's set—that included Janis Joplin, Mama Cass, Roger Daltrey, Eric Burdon, and Brian Jones all singing "Sgt. Pepper's." "We were making quite a lot of noise," Burdon recalled, "and Bill Graham came down from the stage and said, 'Shut the fuck up! You're killing the other acts.'"

Though no one could have predicted the historical importance of Monterey, Jimi was well aware that the show represented the U.S. debut of the Experience, and much was riding on that. "For Hendrix it was a bit strange coming back," observed Noel. "He'd left as an R&B cover-band guy, and he was coming back with two white guys in a rock band. So much had changed for him." Jimi had failed to succeed in the U.S. before, and stardom still was iffy—success in the U.K. guaranteed nothing in America. Wanting to stand out, Jimi spent the afternoon painting his Strat with psychedelic swirls.

Monterey was loosely organized and no exact Sunday lineup had been set. The Mamas and the Papas were to close the show and Ravi Shankar was to open it, but when Jimi and the Who were to play had gone undecided. "By the time Jimi and the Who got to Monterey, we were both desperate to be noticed," recalled Pete Townshend. "We had very short spots, and we were competitive. I *really* did not want to go on after Jimi." Hendrix felt the same about following the Who. The Grateful Dead, also scheduled that afternoon, agreed to play "whenever." Organizer John Phillips finally decided to settle the matter with a coin toss. The winner of the toss would go on the first; the loser would follow. The Who won, and Jimi was a poor loser. "If I'm going to follow you," Jimi told Townshend in a threatening voice, "I'm going to pull out all the stops." Jimi stormed off to find lighter fluid, while the Who came onstage and put on a tremendous show that launched their coming stardom in America. When Townshend smashed his guitar at the end of their set, he did it with such fury that bits struck filmmaker D. A. Pennebaker, who was thirty feet away.

Backstage, Jimi ran into Al Kooper of the Blues Project. The two talked about Dylan, whom Kooper had played with, and Hendrix asked Al if he'd join Jimi onstage for "Like a Rolling Stone." Kooper declined. Next Jimi went over to the Mamas and the Papas' tent, where he talked for a while with Mama Cass and boyfriend Lee Kiefer. "Owsley showed up," Kiefer recalled. "Jimi took acid then. It was the real stuff, this no-bad-trip stuff." It seemed like everyone at Monterey was on Owsley's acid, and Jimi joked that he was disappointed the Grateful Dead would precede him since the drug-soaked audience would be peaking before his set. Jimi timed his own acid trip so that his peak would come during the middle of his performance.

When it came time for the Experience to play, Brian Jones came onstage for their introduction. "I'd like to introduce you to a very good friend, a fellow countryman of yours," he told the crowd. "A brilliant performer, the most exciting guitarist I've ever heard: the Jimi Hendrix Experience." The band began with "Killing Floor" and then played "Foxy Lady." It wasn't until the third song, "Like a Rolling Stone," that Jimi began to win over the crowd—his album wasn't out in the U.S., and it was the only song the audience could recognize. "By then you would have seen thousands of O's because everyone's mouth was open," recalled crowd member Paul Body. "We'd never heard anything like it, and we'd never seen anything like him." Jimi wore a yellow ruffled shirt, tight red pants, his embroidered military jacket, and a headband, and he did all the usual tricks like playing with his teeth, playing behind his back, and playing between his legs. But those pat gimmicks were also backed up by innovative songs and a solid band that had been touring for the past seven months. "We destroyed the place," said Noel. "We just nailed it. That made the band in America."

Jimi's only real miscue came at the end of "The Wind Cries Mary" when his guitar went wildly out of tune. Switching instruments was not an option: Jimi had painted the Strat for the occasion. He plowed through "Purple Haze" using feedback, which didn't need to be in tune. Next, he told the audience, "I'm going to sacrifice something right here that I really love. Don't think I'm silly doing this because I don't think I'm losing my mind. This is the only way I can do it." Launching into "Wild Thing," he called the song "the English and American combined anthems." Two minutes into the number, he grabbed a can of Ronson lighter fluid and set the guitar ablaze. He straddled the instrument as he shot the fluid on it, and eventually knelt over it, moving his fingers like a voodoo priest. Jimi had done this trick before, but never before movie cameras or before twelve hundred journalists, which was the estimate of the number of writers, critics, and reporters who had come to Monterey. Pete Townshend was sitting in the audience next to Mama Cass during Jimi's show. Cass turned to him as Jimi smashed his burning guitar, and said, "He's stealing your act." "No," quipped Townshend, "he's *doing* my act." As Jimi walked offstage, still smelling like lighter fluid, Hugh Masekela began screaming, "You killed them!" Andy Warhol and Nico were the first to greet Jimi. Before the show they had paid him no attention, but now they kissed him on both cheeks and embraced him the way two grandes dames would welcome a new debutante. Nico later described Jimi's Monterey performance as "the most sexual" performance she'd ever seen.

Monterey made Jimi Hendrix a star in America, but the effect wasn't instantaneous. It would be almost six months before D. A. Pennebaker's film of the festival opened, and it took time for the phalanx of reporters to file stories across the nation. Pete Johnson wrote in the *Los Angeles Times* that by the end of the set "the Jimi Hendrix Experience owned the future, and the audience knew it in an instant. When Jimi left the stage he graduated from rumor to legend." Virtually every report on the festival mentioned the Experience—good or bad—as its most memorable act. Jimi had wondered whether he could make it in America; Monterey proved he could. "It was his coming-out party," Eric Burdon observed. "He was ready to drop the brick and build the monument."

Not all the reviews were positive, but even the negative ones created controversy, which to an unknown act was still useful. Robert Christgau in *Esquire* called Jimi a "psychedelic Uncle Tom," while Jann Wenner, who would later start *Rolling Stone,* reviewed the show for *Melody Maker* and wrote, "Although he handled his guitar with rhythmic agility and minor drama, he is not the great artist we were told." Pete Townshend was disappointed that the show had relied on so many stunts. "When Jimi went on and started doing the same gimmicks we had done—and they were just gimmicks—I realized I had underestimated Jimi's readiness to play the fool to get attention. He didn't need to do it. We're talking crass, show business nonsense here. My guitar smashing started as a serious art-school concept with a clear manifesto." If Townshend had attempted to discuss "manifestos" with Hendrix, Jimi would have in all likelihood smashed the guitar on Pete's head.

The day after Monterey, Jimi ran into Townshend at the Monterey airport. In an attempt to deflate the tension from the previous day, Pete said, "Listen, no hard feelings. And I'd love to get a bit of that guitar you smashed." Hendrix fired back an icy glare and called Townshend a cracker. It was rare for Jimi to use racist names against whites, but when he was angry, as he was in that airport, a torrent of obscenities could flow from his mouth. Townshend was bowled over by Jimi's venomous display; back in England they had frequently discussed the role of race in music. "We had talked a bit about the fact that he had taken 'back' the black blues that artists like the Stones and Clapton had appropriated from the States, then sold back to the States as though it was British and white," Townshend recalled. "That had always been discussed between us as a terrific and allowable irony, of course." A few months after Monterey, Townshend and Hendrix would patch up their friendship, and it would evolve into a lasting one, but at the Monterey airport they parted with acrimony. Though Jimi had aced his Monterey show and had every reason to be elated, he boarded his plane with a grimace on his face, still steaming from his encounter with Townshend, and realizing—perhaps for the first time—that along with fame came jealousy, subterfuge, and envy.

∾∾∾

MONTEREY HAD CREATED a lot of press for Jimi, but celebrity and financial success did not always jibe. After the concert, they had received an endorsement deal from Sunn Amplifiers, which gave them free gear, and a contract with Michael Goldstein to serve as the group's publicist in America, but they still lacked bookings. Their only booking came from Bill Graham, who asked them to open a few shows at the Fillmore in San Francisco. They played only one night as openers and the crowd response was so great—this on a bill that included Janis Joplin's Big Brother—they were moved into the headlining slot for a week. During this run of shows, Jimi came to know Janis and legend suggested they had sex in the Fillmore backstage bathroom between sets. Though neither principal ever directly confirmed this tryst, their various bandmates all believed it to be true. Jimi was still living with Kathy Etchingham back in London, yet he behaved on the road as if he were single. Janis would have been a more than willing partner, and perhaps the initiator of any carnal romp, and the idea of these two rising stars humping against a backstage wall became as enduring a part of the storied Fillmore's history as was the music performed onstage.

July began with a show in Santa Barbara, and the group's first L.A. gig at the Whisky A Go Go. The Whisky show drew an all-star crowd of onlookers that included Mama Cass and Jim Morrison. Legendary rock groupie Pamela Des Barres was at the Whisky and felt it marked Jimi's ascension to stardom in L.A. "No one in L.A. even knew who he was before the gig," she said. "Everyone knew afterward." Later Jimi hit on Des Barres, who, surprisingly, felt his sexual presence was too strong for her, early as it was in her groupie career. "He just oozed sexuality," she recalled. "There was an obvious magnetism he had. I just couldn't do it at the time." At a party in Laurel Canyon, Jimi met a more willing partner in Devon Wilson. A tall, attractive African American, Wilson was one of the first rock "supergroupies." She had been born as Ida Mae Wilson, but at fifteen had picked up the name Devon working on the streets as a prostitute. She had stepped up to the title of groupie by 1967, and for the next three years she would be an on-and-off partner in Jimi's bed. Devon was exceptionally beautiful, and extremely bright; she looked a bit like a curvier version of Josephine Baker. Had it not been for her constant struggle with drugs, which frequently gave her a ghost-like complexion, Devon could have been a model; instead, she found the power and identity she craved by attaching herself to the biggest rock stars of the day. Once she had Jimi in her sights, she pursued him relentlessly.

The day after their Whisky show, the Experience flew to New York for two club dates, and then jetted to Jacksonville, Florida, to start a tour as opening act for the Monkees. Michael Jeffrey had arranged this peculiar booking. When Jeffrey had informed Chas Chandler of the gig, Chandler's response was "Are you out of your fucking mind?" The Monkees were a pop phenomenon and their entire tour was sold out, but the pairing would prove to be one of the oddest in the annals of rock history. "Our audience didn't exactly dig him," recalled Monkee Peter Tork. In fact, the only new fans won over to the Experience were the four members of the Monkees. "We'd get there early and watch him from backstage," said Tork. "What he did was simply exquisite. I loved to watch the way his hands worked—it came so easily to him it looked as if he wasn't playing at all." Tork thought Jimi's guitar playing was as effortless as "the royal wave" from the Queen, a physical movement done with ease so it could be repeated all day without strain. "Most guitar players have so much tension in their arms, they hunch over," Tork observed. "But the easier you are—and Jimi was extraordinarily easy with it—the wider your range of expression."

Jimi's love of playing did little to improve his mood, however; opening for a teen sensation felt to him like backsliding, and other than the fact that the Monkees had an unceasing supply of powerful marijuana, he saw little in favor of the tour. Chandler convinced the promoters to drop the Experience after only eight shows. Yet in the spirit of controversy that surrounded Jimi, Chandler issued a bogus press release stating that the Experience had been kicked off the tour because "the Daughters of the American Revolution" had complained that his show was "too erotic." The members of the DAR probably weren't Hendrix fans, but the press release was completely fabricated. Still, getting kicked off a tour for being too erotic was great publicity and a headline in the *N.M.E.* further fueled the controversy: HENDRIX: DID HE QUIT OR WAS HE PUSHED?

The tour cancelation left a major void in the Experience's schedule. They filled it by going back into the studio in New York and by scheduling a handful of club shows. One of the only venues that would book them at the last minute was the Café Au Go Go in the Village. It had been less than a year since Jimi had played the Au Go Go as Jimi James, an unknown. Now he was back in the same club where he'd been snubbed by Junior Wells and where he'd backed up John Hammond. The hall was small enough that the gig paid only a fraction of what the Experience could make in the U.K., but nonetheless it must have felt victorious to see lines around the block every night. One of the first things Jimi did in New York was to track down Charles Otis and pay back the forty dollars he'd borrowed prior to leaving for England. Finally being able to pay back a loan felt vindicating, but better than that was the fact that he had accomplished exactly what he had told everyone in the Village he would do: As improbable as it was, he had gone to London and returned a star.

# CHAPTER SEVENTEEN

# BLACK NOISE

NEW YORK, NEW YORK
*August 1967–February 1968*

*"He played with no hands at all, letting his wah-wah pedal bend
and break the noise into madly distorted melodic lines. And all
at top volume, the bass and drums building a wall of black noise
heard as much by pressure on the eyeballs as with the ears."*

—from a February 23, 1968, *New York Times* article headlined THE BLACK ELVIS?

THE EXPERIENCE SPENT the next month doing club dates in New
York, which gave Jimi time to reconnect with his uptown friends. Few
in Harlem were hip to the English music scene, and Jimi brought along
a copy of the U.K. release of *Are You Experienced* to convince his
friends that he truly was a sensation in London. "We didn't realize that
he had become successful," recalled Tunde-Ra Aleem. "We thought
James Brown was successful, and we weren't so sure about Jimi because
we had never heard about him." His clothes appeared strange to the
Aleems, but when Jimi pulled a handful of LSD tabs out of his pocket,
they knew he wasn't the same shy boy they had once known. When they
listened to his album, however, the Aleems weren't sure Jimi was telling

the truth when it came to his stardom. "We thought, 'Poor Jimi, he's not going to make it,'" Taharqa recalled. The Aleems had become major players in the Harlem music scene and arranged for him to meet with influential black DJ Frankie Crocker, thinking the connection might get Jimi airplay on black radio. Crocker hated the record, the meeting was an embarrassment for all involved, and Jimi left downcast.

One night Jimi went with the Aleems to Small's Paradise, thinking perhaps he would return to this old stomping ground as a conqueror. Instead, he found that the freaky clothes he'd bought in San Francisco were in such contrast to African American dress styles that he was taunted. A fight was averted only after the Aleems stepped in and apologized for Jimi's faux pas. "Jimi was wearing this giant witch hat," Tunde-Ra said. "Everyone else was wearing little hats called 'stingy brims.' And he was wearing these giant bell-bottoms; everyone else had on tight-legged pants. Whatever we wore, he had more. He had more hair, more pants, he had more of everything. But he wasn't popular in the black community."

His reception was decidedly more positive in the Village, where many had heard import copies of his British singles. When he visited the loft of Buzzy Linhart, where drugs and music flowed freely, he was treated like a celebrity. "We had a literal ton of red Lebanese hash that someone had flown in on a private plane," Linhart said. "Jimi would come by all the time, as would Dylan, Roger McGuinn, David Crosby, and others." Perhaps it was the desire to run into Dylan—whom he perennially missed—or maybe just the hash, but Jimi stopped by frequently, and jam sessions often ensued. One night, Jimi took acid and played for eight straight hours, wowing the other musicians in the loft with his stamina.

Even Greenwich Village had changed in the year that Jimi had been gone. The beatniks had given way to the hippies, heads, and flower children. Style of dress, drug use, and music were the bonds that united or separated youth, rather than race, which became less meaningful within the counterculture. The Experience were playing for two weeks at the Salvation Club that month, and on breaks Jimi began to regularly visit the offices of *Crawdaddy,* one of the first rock magazines. While the idea of a musician trying to influence the press might have motivated some, Jimi never gave the impression this was his goal: "We'd talk about music, but sometimes he'd just stop by to smoke pot," *Crawdaddy* editor Paul Williams recalled. "If you were part of the psychedelic scene, you were outlaws together, and part of the same head community. At that particular moment, it was safer and more comfortable for Jimi with white hippies than it was in the African American world." Jimi became such a fan of *Crawdaddy* that when the magazine ran a picture of him, with a short review, he took a stack of the issues and handed them out to attendees at a nearby Byrds concert. He would shout, "My name is Jimi Hendrix. Read this magazine! There's an article about me in it." Only a few in the crowd showed any recognition. The incident demonstrated how unknown Jimi still was in America. In London, he had fans chasing him down the street trying to trim his hair; in America, he was passing out pamphlets.

Jimi met up with his old bandmate Curtis Knight that August and played demos from *Axis* for him. "I'm really getting into something now," he told Knight. The two wanted to go to dinner, but Jimi had no cash. Knight suggested Jimi borrow money from Ed Chalpin, the same producer Jimi had signed a contract with for a one-dollar advance in 1965.

At two in the morning, Knight and Hendrix dropped by Chalpin's apartment and woke him. They all three then went to dinner at a diner. The oddness of this evening can't be overestimated, and it speaks to core contradictory parts of Jimi's nature: He universally placed music above the business of music. It was as if whatever gene allowed Jimi to live in the moment, and thus gave him creativity, canceled out his ability to carefully consider business deals. The contract Jimi had signed with Chalpin had come back to haunt him: Once Jimi had become famous in England, Chalpin sought to halt any future recordings by the Experience. Chalpin was Jimi's opponent in their court case, yet Hendrix welcomed him as an old friend and appeared to hold no bitterness.

Chalpin recalled his dinner with Jimi and Knight as a friendly affair, and afterward he loaned Jimi a small amount of money. And in a decision that seems unbelievable but was captured on audiotape, Jimi went into the studio in the middle of the night and cut six more tracks for Chalpin. During the recording, Jimi did warn Chalpin that his name should not appear on any release. "You can't, you know . . . put my name on the thing," he warned. "You can't use my name for any of that stuff." Chalpin recalled that Jimi's attitude was affable, and not what one might associate with a combatant in a legal battle. "He loved how I recorded him in 1965, and he came back in 1967," Chalpin observed. Jimi seemed most interested in demonstrating his mastery of the wah-wah pedal. Chalpin taped the session and eventually released it under Jimi's name, which complicated their legal issues even more. If this session weren't strange enough, Jimi returned one more time that August and did another session with Chalpin and Knight.

In August, the Experience played a few more New York dates and a handful throughout the U.S., including a Hollywood Bowl show where they opened for the Mamas and the Papas. On August 21, they flew back to England, their first visit home in almost three months. Their arrival in the U.K. was reason for feature stories in two major newspapers, and they appeared on several television shows to support their most recent U.K. single, "Burning of the Midnight Lamp." Jimi and Kathy Etchingham had a warm reunion, but it wasn't long before they were fighting again over her cooking.

It wasn't until September 1, 1967, that *Are You Experienced* was finally released in America on Reprise Records. The U.S. album left off "Red House," "Can You See Me," and "Remember," but it did include the singles that had been omitted from the U.K. album: "Hey Joe," "Purple Haze," and "The Wind Cries Mary." To confuse matters, the spelling of two song titles had been changed ("Foxy Lady" became "Foxey Lady" and "Are You Experienced?" now had a question mark, as did the album title). Most of the reviews in America were positive, particularly those in

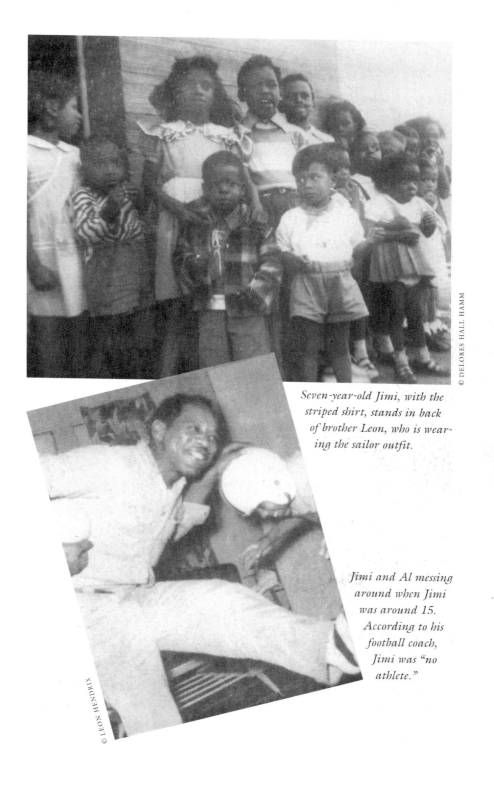

Seven-year-old Jimi, with the striped shirt, stands in back of brother Leon, who is wearing the sailor outfit.

Jimi and Al messing around when Jimi was around 15. According to his football coach, Jimi was "no athlete."

*Jimi and Al posing with the football uniform.*

*Jimi, with guitar, onstage with the Rocking Kings, 1960.*

*Jimi holding his guitar in his army barracks. Jimi named the guitar "Betty Jean" after his high school sweetheart. This is one of the only known photographs of Jimi with the guitar with his girlfriend's name painted on it. A Bo Diddley album is to the left.*

*Jimi sent his high school sweetheart this photo on September 22, 1961. Though the fake tropical background makes it look exotic, he spent most of his enlistment in Kentucky.*

*Jimi with an army buddy in the photography studio, in a shot he sent to his girl-friend. "Part of the picture didn't come out so good," he wrote on the back, "but here darling, please accept it in your heart."*

*Jimi, left, sent Betty Jean Morgan this photo in May 1962. On the back he wrote that the King Kasuals had added background singers.*

*Jimi in one of his last back-up gigs at an Atlantic Records party with Wilson Pickett. Just a few weeks later, he became a band leader.*

*Jimi backstage at the Café Wha? in the summer of 1966. He's holding a Howlin' Wolf album. He is sporting a Dylan-like hair-style he created by using curlers. He would soon switch to the Afro.*

*The Jimi Hendrix Experience. Drummer Mitch Mitchell, Jimi, and Noel Redding.*

*Backstage February 12, 1968, at Jimi's Seattle homecoming show. Brother Leon, in white coat, is turning toward Jimi; stepmother June is to Jimi's left; and father Al has his hand in front of his face.*

*February 12, 1968, Jimi and Al Hendrix. Prior to this show, Jimi had not seen his father for almost seven years.*

*Backstage February 12, 1968.*

*Jimi jokes while trying on his brother Leon's glasses. Jimi had poor vision but refused to wear glasses.*

*Backstage February 12, 1968.*

*Jimi backstage at New York's Philharmonic Hall, November 28, 1968, one day after he turned twenty-six.*

*Jimi in one of his Corvettes. He frequently wrecked cars due to his poor vision and reckless driving.*

*Jimi with longtime girlfriend Kathy Etchingham in their London flat.*

*Jimi backstage surrounded by police. He once wrote in his diary, "Can you imagine Southern police protecting me?"*

*Jimi in Hawaii with a lei, February 1969.*

the underground press, but a few were evidence of how revolutionary Jimi's style was. When Chas Chandler saw a horrid review in the *New York Times,* it vindicated his earlier decision that Jimi had to go to England to break: "The disc itself is a nightmare show with lust and misery," the review read. The *Times* thought even less of the album cover and suggested it "reinforced the degeneracy theme with the three sneering out from beneath their bouffant hairdos, looking like surreal hermaphrodites." Jimi had been called many outrageous things in the English press, but it took the *New York Times* to call him a hermaphrodite. A few months later, the *Times* wrote a laudatory piece—by then, Jimi was too popular to write off.

In America, particularly with what was now being called "the younger generation," outraged mainstream newspaper writers could do little harm to a rock musician. Far more important was FM radio and *Are You Experienced* became one of the first staples of that frequency dial. In England and Europe, in contrast, Jimi was a pop star and was more likely to be on television and get singles played on commercial radio stations. The U.S. album also benefited from the fish-eye cover photograph that the *New York Times* had said made Jimi look like a man/woman. There were few rock stars as photogenic as Jimi—who looked handsome in virtually every frame shot of him—but this particular photograph by Karl Ferris was one of the finest psychedelic images of the decade. Shot from below, from the perspective of Jimi's crotch, it gave an *Alice in Wonderland* appearance to the band and suggested that within the album cover, a hallucinogenic world awaited. The combination of the cover and the groundbreaking music inside propelled the album to become one of the fastest sellers in the label's history, outselling Reprise's biggest artist, Frank Sinatra. As a Seattle adolescent, Jimi had worshiped crooners like Dean Martin and Sinatra. To outsell Sinatra was a milestone that he had never imagined was within the realm of possibility.

❧

NOT LONG AFTER he arrived back in England, Hendrix and Kathy Etchingham moved into a flat on Upper Berkeley Street. They were still sharing with Chas and his girlfriend, and Chas took the best room in the new apartment. Despite Jimi's star status, Chas was still Jimi's boss, and their relationship was messy: Chas served as artistic director, mentor, friend, employer, and even occasionally as a bodyguard. During one incident in a pub, he pummeled a drunk who threatened Jimi. "They would talk about science fiction, and they would play Risk together," recalled Eddie Kramer. "There was so much trust that when Jimi walked into the studio, he trusted Chas to help him realize his dream." Even with their closeness, Chandler and Jimi fought in the studio, typical of a manager and a temperamental artist. "Jimi was exerting his power," recalled road manager Neville Chesters. "By then, he knew what he wanted, and what he wanted it to sound like. Chas liked songs to be tight and short; Jimi wanted the songs to extend and stretch out." For his first year with Chandler, Jimi had let Chas make most decisions—he had basically been along for the ride—but once he found success, Jimi no longer was willing to defer all to Chandler.

The band's organization displayed some similarity to a dysfunctional family. Michael Jeffrey handled most business arrangements, in the father role, which chaffed at Chandler, who was always treated as the junior partner. Their office had begun paying many personal expenses of the band members and their girlfriends, and though money was steadily coming in, their bills were still larger than their income. "I had to pay the rent for their flats," recalled office manager Trixie Sullivan. "And they took taxis or limousines everywhere and charged them to the company." Jeffrey's primary office duty was to put off creditors who were hounding them, something Chandler was rarely entrusted to handle. To refill their coffers the band began a short tour of Europe in September 1967. They were huge stars in Sweden, and sold sixteen thousand tickets in Stockholm alone.

In the U.K., "Burning of the Midnight Lamp" became Jimi's first single to fail to break the top ten, yet the band's earlier hits were still getting airplay. The BBC taped the band playing live on October 6, and in a joyous jam after the taping, Stevie Wonder sat in on drums with Jimi and Noel. October was taken up with session work on *Axis* and a scattering of U.K. concert dates, mostly in the north. Though they were stars in London, some of their shows in outlying cities were poorly attended. At one, Jimi joked with the crowd, "thank you both."

By the end of October, *Axis: Bold as Love* was finished. For this record, management had decided that the U.S. and U.K. releases would have identical covers. When press agent Tony Garland first brought out a mock-up of the quasi religious-looking artwork, Hendrix disliked the Hindu-inspired design. "You got it wrong," Jimi said. "I'm not that kind of Indian." But Jimi grew to appreciate the arty cover, which Track Records had paid over five thousand dollars to produce, if only because it fit the trippy nature of the music inside.

Many bands suffer a sophomore slump with their second record, but in Jimi's case, *Axis* was a more mature album, and one that reflected a new cohesive sound. In 1966, singer Kim Fowley had asked Jimi what his "scene was," and Jimi's response could have served as a one-line description of *Axis*: "Science fiction rock 'n' roll," he said. The album began with "EXP," wherein Jimi pretended to be his Village friend Paul Caruso talking about UFOs on the radio. Even when the songs weren't science fiction in subject, they sounded extraterrestrial and dreamy. In the studio, Jimi experimented with Mayer's many effects boxes, with panning, and with stereo phasing. "There was nothing we wouldn't do, or that we wouldn't want to try for him," recalled Eddie Kramer. "The rules were there were no rules."

By the time of the recording of *Axis,* Jimi was more comfortable in the studio, though he still struggled with singing. Each song typically began with the band cutting instrumental tracks; vocals were added later. When it came time for Jimi to sing his vocal track, he insisted the studio be emptied of the many groupies and hangers-on milling about. Even with that, Jimi wasn't always pleased with his voice: At the end of "Spanish Castle Magic," his song about the legendary Northwest club, he muttered, "I can't sing a song." Yet when it came to guitar parts—

like the delicate work required on the magnificent "Little Wing"—he was fearless.

Chandler and Jeffrey had originally considered naming the band "Jimi Hendrix and his Experience," but thought that too confusing, yet the name would have been a better description of how the band operated in the studio by the time of *Axis*. Jimi complained to Redding and Mitchell that he wanted more from them, but when the other band members offered up ideas, they were frequently rebuffed. Still, Jimi allowed Noel's "She's So Fine" to appear on *Axis*. The song also sowed a seed of future discontent when Jimi decided it wouldn't be released as a single, which made Noel resentful. Noel also complained that Jimi showed him the bass parts he wanted before a recording session and sometimes Jimi cut Noel out of the mix and recorded the bass parts himself. Mostly this move sprang from Jimi's perfectionism—if he had been proficient on drums, he might have handled Mitch the same way.

After final mixes were done for *Axis* but before the album was released, Jimi was back to recording again, cutting a rough demo called "Angel." The song reflected the increasing self-reference of his writing, a trend that had started with "Spanish Castle Magic" and "Castles Made of Sand." Jimi never directly addressed the subject of "Angel," but it featured a female figure coming "from heaven" for support. One line reads, "Silver wings silhouetted against a child's sunrise." Thematically, "Angel" was very similar to "Little Wing," which also told a story of a female figure walking in the clouds and looking over the song's central figure. When a journalist asked Jimi to explain "Little Wing," he said it had been written in Monterey: "I figured that I take everything I see around, and put it maybe in the form of a girl . . . and call it 'Little Wing,' and then it will just fly away." Jimi's comments masked what in all likelihood was the true subject of these two confessional ballads: He later told his brother Leon that both songs were about their mother, Lucille.

*Axis: Bold as Love* was released in the U.K. on December 1, 1967 (it would come out in the U.S. a month later). The British reviews were glowing. "A hit record with no doubts," wrote *Record Mirror*. "It's too much," raved *Melody Maker* in a review that read more like an endorsement of a new religion: "Amaze your ears, boggle your mind, flip your lid, do what you want but please get into Hendrix like you never have before." Jimi's own explanation of the album was equally celestial: "We've tried to get most of the freaky tracks right into another dimension so you get that sky-effect, like they're coming down out of the heavens."

❧

THE EXPERIENCE WERE in the middle of another English tour when *Axis* came out, so there was little time to savor their success. This particular tour matched them with Pink Floyd, the Move, and the Nice. It began at London's Royal Albert Hall in a show billed as "the Alchemical Wedding" because of the outlandish nature of the bands involved and their drug-soaked sounds. Jimi came up with a nickname for the perennially morose Syd Barrett of Pink Floyd, calling him "laughing Syd Barrett." Hugh Nolan in *Disc* wrote that Jimi's "hysterically exciting act provides what must be the most crashing, soulful, thrilling finale any pop bill could hope for—short of, perhaps, the Beatles." In the typically brutal pace of the Experience's tours, which usually featured two performances a night, this road trip had them playing thirty-two shows in twenty-two days.

Jimi turned twenty-five in the middle of the tour, and the crew gave him a birthday cake. When he returned home to London, Etchingham gave him a basset hound as a gift. Jimi named the dog Ethel Floon, but usually called her "Queen of Ears." Jimi had often talked about his childhood dog Prince, and it was in an effort to recapture those fond memories that Etchingham had purchased the dog. But where Prince had been independent, Ethel proved impossible even to housebreak. Jimi and Kathy would walk the dog occasionally in Hyde Park, a sight that was sure to turn heads, but eventually the dog became too fat for their flat. Etchingham found a country house for Ethel and she was shipped off.

As 1967 and a whirlwind year of touring came to an end, fatigue and exhaustion set in. In a year-end interview with *Melody Maker,* Jimi suggested for the first time that his rocket-like ascent to stardom was taking a toll. "I'd like to take a six-month break and go to a school of music," he said. "I'm tired of trying to write stuff and finding I can't. I want to write mythology stories set to music based on a planetary thing." He also suggested that though he intended to keep a core band of Mitch and Noel, he planned to supplement them with other musicians. In an effort to cope with their burnout, the band had increased their intake of uppers and downers, using them almost daily to get to sleep or wake up. Noel Redding wrote in his memoir that the drugs became a game of "I can take more than you." Jimi's tolerance was greater than anyone else's in the band or crew, and if Noel took two tabs, Jimi took four. The band's reputation as drug users began to attract both dealers and groupies who brought a compendium of every drug imaginable into their dressing rooms. Noel recalled being offered a line of cocaine that turned out to be heroin; he snorted it and became sick.

The band's exhaustion came into play when they began a January tour of Scandinavia. On their first day in Sweden, and before they'd even played a single show, Jimi got drunk and trashed his hotel room. Redding detailed the circumstances in his memoir: "We all got rotten drunk. Jimi had been hanging out with this gay Swedish journalist. Perhaps he was putting ideas in Jimi's head, but Jimi suggested we should have a foursome." Redding called the idea absurd but the Swede kept insisting. No sexual act ever commenced and instead Jimi smashed up his hotel room, for which he was arrested. He was released with a fine, but the legal fees cost the band a third of their earnings from the tour. The incident was a financial setback, but the greater price was the humiliation Jimi paid in the headlines—in 1968, trashing a hotel room still constituted an embarrassment for a pop star.

Jimi and Noel slept with hundreds of young women on the road, and they were often competitive when it came to bedding groupies, a perennial point of contention between them. In his memoir, *Are You Experienced?*, Noel Redding described touring as an "overdose on sex." Redding's story of Jimi and the Swedish journalist's proposition is not the only tale that hinted at Jimi's bisexuality—the same qualities that

*Jimi Hendrix and his mother Lucille in the first photo taken of the baby.*

*When Jimi's Aunt Delores sent this photo to Jimi's father Al, she wrote an inscription that said, "To my Daddy with all my love, Baby Hendrix." She called Jimi "baby" to avoid his original given name, which Al thought referred to another boyfriend.*

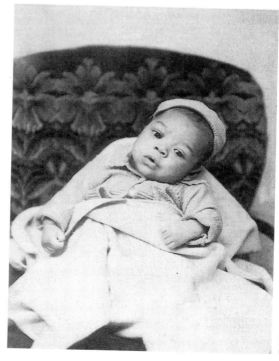

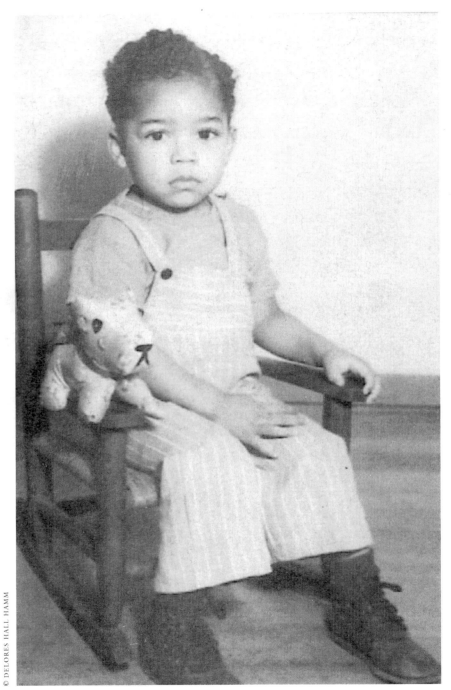

*Jimi's Aunt Delores took this photo when Jimi was three years old. The original caption identified him as "Buster," his family nickname.*

*Monika Danneman. Jimi would die sleeping next to her.*

*Jimi's funeral at Seattle's Dunlap Baptist Church.*

*Jimi in Hawaii, 1970. Hendrix once said that in death "all you're doing is getting rid of that old body." He died at twenty-seven.*

made him sexually interesting to women also attracted an occasional proposition from a man. There were at least two instances in which Jimi was the one doing the propositioning, though both incidents involved significant amounts of drugs. CSNY drummer Dallas Taylor got a call one night from his girlfriend, who asked him to come over. When Taylor arrived, he found the girlfriend in bed with Jimi—both were naked and very stoned. "It was heartbreaking," Taylor recalled. Rather than acting shocked, Jimi invited Taylor to join them in a threesome; Taylor declined and left. Arthur Lee also told a story of Jimi trying to involve him in a threesome. Whether these stories truly represented bisexuality or were simply part of a drug-infused mania is impossible to determine.

What was certainly sexually odd about the bacchanalian antics of the Experience on tour was the informality of their cavorting with groupies—it wasn't uncommon for copulation to take place backstage in full view of others, and partners were often switched. "They all shared the girls between them," observed office manager Trixie Sullivan. "The girl first slept with the roadie, and then worked her way up." Jimi always spoke of "free love" as if it were a tenet of his philosophy of life, but that freedom came with a price. "The big joke was you had to send the whole lot of them round to the doctor because a groupie had given them all the clap," Sullivan added. In the pre-AIDS world, complications could still result from such promiscuity: gonorrhea or some other sexually transmitted disease; jealous lovers in a rage; and pregnancy. The latter was the scariest prospect to Jimi, but not scary enough to make him use contraception.

During the Sweden trip, one of Jimi's lovers was university student Eva Sundquist. He'd met her in a train station on a previous tour and pursued her relentlessly, even calling out her name from the stage and announcing what hotel he was in, on the chance she might come to it. "He would send me his touring schedule in advance," Sundquist told the *Daily Mail*. "I was living with my family, and my father disapproved of the relationship. He couldn't come to my place, so I used to go and see him at various hotels. He was always the perfect gentleman, really kind and sweet." According to Sundquist, in January 1967, she lost her virginity to Jimi during the same tour that saw his arrest for trashing his hotel room.

∽⌒∾

AT THE END of January, the Experience headed out for their first large-scale tour of America. *Are You Experienced* had already sold over a million copies in the States, making it a huge hit, though the U.S. reviews for *Axis* were only lukewarm. *Rolling Stone* said Jimi sounded "like a junk heap," his songs were "basically a bore," and called to task his singing. Other reviews were more effusive, but a theme recurred in many of the notices: Critics were quick to call Jimi "one of rock's greatest guitarists," but his overall artistry, or his skill as a songwriter, were attributes mentioned further down in any review, if at all. Like it or not, the public image of Jimi Hendrix had already been cemented as a guitar god, and nothing would change that.

Publicist Michael Goldstein had been directed to create "an event" to kick off the U.S. tour. Since Soft Machine and the Animals were also clients of Jeffrey/Chandler, these other groups were included in a press conference, which Goldstein had named "The British Are Coming." His plan was to have them land in a helicopter on top of the Pan Am Building and hold the press conference there. The idea failed when weather prevented the helicopter from flying and the groups had to come in by bus. Nevertheless, a dozen magazines and radio stations interviewed Jimi.

One of those interviews was with Michael Rosenbaum of *Crawdaddy,* where Jimi was given the space to expound on a number of his beliefs. In most of his interviews, particularly with the music press, Jimi spoke in a street speech pattern, using "groovy," "you know," and "cool" at every turn. His lingo made him appear hip, but it also had the advantage of making him appear more opaque. He repeated the fabricated story about the Daughters of the American Revolution getting him kicked off the Monkees tour and said, "The little kids they dug us."

When asked about the song "Bold As Love," Jimi spoke of how certain colors matched certain emotions and he sought to play those colors. He said there were only three songs on *Axis* that he liked ("Bold As Love," "Little Wing," and"Little Miss Lover"), and threatened, "Our next LP is going to be exactly the way we want it or else." These were hardly the comments of an artist promoting a new record, and his publicists moved to control his off-the-cuff statements.

The tour itself started in San Francisco with shows at the Fillmore and Winterland. Michael Lydon, under the headline THE BLACK ELVIS? raved about the show in the *New York Times*. In San Francisco, Jimi found himself topping a bill over Albert King. Hendrix had first met King back in Nashville with Johnny Jones, and it must have been bizarre to see Albert open for him. Although King later recalled the re-union as warm, he was not the kind of bluesman to cede the stage to anyone. "That night I taught him a lesson about the blues," King later told *Musician*. "[Jimi] had a row of buttons on the floor, and a big pile of amplifiers stacked on one another. And he'd punch a button and get some smoke. . . . But when you really want to come down and play the blues, well I could have easily played his songs, but he couldn't play mine." King must have missed part of Jimi's set, which now included a slow-burning number he called "Catfish Blues," an update on Muddy Waters's "Mannish Boy."

Few at the San Francisco shows would have agreed with Albert King's assertion. Bill Graham, in his memoir *Bill Graham Presents,* called Jimi "a combination of the ultimate trickster and the ultimate technician with great emotional ability." Graham also thought Jimi's ability to appeal across racial lines was unique. "After Otis Redding," Graham wrote, "[Jimi] was the first black man in the history of this country who caused the mass of white females in the audience to disre-gard his race and want his body. . . . After Otis, he was the first black sex symbol in White America." The truth of Graham's observation was reflected in the growing number of female fans Jimi now drew, many attracted as much by his sexual charisma as his guitar skill.

After San Francisco, the Experience played a handful of dates throughout California, ending with a February 11 show in Santa Barbara. Most of the tour was sold out and Jimi had proven that his popularity in America could match what it was in Britain. Yet not long after the Santa Barbara show, Noel noticed that Jimi was nervous and edgy. He understood why only after he examined the tour itinerary and saw that their next stop was Seattle, Washington.

# CHAPTER EIGHTEEN

# NEW MUSIC
# SPACEQUAKE

SEATTLE, WASHINGTON

*February 1968–May 1968*

*"Hendrix, like the Fugs, is a valid art tremor in the New Music spacequake. To ignore his savage discourse is to leave ourselves at the mercy of some new meaning that may lurk in ambush at the center of a primitive blaze."*

—TOM ROBBINS in the *Helix*

BY THE TIME of his first major tour of the U.S. in early 1968, any kind of normal life for Jimi Hendrix had long since been replaced by the itinerant lifestyle of a touring musician. On this tour alone, the Experience would play in forty-nine cities in fifty-one days, with most of their offstage time taken up by travel. Road manager Neville Chesters computed that he drove eighteen thousand miles during the tour, which was just the first of three the band undertook that year. Their tours frequently suffered from bizarre routings, forcing them to travel long distances to one appearance and then backtrack for the next. They continued to suffer from a cash crunch, and Michael Jeffrey felt they couldn't turn down any dates, even if a last-minute booking required the band to travel all night. For their 1968 Seattle show, the Experience flew from Santa Barbara to Seattle then back to Los Angeles the next morning. The band took planes between some stops, but most travel was done by car and they often endured hours together in the backseat of a rented station wagon.

No show on the entire tour had Jimi more nervous than the February 12 booking at the Seattle Center Arena. He had not set foot in his hometown for seven years and the circumstances of his last visit could not have been more different: Back in 1961, he'd been on leave from the army and in uniform. So much had occurred in his life since then and much had changed within his family. With his father's remarriage, Jimi had a new stepmother along with five stepsiblings. His brother Leon had been a kid when Jimi left home; he was twenty now, and a handsome young man, though he still hadn't settled into adulthood. Leon had become a street hustler, working out of a downtown pool hall, a fate that had probably awaited Jimi if he had stayed in Seattle. If all of that wasn't enough, the Seattle show—despite being a last-minute booking, advertised with just a week's notice—was sold out.

The week before the concert, promoter Pat O'Day phoned Jimi and asked if there was anything special he wanted to do in Seattle. Jimi said he wanted to play a free show for students at Garfield High School. O'Day replied that he would try to set that up. Jimi also came away from the conversation with the impression that he would be receiving the ceremonial key to the city, though O'Day doesn't recall this being discussed. Nonetheless, when Jimi did an interview that week with the *Sunday Mirror,* he referred to what he thought was this upcoming honor, saying how surprised he was that his luck in Seattle had so drastically changed: "The only keys I expected to see in that town were of the jailhouse," Jimi remarked. He had left Seattle in 1960 facing a five-year jail term for riding in a stolen car. He was coming back as a hero to play a sold-out show.

When their plane arrived on the afternoon of the concert, Jimi was the last person off. Leon, like the rest of the family, hadn't seen him in years, and was surprised at his big brother's appearance: "He had on this giant hat, and a red velvet shirt. He had all this hair and he looked just wild!" Leon, in contrast, wore a stingy-brim hat and straight-legged pants. Jimi was startled by Al's appearance—his father had aged considerably and had shaved off his mustache for the first time in his life. It was also the only time Jimi had ever seen his father wear a tie. Prior to arriving in Seattle, he had mentioned to one interviewer that he was fearful his father might grab him and cut off his hair. Instead, Al took Jimi's hand, put his other hand on his back, and said, "Welcome home, son." It was a warm reunion, and the new marriage appeared to have softened Al. Jimi met his new stepmother, June, and took a liking to her.

While the rest of the band went to their hotel, Jimi was whisked to Al's house, where he held court for friends and neighbors. Some of the gathered throng began drinking Al's bourbon, but before Jimi took a sip, he asked Al for permission, a sign of how much, even at twenty-five, he still deferred to his father. Aunt Delores and Dorothy Harding came by, and Jimi began telling stories of swinging London. "He looked so grown up," Delores recalled. "He was like a hippie!" Jimi asked Leon about his friends from the neighborhood and found that many—including Terry Johnson and Jimmy Williams—were serving in Vietnam. African Americans made up a disproportionate percentage of the soldiers in Vietnam, and it was never far from Jimi's mind that he might have been stationed there had he not left the service.

When it came time for Jimi to get ready for the night's concert, he asked Ernestine Benson to curl his hair. "The problem with my life to-day," he told her, "is that I have to take a pill to sleep, and a pill to per-form." This kind of confession, which illustrated the downside of fame, was rare for Jimi, but with someone like Ernestine, he simply couldn't lie. When he complained of touring, she feared he might start to weep. She helped curl his hair, but also offered him advice: "You got to take some time off." Though Jimi was an adult now, Ernestine came away feeling as though he wasn't all that different than the latchkey child she had once watched over—he seemed just as lost.

At the show that night, Jimi's entire family was seated in the front row. Linda Jinka, one of Jimi's new stepsisters, held up a sign that read, "Welcome home Jimi, love, your sisters." While the seating was arranged to honor the family, it put them directly in front of the speakers, and Al watched some of the deafening show with his fingers in his ears. As for the performance, the band played a standard nine-song set with the greatest crowd reaction coming on "Foxy Lady" and "Purple Haze." Jimi named off the area's high schools and got the biggest round of applause when he mentioned Garfield. Tom Robbins reviewed the show for the *Helix* and called Jimi "a black dwarf cowboy Oscar Wilde in Egyptian drag" with a voice "like raspberry preserves— thick and sweet." Still, Robbins found Jimi's showmanship worth applauding: "Despite the shallowness of much of his sound, Hendrix is a hotly exciting performer. What he lacks in content, he makes up in style. He is, in fact, a master stylist; an outrageous exponent of high black showmanship. He is Adam Clayton Powell on DMT and freaking fine, thank you." Most in the audience were less discerning: Jimi was simply a hometown kid who had made good, and would have been applauded simply for walking onstage.

An after-show party was held at the ritzy Olympic Hotel. As the most posh hotel in town, it was a far cry from the Seattle fleabags with one gas burner where Jimi used to live as a child. Jimi ordered steak from room service and insisted his family do the same on his tab—it may have been the first time in Jimi's life he ever bought his father a meal, and that alone offered great personal satisfaction. Jimi gave Leon fifty dollars, and told Al that if he needed anything to let him know. Around midnight, Jimi's manager reminded him of his appearance scheduled at Garfield High School at 8 AM, just a few hours away. Disregarding the suggestion that he call it an early night, Jimi returned to Al's at 1 AM and played Monopoly. Throughout the night, Jimi and Leon joyously drank Al's bourbon. Jimi was disappointed that Leon was hustling and he told his brother to straighten out, but his exhortations would have little effect: Jimi knew that Leon's childhood had been as difficult as his own, and there had not been the saving grace of the guitar for Leon. Though Leon displayed artistic skill, being Jimi Hendrix's kid brother had disadvantages, and Leon was constantly compared to his older, more talented sibling.

At 7:30 AM, journalist Patrick MacDonald arrived at Al's house to pick Jimi up for the Garfield assembly—MacDonald had been asked to make sure Jimi showed up on time. When they arrived at Garfield, promoter Pat O'Day met them with a limousine, which Jimi expected to contain Noel and Mitch. The car was empty; O'Day had been unsuccessful in waking the band or roadies and he had failed to find an instrument for Jimi. O'Day was surprised that Jimi was wearing the same clothes he'd had on during the previous night's concert; he hadn't showered, nor had he slept; and he was hungover. "He was not capable, or able, to play, or really to speak," observed Garfield principal Frank Fidler, who had known Jimi since junior high. The idea of having Jimi perform was abandoned; O'Day suggested he just speak and answer questions from the students.

The assembly was held in the Garfield gymnasium, the only facility that could hold all twelve hundred of the school's students. O'Day gave a short introduction, telling the crowd that Jimi had once been a Garfield Bulldog but had gone on to international fame. "Kids had already begun to heckle," recalled Peter Riches, who photographed the event. "Many obviously had no idea who Jimi was." In a strange twist of circumstance, some of the hecklers were African American students who were unaware of Jimi's music, which wasn't played on black radio, even in Seattle; some also felt his style of dress inappropriate. "At the time Garfield was highly politicized and the Black Power movement was blooming," recalled student Vickie Heater. "To have this strange, hippie musician come along bothered kids."

During interviews with journalists and in television appearances, Jimi could be charming and speak off-the-cuff. But at Garfield—hungover and as nervous as he'd ever been in his life—his courage failed him. At a loss for words, Jimi mumbled, "I've been here, and there, and everywhere, and it's all working." He then paused for a long time before stating that he'd written "Purple Haze" for Garfield—the school colors were purple and white. And with that, Jimi's short speech came to an end. The audience began to whistle and heckle.

O'Day grabbed the mic and encouraged questions. One boy raised his hand and asked, "How long have you been gone from Garfield?" Jimi had been gone for exactly seven and a half years, but the question stymied him. He put his head down and mumbled, "Oh, about 2,000 years." Another student asked, "How do you write a song?" Jimi paused for a moment and again looked at the floor. "Right now, I'm going to say goodbye to you, and go out the door, and get into my limousine, and go to the airport. And when I get out the door, the assembly will be over, and the bell will ring. And when I hear that bell ring, I'll write a song. Thank you very much." With that, he walked out. The entire assembly had taken less than five minutes.

A number of students booed, and the principal ordered everyone back to class. O'Day and Patrick MacDonald went to locate Jimi but were unable to find him. They first searched the limo and then the gym, but Jimi wasn't to be found. Then MacDonald began to comb the coach's offices, and in a darkened office he spotted a solitary hunched-over figure. MacDonald asked if he was okay. "Yeah," Jimi replied. "I just can't face an audience without my guitar. I don't feel well." They went to the limo. Near the car, MacDonald asked Jimi to autograph his press kit. Before signing it, Jimi began to read the bio. "I've never seen this," he said, and for the first time that day he brightened. The press kit took three years off his age, distorted much of his early history, and contained many fictions. "This is hilarious," Jimi said, laughing. He climbed in the limo and, with the door still open, apologized for his be-havior at the assembly. "It was so strange how bad the whole thing turned out," O'Day recalled. "It had all been his idea. He had wanted so badly to go back to the school he'd gone to. It was supposed to have been a homecoming. When he got there he was scared shitless." Per-haps, like many who have difficult high school years and rush to their ten-year reunion hoping to reinvent themselves, Jimi had wanted to fi-nally come back to Garfield High as the hero. Instead, he left the school as he had seven and a half years before, with the acrid bitter taste of disappointment and embarrassment in his mouth.

✑✑✑

JIMI'S CRAZED TWENTY-FOUR hours in Seattle had left him physically and emotionally drained, but he had no time to rest. The band would play thirteen shows over the next fourteen days. On February 25, they rolled into Chicago for two sold-out shows at the Civic Opera House: a rare matinee at 3 PM, and an evening show at seven. After they had completed the matinee, the band took a limo back to their hotel. As they drove down Michigan Avenue, a car pulled next to them, and a young woman leaned out of the window and pointed to lettering on her briefcase. It read: "Plaster Casters of Chicago." Jimi gestured for them to follow.

When they arrived at the Chicago Hilton, the three members of the band climbed out of the limo and stood on the sidewalk. As was usually the case, the Experience had no bodyguards. Three young women ran up to them excitedly. "We are the Plaster Casters from Chicago," one announced, "and we want to plaster-cast your Hampton Wick." Cynthia "Plaster Caster" Albritton, the twenty-year-old leader of the crew, had come up with the "Hampton Wick" description because she thought talking Cockney would make her Chicago accent seem more worldly. Jimi's response: "Oh, yeah. I heard about you. Come up to the room." The groupie circuit in America was tight-knit, and a woman in L.A. had tipped Jimi off that Cynthia was making plaster casts of rock stars' genitalia. Despite the fact that she had printed up T-shirts, Cynthia was still a novice and had yet to actually cast any stars. Jimi agreed to be the first subject; Noel volunteered to go second; and Mitch, in a rare moment of clarity, politely declined.

The women followed Jimi to his room. Cynthia retreated to the bathroom to begin the delicate process of mixing the dental plaster used in the castings while the other two women began working on Jimi. One woman took notes on a clipboard like a scientist, although never having even seen a penis before, she could barely contain her surprise at the proportions of Jimi's member. "We were not prepared for the size of it," Cynthia wrote in her notes later. As Cynthia mixed the plaster, another girl began to orally stimulate Jimi. Once he was aroused, they stuck a vase filled with plaster around his penis, and he was told to stay still—and turned on—for one full minute while the plaster dried. Cynthia's notes read: "He has got just about the biggest rig I've ever seen! We needed to plunge him through the entire depth of the vase." The whole process, as Noel Redding would later say of his own casting, was "more clinical than erotic." The room was silent during the molding. "It wasn't very sexy, really," Cynthia recalled. "Jimi was one of the first molds we ever did, and we didn't lubricate his pubs enough. A lot of his pubs got stuck in the plaster, and there was only one way to remove them, which was pull them individually." To remove the hair took the better part of ten minutes. Jimi, no longer a cooperative model, began to use the now-hardened mold for self-stimulation. "He was bumping and grinding the mold, fucking it really, because being a mold it was the perfect size for him," said Cynthia. As Jimi ground against the mold, in a move that looked much like the way he handled his guitar onstage, tour manager Gerry Stickells opened the door to the room. It said much about the riotous nature of an Experience tour—and Jimi's lifestyle—that witnessing Jimi humping a vase filled with dental mold as a young woman with a clipboard took notes didn't even raise Stickells's eyebrows. "Just, uh, let me know when you're ready" was all the tour manager said before leaving.

The Casters next journeyed to Noel's room, though his casting didn't go as well. Noel wrote in his memoir, "My offering was unusual—a corkscrewed rendition." Noel blamed the inferior cast on bad plaster and on Stickells's opening his door at the wrong moment. At one point Jimi inquired as to what Cynthia intended to do with the casts. "I told him I wanted to put them on display, and he was cool with that," she said. When she later exhibited the casts at an art gallery, one newspaper called the Hendrix cast "the Penis De Milo."

Jimi may have been the Penis De Milo, but he was also a very tired man in the middle of a long tour. At the after-concert party, most of the band and crew hooked up with groupies—Noel and Cynthia went off together—but the Penis De Milo lusted for nothing more than rest, and sat in the corner by himself. As the other members of the band partied away, Jimi fell asleep in a chair, his hat resting peacefully over his face.

༄༄༄

THREE WEEKS LATER in Ottawa, Jimi had a backstage encounter that was far more romantic than his time with the Plaster Casters. He arrived in town to find that Joni Mitchell, whom he'd first met in the Village, was playing down the street. During the early part of the 1968 tour, Jimi began to keep a daily diary. His entry for March 19 read:

> Arrived in Ottawa, beautiful hotel, strange people. Beautiful dinner. Talked with Joni Mitchell on the phone. I think I'll record her tonight with my excellent tape recorder (knock on wood). Can't find any weed. Everything's plastic. Beautiful view. Marvelous sound on the first show, good on the second. Went down to the little club to see Joni. Fantastic girl with heaven words. We all go to party. Oh, millions of girls. Listen to tapes and smoked back at the hotel.

Jimi played two shows in Ottawa at the 2,300-seat Capitol Theatre. In a strange twist that demonstrated how much his popularity had grown in a single year, the Monkees were scheduled to open for him, though they canceled rather than play the gig. Onstage in Ottawa, Jimi made what would soon become his standard reference to the Vietnam War: "Instead of all that action happening over there, why doesn't everyone just come on home, and instead of M16 machine guns, hand grenades and tanks on their backs, why don't they come back with feedback guitars on their backs? That's better than guns."

The next day Joni was again the highlight of his diary entry:

> We left Ottawa City today. I kissed Joni goodbye, slept in the
> car a while, stopped at a highway diner, I mean a *real* one,
> like in the movies. . . . Nothing happened in Rochester to-
> night. Went to a very bad, bad, bad tasting restaurant. Thugs
> follow us. They probably were scared, couldn't figure us out.
> Me with my Indian hat and Mexican mustache, Mitch with
> his fairy tale jacket, and Noel with his leopard-band hat and
> glasses and hair and accent. G'nite all.

Not long after this entry, the sameness of life on the road took over and
zapped Jimi's creative juices. His diary entries were thereafter usually
"S.O.S." for "same old shit." One day that could have stood out was a
visit to Cleveland in March. The band arrived the night before their
concert, and Joe Esterhaus, later known for his screenplays, convinced
Hendrix to jam at a local club so it could serve as color for a *Time* magazine piece. Leonard Nimoy, of "Star Trek" fame, was also present and
partied with Jimi, leading to a strange photo op. Jimi showed Nimoy
the buttons on his hat, which included "Make Love, Not War," "Peace
at Any Price," "LBJ is a Bag," "Stoned," and one he had just bought
that evening, "Let's Brag a Little." That night Jimi hooked up with a
Cleveland groupie. "After a while, you remember the towns you been
in by the chicks," he told a reporter around this time. "We go into a new
town and there's no time to do anything except some chick, so you can't
help remembering the chicks, except that lately I've been confusing the
chicks and the towns." Publicist Michael Goldstein had accompanied
Jimi on this tour just to try to avoid these kinds of quotes, but to no
avail. Jimi rarely listened to the advice of his handlers and keeping him
out of trouble became a full-time task.

The next day the Experience did an appearance for a radio station,
then played the first of two shows scheduled at Cleveland's Public Music

Hall. Immediately after the early show, Jimi left the hall and took a cab to a car dealership. The salesmen in Blaushild's Chevrolet couldn't have been more surprised to see him; the only other celebrity they'd ever helped was Dinah Shore, whose picture adorned their wall. Jimi test-drove a new 1968 Corvette Stingray, then peeled off eight thousand dollars in cash from his take for the night's show and bought the car. He didn't have a driver's license—indeed, with his poor vision he would never have passed the eyesight test. Jimi also didn't have a garage or a residence other than his flat in London. Having purchased a car in Cleveland when he lived in England, he was temporarily stymied about where to put the vehicle. He convinced a salesperson to drive the car to New York City, where his management could store it. Jimi then caught a cab back to the concert hall and began his second show. An hour into the performance, as he was preparing to light his guitar on fire, the show was halted by a bomb threat. When no bomb was found, Jimi went back onstage after the break and announced, "Nobody but Jimi burns a house down," and proceeded to tear through the rest of his set. Far from considering this an extraordinary day in his life, Jimi found these twenty-four hours so normal that his diary entry read "same old shit" once again. The eight grand he spent on the car was a remarkable amount in 1968, particularly for someone who had grown up in such poverty, but once Jimi started making money, he spent it quickly. Even with success, he lived—as he had lived when he was penniless—imagining that each day might be his last. For a man who had grown up with scarcity, he quickly embraced a life of excess.

Even at his wildest, however, Jimi did not approach the excess of Jim Morrison, with whom he had two run-ins that month. The first was in a New York City club, where Jimi was jamming with the Chambers Brothers. Morrison was in the crowd and so inebriated he grabbed the microphone and screamed obscenities and slurs. During the disastrous jam—which was later bootlegged—Morrison crawled over to Jimi and yelled, "I want to suck your cock." Morrison said this loud enough that others in the club, including Janis Joplin, overheard it. Joplin, disgusted at the shambles of the evening, put an end to the festivities by smashing a whiskey bottle over Morrison's head, resulting in her ejection. A month later, at the Experience's Montreal concert, Morrison showed up again and managed to squeeze his way into the front row of the crowd. Security kept pushing him back, so he screamed, "Hey Jimi! Let me come up and sing, man, and we'll do this shit together." Hendrix said no thanks. Morrison then yelled, "Do you know who I am? I'm Jim Morrison of the Doors." Hendrix's response: "Yeah, I know who you are. And I'm Jimi Hendrix."

April 5, 1968, was one of the few truly exceptional nights of the mad tour. Two shows were scheduled for the three-thousand-seat Newark Symphony Hall. As the band drove in from New York, their limo passed a tank in the street and they wondered if a war had broken out. In a way it had: Dr. Martin Luther King Jr. had been assassinated the day before, but Jimi hadn't heard about the event until he'd arrived in Newark, where riots were predicted. When their white limo driver heard the news, he refused to drive unless Jimi sat in the front seat next to him.

At the hall, police ordered Jimi to play the first of the two shows and cancel the second. Only four hundred people had arrived by showtime. Jimi told them, "This number is for a friend of mine," and he broke into a long, mournful blues instrumental. It was Jimi's way of honoring the loss of Dr. King, and the performance was so poignant that many in the audience were moved to tears. While the band played, gunshots rang outside the hall. After an hour of improvisation, Jimi put his guitar down and walked offstage. There was no applause—the crowd knew it had been a funeral dirge. Jimi's eulogy wasn't over, however; back in New York City that same night, he jammed with Buddy Guy at the Generation Club. That next week, without any publicity, Jimi sent five thousand dollars to a memorial fund in Dr. King's honor. Dr. King's message of racial unity and nonviolence had resonated deeply with Jimi, who preferred to avoid direct confrontation in any area of life. "When the power of love overcomes the love of power," Jimi once said, "the world will know peace."

Hints of social consciousness began to appear in songs Jimi was writing that spring, most of which he planned for his third album, *Electric Ladyland*. In "House Burning Down," he had urged people to "learn instead of burn," a sentiment that echoed Dr. King. This song and several others were worked on in sessions at the Record Plant in April and early May. Even on days when they completed a full eight hours of recording, Jimi would go out to jam in local clubs. The Generation Club on West Eighth Street was one of his favorite haunts, as was the Scene club. Jimi was living in the Warwick Hotel at the time, and he used his room as an informal studio to cut demos of songs. After throwing a particularly wild party for guitarist Mike Bloomfield—attended by Truman Capote, among others—Jimi was kicked out of the hotel and moved to the Drake on Fifty-sixth Street.

Though Jimi's records were still selling well, the band was burning through cash as fast as they could earn it, and pressure increased to finish another album. In the U.K., Track Records had issued *Smash Hits* on April 19, a greatest-hits package. That briefly eased the pressure, but the biggest concern remained the next studio album, which was coming along very slowly. Jimi had begun to insist on multiple takes for every song. Unhappy that his previous two albums had not captured his work as he intended, Jimi was no longer willing to listen to Chas Chandler or the rest of the band. "Jimi had attempted to take over," Noel Redding recalled. "I would frequently walk out of the sessions, and, admittedly, I'd slag Jimi." One of Noel's diary entries from the following year would sum up the stress the band was under: "The pressure from the public to create something even more brilliant each time, while basically expecting us to stay the same, was crushing." Chandler also became perturbed over the number of hangers-on Jimi would invite into the studio. Their sessions took on the feel of an extended party, which was a major shift from the way the first two albums were made. The strong work ethic that had carried the band through their early records was abandoned in favor of a laid-back, jam-heavy approach to recording. Frustrated, Chandler retreated from his role as producer that spring.

Noel stormed out of a session in early May and consequently missed the recording of "Voodoo Chile." This session, typical of many in this period, sprang from a jam at the Scene club earlier in the night. When the club closed, Jimi's full entourage moved to the Record Plant. "Jimi invited *everyone* back to the studio," recalled Jack Casady. "There were at least twenty people, and most of them didn't belong there." At around 7:30 AM, the formal recording for the day started with a lineup of Jimi on guitar, Mitch Mitchell on drums, Traffic's Steve Winwood on organ, and the Jefferson Airplane's Jack Casady on bass. The song took only three takes, though they were lengthy: The released version would clock at fifteen minutes, the longest official Hendrix studio cut. After a few takes, Casady had to leave for another gig, but their final run-through of "Voodoo Chile" ended up as the master. The session, like others that year, had been very different from the tightly controlled productions Chas had run for the first album, but the spontaneity fit Jimi's evolving muse. "Voodoo Chile" would prove to be one of his most enduring songs.

By mid-1968, Jimi's entire life revolved around music. If he wasn't in the studio, he was at a jam session. If he wasn't jamming, he had a concert to do. He was adrift without the guitar or without a concert stage. When the band's final date of their U.S. tour at the Miami Pop Festival was rained out, Jimi initiated a jam in the hotel bar that included Frank Zappa, Arthur Brown, and John Lee Hooker. "It was probably the best music I've ever heard in my life," recalled Trixie Sullivan. While in Miami, Jimi had to climb through a bathroom window to escape the hotel because the band—despite earning half a million dollars that tour—didn't have enough cash to pay their bill. The Experience's first tour of the United States had come to an end with the same kind of lunacy that had marked virtually every one of its shows. Jimi didn't write anything in his diary on the day of Miami Pop, but one can imagine that if he had, like so many others in that mad spring it would have been just another dose of the "same old shit."

# CHAPTER NINETEEN

# THE MOON FIRST

NEW YORK, NEW YORK

*July 1968–December 1968*

*"Hendrix is amazing, and I hope he gets to the moon first. If he keeps up the way he's going here, he will."*

—from the *Rolling Stone* review of *Electric Ladyland*

By MID-1968, THE machine that had created the Jimi Hendrix Experience two years earlier was falling apart. Frustrated by their slow progress in the studio, Chas Chandler quit as Jimi's producer. He also stopped being Jimi's comanager, though the circumstances of his departure are still in debate: Chas always maintained he quit outright, but office manager Trixie Sullivan recalled Jimi being given an option of choosing either Chas or Michael Jeffrey. "It was Jimi's choice to stay with Mike," Trixie said. "Chas never forgave him for that." Jeffrey bought out Chandler's share for $300,000. Despite his initial anger, the shift may have improved Chandler's health—the difficulties of working with Jimi had been so great Chandler had begun to lose chunks of his hair from a stress-related disease called alopecia. Still, for Jimi the loss was significant, as Chandler had been the true mastermind who had created the Jimi Hendrix Experience. "Chas was one of the only people who told Jimi a straight story," observed Kathy Etchingham. "When Jimi lost him, he was then only surrounded by yes men." Jeffrey chose not to involve himself in most creative decisions as long as Jimi was willing to tour and record. Chandler, in contrast, was one of the few who would tell Jimi that an idea was misguided.

Chas would later accuse Jeffrey of becoming "acid buddies" with Jimi to ingratiate himself to his client. Jimi was indeed taking more acid; he felt the drug was aiding his songwriting, and it allowed him a brief period of escape from being Jimi Hendrix. "Acid really freed him up," recalled Jimi's friend Deering Howe. "It got him above being rock 'n' roll, above being black, above the pressures of fame. It took him to a place where he was free of all that." Nonetheless, whenever journalists asked Jimi about acid, he was very careful not to sound like an endorsee. "If I were to take LSD, then [I'd take it] only for my personal entertainment, for fun, or just because it pleases me, [not] for psychological reasons," he said in 1967. More often Jimi deflected questions about his drug use. "Music is a safe type of high," he would frequently suggest.

The split with Chandler meant a location change for Jimi; apart from the artistic significance, they were still living in the same apartment. Etchingham leased a new flat at 23 Brook Street in the Mayfair neighborhood of London. The new flat took up two levels of a Georgian house, with a café on the street level. The house next door had once been the residence of George Frideric Handel, which Jimi later said was inspirational to his own songwriting. Because of Jimi's celebrity, the rent had to be paid six months in advance, but in this location he could make all the noise he wanted.

Another lease was also on Jimi's mind that summer, as he and Michael Jeffrey had entered into an arrangement to take over the now-closed Generation Club at 52 West Eighth in New York City. The club had been one of Jimi's favorite jamming spots, and though their initial concept had been to reopen it, they eventually decided to build a studio.

Part of the reason for this shift was the astronomical studio bills that the lengthy sessions for *Electric Ladyland* were generating—they could have bought a studio for what it cost for them in rentals for that one album alone.

By mid-1968, both Jimi and Jeffrey were spending increasing amounts of time in the United States, where the band could generate more revenue touring. "I'm an American," Jimi told *Melody Maker*. "I dig Britain, but I haven't got a home anywhere." Mitch Mitchell was more succinct when he told the same magazine, "Let's face it, America is where the big money is." Only the U.S. had the large arenas that the band was now playing.

In a significant sign of the larger shift in their operations, Jeffrey set up a management office in New York, closing their London office down after the rent went unpaid and the furniture was repossessed. "When I went back to London to get our things," Trixie Sullivan recalled, "everything was gone, even the telephones. There was just a big pile of paper in the middle of the floor." Though the Experience were earning increasingly large paydays, expenses had also ballooned, and the entire operation seemed moments away from collapse. Noel Redding, among others, regularly complained that he thought Jeffrey was stealing from them. "The problem was," Trixie observed, "we never even knew how much money we had. And the way they all lived, including Mike and Jimi, was 'let's spend it all now.'" When Jimi would hear that the gate for a particular concert was ten thousand dollars, he would frequently spend that amount on jewelry or clothes without taking into account the expenses of putting on the show, or the 10 percent that went to Jeffrey's offshore company Yameta for management fees. Their bills for limousines alone ran thousands per month. "Jimi might spend ten thousand dollars in a boutique on a girl he just met, and then never see her again," Trixie added. The band's tab at London's Speakeasy, where they would eat most meals, ran upward of four thousand dollars a month. Litigation expenses from ongoing lawsuits with Ed Chalpin over his original PPX contract were costing Jimi thousands as well.

Both Hendrix and Jeffrey could be generous to a fault, and Jimi frequently gave money away. In 1968, he began to pay Fayne Pridgeon's rent as a way of compensating her for supporting him when he was penniless. After his first Seattle visit, Jimi had sent ten thousand dollars to his father for a new car and truck.

Jimi also supported a number of causes, sometimes privately. When Abbie Hoffman and the Yippies were looking for a financial backer for a scheme to anonymously disseminate marijuana, Jimi gave ten grand to the effort. The concept was to mail the marijuana to individuals randomly picked out of the New York City phone book. The joints would come with a letter that pointed out that the recipient was now a criminal and detailing how many people were in prison for pot possession. Though the Yippies' original plan to mail fourteen thousand joints was derailed by the labor it took to type the envelopes and roll the marijuana, they did manage to send several thousand out and the event made the television news. Jimi's sponsorship of the prank wasn't revealed until years later.

ာ

AT THE END of July, the Experience began their second U.S. tour in Baton Rouge, Louisiana. It was their first show in the Deep South, and Redding and Mitchell were surprised to find Jimi edgy. He complained that he was apprehensive whenever he found himself in a state where segregation was still the de facto norm. The band missed a plane and had to drive to Shreveport, which furthered Jimi's anxiety. When they stopped for lunch, Jimi told his bandmates he couldn't go into the restaurant they'd selected. "I didn't believe that was possible, even in Louisiana," Noel recalled. Redding convinced Jimi to accompany them. Jimi was the only African American in the restaurant, and though they were served, they drew many glares and quickly left. A few days earlier, they had run into legendary rocker Jerry Lee Lewis at an airport—Lewis had failed to recognize Hendrix.

Seattle's Pat O'Day was now promoting most of Jimi's concerts and he recalled that at several Southern shows racial tensions were high. At one, Jimi walked through the backstage door with a blonde on his arm and a police officer, hired to protect the star, pulled a gun on him. The officer screamed, "The nigger has no right to have his hands all over that girl." O'Day wondered if his famous client would meet his end in a racially motivated shooting. One of O'Day's partners stepped between Jimi and the gun, but two other officers arrived and also drew their weapons. Eventually, the police put down their pistols, but they and the entire security force walked off the job that night in protest. "They left the show because they couldn't stand the idea of a black man with this white girl," said O'Day. Afterward, O'Day was furious, but Jimi remained calm. "Fifty years ago," Jimi told him, "I couldn't have even walked into this auditorium. And fifty years from now, no one is going to care." In Jimi's personal diary, he was similarly philosophical. On the day of the incident, he wrote: "We could change America, not from white to black but from old to young. . . . Can you imagine Southern police protecting me?" The diary entry ended with a note on his bed partner that night, who surely would have upset the police: "Came back to the hotel, got stoned and made love to 'pootsie,' a tall Southern blonde."

The tour hit Seattle that September, and Jimi's second visit to his hometown went easier than the first, but it was still eventful. He spent much of the brief visit partying with Leon, which infuriated Al, who had wanted to show off his famous son. "We came home real late," Leon recalled, "and the house was still full of people waiting for Jimi to show up. My dad was waiting in the doorway holding his belt in his hand. He said, 'You boys go in the room, you're getting a whipping for this.'" Jimi and Leon looked at Al incredulously, wondering if they were truly going to get whipped in front of a houseful of neighbors. Jimi was twenty-five and Leon was twenty. Several neighbors intervened and Al put the belt away but stayed angry through the night.

Jimi drove to his next show in Vancouver, Canada, with his family rather than travel with the band. They took the new car Jimi had bought for Al and in piled Jimi, Leon, Al, Al's new wife, June, and seven-year old Janie, June's daughter whom Al had adopted that year. When they stopped for lunch at a Denny's near Mount Vernon, Washington, they sat in the restaurant for an inordinate period of time without being served—Jimi must have thought he was back in Louisiana. The other patrons stared at them; they were the only nonwhites in the place. "We were sitting there for a long time," recalled Leon. "Finally, this little girl came up and asked Jimi for his autograph. Her parents were trying to hold her back, but she started screaming, 'That's Jimi Hendrix.' She ran over to the table, and Jimi gave her an autograph." Only after a flurry of other patrons recognized Jimi was the family waited on. Even in his home state, only Jimi's fame could ensure the same treatment that whites were afforded at all times.

In Vancouver, Jimi was pleased to be able to play for his grandmother Nora, to whom he dedicated "Foxy Lady." Nora later gave her concert review to a TV reporter: "The way he was picking that guitar, oh, my gracious! I don't see how he could stand all that noise." Jimi also met up with his cousins Diane and Bobby and his aunt Pearl. Pearl had raised him for one year of his childhood, and he turned to her as he would to a mother and complained about his hectic schedule. "Jimi was already in a funk then," cousin Diane Hendrix recalled. "He was crying to my mom. He wanted out. He didn't want to go back on the road." Still, Jimi told Pearl he had no choice: His management, crew, and band were all counting on him for their livelihood, and there were now thirty people on his payroll. This same complaint would be often repeated over the next two years, though Jimi seemed incapable—perhaps driven by his early childhood scarcity issues—of turning down a tour or saying no to work.

Two days later the Experience was in Spokane, Washington, where a critic for the *Spokane Daily Chronicle* noted, "Hendrix steals the show. . . . He's so physically beautiful, and such an accomplished musician, that it's impossible to take your eyes off him." After the concert, a roadie invited eighteen-year-old Betsy Morgan to a postshow party at the Davenport Hotel. Morgan's concert seats had been so far from the stage that she didn't initially recognize Mitch and Noel, who were hosting the party. "They looked like munchkins in person," she recalled, "because they were so short, and they had these long noses." When Jimi approached her, she didn't recognize him, either. When he finally introduced himself, she blushed from embarrassment. He asked if she wanted to go to his room and listen to his new album, *Electric Ladyland,* which he said was about girls like her.

In the elevator, he tried to kiss her. Morgan, who was still in Catholic high school, turned her head to the floor and deflected him. "Have you ever seen the plaid carpet on this floor?" she said.

"Does the fact that I'm black have anything to do with it?" he asked of her rebuke.

"Of course not," she replied, "but I just met you." With that, the evening shifted, and Jimi's mood lightened. He could easily have dumped Morgan and quickly found another willing bedmate, but instead he was amused by her. As the elevator opened, he moved his arm to hold the door as one would do for a princess, and said to Morgan, "Our floor, madam."

In his room, Jimi opened up his wardrobe, and for the better part of an hour, he and Morgan tried on clothes, playing dress-up while they listened to his new album. They were like two girlfriends at a Saks Fifth Avenue sale as they experimented with different ensembles, giggling all the while. "He had this boa, and he would sashay across the room wearing it like an old movie star," Morgan remembered. There were velvet clothes and bright aqua suits. Eventually, they sat on a couch and began to talk of their backgrounds and life stories. The conversation touched on her school, current fashions, and local happenings. "He wanted to know if I had a curfew," Morgan said. "He wanted to know everything about what it was like to go to an all-girl Catholic high school." Some seducers might have used this as a way to steer the conversation back toward sex, but Jimi remained a gentleman. "He was better behaved than the boys I was dating from Gongaza Prep," Morgan observed.

Though he had lived a storied life, Jimi found it tiring to talk about himself, and he enjoyed hearing someone else's burdens. One of his personal gifts was the ability to put others at ease and make them feel important. He listened as Morgan detailed her experience at the Sky River Rock Festival, the Northwest's first large-scale festival. "I told him how I'd lost my shoes, about all the mud, how I'd lost my ride, and about all these drugged-out people there," she said. Though pot had been openly smoked at the earlier party, Morgan didn't witness Hendrix take a single drink of alcohol or use any drugs. He drank only coffee, holding the cup like an English gentleman.

At Sky River, Morgan had run into someone who had said he had gone to school with Jimi, and sure enough Jimi knew the guy. As the night wore on, Jimi never mentioned a need to sleep, and though he appeared tired, he never moved from the sofa. She asked if the line in "Purple Haze" was "Excuse me while I kiss this guy," and he had a belly laugh at that. She would later recall him as seeming "lonely," and as a man with "a deep sadness" despite his outward levity.

At nine in the morning, Jimi had to leave. They had spent eight hours talking, and he was traveling to Portland in a few minutes. He walked her down to the lobby and gave her twenty dollars for cab fare. There was awkwardness to their parting: She knew her friends wouldn't believe she'd met him, so she asked for an autograph. He was gracious and wrote, "To Betsy, what a wonderful evening we spent together." He put schoolgirl Xs and Os underneath. As she jumped in the cab and read the note, she realized they had never even kissed.

⚮

A WEEK LATER the tour hit Los Angeles for a sold-out show at the eighteen-thousand-seat Hollywood Bowl. The orchestra pit in front of the stage had been filled with water, and the crowd soon made it a wading pool, giving the show an air of triumphant chaos. Jimi dedicated a song to drummer Buddy Miles, who had become a close friend, only to watch security beat up Buddy when he attempted to climb onstage. The eleven-song set included "The Star Spangled Banner," a number Jimi had begun playing earlier that year, remaking it as an extended guitar solo. Many critics felt it disingenuous. Nat Freedland in the *Free Press* called the song "a lengthy, discordant treatment—which just isn't a freak-out tune, let's face it."

Taking advantage of a short tour break, Jimi rented a mansion in L.A.'s Benedict Canyon that had been used by other touring rock bands including the Rolling Stones. Though he was there for only a month, it was the fanciest house Jimi had ever lived in. Actor Buddy Ebsen, who was then enjoying a hit with the sitcom "The Beverly Hillbillies," lived next door and must have imagined he was seeing a real-life mutation of his television show as he watched Jimi move into the affluent neighborhood. Though the band had a few shows scheduled that month and did some recording, these four weeks in L.A. represented the first break Jimi had taken in two years. He'd had his Corvette driven out from New York, but because of his poor eyesight, he totaled the car the day it arrived; he later purchased another. On his days off, Jimi did pretty much what he had done in New York and London—he slept late and went out every night to play at the clubs on Sunset Boulevard. At the Whisky A Go Go, he met a waitress named Carmen Borrero, who was a former Playboy Club bunny. A stunning Puerto Rican blonde, she soon became his favorite companion.

Jimi's entourage in Los Angeles also grew to include his brother Leon. Leon had recently joined the army but had gone AWOL to hang out with his famous brother. Leon found that being Jimi's handsome younger brother had advantages. Backstage at a show, he found "a pile of cocaine, Johnny Walker, weed, and all kinds of shit right out there," Leon recalled. After another show, Jimi took Leon to a party at Eric Burdon's house that dozens of Playboy models attended. Jimi told Carmen Borrero, "That's my little brother; he's a big-time goof, but bear with him and give him anything he wants."

Leon was only twenty but he was an experienced hustler and felt that Jimi was being hustled by his management, an opinion he frequently voiced. This career advice annoyed Jimi—perhaps because it had some ring of truth. A far greater infraction came when Leon took Jimi's limousine for an extended ride. "Jimi had three limos, and that's where he kept his stash," Carmen recalled. "Jimi was furious when his wheels, and his stash, were gone."

Leon took full advantage of the fact that there were more groupies than there were Hendrixes. "Every model in L.A. was after Jimi," Leon said. "And they couldn't get to Jimi, so they'd come to the little brother. And afterward, they'd say, 'You tell your man that was the best pussy you ever had, and tell him about me.'" Leon was eventually shuttled out of Jimi's orbit when the next leg of the tour began and management gave Leon the wrong schedule, but the bevy of groupies continued to be a logistical annoyance for Jimi. "They would show up at all hours of the night," observed Carmen. "They'd sleep in front of his door." Jimi slept with some—even as he dated Carmen and still professed his love for Kathy Etchingham back in London—but even his legendary sexual appetite wasn't as large as the army of women who wanted to bed him.

The Los Angeles music scene was awash with drugs during the late sixties, and Jimi's fame attracted dealers the same way it drew in groupies. Cocaine, Seconal, quaaludes, and heroin became part of the landscape, and particularly when taken with alcohol, they were incendiary ingredients for Jimi. When Jimi mixed drugs with alcohol, he went into a kind of madness, as was the case after the Benedict Canyon house was burglarized and his guitars, clothes, and a book of lyrics were stolen. Paul Caruso, Jimi's old friend from the Village, was in L.A. at the time, and in an acid and alcohol rage, Jimi blamed Caruso for the theft. "He thought it was me because I was this hippie who didn't have any money," Caruso said. Caruso told Jimi he had no involvement in the theft, but Jimi was undeterred. "When was the last time you really felt something?" Jimi asked, and then punched Caruso in the stomach. "He hit me so hard it knocked the wind completely out of me," Caruso recalled. "I started to run down the hill, and he was throwing rocks and sticks at me." Caruso ran into the Whisky A Go Go, which they were near, and went up to Noel and told him Jimi had gone mad. "Bash him in the face" was Noel's advice. "He's got it coming." Noel felt that Jimi's increasing drug-induced paranoia deserved punishment rather than sympathy.

An even more dramatic incident happened a few days later between Jimi and Carmen Borrero. Though openly unfaithful, Jimi was nonetheless jealous of Carmen's friendships with other men, particularly Eric Burdon. "Jimi was drinking, and he could not drink," she recalled. Thinking she was involved with Burdon, Jimi threw an empty vodka bottle at Carmen and hit her above the eye. "They had to rush me to the hospital, and they were afraid I was going to lose my eye," she said. Eric Burdon was shocked to see the normally placid Jimi turn violent. "It was the beginning of a seed of tragedy because he started lashing out at other people," Burdon recalled. "He apologized later, and he told me a bit about how he'd grown up with brutality. It was this circle of brutality." Jimi rarely blamed his childhood for his struggles; it was more common for him to blame drugs.

Drugs, however, never had the negative effects on Jimi that alcohol had. When he drank, he would trash hotel rooms, much as he had done in Sweden earlier in 1968. "He'd smash the shit out of them," recalled his friend Herbie Worthington. "You wouldn't expect somebody with that kind of love to be that violent." Despite the quantity of drugs Jimi consumed, alcohol had the more damaging effect on his personality, just as it had played a significant role in the darkness of both his mother and father. "He just couldn't drink," Worthington observed. "He simply turned into a bastard."

∽∾∾

ON SEPTEMBER 2, 1968, at 4:30 AM, in a hotel room in Denver, Jimi wrote out his final instructions on how the cover for *Electric Lady-land* was to be constructed. He wanted to use photographs by Linda Eastman (who would later marry Paul McCartney) and he had jotted out liner notes that he titled "Letter to the Room Full of Mirrors." The line "Room Full of Mirrors" had become one of Jimi's favorite ways to describe his crazed experience as a superstar: Like a carnival mirror, his fame had distorted so much that it had become a prison of sorts. Jimi had already written and recorded one version of "Room Full of Mirrors" earlier in 1968, and later he would record at least one more, as the concept was one he found fascinating and kept returning to. Jimi's five pages of liner notes, written on stolen hotel stationery, were a rambling discourse on many topics including some self-reflection. "It wasn't too long ago, but it feels like years ago, since I've felt the warm hello of the sun," it began. He went on to speak of Ethel, his basset hound; a border guard; a velvet horse; and a "liquid rainbow." He also wrote out detailed instructions to the printer for the LP. "We have enough personal problems without having to worry about this simple, yet effective, layout," he warned.

For all of Jimi's detailed notes, his label ignored most of his requests. Reprise rush-released the double album on September 17 in the U.S. and it went almost immediately to No. 1 on the *Billboard* charts, a rare feat for a two-LP set. Buoyed by Jimi's magnificent cover of Bob Dylan's "All Along the Watchtower," which also became the Experience's biggest-selling single in the U.S., the album stayed at the top of the charts for most of the rest of the year. "All Along the Watchtower" became ever present on the radio and many critics ranked it as one of the only Dylan covers that topped Dylan's own version. The suggestion that Jimi had outdone his idol must have been some of the sweetest recognition Jimi ever received.

In the U.K., the album's release was complicated by an outrageous cover design. A photo shoot was set up with twenty-one women; the idea originally called for the women to surround Jimi as if he were a god. Jimi had already been explaining in interviews that the title *Electric Ladyland* referred to his nickname for groupies. "Some people call them groupies, but I prefer the term 'Electric Ladies,'" he explained. Still, Jimi had second thoughts about the cover shoot and failed to show. The women were then asked if they would disrobe for more pay. The resulting cover of the nude women—which Jimi said he hated—created a controversy that stirred up attention for the album's release. Unfortunately, the cover was so risqué that many shops refused to carry it, or insisted it be wrapped in a brown paper bag. The album went only as high as No. 5 in the U.K., in all likelihood hampered by the distribution issues caused by the cover.

*Electric Ladyland* had been such a difficult album it had cost Jimi his producer, Chas Chandler. Though the record would later be generally accepted as Jimi's studio masterpiece, the contemporary reviews were mixed, with many critics challenging the length of the sixteen-song double album. Frank Kofsky in *Jazz & Pop* wondered whether it was "absolutely essential that we be given a long and sometimes monotonous double album." Jimi felt the opposite and said in interviews that he would have preferred a triple-LP set. "We really got about half of what we wanted to say in it," he explained.

Most critics couldn't avoid calling *Electric Ladyland* a "concept album" or contradictorily suggesting that it didn't have a strong enough sense of cohesion. "Hendrix is a good musician and his science fiction concepts surmount noise," Tony Glover wrote in the *Rolling Stone* review. "There isn't really a concept (no *Sgt. Pepper* trips here)—instead there's a unity, an energy flow." Glover went on to call the set "an extended look into Hendrix's head. . . . Hendrix: psychedelic superspade? Or just a damn good musician/producer? Depends on whether you want to believe the image or your ears."

It wasn't just in *Rolling Stone* where Jimi's race became part of the critical analysis—he was called a "superspade" in a number of magazines at the time. The *East Village Other* headlined their *Electric Ladyland* review HENDRIX: THE CASSIUS CLAY OF POP? while critic Richard Goldstein called Jimi an Uncle Tom because he had attracted a largely white audience. Even *Ebony* magazine couldn't avoid stereotypes when describing Jimi. "In repose, he looks like a cross between Bob Dylan and the Wild Man of Borneo," their piece read, reprising the metaphor from the early British press.

By late 1968, Jimi found that every move he made—or didn't make—had ramifications that were racial, social, and political. In late November 1968—just days after he had turned twenty-six—he was walking in Greenwich Village with the Aleem twins when a vendor hawking the Black Panther newspaper spied them. "Jimi Hendrix! Jimi Hendrix! *You* sure can afford a dollar for the Black Panther paper!" the vendor yelled. "Sure, man," Jimi mumbled as he stuck a bill in the jar and walked on. The vendor then held the dollar aloft and began bellowing so that everyone in the vicinity could hear: "JIMI HENDRIX WANTS A PANTHER NEWSPAPER!" The vendor became confrontational with the Aleems, putting the jar in front of their faces and asking, "Jimi *Hendrix* buy a Black Panther paper and y'all don't?" The Aleems were lifelong residents of Harlem, where the Black Panthers, Black Muslims, and other groups were all fighting for turf in 1968. "We happened to be affiliated with the hustlers, and we weren't going to be intimidated by the Panthers," Taharqa recalled. As the vendor continued to shake the money jar, the twins brushed it aside and walked by. "Jimi Hendrix *wanted* the Black Panther paper," Tunde-Ra said. "We *don't*."

As Jimi's celebrity grew, so did the number of people who sought to use him as a spokesperson for their own cause. In London the year before, Michael Abdul Malik, a black anarchist who went by the name Michael X, demanded a meeting with Jimi. Kathy Etchingham recalled that Jimi was afraid to meet with X, but more fearful of saying no since X was also a well-known criminal (he would later be convicted of murder and executed). Jimi agreed to meet with him, but took Etchingham along. Rather than talk politics, X spent the entire evening berating Jimi for having a white girlfriend. Jimi left the flat as soon as he could. On the way home, Etchingham recalls that Jimi stopped on the street and for several moments his entire body shook with both anger and fear. He was "Jimi Hendrix," one of the biggest pop stars in the world, but he was also increasingly a target.

# CHAPTER TWENTY

# ELECTRIC CHURCH MUSIC

LONDON, ENGLAND

*January 1969–May 1969*

*"We play our music, 'Electric Church Music,' because it's like a religion to us."*

—JIMI HENDRIX to HUGH CURRY of the CBC

THE BEGINNING OF 1969 was the beginning of the end of the Jimi Hendrix Experience. In several interviews, Jimi spoke of his desire to work with other musicians. "Very soon, probably in the new year, we'll be breaking the group apart for selected dates," he told *Melody Maker*. Jimi implied that the break would be temporary, and that he would add other musicians as needed, which was how *Electric Ladyland* had been recorded. But by 1969, relations between Jimi and his two bandmates had changed enough that the British papers were already describing Noel Redding as "ex-Experience," though he was still in the group. The trio had once traveled everywhere together, even during their leisure time, but on off days they now went their separate ways. "After Chas Chandler left, things began to drift apart," Noel said. "We were so overwhelmed by the money and the glamour of being so-called pop stars,

we all forgot we were people." Noel and Jimi now treated each other
with outright hostility, while Mitch tried to stay out of the line of fire.
When the band's 1968 U.S. tour ended, Mitch and Noel hurried to the
U.K. for the holidays, while Jimi stayed in New York and continued to
jam nightly in clubs. He arrived in the U.K. on January 2—it was the
first time in almost six months that he was back at his own apartment
and back with Kathy Etchingham.

Jimi did a number of interviews with the press in January, all conducted in the Brook Street flat. With Chas gone, he decided to stop pretending to be a bachelor and to publicly introduce Etchingham as his
girlfriend. His disclosure may have been provoked by rumors in late
1968 that Jimi was already married. When the *Disc and Music Echo* had
asked about those reports, Chas denied them and expressed shock: "If
he had planned to wed, everyone would know about it because I would
capitalize on it for the publicity." And as if to maintain Jimi's sexy image, Chandler had added, "He has hundreds of girlfriends." To Chandler, any press that made Jimi sound controversial, and available, was
good press. Jimi decided to put a stop to all that and debuted Kathy to
the *Daily Mirror* as "my girlfriend, my past girlfriend and probably my
future girlfriend. My mother and my sister and all that bit. My Yoko
Ono from Chester." Etchingham felt some level of vindication in Jimi's
public acknowledgment of a relationship that had already run two years,
but she would have felt even better had Jimi stopped cheating on her.

On January 4, 1969, the Experience appeared on the BBC's live
television program "Happening for Lulu." Exposure on television had
been essential in launching the band two years before, but by 1969,
Jimi had little patience for the artificiality of the medium. The Experience was scheduled to play two songs and Jimi was to end the show
with a duet with host Lulu. Instead of sticking to that script, after a performance of "Voodoo Child" and as Lulu was speaking, Jimi played
feedback. Unnerved, Lulu finished her introduction: "They're gonna
sing for you right now the song that absolutely made them in this country, 'Hey Joe,' and I love to hear them sing it." They played about two
minutes of "Hey Joe" before Jimi paused: "We'd like to stop playing

this rubbish and dedicate a song to the Cream, regardless of what kind of group they may be in. We dedicate this to Eric Clapton, Ginger Baker, and Jack Bruce." With that, the band broke into "Sunshine of Your Love." As the Experience played a lengthy version of the song in honor of the Cream's recent breakup, off camera the stage director was signaling at Jimi to stop. Hendrix's response, which only the director could see, was to gesture with his middle finger. The Experience kept playing, eventually using up all the remaining time on the live show. When they finally ended, the producer was furious. "You'll never appear on the BBC again," he threatened. While the event looked spontaneous, Jimi told Etchingham he had planned it all along. "I'm not going to sing with Lulu," he told Kathy. "I'd look ridiculous."

Three days later Jimi let Hugh Curry of the Canadian Broadcasting Channel into his apartment for a lengthy television interview. It was one of the many interviews that month during which Jimi began to introduce the concept of "Electric Church" or "Sky Church" music. "We [call] our music," he told Curry, "'Electric Church Music,' because it's like a religion to us." When Curry suggested that "Electric Church Music" might have made a better title than *Electric Ladyland,* Jimi smiled. "Well, some ladies," he said, "they're like church to us, too." Etchingham was just off camera as he said this; she had long ago learned that any attempt to domesticate Jimi Hendrix would fail.

❧

THE NEXT WEEK the Experience began another tour of Europe, starting in Göteborg, Sweden. Chas Chandler was visiting the city and attended the show. He later said Jimi asked him to rejoin his management, but he refused. Chandler's review of the performance was that the band he once directed had taken a turn for the worse. They were no longer playing as a unit, he said, calling it a "dire concert."

In Stockholm the next evening, at the first of two shows, Jimi dedicated the night to Eva Sundquist, his favorite groupie in Sweden. "She's a goddess from Asgard," he said. After the show, Jimi spent the night with her at the Hotel Carlton. A week earlier Jimi had been professing his love for Etchingham in the press; in Sweden, he was brash enough to invite Eva to his room from the public forum of the stage. The night would have lasting implications—Eva Sundquist became pregnant from their tryst.

As for the show itself, Jimi said, "We're gonna play nothing but oldies-but-baddies tonight. We haven't played together in about six weeks, so we're going to jam tonight, and see what happens. Hope you don't mind; just gonna mess around and see what happens." As an aside to Redding and Mitchell, but audible to many in the audience, he added, "You wouldn't know the difference, anyway." This affront to his audience would have been unheard of a year earlier. By 1969, Jimi was complaining to all who would listen that his audience didn't understand him and his fans only wanted to hear the hits. "He said he was sick of playing the hits and that he wanted to evolve," Etchingham said. "But he'd still always play the hits." This contradiction—of cursing his audience but nonetheless crafting his show to please them—sprang from Jimi's fear of losing a fan base that had been so hard-won: Even as his crowds had mushroomed, he often talked about his early struggles and could not seem to escape a fear that those hard times would return. That night the band performed "Hey Joe," their biggest hit in Europe.

The Stockholm show earned the Experience their first bad reviews in Sweden. "Hendrix was listless and tired," critic Ludvig Rasmusson wrote. "He seemed like he had a desire to run away from it all. The joy of playing was gone. He played his guitar carelessly. . . . All the other things were gone—liveliness, engagement, impudence, and poetry." Rasmusson had even harsher words for Noel and Mitch, whom he called uninspiring. "It is strange that [Jimi] has put up with these two unimaginative musicians for this long." The criticism of the band was unfair; Mitch and Noel were talented musicians but they did rely on Jimi's energy to either drive the show forward or sink it. Noel later attributed the poor show to the difficulty of finding drugs in Sweden. "In desperation," he wrote in his memoir, "I went out between shows and with much persistence managed to score a leaper." The band broke up this methamphetamine pill and snorted it. Where once music had been the cohesive force within the band, their never-ending tour had turned them into road zombies and the temporary escape offered by drugs became their strongest bond. Noel's diary, which had once been a detailed log of their musical accomplishments, soon read like a pharmaceutical reference guide. As for Jimi's journal, it was abandoned.

Just a few days later, in a hotel bar in Düsseldorf, Germany, Jimi met Monika Dannemann, a tall blond ice-skating instructor from a wealthy family; she'd attended the previous night's show and had gone to the hotel hoping to meet Jimi. He spent the afternoon talking with her. Her story, years later, was that she stayed with him the next few days.

After the short continental tour, Jimi had concerts on February 18 and 24 at London's Royal Albert Hall. The shows were important enough that the Experience rehearsed, an event that was now rare. The band was nervous about these concerts because they were to be filmed. A duo of American filmmakers, Jerry Goldstein and Steve Gold, had formed a joint venture with Jeffrey to produce a documentary on the Experience.

While the rehearsals had gone well, the first concert did not, as a result of Jimi's having snorted too much cocaine. "He was so stoned, he was legless," recalled Trixie Sullivan. "I had to push him onstage." Worse yet, Jimi had begun to apply the same loose improvisational style of his club jamming to the Experience's live show. If the show was a letdown, true-to-form Jimi put on an impromptu jam later that evening in his flat that had all the inspiration the concert lacked: He played "Hound Dog," a song made famous by Elvis, on acoustic guitar sitting on his bed while Steve Gold filmed him. Jimi had been practicing "Hound Dog" since he was a kid playing broom guitar, and his version had warmth, humor, and energy, all traits lacking onstage at the Royal Albert Hall.

A week later, the second Royal Albert Hall show was better, and Jimi appeared to be back on his game. The Experience rarely encored, but they came back that night and played "Purple Haze," "Wild Thing," and "The Star Spangled Banner." The concert ended in a near riot as fans tried to climb on the stage; it was a fitting ending for a show that would be Jimi's last in Britain for eighteen months.

✌︎✌︎

AFTER THE LAST Albert Hall gig, Jimi had three weeks in London before heading to America for studio sessions and another tour. On one of his off days, he made an unusual home recording in his Brook Street flat: a three-minute spoken-word version of "Room Full of Mirrors." On the track, Jimi unleashed an inner monologue about demons, Gods, and lost little boys: "Call out your loved ones, you better call a little louder because you will be lost very soon. You'll be lost within yourself, past dimensional stage, you'll be lost in vacuums. I turn to the world; what has the world to offer me except pats on the back?" One line, shouted, sounded like Jimi was possessed: "Tell this idiot to get the hell out of me, and get me out of this damned mirrored room!" Music had once offered Jimi a way to imagine a life different from the grueling circumstances of his youth. Though his musical gift had indeed given him success, it had not proved to be the panacea he had expected. Like his "Room Full of Mirrors" spoken-word performance, Jimi's career was now something he wanted to escape—it was no longer the fairy-tale dream that he had sought for so many years.

When he wasn't exploring his psyche, Jimi was conducting interviews with the press, though he rarely discussed anything intimate in these chats. He did two dozen interviews in the first two months of 1969. Now that his management no longer had a London office, Jimi conducted interviews in his flat, offering journalists the kind of access few performers of his stature allowed. When one writer joked how much easier it was to contact Jimi than Paul McCartney, Jimi replied, "I'm not Paul McCartney." "He was always open, maybe too open," observed Kathy Etchingham. "If somebody knocked on the door, Jimi would be the first person to open it, and a crowd of people would pile in." So many people had their phone number that Etchingham had a second line put in. When that number became widely circulated, Kathy began to leave the receiver off the hook. "We'd get calls all morning, and all night," she recalled.

Many of the calls were from groupies-in-waiting and some came from journalists. Occasionally, the two were one and the same. One writer said she wanted to be photographed in her underwear with Jimi—he kicked her out. Sometimes, though, Jimi was the one doing the seducing. When *International Times* writer Jane Mendelssohn arrived for an interview, Jimi answered the door naked. As they entered the flat, he climbed into bed. Next to his bed were pot, hash, pills, and numerous bottles of alcohol. He offered her amyl nitrate. Naked and stoned, Jimi lay in the bed for the three-hour interview, and when Mendelssohn had still more questions, he invited her back the next day, perhaps hoping that he would finally be able to seduce her. The only questions he refused to answer were ones about his family.

When Mendelssohn asked Jimi about an interview in which he'd suggested it was time for a change from "the pretty songs" of the Beatles, he gave a discourse on the British press, which also suggested how the media were complicit in creating his "wild man" persona. "Which paper was that in?" Jimi asked. "*Sunday Mirror*. Well, most of those papers are all screwed up anyway. They come over here and they do their interviews, we turn the cats on, you know, give them wine and all that, and they go back and they're so stoned they don't know what they are writing about." He then hinted at his own true biography: "If I wasn't a guitar player, I would probably be in jail." To the question of what motivated his songs, he replied, "Well, honest to God truth, on the first LP I didn't know what I was writing about. Most of the songs, like 'Purple Haze,' and 'Wind Cries Mary' were about ten pages long, but then we're restricted to a certain time limit, so I had to break them all down, so once I'd broken the songs down, I didn't know whether they were going to be understood or not. Maybe some of the meanings got lost, by breaking them down, which I never do any more." He complained about his schedule: "I've had no time off to myself since I've been in this scene. . . . Most people would like to retire and just disap-

pear from the scene, which I'd love to do, but then there's still things I'd
like to say. I wish it wasn't so important to me. I wish I could just turn
my mind off." The very traits that had made Jimi a star—ambition and
talent—made it impossible for him to step back from his career and
have a life offstage.

In most interviews, Jimi was asked about the political and social
movements of the day: drugs, Black Power, and the Vietnam War. Jimi
usually sidestepped these questions, though he did tell Mendelssohn,
"There's certain people on this earth that have the power to do different
things, for instance in the Black Power Movement, they're using it
wrongly. . . . Protest is over with. It's the solutions everyone wants
now, not just protest." In one interview that month, Jimi compared
U.S. troops in Vietnam to D-day: "Did you send the Americans away
when they landed in Normandy? That was also purely interference. No,
but that then was concerning your own skin. The Americans are fighting in Vietnam for the complete free world. As soon as they move out,
they'll be at the mercy of the communists. For that matter, the yellow
danger [China] should not be underestimated. Of course, war is horrible, but at present, it's still the only guarantee to maintain peace." Jimi's
attitudes on the war would shift over the next year, but in a time when
critics were ascribing an antiwar bent to his songs, his personal beliefs
were surprisingly hawkish. Buck Munger worked for Sunn Amplifiers
and managed to get Jimi an endorsement deal with free gear. Yet when
Munger and Hendrix got together, rather than amps, Jimi talked Vietnam with ex-Marine Munger. "He wanted to be updated on what units
were taking losses," Munger recalled. At that time, Jimi felt the Com-
munist threat was real, and that the war was a necessary one—a stance
that had been indoctrinated into him during his time in the service.

The Brook Street flat was near the American embassy in London,
and Eric Burdon remembered sitting on Jimi's roof one day as a massive anti–Vietnam War demonstration took place in the streets below.
Burdon asked what Jimi thought about the protesters. "His reaction
was quite a surprise to me," Burdon recalled. "He said he was still a sol-

dier, and still trained to think like one. He was pissed about the protests." As the demonstration became louder, Jimi grew visibly angered. Jimi said: "When the Reds come down from China and they take over North Vietnam, and South Vietnam, and then they go for Japan, and beyond, then are you going to understand why the U.S. is there fighting these guys?" What Jimi never told another soul—not Etchingham, not even his closest friends—was that had he not feigned homosexuality to an army psychologist, he might have been one of those soldiers fighting in Vietnam.

∽∾∾

ON MARCH 13, Jimi and the band left London for a month of New York studio sessions prior to the start of an April U.S. tour. Jimi had decided to have Kathy Etchingham join him a week later and accompany him on the tour—the first time he had ever brought his girlfriend on a tour. Yet before Kathy arrived, Devon Wilson moved to solidify her position as Jimi's favorite groupie. The relationship between Jimi and Devon was unusual: Though the two did sleep together at times, their union bore more similarities to that of two great rivals or two siblings. Devon was constantly informing Jimi of the other A-list stars she had bedded—which occasionally included women, as Devon was bisexual—and Jimi bragged about the other groupies he'd been with. Devon told everyone that she was Jimi's girlfriend—and observing the way she ordered people around at his concerts, some thought this to be the case. Yet she also served as a gofer for him, particularly when he needed someone to score drugs, which soon became more important to their relationship than sex. By 1969, Devon was increasingly strung out from snorting cocaine and heroin; more and more Jimi was joining her in these vices. "They were these two birds of a feather," recalled Jimi's friend Herbie Worthington, who often observed them. "She was this major groupie, but she was also very smart, and very loyal to Jimi. And if you want to control somebody, there's no better way than to get high

with them." Devon had followed Jimi to England on at least two occasions. Etchingham felt less jealous of Devon than other women, if only
because she observed Jimi treating  Devon more like an employee than
a lover. "She used to sit at the end of our bed and bring tea," Kathy
said. "She was just somebody who hung around, and obviously she was
besotted by him. She was the type who would ring on the doorbell, and
she would keep ringing until you answered."

By the time Etchingham arrived in America and rang the doorbell
of Jimi's suite at the Pierre Hotel, Devon had been wise enough to va-
cate. As Kathy would write in her memoir, *Through Gypsy Eyes,* Jimi
seemed like a different person in New York: "[He was] trailing an enormous entourage like the colorful leader of some circus freak show. . . .
There never seemed to be less than twenty people." To Etchingham, the
women were "obviously whores, and the men all appeared to be pimps
and drug dealers, with their cool shades and little spoons hanging
round their necks." When she asked Jimi who they all were, he replied,
"My friends."

Later, in Jimi's posh suite, Etchingham encountered one of those
"friends," a drug dealer. "He looked like Columbo," Kathy recalled.
"He had a raincoat on, and a limp; he told us he'd once been shot in the
leg. He was about fifty, which to us in our twenties seemed old." More
ominous than his appearance was a duffel bag the man carried: it was
filled with packets of cocaine and a .45-caliber revolver. Kathy had
never even seen a gun before. At the sight of the weapon, and what had
become of her Jimi, she decided to return to England immediately. The
move would mark the end of her romance with Jimi, which had begun
on the day he had first arrived in England. "I knew there were no long-
term prospects with Jimi," she said. "There was no way I was going to
tame him. I wanted a decent family." Jimi had spent much of his youth
worrying about surviving day to day; other than a few foster families he
visited, he had rarely ever witnessed a functional two-parent family, and
his own mother and father were hardly role models. Long-term relationships required commitment and intimacy, two traits that Jimi had

very little experience with. "Jimi wanted a family as well," Kathy observed. "He just didn't know how to get it."

ᘐᗩᗢ

THE EXPERIENCE'S SPRING tour of the U.S. would see them play twenty-nine shows over the course of ten weeks, to a total audience of 350,000 fans, with a take of over $1.3 million. In the manner that had become typical of their tours, most of Jimi's time would be taken up by travel, doing press or promotions, or trying to cram in the odd studio session during an off day. By the second date of the tour, Jimi was already complaining of exhaustion, and in his interviews, he was far more irritable than he'd been in Britain. He'd cut his hair and found that most journalists tried to ascribe some major significance to this.

Crowd violence or gate-crashers marred many shows on the tour. Racial politics also came into play when Black Power advocates would show up backstage and criticize Jimi for using white musicians and a white promoter. "They called him an Uncle Tom," promoter Pat O'Day recalled. "I reminded Jimi that we worked for him, not the other way around." Jimi tried to think of people as raceless—it was what he had learned growing up in a diverse neighborhood in Seattle—but he found that in the public spotlight, he could never escape the fact that he was black and that most of his fans were white. It was one of several reasons the FBI began to investigate Jimi that year—the ability of his music to cross the deep divide of race in America made the government fear him.

At a show in Oakland on April 29, it was Jimi's personal past that he couldn't escape. After the concert, a note was delivered backstage from Diana Carpenter, his girlfriend in the New York days when Jimi had struggled to find enough to eat and she worked the streets as a prostitute. Jimi sent word back that she was to follow his limo to the airport. There in the terminal, as he waited for a flight, they talked for the first time in three years. What might have been their warm reunion was derailed when Diana handed Jimi a snapshot. "This is your daughter,

Tamika," she announced. "She's two years old." Jimi held the picture in his hands. "She has my eyes," he remarked. For the next hour, Jimi put his head on Carpenter's lap and talked about how tired he was of touring and his lifestyle. He didn't ask much about his daughter and talked instead about his own exhaustion. Still, Jimi took the picture of Tamika with him when he boarded his plane.

A week later the band was in the Midwest playing the Cobo Arena in Detroit. The next morning they checked out of the Pontchartrain Hotel and took a quick flight to Toronto. As he was going through Canadian customs at 9:30 AM, Jimi's bags were searched. The officer found the tiny snapshot of Tamika Carpenter along with a postcard, a bottle of Avocado Cream Shampoo and one of Avocado Cream Rinse, some Vitamin C pills, and a book titled *You Can Change Your Life Through Psychic Power*. But underneath those items, according to the Royal Canadian Mounted Police who were doing the searching, there was a small glass vial. Inside were six cellophane packages of white powder and a small dark residue of resin. A mobile drug-testing lab was called in, and at one thirty in the afternoon Jimi was arrested for possession of heroin and hashish.

# HAPPINESS AND SUCCESS

TORONTO, CANADA

*May 1969–August 1969*

*"The Hendrix concert grossed around $35,000 of YOUR bread!*
*That's $19,000 to the performer. Okay, who is the villain here?*
*That's right, kiddies, our HEROES are screwing us! Hendrix*
*and others have copped-out to the American standard of*
*happiness and success."*

—from the *Door* underground newspaper

By FAR THE most extraordinary aspect of Jimi Hendrix's drug bust in
Toronto on May 3, 1969, was how little press it generated. Although
Jimi was arguably the biggest rock star in America at this juncture, his
arrest only made a few Toronto papers. The first major U.S. outlet to
carry the story was *Rolling Stone,* a full four weeks later, and that account was predictably sympathetic to Jimi, going so far as to imply that
he'd been framed. "I stopped the story from going out on the wires,"
said Michael Goldstein, Jimi's public relations manager. Goldstein
bribed an Associated Press editor with a case of liquor to keep the scan-
dal out of the newspapers. Jimi's big concern was that the arrest would

cause cancellations on the lucrative tour; thanks to Goldstein, the news didn't break until the tour was near completion.

As for the drugs, Jimi categorically denied they were his. As the Mounties pulled the vial out of his bag, Jimi shook his head in disbelief. The Experience had been tipped off before arriving in Toronto that a search might take place, and everyone other than Jimi had made careful checks of their luggage. Just to avoid this sort of incident, Mitch Mitchell went through customs in a suit without pockets. By 1969, many high-profile rock stars, including members of the Stones and the Beatles, had been busted for one drug or another. The circumstances of Jimi's bust raised questions about advance planning, as it was usually customs agents who made such arrests, not Mounties. "The Mounties do not customarily wait at the airport to make dope busts, as they did in Hendrix's case," *Rolling Stone* reported. Jimi would later argue in court that the drugs were slipped into his bag by a fan back in Los Angeles and that he didn't notice them. Privately, he blamed a disgruntled groupie who, he said, had planted the drugs and called ahead to the Canadian police. When the news of the bust finally did break, Jimi suggested the arrest was emblematic of a larger battle between youth and authority: "All of that is the Establishment fighting back," he told reporters. "Eventually they will swallow themselves up. But I don't want them to swallow too many kids up as they go along. Put that down, I know what I'm talking about."

Jimi was released in time for the evening concert in Toronto, and the band went onstage without any mention of the incident, though Mounties escorted them there. During the show, Jimi changed the lyrics to "Red House" and sang, "Soon as I get out of jail / I wanna see her." He was arraigned two days later and, after posting ten thousand dollars bail, was allowed to continue the tour. His trial was set for June 19. During that waiting period, Jimi lived with the very real fear of conviction—he faced as many as ten years in prison.

The band immediately went back on the road, playing East Coast dates and trying to cram in session work at the Record Plant on off days. They drew eighteen thousand fans to a sold-out show at Madison

Square Garden, though you could also catch Jimi in a New York club almost every night for free. One of those club jams that month paired Jimi with Stephen Stills and Johnny Winter. "He wanted to play the songs he grew up on: Freddie King, Earl King, and Muddy Waters," Winter recalled. "When I played with him, I deferred and let Jimi play lead." The jam lasted until three in the morning, at which point Jimi suggested they move to the Record Plant. That night he cut Guitar Slim's "The Things I Used to Do," using Winter on bottleneck guitar.

Though Jimi was now the highest-paid rock musician in the world—he'd made fourteen thousand dollars a minute for his Madison Square Garden concert—that popularity came with increasing criticism from anarchists who demanded he play for free. The higher paydays also increased expectations from the audience and the critics. After Jimi complained about Madison Square Garden's revolving stage, the *Village Voice* review rebuked him: "He should bitch with all the bread he walked off with? A performer with Hendrix's options is responsible for his audience, and for where he plays." A little later in the tour, the *San Diego Door* criticized Jimi's ticket prices of $5.50: "The Hendrix concert grossed around $35,000 of YOUR bread! That's $19,000 to the performer. Okay, who is the villain here? That's right, kiddies, our HEROES are screwing us!"

∽∾

THREE WEEKS AFTER his Toronto bust, Jimi flew from New York to Seattle for a concert at the Coliseum. As usual, he was nervous about visiting his hometown, particularly with his arrest unresolved. He had Carmen Borrero accompany him, perhaps thinking a girlfriend would provide a buffer between him and his inquiring relatives. Jimi's management had booked him in a hotel in Seattle's U District, and they gave specific instructions to the road crew to keep his itinerary secret so that he could control how much time he wanted to spend with relatives.

As he had done before, Jimi dedicated the show to his family and Garfield High School. As the show came to a close, a thunderclap

sounded outside the hall, a downpour began outside, and it seemed like
the gods had announced that the show was over. Backstage, Jimi spent
time entertaining his family, though because of the weather, most
didn't linger. Eventually, Jimi was alone with Carmen and only a few
fans. It was an era when concert security was loose, and random fans
could walk into the dressing room if they bypassed one police officer.
Jimi told Carmen he wanted to show her his Seattle roots. "You got a
car?" he asked one surprised fan nearby who was clutching an album
cover for an autograph. The teenager was too shocked to reply but nod-
ded his head yes.

An hour after the show ended, Jimi walked in the rain to the kid's
car. Carmen thought the idea unsafe and argued with Jimi. "I told him,
we knew nothing about this kid," she said. "We were both still tripping
from acid, so I'm not sure Jimi was thinking straight." Carmen's concerns increased when they found out the kid's car was a Volkswagen
Beetle with springs sticking out of the seats. The boy apologized for the
state of the vehicle and said that he was planning on selling the car the
next day for sixty dollars. Jimi, who was used to limousines, got in the
backseat with Carmen and the teenager drove. Through rusted out
holes in the floorboard, Jimi and Carmen could put their feet on the asphalt below. As the boy cautiously moved the car forward, Jimi called
out several Seattle locations.

Over the course of the next two hours, the teenager followed
Jimi's directions and drove from house to house as Jimi retraced the arc
of his youth. He pointed out the ramshackle homes he'd lived in, the
clubs he'd played in, the lawns he'd helped his father mow. They
stopped at a drive-in hamburger stand on Madison Street; it was directly across from the parking lot where Jimi had played his last local
concert with the Tomcats before entering the army seven years before.
This was the very hamburger stand where Jimi had always wanted to
take his junior high school girlfriend, but he'd never had ten cents for a
burger. He didn't have any money this day, either, since he rarely carried cash; the teenage fan had to buy his hamburger.

The rain stopped while they dined on burgers and fries in the backseat of the tiny Volkswagen. No one at the burger joint recognized Jimi—as his only retinue was the starstruck teenage driver, the context was probably too bizarre for anyone even to imagine. After the food, they drove to the parking lot of Garfield High School, where Jimi pointed to windows on the building and told Carmen what classes were held there. The building had a pull that found him returning with a regularity that was in contrast to the infrequency of his attendance as a student. Since his fame, Garfield had taken on a mysterious allure that saw Jimi dedicate all his Seattle shows to the school from which he flunked out. Eventually, the tour of Jimi's domiciles recommenced. Though Carmen had already heard many stories about Jimi's childhood, she was surprised at the sheer number of different homes, apartments, hotels, and boardinghouses he had lived in. "On every block there was someplace he had stayed," she recalled. "He had stories about every one."

They drove down the stretch of Jackson Street that had been the entertainment district back when the region's black community was more insular; many of those storefronts and clubs were now closed. Since Jimi's childhood, Seattle's African American population had grown substantially and become markedly more political—blacks were no longer willing to accept subpar housing, employment discrimination, and inequitable access to education. The day before Jimi's concert, a huge demonstration by the Central Community College's Black Student Union had crippled Seattle and been the talk of the town. The Seattle Black Panthers were one of the most active chapters in the nation, and also one of the first offices to accept membership from other minorities. Mike Tagawa, who had gone to Garfield with Jimi, joined in 1968: "I said, 'I'm not black.' They said, 'You ain't white, either.'" In 1968, armed Panthers had occupied a Seattle high school when they'd heard reports of racism in the school. Seattle was also home to a number of extremist anarchist groups, and in 1969, Seattle's sixty-nine bombings would rank the city number one in the nation in per capita bomb incidents.

At three in the morning, Jackson Street was quiet as the Volkswagen lumbered down the road. Jimi pointed to boarded-up buildings that had once hosted music legends like Ray Charles, Quincy Jones, and Bumps Blackwell. At one particular corner, where an old hotel still stood, Jimi gestured and said, "That's where my mother lived." Carmen was briefly taken aback: She had heard Jimi talk about Lucille many times—he had even said that should they have a child, he wanted any daughter to be named Lucille—but Carmen hadn't realized that Lucille lived in many of the same places as Jimi. "He had so idealized his mother," she said. "I had forgotten she had been a real person." On a previous visit to Seattle, Jimi told friend Pernell Alexander he wanted to visit his mother's grave, which was in Renton, south of Seattle. He hadn't made the trip then, and he brought up the idea now to Carmen and the teenager at the wheel. It would have been a thirty-minute drive, and the kid was tired, as was Carmen. "We were flying out in just a few hours for a show Jimi had in San Diego that evening," Carmen recalled. Even Jimi let loose with a yawn, and with that, he directed the teenager north toward his hotel and away from the markers and the ghosts of his past. As they drove, the roads were puddled with water, and the street-lights reflected off the wet asphalt guiding them home.

❧

THAT SAME MONTH Jimi had caused a stir in Britain with an interview in the *N.M.E.* in which he said he might want to take a year off. Doing press in L.A. during a tour break, he told a different story, suggesting to *Rolling Stone* that he'd soon be touring with a different band; when he announced this, he had yet to discuss it with the members of the Experience. Jimi also told the magazine that he was writing songs with the Aleem twins—who had formed a group under the name Ghetto Fighters—for an album he planned to produce with them. In a different interview, he said his future direction might be toward "symphonic things. So then the kids can respect the old music, the traditional, you know, like classics. I like to mix that in with the so-called-rock today."

On June 19, Jimi flew to Toronto, where he appeared in court for a preliminary hearing. It was the first time he had worn a proper suit since he'd played with Curtis Knight and the Squires. At the hearing, his case was set for a full trial on December 8. He flew back to Los Angeles, where, on June 22, the Experience were set to play the Newport Pop Festival, a gig that would earn them $100,000, their biggest one-night fee yet.

Despite the large payday, the show was lackluster. Noel later argued Jimi's sour mood was due to the distraction of the court hearings. Feeling remorseful about his performance, Jimi returned the next day unannounced and, without additional pay, jammed with Buddy Miles and Eric Burdon.

The same pattern of dynamic jams and uninspired shows continued the next week when Jimi flew to Colorado in advance of the Denver Pop Festival. On an off night in Denver, he called up musicians Herbie and Billy Rich and asked them what they were up to; they had a wedding reception gig that night and didn't have time to see Jimi. Later, at the reception, which was in a public park, the Riches were surprised to see a limousine pull up. Instead of the bride and groom, Jimi climbed out. He joined them onstage, and since the park was public, a huge crowd gathered. "He only played for about fifteen minutes before it got out of control," Billy Rich recalled. "Everybody in the park ended up coming to the wedding to see Jimi play."

The next day, before his show at Mile High Stadium, Jimi dropped acid with his friend Herbie Worthington. "I had one tab of purple Owsley," Worthington recalled. "He said, 'We've got to split it.' And I said, 'No. I know how much you take, and if you're going to get high, you'll have to take it all.'" Jimi insisted they split the tab, and after doing so, they headed to the concert. Before the show began, a journalist spotted Noel Redding, and having heard reports that Noel was out of the group, he came up and asked, "What are you doing here? I thought you had left the band." It was the first Noel had heard of it. The rumors were the result of Jimi complaining in front of writers.

If there was a nadir to the history of the Jimi Hendrix Experience, it came in Denver—which would also prove to be the last Experience show ever. Outside the stadium, fans had rioted, demanding the festival be free. When the show began, Jimi seemed out of it, perhaps a result of the acid, or maybe something else he had taken, since performing on acid usually put him in a pleasant mood and not the sour one he exhibited that night. Rather than entertaining the crowd, Jimi antagonized them, changing the lyrics of "Voodoo Child" to "Gonna make a lot of money and buy this town / Gonna buy this town and put it all in my shoe." At one point during the set, he announced, "This is the last gig we'll ever be playing together." Spurred on by that declaration and by continual clashes with police, rioting broke out among the seventeen thousand people inside the stadium, with many trying to climb onstage. When the police shot tear-gas canisters into the audience, Jimi joked, "We see some tear gas—that's the sign of the Third World War." But as the gas began to drift onstage and engulf the band, the three members of the Experience put down their instruments and fled. Their last moment onstage as a band looked like something out of a horror film as they bolted at breakneck speed from the surging crowd and cloud of gas.

Road manager Gerry Stickells had procured a U-Haul truck, and he pushed the group and Herbie Worthington into the back, pulled the door down, and locked it. Stickells then attempted to drive through the massing crowd. Tear gas had engulfed the entire stadium, and to evade it, fans had climbed on the top of the truck. The weight of the fans began to snap the roof supports of the panel truck. The band sat inside in darkness, but could hear people on the roof. "They were pounding on the doors and the roof, and you could see the sides of the van start to buckle," Herbie Worthington recalled. Jimi was silent. The only one who spoke was Noel, who had decided that if he survived this moment, he was getting on a plane to England and never coming back. Still, even in his state of abject fear, he made a joke. "That's my leg, mate, and I don't know you that well," he said to Worthington, who was sitting next to him. The Experience had been together for three tumultuous years, and Noel's sense of humor had been one element that had helped hold them close during difficult times. Now Noel joked that it was all going to end with their deaths in the back of a U-Haul and they'd never get a chance to spend their money or enjoy their fame. Though it took them an hour to drive a hundred yards, Jimi, Noel, and Mitch survived the Denver Pop Festival. They would never again play together as a trio, though.

Noel took a plane to England the next day, while Jimi flew to New York and checked into the Hotel Navarro. One day later, Jimi heard that his friend Brian Jones of the Rolling Stones had drowned at his Sussex home. Jones was only twenty-seven years old.

*∽∾∾∾*

ON JULY 10, Jimi was scheduled to appear as a guest on the "Tonight Show" with Johnny Carson. As soon as Noel split, Jimi attempted to track down Billy Cox, his old army buddy, to offer him the job of bass player. Billy had moved, however, which made locating him difficult. "I used to live next to a TV repairman," Cox recalled. "Jimi called up that TV guy and told him he'd give him some money if he found me." Once located and brought to New York, Cox began to rehearse with Mitch Mitchell. Jimi said that the loss of Noel Redding was no great setback, but the record would indicate otherwise: Over the next six months, Jimi would play only one festival date, one free street fair, and two proper theater concerts, by far the quietest period of his professional career. He still jammed in clubs occasionally, but even those appearances were more selected.

Jimi used the new trio on the "Tonight Show." Johnny Carson was ill that night and Flip Wilson was recruited as guest host. *Rolling Stone* called the appearance "a disaster," citing Jimi's excessive giggling and gum chewing, which made it hard to understand what he said; Jimi obsessively chewed Blackjack licorice gum, particularly when he was nervous. The magazine was even harder on Wilson, who, they wrote, "tried to hip-talk himself onto Hendrix's level while patting a huge watermelon on his desk." After Jimi's brief chat with Wilson, he moved to the stage for his first public performance with the rhythm section of Cox and Mitchell. They played "Lover Man," which Jimi dedicated to Brian Jones. Cox and Mitchell sounded fine, but unfortunately Jimi's amplifier blew up, which derailed the live broadcast.

By the summer of 1969, Jimi had shifted most of his life from London to New York. With Kathy Etchingham gone, Carmen Borrero or Devon Wilson became his preferred concubines. In London, his circle of friends had primarily included musicians or Mitch, Noel, and Chas. In New York, his friendships expanded to include contacts outside of the music business and outside of his band. Jimi first met Deering Howe in 1968 when Howe's yacht had been rented for the band to take a one-day cruise, and Deering became one of Jimi's closest confidants after that. Howe's family owned several Manhattan hotels and he was a music fan but not directly involved in the music business. "I think part of the attraction was that I came from money and there was nothing I wanted from him," Deering recalled. "We had almost nothing in common except for a love of music."

In addition to Deering, Jimi met and befriended two women who ran a boutique where he shopped. Colette Mimram and Stella Douglas were both more cultured than Jimi, and he found that appealing, along with their fashion sense. "He was simply a charming gentleman," Colette recalled. "I think he gravitated to us because we were outside his world. In his world, everybody was after him for something, no one had a job other than Jimi, and he thought they all wanted a handout." With Colette, Stella, and Deering, Jimi developed his first adult friendships that were outside the music industry. "We'd expose him to a certain refinement that he had never experienced before," Colette noted. Deering even taught Jimi how to order wine and a meal in a fine restaurant, something Jimi had never done before.

That summer, Colette, Stella, Jimi, and Deering dined together often, forming a salon of sorts. "It was almost like something out of the twenties," Deering recalled. "We were a group of people who would gather and eat together and talk." The frequent dinners were relaxed and served as breaks from the stress of Jimi's career. One rule was that business was never to be discussed. With his friends, Jimi talked about art, philosophy, religion, and politics. He found the group fascinating, if only because he felt like a cultural apprentice around them, the opposite of his experience as a musician, where he was the trendsetter.

Jimi's interest in areas other than music was an immediate concern to Michael Jeffrey, who desperately needed him to finish a new album. In an effort to speed up that process, Jeffrey rented a country house for Jimi that summer. Jeffrey himself had a home near Woodstock, and the rental was ten miles away near Shokan. The Shokan house was an eight-bedroom stone mansion on ten acres, complete with a riding stable, horses, and a swimming pool. The rent was three thousand dollars a month, but Jeffrey felt that if a new album resulted from the stay, it was money well spent. Jeffrey even hired a cook and a housekeeper so that all of Jimi's needs would be met.

In the Shokan house, Jimi began to refigure his next musical move. He decided to use Noel's departure as an excuse to build the large-scale band he had always wanted. He first hired Larry Lee, the Nashville guitarist he had played with years before, for rhythm guitar. Next Jimi added two percussion players, Jerry Velez and Juma Sultan. He had met both in New York clubs, and Sultan already lived on a farm near Woodstock. Lee, Sultan, Velez, and Billy Cox all moved to the Shokan estate and began the process of forming a band. Their cohesion was compromised by the fact that the group still didn't have a drummer—it was unclear whether Mitch Mitchell, who was back in England, would fill that role. The confusion among the new group was exacerbated when Jimi left the house to go to New York City for the day and didn't return. When one of the players called Jeffrey, they discovered Jimi had left for Morocco.

Jimi had originally gone to New York to see off Deering Howe, who was traveling to Africa to meet up with Colette Mimram and Stella Douglas. Deering urged Jimi to join them, arguing that there was no reason to earn money if one couldn't spend it. In a rare flouting of his tendency to follow orders from management, Jimi agreed. He phoned Michael Jeffrey, who was furious but couldn't stop Jimi, and he phoned the police in Toronto, who had to approve any travel outside the United States. With the drug charges still hanging over him, Jimi desperately needed a break, and the Royal Canadian Mounted Police were kind enough to approve his trip.

Jimi spent nine days in North Africa, and they were, in all probability, the most joyous of his entire life. "It was the best, and maybe the only, vacation he ever had," recalled Deering. Jimi and Deering landed in Morocco, where they met up with Stella and Colette, who hadn't known Jimi was coming and were delighted to see him. They rented an ancient Chrysler and used it to travel across the desert and to visit famous sites. They spent the trip buying rugs and clothes, eating, talking, and resting. "Jimi had a ball," Deering recalled. "It was amazing to watch him, as a black man, experience Africa. He loved the culture and the people, and he laughed more than I'd ever seen him laugh." In Africa, Jimi found a place where his race didn't matter, but equally important, neither did his fame. Jimi was the biggest star in the world that year, yet in Africa, no one knew who he was. The trip felt like a reprieve from fame, as he was able to drop his rock-star persona and enjoy life. "The vacation seemed to give him nourishment," Colette said. "It recharged him." Jimi was recognized only a few times; once, two actors from New York recognized Jimi and befriended him. He went one night and read one man's poetry, thankful that someone else was providing the entertainment. "We talked about theater, art, Africa, but never music," said Deering.

On August 6, Jimi flew back, leaving his friends still enjoying their extended vacation. Yet his own vacation, it turned out, was not completely over: On a layover in the Paris airport, he ran into Brigitte Bardot. Jimi would later tell Deering that on the spot he decided to miss his flight in an effort to bed the famous actress: He succeeded, and for two days he had a secret fling with Bardot while his management searched unsuccessfully to find him. It was a crazy idea—missing a flight on the chance of seducing a famous French actress—but it illustrated the kind of joie de vivre that characterized Jimi's life. What was truly insane, though, was that Jimi virtually had to go underground to escape the demands of his management and his career. He had striven so hard to find fame on the streets of New York and touring in the Chitlin' Circuit— once he found it, he wished only for anonymity.

When Jimi did finally arrive back in America, his trip seemed to have revitalized him musically. He came back wanting to play acoustic rather than electric guitar and was inspired by the African music he had heard in Morocco. In jam sessions at the Shokan house, he explored this territory, making a number of recordings that featured just him and Juma Sultan. "They were only his acoustic guitar and my percussion," Sultan recalled. "It was phenomenal—a sound somewhat like Wes Montgomery or Segovia, but with a Moroccan influence."

Though Africa had widened Jimi's musical vision, one incident that occurred on the trip stuck with Jimi more than any other and soon gave him nightmares. Colette Mimram had relatives in Morocco, including a grandfather who was a tribal leader. The grandfather had recently remarried and his new wife was a renowned clairvoyant who worked for the King of Morocco. When the old woman met Jimi— despite knowing nothing of his history or career—she announced that he had a "forehead" that indicated artistic genius. Jimi and his friends found it warmly amusing as she began to run her fingers over his head, reading the lines on his face. The woman spoke French, so her words had to be translated for Jimi and they made him laugh. Later that night, the old woman told Colette, in French, what sounded like an ominous warning: "You will not be friends with this man in a year's time because of other women." The prophecy surprised Colette, but in the carefree era of the sixties, making such a prediction hardly required a great psychic mind. What happened later that night, however, shook Colette and positively spooked Jimi.

The woman had suggested that she read Jimi's tarot cards, and he agreed. He and his friends gathered around a table as the woman dealt a tarot deck. The first card she pulled was the Star. This brought smiles to everyone except the fortune-teller, who didn't know that Jimi was famous. She told him that the card meant "grace" and that he would soon be around a large number of people. The next card that came from the deck brought a decidedly different response from Jimi: It was the Death card. The old woman immediately began telling Colette that the card did not mean that Jimi would die soon—that it could also mean rebirth. But during the few moments it took for Colette to translate, Jimi stared transfixed at the card. "I'm going to die!" he cried. His friends immediately gathered around him and told him that the tarot had many different interpretations and that he should not take random cards dealt by an old woman as an omen.

Some might have been able to shrug off the card, but Jimi—who, in 1966, had dreamed he would become a star and saw that dream come true—could not forget it. Over the next few months, he kept echoing the forecast that he was doomed. "Sometimes it would be 'I'm going to die in three months,' and sometimes it would be that he was only going to live for 'six months,'" Colette recalled. "But he kept repeating that he was going to die before he was thirty." On one occasion when Jimi spouted this prediction, Colette told him, "Don't talk like that, Jimi—it's so negative."

"It's not negative," he replied. "It's just the way it is. I'm sorry. I'm not ready to go."

Whether he was ready to go or not, once he was back in America, those visions of doom had to be put on hold, at least temporarily, as Jimi needed to rehearse his new band. Less than two weeks after he returned to the U.S., he was scheduled to play a festival in upstate New York, not far from the Shokan house. Jimi had already played a dozen such festivals over the last three years, and this one wasn't expected to be as large as several he had already done—but then again, the Moroccan soothsayer had predicted he would be in a large crowd. The festival was to be held in Bethel, New York, and the original poster billed it as "An Aquarian Exposition," but it would be known for the ages as Woodstock, and Jimi Hendrix—fresh from the arms of Brigitte Bardot and the spooky world of fortune-tellers—was to be the headlining act.

# GYPSY, SUN, AND RAINBOWS

BETHEL, NEW YORK
*August 1969–November 1969*

*"We decided to change the whole thing around and call it 'Gypsy,
Sun, and Rainbows.' For short, it's nothin but a 'Band of Gypsys.'"*
—from JIMI'S introduction at Woodstock

THE WOODSTOCK MUSIC and Arts Fair, scheduled from August 15
through 18, was originally supposed to take place in Wallkill, New
York. When local residents complained, the concert was moved at the
last minute to the farm of Max Yasgur in nearby Bethel. Roughly sixty
thousand advance tickets had been sold, and the promoters predicted a
hundred thousand attendees at most. When the organizers first approached manager Michael Jeffrey about booking Jimi, they settled on
a fee of thirty-two thousand dollars, expecting the festival to be modest
in size. Jimi was the highest-paid performer at the event, but this fee
was considerably less than he'd earned at other shows. Jeffrey had a
house in Woodstock, and knowing that it was a solid two hours north
of New York, he also didn't expect many fans to make the trek.

Once Jimi returned from Africa, he began rehearsals in earnest. He held auditions for a new drummer but eventually settled on bringing Mitch Mitchell back. When Mitch arrived from London, he found that the tight ensemble of the Experience was a thing of the past. "The band was grim," he would later write in *The Hendrix Experience,* "a shambles." Mitch said it was the only band he had ever played with that did not get better with practice. Juma Sultan and others in the group disputed Mitchell's assessment and argued that Mitch wasn't used to the Latin rhythms they were using. In any case, as a full band, the group had only had a week of rehearsal prior to Woodstock—their rawness would show in their performance.

By the time the festival began on Friday, things were already unraveling in Bethel. Rather than the expected 60,000 ticket holders, somewhere around 800,000 people made the trip. At least 200,000 of them became so hopelessly stuck in traffic that they turned around and went home. Though the festival site was only a hundred miles from New York City, the drive took ten hours that day, and traffic was blocked for the last twenty miles. Many attendees simply abandoned their cars and walked. By the time Richie Havens officially began the festival on Friday night, 186,000 tickets had been sold, but at least twice that many people had come in after the fences were torn down and promoters were forced to declare it a "free festival." Jimi and his band were still at home when they watched reports on television of the New York Thruway being shut down. "No one knew, no one suspected, no one had any idea," recalled Billy Cox. "We had thought it was just a gig where a lot of good musicians were going to be."

On Saturday, the headline of the New York *Daily News* blared TRAFFIC UPTIGHT AT HIPPIEFEST. By then an estimated 450,000 people were at the site, making use of only six hundred Porta Potties. Officials were flying in emergency food and medical staff by helicopter. Over the weekend, there would be three deaths, two births, and over 400 people seeking medical attention because of bad acid trips. Organizers were already handing out leaflets under the headline SURVIVE containing such practical tips as avoiding the "light blue acid" and "don't run naked in the hot sun." Those successful enough to get near the stage saw some stunning musical performances on Saturday: Santana, the Grateful Dead, Janis Joplin, the Jefferson Airplane, and Sly and the Family Stone. The Who went on at three in the morning, and the highlight of their set, and perhaps the entire festival, was Pete Townshend whacking Abbie Hoffman with a guitar to get Abbie off the stage.

Jimi was scheduled to close the three-day festival at 11 PM Sunday. One benefit of the Shokan house was that Jimi was nearby, yet organizers still arranged for him to take a helicopter from a local airport. When he and the band arrived at the airport, it was raining and no flights were taking off. They were stuck with a number of bands, including Crosby, Stills, Nash and Young. Gerry Stickells eventually commandeered a truck and drove them the last few remaining miles. Neil Young would later tell *N.M.E.* that the scene at the airport was more memorable than the concert. "Stealing a pickup truck with Hendrix is one of the high points of my life," Young said.

When the band arrived at the venue, they were told the show was running three hours late—in fact it was nine full hours behind by that point. Promoters offered Jimi the chance to play at midnight, when the crowd would be lively, but Jeffrey insisted that he close the show. Jimi and the band spent most of the night in a cottage a few hundred yards from the stage, where they smoked pot and played acoustic instruments, waiting for their cue. The band that played before Hendrix was Sha Na Na, hardly an auspicious lead-in. Even before Jimi and his band went on, Jimi was arguing with the festival promoters: He wanted to do two songs acoustically, but the promoters axed the idea.

By the time Jimi was introduced—"Ladies and gentlemen, the Jimi Hendrix Experience"—it was eight thirty Monday morning. The majority of the crowd had departed during the night, and only forty thousand were on hand for Jimi's show. The sparse audience hardly mattered, as the film crew remained, and the daylight made Jimi's portion of the show look all the better in the resulting *Woodstock* movie, which would be seen—as D. A. Pennebaker's movie of the Monterey Pop Festival had been—by millions more than attended the festival.

Jimi walked onstage wearing a red headband and a white beaded jacket with fringe he'd purchased from his friends Colette and Stella's boutique. He was carrying his white Strat, and unhappy with the introduction he'd been given, he spent the next few minutes correcting it. "Yeah, well, dig, we'd like to get something straight," he said. "We got tired of 'the Experience' and every once in awhile we was blowing our minds too much, so we decided to change the whole thing around and call it 'Gypsy, Sun, and Rainbows.'" He then introduced his five-piece band. As Jimi spoke, an audience member loudly yelled, "Jimi, are you high?"

Jimi ignored that comment and continued. "Okay, give us about a minute and a half to tune up. We only had about two rehearsals, so [we'll] do nothing but primary rhythm things, but, I mean, it's a first ray of the new rising sun, anyway, so we might as well start from the Earth, which is rhythm, right? Can you dig that? When you get your old lady, your woman, that makes the melody, right? I have mine, thank you very much." And with a count-in, Jimi began "Message to Love," the first number of a sixteen-song set that would run two hours and rank as the longest show of Jimi's career.

Jimi's performance at Woodstock was fluid, loose, and appeared unrehearsed; prior to going onstage, he had written out only a rough set list with eight songs, half of what they played. Parts of the show were majestic, such as "Voodoo Child," which got a masterful treatment, and parts were amateurish, such as a song Jimi introduced as "Jammin' at the House," an instrumental the band had not yet perfected. "None of our numbers really gelled," Mitch Mitchell later wrote in his autobiography. "They just turned into long jams." Some of those jams, though, were dazzling, as was the case with a cover of Curtis Mayfield's "Gypsy Woman" sung by Larry Lee with a delicate Jimi guitar solo. Many in the audience were disappointed that Jimi wasn't singing, and many songs, like a Larry Lee original called "Mastermind," were completely unknown to the crowd. The band's performance wasn't helped either by the fact that Jimi, and to a greater degree Larry

Lee, suffered from severe tuning problems. At one point during the show, Jimi joked, "We'll just play very quietly and out of tune."

As the show progressed, more of the crowd began to filter out, a turn of events that Jimi felt compelled to comment on. "You can leave if you want to," he said. "We're just jamming, that's all. Okay? You can leave, or you can clap." And with that Jimi began the introduction to "The Star Spangled Banner." The number had been in his set for a year and had been performed on at least three dozen occasions, yet for the forty thousand or so people who remained at the festival—and those who later saw the Woodstock film—the song defined the three-day concert. "I was working in the 'bad trip tent' as a nurse when he started to play it," recalled Roz Payne. "Everything seemed to stop. Before that, if someone would have played 'The Star Spangled Banner,' we would have booed; after that, it became *our* song." Al Aronowitz, pop critic for the *New York Post*, was even more enthusiastic: "It was the most electrifying moment of Woodstock, and it was probably the single greatest moment of the sixties. You finally heard what that song was about, that you can love your country, but hate the government."

The song had long been a showcase for Jimi to display his innovative use of feedback, with his guitar mimicking the sounds of rocket explosions and ambulance wails. Jimi's version was the rare example of a musical performance that challenged the listener to hear the song any other way in the future. Through feedback and sustain, he had taken one of the best-known tunes in America and made it his own. For Jimi, it was a musical exercise, not a manifesto. If he had any intention of making a political statement with "The Star Spangled Banner," he didn't speak of it to his bandmates, friends, or even later to reporters, who consequently hounded him with questions suggesting such a motivation. At a press conference three weeks later, he said of the song: "We're all Americans . . . it was like 'Go America!' . . . We play it the way the air is in America today. The air is slightly static, see." If he meant the song as an anti–Vietnam War screed, as pundits quickly suggested, he never stated this. In fact, earlier in his set, Jimi had dedicated

"Izabella" to soldiers in the army. Ultimately, however, Jimi's pro-army stance or his own political beliefs hardly mattered—the song became part of the sixties Zeitgeist, captured forever on film as an antiestablishment rallying cry.

Jimi followed "The Star Spangled Banner" with "Purple Haze," which got a more visible response from the crowd that morning. He ended with "Villanova Junction" and was called back for an encore. He chose "Hey Joe," the very song that, just three years before, he had been playing to a handful of teenagers in a basement Greenwich Village club. When he finished, the Woodstock Music and Arts Fair officially ended. Jimi walked offstage and collapsed from exhaustion; he had been up for three days straight.

Shortly after Woodstock, Jimi wrote a poem about the event. It read: "500,000 halos outshined the mud and history. We washed and drank in God's tears of joy. And for once, and for everyone, the truth was not still a mystery."

৶৶৶

AFTER WOODSTOCK, JIMI took his new band into the Hit Factory in New York and cut half a dozen songs, including "Machine Gun," which would become one of his signature tunes. He also ran the band through rehearsals for an upcoming show that was decidedly more important to him than any other that year—a free street fair in Harlem. It was to be his first show uptown since his days at Small's Paradise, and he was more anxious about playing this gig—to an African American audience—than he had been about Woodstock. The show was to benefit the United Block Association (UBA), but the idea for the gig grew out of the Aleem brothers' concept that a Harlem show might finally get Jimi on black radio. The Aleems had originally hoped to do the show at the Apollo, but the historic theater—where a penniless Jimi had won an amateur show in 1964—rejected the idea. "They didn't want him," Tunde-Ra Aleem recalled. "They were afraid that there would be too many white folks."

In most instances, Jimi's approach to race was rooted in the multiculturalism he had learned back in Seattle at Leschi Elementary. "He believed that color was what was on the outside, not what was inside," Colette Mimram observed. Still, the fact that Jimi had not found a large audience in the black community was a concern for him. "He felt his audience was white, but he wanted the black audience, where he felt he wasn't accepted," Colette added. He was recognized uptown, however: When Colette and Jimi attended an Al Green concert at the Apollo, Jimi left early because he was being recognized by so many African Americans in the crowd.

By 1969, Jimi found that, like it or not, as the most popular African American entertainer in the world, there existed numerous groups who sought to attach themselves to him for reasons of race; some suggested he owed something to the black community, an idea Jimi flatly rejected. The Black Panthers had made extensive attempts to involve him, and while he had been quietly supportive, he didn't want to be a spokesperson for a group he felt advocated violence. He was asked about the Panthers in virtually every interview he did that year, and he usually sidestepped the question. If pressed, he'd admit, "I naturally feel a part of what they're doing, in certain respects, you know. But everybody has their own way of saying things. They get justified as they justify others, you know; in their attempts to get personal freedom. That's all it is." Jimi had the ability to answer a question with a response so wide-ranging it hardly was an answer at all. This fluidity furthered his phantom-like nature, and even those who were close to him felt as if they were never really sure what he thought. He also changed positions frequently, another reason different groups felt he spoke to their individual causes. In politics, as in his personal life, Jimi had difficulty with saying no or with handling himself in direct confrontations—others sought to use this to their advantage.

One of the factions trying to attach themselves to him that summer was a cabal of Harlem gangsters who attempted to extort him into playing for them. Jimi found out about this hustle when he saw posters strewn all over Harlem announcing a concert he had not agreed to give.

Walking with the Aleems on 125th Street, he witnessed someone putting up the posters and for a moment it seemed as if he would assault
the man. As if by cue, one of the promoters, a mobster, appeared with
two thugs. Guns were pulled and pointed at Jimi, with fingers on the
trigger. "They were going to *shoot* Jimi right there," Taharqa said. The
situation was resolved only when the Aleems mentioned their own connections to Harlem kingpins, which led the gangsters to back down.
This incident was part of the impetus for the UBA benefit: The Aleems
argued that if Jimi didn't plan a Harlem concert of his own volition,
he'd be forced into one.

Michael Jeffrey was against the idea of doing the UBA show and
felt threatened by the growing influence of the Aleems. "Jimi was
conned into doing that show," observed PR man Michael Goldstein.
"It was a time when any black hustler who could get near him was saying 'You shouldn't have any white people around.'" Jeffrey may have
been against the idea for strictly financial reasons, though: Jimi was not
getting paid for his appearance at the free show, and the only way to
raise money for the cause was for Jeffrey to seek sponsorship. Ultimately, Warner Bros. Records made a large donation.

Jimi held a press conference in a Harlem restaurant two days before the show. Wearing a black robe he'd purchased in Africa, he looked
resplendent as he spoke to a dozen reporters. This was his first public
appearance since Woodstock, and the majority of the questions were
about that festival and "The Star Spangled Banner." Jimi said he'd been
impressed by the nonviolent nature of Woodstock and hoped the UBA
show would bring that same sense of unity to Harlem, where "they're
tired of joining street gangs, they're tired of joining militant groups,
they're tired of hearing the President gab his gums . . . they want to
find a different direction." When asked if the UBA show was a "black
Woodstock," he replied, "We'd like to have more festivals in Harlem
where we play for three days. . . . A lot of kids from the ghetto, or
whatever you want to call it, they don't have enough money to travel
across the country to see what they call these festivals."

The afternoon of the show, Jimi drove to the site in his Stingray with Mitch, parked the car on the street, and before he'd even gotten out, his guitar was stolen from the backseat. Fortunately, in the small world that was Harlem at the time, the Aleems discovered who had taken the instrument and forced the person to give it back.

The UBA festival was an all-day affair held on 139th Street, and Jimi was scheduled to play in the evening. Five thousand people had gathered for the event, which also included music from the Sam & Dave band, Big Maybelle, Chuck-A-Luck, Maxine Brown, and J. D. Bryant, all playing on a tiny stage that faced Lenox Avenue. Before the show, Jimi spoke with a *New York Times* reporter: "Sometimes when I come up here, people say, 'he plays white rock for white people. What's he doing up here?' Well, I want to show them that music is universal—that there is no white rock or black rock." Despite his equanimity, tensions were high. "A lot of black people in the neighborhood didn't even know who Jimi was," Tunde-Ra Aleem said, "but so many white people were in the street they became curious."

Trouble began to brew before Jimi even took the stage. He was standing with Carmen Borrero watching the other bands when several people chastised him for having a Puerto Rican girlfriend. "They saw Jimi with what they thought was a 'white bitch,' and they threw stuff at me," Borrero recalled. Carmen's blouse was ripped in the tussle that broke out.

It was midnight before Jimi took the stage and many had left by then. Jimi had to follow Big Maybelle, a two-hundred-and-fifty-pound R&B singer. When Maybelle refused to do an encore the crowd booed, and continued to boo when the first musician to follow her onstage was Mitch Mitchell. "People were annoyed because Mitch was a white kid in Harlem," Taharqa Aleem said. Jimi came onstage wearing white pants, and even the color of his clothing earned catcalls from the crowd. As Jimi began to tune his guitar, someone threw a bottle onstage, which smashed against an amplifier. A few eggs followed, and broke against the stage. Many in the crowd began to go home; by the time Jimi started, there were only five hundred people left. Less than three weeks before, Jimi had headlined the single biggest American concert of the decade to the adoration of all; in Harlem, playing on a four-foot stage for free, he was dangerously close to being upstaged by Big Maybelle—or being bonked by a bottle. "He had to act really quick," Taharqa observed, "or a riot could have happened."

He began with "Fire" and followed that with "Foxy Lady." By the time he got into "Red House," its bluesy flavor softened the tough crowd. He followed with "The Star Spangled Banner," the same version he'd played at Woodstock, but away from the throngs of reporters and film cameras, it paled in comparison with "Voodoo Child," which he introduced as "the *Harlem* National Anthem." By the time Jimi finished his set, there were fewer than two hundred people remaining, but he had survived one of the toughest audiences he ever faced. Juma Sultan, the band's percussionist, summed it up best when he called the show "a draw." After the concert, Jimi walked with Carmen to his car and found a parking ticket tucked under his windshield wiper.

❧

FIVE DAYS AFTER the UBA benefit, the lineup that Jimi called Gypsy, Sun, and Rainbows played their last show. An appearance at the Salvation was intended as a press showcase, but Jimi went on so late that most journalists had left. When the band did begin, problems with the sound system prevented Jimi from singing. "A gig he may not have been too eager to do in the first place had turned into a disaster," reported *Rock* magazine. Two weeks later, Jimi dismantled the large band, though he continued to play with Billy Cox.

The Salvation was also the setting for one of the most peculiar incidents in Jimi's life: He was kidnapped one night after a jam session at the club. He left with a stranger to score cocaine, but was instead held hostage in an apartment in Manhattan. The kidnappers demanded that Michael Jeffrey turn over Jimi's contract in exchange for his release. Rather than agree to the ransom demand, Jeffrey hired his own goons to search out the extorters. Mysteriously, Jeffrey's thugs found Jimi two days later at the Shokan house, unharmed.

It was such a strange incident that Noel Redding suspected that Jeffrey had arranged the kidnapping to discourage Hendrix from seeking other managers; others, such as office manager Trixie Sullivan, argued the kidnapping was authentic. "There were a lot of junior Mafia in New York that wanted to muscle into the music business," she said. "They snatched Jimi, and Mike had to meet a guy, someone who was very much into the Mafia, and Mike was taken by guys with machine guns, and it was negotiated. I remember Mike telling me that there were men in trees with guns." Sullivan said Jeffrey carried a gun at times because of this kind of looming threat. Jeffrey talked the kidnappers into releasing Jimi rather than risk the wrath of his own mob contacts. Juma Sultan, who had lived in the Shokan house with Jimi earlier that summer, recalled a time just a few weeks before the kidnapping when Jeffrey and a driver came to the house to talk business with Jimi: As Jeffrey and Jimi chatted, the driver pulled out a .38 and started firing into a tree in the front yard. Sultan was convinced the visit was undertaken to send a message to Jimi that Jeffrey was indeed the boss, the same theory Noel used to explain why he thought Jeffrey was behind the snatching.

When *Rolling Stone*'s Sheila Weller did a profile of Jimi that September, there was no mention of the kidnapping or gunplay. In an article headlined, I DON'T WANT TO BE A CLOWN ANY MORE, Jimi came off as self-effacing, polite to a fault, and charming. He pawed through his extensive record collection in front of Weller, which included everything from Marlene Dietrich to Wes Montgomery to Blind Faith. He was most effusive about Bob Dylan, explaining, "I love Dylan. I only met him once, about three years ago, back at the Kettle of Fish on MacDougal Street. That was before I went to England. I think both of us were pretty drunk at the time, so he probably doesn't remember me." As he responded to Weller's questions, Jimi played along on his guitar to a Dylan record.

If Jimi's reminiscence is true, it contradicted Deering Howe, who one day that fall was walking down Eighth Street in New York City with Jimi when they spied a figure on the other side of the road. "Hey, that's Dylan," Jimi said excitedly. "I've never met him before; let's go talk to him." Jimi darted into traffic, yelling "Hey, Bob" as he approached. Deering followed, though he felt uneasy about Jimi's zeal. "I think Dylan was a little concerned at first, hearing someone shouting his name and racing across the street toward him," Deering recalled. Once Dylan recognized Jimi, he relaxed. Hendrix's introduction was modest enough to be comic. "Bob, uh, I'm a singer, you know, called, uh, Jimi Hendrix and . . ." Dylan said he knew who Jimi was and loved his covers of "All Along the Watchtower" and "Like a Rolling Stone." "I don't know if anyone has done my songs better," Dylan said. Dylan hurried off but left Jimi beaming. "Jimi was on cloud nine," Deering said, "if only because Bob Dylan knew who he was. It seemed very clear to me that the two had never met before."

This chance street meeting would be their only confirmed in-person interaction, but a mutual admiration continued in private. Michael Goldstein, who did PR for both artists, received a phone call from Albert Grossman, Dylan's manager, requesting a private meeting. Grossman passed over a reel-to-reel tape of unreleased Dylan songs that he hoped Jimi might cover. "Bob really likes how Jimi does his songs, and here are a bunch of new ones," Grossman explained. Jimi eventually cut three of those songs as demos, which enraged Michael Jeffrey, who didn't want him doing covers and forgoing writing royalties.

If Jimi continued to hold Dylan in awe, Mick Jagger had the opposite effect on him. Deering Howe was also close with Jagger, and his penthouse apartment was the setting for late-night jam sessions featuring Jimi and Mick. Devon Wilson had managed to add Jagger to her list of groupie conquests, which led to several uncomfortable scenes. "There were some occasions, at four in the morning, when they all showed up at my apartment," Deering recalled. "Devon loved having Mick on her arm in front of Jimi. Most of the tension was on Devon's part; she had glee at rubbing it in." Jimi wrote the song "Dolly Dagger" after watching Devon seduce Jagger. One line in the song, "she drinks her blood from a jagged edge," was a direct reference to an incident in which Mick pricked his finger and Devon, rather than get him a Band-

Aid, said she'd suck the wound clean. If Jagger was successful in wooing Devon, Hendrix won their musical showdowns at Deering's apartment. "They would jam in private in my penthouse," Deering said. "When you saw Jimi play the blues, on an acoustic guitar, he was never better." Jagger was, for once, speechless.

Jimi turned twenty-seven that November 27, and he spent his birthday watching the Stones at Madison Square Garden. Before the show, he chatted up Keith Richards backstage and asked if Richards had heard from Linda Keith—they both chuckled about their once-heated rivalry over her. Jimi borrowed a guitar and began to play. A filmmaker was capturing the scene for a documentary, and—as if to turn the attention away from Jimi—Jagger repeatedly walked in front of the lens. When the concert itself began, Jimi sat onstage behind Richards's amplifier, visible to the audience as well as to the band. Some might have thought an invitation for Jimi to jam with the Stones on his birthday would have been forthcoming, but Jagger offered no such summons. Mick had too much experience watching Jimi play in Deering Howe's apartment, where on many occasions Jimi's talent had silenced everyone in the room. As one who always sought to be the brightest light in a room, Jagger had no desire to be upstaged at his own show.

# KING IN THE GARDEN

---

NEW YORK, NEW YORK
*December 1969–April 1970*

*"There were so many women after him, it was like he was a king
in the garden."*

—Musician BUZZY LINHART on JIMI'S sex appeal

IN THE FALL OF 1969, Jimi leased an apartment at 59 West Twelfth
Street in Greenwich Village. It was the first and only place of his own in
New York, and he hastily set out to decorate it with help from his friend
Colette Mimram. He covered the walls with bedspreads and prayer rugs
and hung a tapestry over his four-poster bed. In the living room, he
arranged three sofas low to the floor and put throw pillows around the
rest of the room. "The place looked like a Moroccan bazaar," recalled
Colette. "You could imagine a hookah sitting in the middle of the floor.
There were African textiles all over the ceiling."

If his apartment looked exotic, Jimi set out to make his own appearance as straight as possible in preparation for his upcoming heroin-
possession trial. He got a haircut and picked out a blue blazer and gray
slacks. And on Sunday, December 7, he flew to Toronto.

The trial began at 10 AM Monday. It was a twelve-person jury trial, and a judge in a white wig presided over the court in the British tradition. The prosecutor first called the officers who had found the drugs and then the lab technicians who had determined the white powder was heroin. The case seemed open-and-shut and the prosecution rested after three hours of testimony.

Jimi's attorneys couldn't very well challenge the existence of the drugs, so their defense was based on the premise that Jimi wasn't aware of the contents of his bag; they argued that fans often gave the band gifts, including drugs. Jimi was the first witness to testify in his own defense. When asked about his background, he repeated the story that he'd left the military after breaking an ankle, but also claimed he'd "had a few exercises in the Philippines and in Germany," which was patently untrue. He described his music as "electronic blues."

From there, Jimi gave a long description of the number of people who were involved in his tours and what a chaotic mess these were. He described all the various items he'd been given by fans over the years, including teddy bears, scarves, and hashish cookies. Jimi also testified that fans had sent him gifts of LSD through the mail. He was extensively quizzed about his own history with drugs: He admitted to having used cocaine "twice," having dropped LSD "five times," having smoked marijuana and hashish recently, but he claimed he had never done heroin or amphetamines. He argued that his drug usage had diminished over the past year and he was smoking less pot: "I feel I have outgrown it," he said. And central to his case, he told a story of how, on his last day in Los Angeles, he'd complained of a headache and a "girl with a yellow top" had given him a vial, which he thought was Bromo-Seltzer. He'd stuck it in his bag and had completely forgotten about it. He'd had no idea it was heroin.

Upon cross-examination, Jimi admitted he'd seen two people use heroin, but that was the extent of his involvement with the drug. The prosecutor thought this defense was ridiculous and asked, "You are charged with a serious offense and your evidence is you don't really know how it got there, or who put it there?" "Yes," Jimi replied.

The next witness was UPI reporter Sharon Lawrence. She testified she was in the hotel room when Jimi complained of feeling ill and recalled a fan passing him something. The prosecutor again indicated his disbelief at this, but Lawrence said that she noticed small details. Then Chas Chandler testified, charming the jury with his Newcastle accent and noting that the band was deluged with gifts from fans. He also said gifts of drugs had been common when he was in the Animals: "The general policy was never to eat cakes that arrived in the dressing room," he said. With that, the case went to the jury, who deliberated for the longest eight hours of Jimi's life. They returned a not-guilty verdict. Jimi said it was "the best Christmas present I could have." He flew back to New York and immediately got extremely stoned on hashish.

Two months after the trial, *Rolling Stone* asked Jimi about his comment in Toronto that he had outgrown pot. He was barely able to stop laughing long enough to answer: "At least, stop it from growing." The reporter asked the same question again. "I don't know," Jimi replied with a huge laugh, "I'm too . . . *wrecked* right now." The quip was typical of his deadpan comic touch, but this particular nugget was too funny even for him to keep a straight face—he fell over laughing.

If the verdict had felt like a reprieve, there were plenty of other pressing issues to worry Jimi. The studio he and Michael Jeffrey were constructing, which would eventually be called Electric Lady Studios, was taking considerably longer than planned and costing more than budgeted—the two had spent $369,000 already and had been forced to borrow another $300,000 from Warner Bros. to finish it. To make financial matters worse, Ed Chalpin had finally settled with Jimi and his U.S. record companies over the PPX contract—the case overseas was still unresolved. The U.S. settlement gave Chalpin a cut of Jimi's three studio albums to that point, plus the entire profit from whatever his next album might be, which Chalpin had arranged to release through Capitol Records. Knowing that his next LP would benefit Chalpin, and not his own coffers, Jimi decided in early December to do a live-performance disc, recorded at four year-end shows scheduled at the Fillmore East.

He then set about forming his next band. He considered a number of players and talked about bringing in Jack Casady from the Jefferson Airplane, Steve Winwood from Traffic, and forming a "supergroup" of sorts. But those arrangements would have been complicated and were abandoned. Jimi was also interested in playing with Buddy Miles, whom he had befriended during the previous year, and he chose to form a trio with Buddy and Billy Cox. "He wanted a black band and a black drummer," Buddy recalled. "He wanted to get together with the roots, going back to what he really loved, which was basically soul, R&B, and blues." Buddy was a multitalented drummer who could also sing, something Jimi had wanted in a bandmate for some time. Jimi decided to call the group Band of Gypsys. The name came from a Mitch Mitchell comment on Jimi's usual backstage entourage ("It's like a band of gypsies"), but ironically Mitch was not part of the group, the first time in three years Jimi had not used the drummer. The name may also have been influenced by stories Jimi heard from his light-skinned mother, who was frequently mistaken as a child for a Gypsy; the choice of the misspelling of *gypsies* was a typical Jimi touch. The group spent ten days rehearsing in late December, and out of those sessions they wrote several new songs.

One of the newer numbers was "Earth Blues," which featured backing vocals from Ronnie Spector of the Ronettes. Spector had stopped by Jimi's apartment that December and found him in bed with five women. "They were lazing around, fighting over who was going to light his cigarette or bring him a drink," she recalled. "It was like he was a sheikh. He was laying there like the king." Once Jimi had a permanent address, he found himself swarmed by young women, even though he had regular girlfriends in both Devon Wilson and Carmen Borrero. His apartment building had a doorman who would call him when girlfriends showed up unannounced. Jimi was rich, talented, and handsome, and there were many who wanted to have a real relationship with him, but more often he found himself attracting groupies, at least partially on the reputation of his plaster cast. To them, he was simply a sexual conquest, as they were to him, though for Jimi, the numbers had become meaningless. "There were so many women after him, it was like he was a king in the garden," recalled Buzzy Linhart. "He was being treated like an object, though. There wasn't much romance to it." Given all the loss he had known as a child, it is also possible that he was afraid to get too close to anyone for fear of being abandoned again. Quick and almost anonymous sexual relationships represented no emotional investment, and therefore little risk of getting hurt.

Ronnie Spector was interested only in a professional relationship with Jimi, though he openly flirted with her, even when he was surrounded by a bevy of other women. In the studio, Ronnie found Jimi to be a greater perfectionist than Phil Spector, insisting on dozens of takes even after she thought a song had been nailed. When the session ended, Ronnie gave Jimi and his usual entourage of young women a ride home. The next morning, she answered her door and found Jimi leaning against her doorjamb with a coy grin on his face. He was alone. His excuse for stopping by was that he'd left the master tapes in her car; Spector suspected that his real intention was to bed her. Married at the time, she smiled, thanked him for the session, found his tape, and sent him on his way. "He was like a black Hugh Hefner," Spector said. Few women could resist Jimi's sly seductive technique, but Spector was no fresh-scrubbed ingenue.

✂☙❧

CARMEN BORRERO WAS Jimi's choice of date for Christmas 1969, which he spent at Deering Howe's penthouse apartment atop the Hotel Navarro. It was a setting out of the pages of *Town & Country:* The ten-room apartment had two living rooms, giant windows facing Central Park, and an oversize Christmas tree that framed the fabulous view. When Jimi and Carmen arrived, a light snowfall had begun. Jimi was dressed in a lizard-skin jacket and festive red velvet pants. They ate a fine meal and drank Dom Pérignon out of crystal flutes. Jimi remarked that it was the best Christmas he had ever spent—it was quite a contrast to those spent as a youth in poverty.

For the holiday, Jimi gave Carmen a pair of diamond earrings and a diamond ring. The ring was meant as an engagement ring, but Borrero said they never seriously talked about marriage. "That marriage would have been with three people: Jimi, Devon, and I." Devon Wilson remained the biggest impediment to anyone seeking a relationship with Jimi. "Devon had been a junkie for a long time by then," Carmen said. Through Devon, Jimi began snorting heroin: "He started playing with that through the nose," Borrero said. Jimi's true drug history, of course, was very different from what he admitted to in the Toronto courtroom. "He liked creative drugs, but he couldn't stand heroin," Colette recalled. "He tried it, but it was not what he wanted to do."

Alcohol, however, was always the most dangerous drug for Jimi, and fueled another incident of violence between him and Carmen. After drinking whiskey, he went into another jealous rage. "He was going to throw me from a window," she said. Instead, for the second time in their relationship, Jimi hit her with a bottle, which caused her to be taken to the emergency room. "I had to get Miles Davis's girlfriend to come and take me. I didn't want to get Jimi arrested," Carmen said.

Though Carmen's relationship with Jimi was tumultuous, there were moments of comedy. Once, while very stoned, Carmen used an Afro pick to straighten Jimi's hair. Accidentally, the joint she was smoking set his hair on fire. Jimi screamed and began to run around the room, before sticking his hair under a water spigot. When the fire was extinguished, clumps of his hair began to fall out. Borrero had to give him a haircut to even it out. "He was obsessed with his hair," she said. "He loved his little curls."

It was at the hairdresser where Jimi first met legendary jazz musician Miles Davis. Jimi had his hair done by James Finney and became one of his first showcase clients. "Finney introduced the 'Blowout' through Jimi," Taharqa Aleem recalled. "Prior to that, it had been 'the Afro,' and before that 'the Conk.'" Miles liked Jimi's hair and also began to go to Finney. The two musicians would also occasionally double-date with their girlfriends. One night, the two couples traveled uptown to Small's Paradise. With Miles in tow, Jimi finally got the reception he had always wanted there. "They put us in a table in the corner," Carmen recalled, "and even put a small curtain around us so we could smoke a joint. They sent over wine and played Jimi's music over the sound system."

Carmen described the relationship between Miles and Jimi as resembling that of a father and son, but it was also clear each admired the other's work. The Aleems once questioned Miles on what he heard in Jimi's music. "It's that goddamned motherfucking 'Machine Gun,'" Miles said, referring to the song that Jimi recorded with the Band of Gypsys. Taharqa commented that he heard similar styles in Miles's own music. "It ain't what you hear," Miles replied. "It's what you *bring* from the subjective to the objective. It ain't about what you hear." Inspired by his friendship with Miles, Jimi began to buy jazz albums, though his musical taste was so eclectic he never limited himself to just one genre at a time. He would frequently go into Colony Records late at night and buy up entire bins of albums by rock, jazz, and classical greats.

Jimi had expressed a desire to record with Miles, and a session was planned pairing them. Jimi's usual approach was to jam first and worry about contracts, record labels, and payments later. Davis, however, was frustrated by how little money he was making in jazz and jealous of how much Jimi was earning. The day before the session, he called Jimi's manager and demanded payment in advance. Miles told Mike Jeffrey he wanted fifty thousand dollars up front. Tony Williams, who Jimi planned to use for a drummer, made an equally large request. Jeffrey refused the outrageous demands and the session never occurred. Prior to the dispute over money, however, Jimi was so certain the session was going to take place that he made efforts to find a superstar bass player. His first choice was Paul McCartney. He went so far as to send McCartney a telegram asking him to play with the group, but that idea, like many others Jimi had, never came to fruition.

There was, however, at least one "summit" between Jimi and Miles, as witnessed by singer Terry Reid. Reid had spent the day with Jimi at his apartment; at one point, Jimi went into the bedroom, but first told Reid a friend was due and to let him in. The doorbell rang and Reid peered through the peephole: "It was like a sci-fi movie because there was this purple person with these shades around his head, and he's standing about an inch in front of the peephole," Reid remembered. "He's standing close enough that all you can see in the viewfinder is his head. I had to do a double take because there is no other human being who looked like that on the whole bloody planet." It was Miles.

Reid opened the door and greeted Miles with a warm smile; in return, he got a scowl. "I knew he hated white people," Reid remembered, "so I tried as hard as I could to be welcoming with my British charm." Miles was dressed in a black leather trench coat. "Come on in," Reid declared with a welcoming gesture.

Miles did not move. "Is Jimi here?" he growled.

"Yeah," Reid said. "He's in the other room, and he said for you to come in." Miles still did not move. "It's okay," Reid answered. "I'm Terry, I'm a *friend*." Miles *still* did not move. Instead of entering, he grabbed the door handle and shut himself out. "It was like a total mind-fuck," Reid recalled. "I looked into the peephole again, and he was standing in the hallway." Reid opened the door once more and urged Miles to enter.

Miles remained motionless. "I want *fucking* Jimi Hendrix to open Jimi Hendrix's *fucking* door," he said.

Reid went and fetched Jimi, who had been in the other room tuning his guitar. "Miles Davis is at the door," Reid said.

"Did you let him in?" Jimi asked.

"I tried to, but he shut the door in my face. He won't come in unless you answer the door."

"Yeah, he's like that," Jimi said with a laugh. Apparently, Miles had played this game on other occasions. Jimi went and opened the door. Miles didn't say a word as he entered, and he and Hendrix retreated to the bedroom. Reid, still situated in the living room, didn't know whether they were doing drugs together—always a possibility—or something else. But his patience was rewarded when he heard the sounds of Miles's muted trumpet drifting out from under the door accompanied by Hendrix's unamplified guitar. "It was truly beautiful,"

Reid recalled. "It was tasteful playing, nothing showy, or over the top. In the jazz context, Jimi was still pushing the limits, and all those jazz guys respected him like they respected no one else in rock."

⤷⤶

MILES DAVIS ATTENDED one of the Band of Gypsys' four New Year's shows at the Fillmore East. With the gospel choir Voices of East Harlem opening, the performances represented a musical departure for Jimi: He played a number of new blues-based songs, reflecting his desire to move away from rock. The group also represented the first time since Curtis Knight and the Squires that Jimi played in an all-black band. They performed Jimi's material, but also some of Buddy's, including the hit "Them Changes," which Buddy sang. The reviews of the show were mixed. The *New York Times* called the first night "mediocre." Mike Jahn wrote, "[Jimi] seems to be more concerned with creating an environment of intense sound and personal fury than he is with performing a particular composition." Chris Albertson in *Downbeat* was kinder: "Hendrix is finding where he should be at, and he might well emerge as the greatest of the new blues guitarists." But what probably made the biggest impression on Jimi was an occurrence he hadn't witnessed for some time: Many in the sold-out crowd walked out during the middle of the show.

After the first set on New Year's Day, even Bill Graham felt compelled to offer a negative review when Jimi came to his office and asked for an opinion. Jimi became angry and cursed Graham, but he later asked if the impresario was staying for the second show. Graham said he was, and that show was remarkably improved. "Aside from Otis Redding," he wrote in *Bill Graham Presents,* "there will never be anything like that [second] show. The man took maybe three steps one way or the other during the whole set. He just played. And he just sang. He moved his body but it was always in time to the music. He was Fred Astaire. Not Harpo Marx. There was grace but *no* bullshit." Halfway through the set, Jimi went backstage and taunted Graham: "Good enough for you, *Jack*?" Graham said it was great. Jimi went back onstage and began "Wild Thing," complete with all the gimmicks Graham had criticized. "All the shtick," Graham wrote. "The *Fire. Throwing. Kicking. Humping. Grinding*. But what he had given them before, that was the real thing."

After the second show ended at 3 AM, Jimi did a short interview with Al Aronowitz of the *New York Post*. When asked the reason for the new band, Jimi said, "I want to bring it down to earth. I want to get back to the blues, because that's what I am." He said he planned to have Buddy do most of the singing. "I'd rather just play," he said. "In England, they made me sing, but Buddy has the right voice, he's going to do the singing from now." Buddy truly had a great blues voice, yet fans wanted to hear Jimi, not the drummer.

Four weeks later, the Band of Gypsys had their next, and last, performance. They were part of the twelve-act "Winter Festival for Peace" benefit at Madison Square Garden. Choosing to appear at the benefit was the most overt protest against the Vietnam War Jimi ever made, though the concert did not go as planned. In what would become a recurrent problem for him, the show ran exceedingly late and the Gypsys did not go onstage until 3 AM when Jimi was in no shape to play. After a disastrous attempt at "Who Knows," a young woman yelled out a request for "Foxy Lady." " 'Foxy Lady' is sitting over there," Jimi yelled back, in a variant of his familiar stage patter, "in the yellow underwear, stained and dirty, with blood." In the middle of the second song, he stopped playing and said into the microphone, "That's what happens when Earth fucks with Space. Never forget that." He then sat down onstage in front of his amps, silent. No audience had ever witnessed a soundless Jimi, and it was disturbing both to the fans and to other musicians who were present. "It was scary," recalled Johnny Winter. "He had to be led offstage." Buddy Miles said the reason Jimi became sick was that manager Michael Jeffrey had given him too much LSD, sabotaging the concert in order to derail the band. "He gave Jimi Hendrix two tablets of Owsley Purple," Buddy said. "I witnessed it and so did my sister." Others told a different story: Johnny Winter recalled that Jimi was already wasted when he had arrived at the hall, and Jimi himself told friends it was Devon Wilson who had spiked his drink. There were a number of incidents that year when Devon dosed Jimi unbeknownst to him; in their strange relationship, control was an even more powerful force than narcotics.

A few days later, Jeffrey fired Buddy, and the Band of Gypsys were no more. "Buddy was forced out," Billy Cox observed, "and I think they wanted to put me out, too." Less confrontational than Buddy, Billy left town and went back to Nashville.

In early February, Jeffrey announced that the original Experience was re-forming and Noel and Mitch were brought over to America for interviews with Jimi. But soon after the articles ran and tickets went on sale for a massive "Experience reunion tour," Jimi decided he didn't want Noel in the band. He phoned Billy Cox and asked him to join again. In his typical nonconfrontational manner, Jimi failed to tell Noel he was out of the group, leaving it to Jeffrey's office. By way of consolation, Jimi played on a solo album Noel was putting together, but it was a small sacrifice—after that session, the two would never play together again.

∽᠀᠐

THE SPRING 1970 tour started April 25 at the Forum in Los Angeles. The show, like many that year, was billed as "The Experience," though small type in the newspaper ad listed Billy Cox and Mitch Mitchell as the band. Cox said Jimi did briefly consider continuing with the name Band of Gypsys. "The next thing you know we were calling it 'the Jimi Hendrix Experience with Billy Cox, a new guy,'" Cox recalled. For his part, Mitch Mitchell was simply happy to be back playing with Jimi once again.

Under any name, the tour drew Jimi some of the best reviews of his career. "Hendrix is a powerhouse of sex and sound," wrote Robert Hilburn in the *Los Angeles Times* of the opening show. Jimi played a few old hits, but over half of the songs were unreleased. Two of them—"Machine Gun" and "Message to Love"—were from the live *Band of Gypsys* album that had come out the day before. "The newer material generated less enthusiasm," Hilburn noted, a pattern that would recur throughout the tour. Jimi also cut back on his guitar gimmicks, which disappointed some in the crowd but left him feeling more energized about his own playing. Though a few critics missed Noel, Mitch was playing better than ever and his jazz-influenced style fit well with the new material. "Mitch was just one bitch of a drummer," said Bob Levine of Jimi's management. "With his ability to improvise, he was the perfect drummer for Jimi."

Though Buddy Miles had been axed from the Band of Gypsys, he was still invited on several tour dates as the opening act, and he continued to have a friendship with Jimi. But even more notable was the third band on the bill in L.A.: Ballin' Jack, Jimi's handpicked selection. The group included Luther Rabb and Ronnie Hammon, both from Seattle. Luther had been a member of Jimi's very first band, the Velvetones. Jimi had often talked about having his old cohorts join him on the road, though the four dates Ballin' Jack played were the first and only time he got this wish. He was generous to his old friends: They were well paid and given a full, rather than abbreviated, set. "Jimi would literally give you the shirt off his back," Hammon recalled. "One night, he was coming offstage, and I said, 'Nice shirt.' He ripped it off and handed it to me." He gave Luther a festive coat he'd bought in London because he thought Luther looked better in it than he did.

Luther, who had known Jimi since junior high, was concerned by what he saw as Jimi's drug problem only a year after the heroin bust in Toronto. "He was over the line," Luther recalled. "He was aware that it was hurting him. He was making efforts, but somehow, through management or someone, people were always funneling drugs to him." Whether it was uppers, downers, cocaine, or heroin, there always seemed to be drugs in Jimi's dressing room. Luther was one of the few around him who addressed the point directly—most were too afraid. "He said he was going to quit just to shut me up," Luther said. Instead, not long after their confrontation, Ballin' Jack was moved to a different hotel than the one Jimi was in.

Despite those issues, touring with his Seattle friends brought Jimi a levity he rarely felt on the road, and Ballin' Jack's dressing room became his sanctuary. Before a show, he would smoke marijuana, and prior to walking onstage, he'd exhale in Ronnie Hammon's face, asking "Does it smell like wolf pussy?" If Hammon told him his breath was bad, Jimi would chew gum. "He chewed a lot of gum," Hammon said.

Yet, perhaps, the greatest relief Jimi found with his old friends was musical. As the tour wore on, he felt compelled to play more of his hits. Jimi once told Luther that he wore outrageous stage clothes because he wanted crowds to come back the next time he passed through town, if only to see what he was wearing. "He hated singing those hits," said Luther, "but he felt he had to. He still had an 'act,' much of it was rooted in 'The Show,' and he felt he had to do things like play behind his back because that's why people came to see him." To help stomach "The Show," Jimi visited the Ballin' Jack dressing room, where they'd play "It's Alright," "Further On Up the Road," and other standards. "He'd call that private show he did with us 'The Seattle Special,'" Luther said. "The people in the audience didn't get to hear it, but it was the best stuff he would do all night."

Only a week into the tour, Jimi was already struggling with the grind, and in Madison, Wisconsin, he came onstage drunk. In a slurred voice, he suggested that the Vietnam War might be the end of America: "Next thing you know every one of us will be completely wiped out because of some shit that old people said." It was less a statement of his political views—which shifted depending on whom he was talking to—and more a reflection of an increasing paranoia. Onstage, he joked that he needed a joint and explained that "Room Full of Mirrors" was about "when you get so high that all you can see is you, your reflections here and there." In two intros that night, he mentioned Christ. Juma Sultan, of the Woodstock band, recalled that by 1969, Jimi was increasingly reading the Bible: "He kept it open in his house, and he was reading it closely, probably for the first time in his life." Drugs, religion, and women were just a few of the many things Jimi grasped at, searching for a foundation in a life that was ever more out of control.

In Madison, Jimi had taken too much of something in addition to the alcohol, and his stage rap took on a tone of desperation. Before "Ezy Ryder," he said the song was inspired by the movie, but his rambling rap also touched on mortality, which had become an increasingly frequent theme for him since his trip to the Moroccan tarot-card reader: "I was trying to help us, but it just blew up at the end, you know what I mean? And that was only one-third of our life, you know, and we have to get blown-up, and then we go on to something better, right? Definitely. If you don't think that, you might as well die now. Oh, Lord, I'm dying."

# MAGIC BOY

BERKELEY, CALIFORNIA
*May 1970–July 1970*

*"Here's a story . . . about a cat . . . he goes on the road to be a
voodoo child, and comes back to be a magic boy."*
—Jimi's introduction to "Hear My Train A Comin' "

ON MAY 30, 1970, the band arrived in Berkeley, California, for two shows at the Community Theater. The last time Jimi had spent any extended time in Berkeley was back when he was a three-year-old living with Mrs. Champ; it was also the city where he first met his father. If he felt any nostalgia, he didn't speak of it, and the Berkeley of 1970 was a far cry from the place he had experienced as a toddler. The campus of the University of California was a battleground for protests, and Governor Ronald Reagan had called out two thousand National Guard troops to fight thirty thousand students; the resulting riots caused 128 injuries and one death. Reagan's infamous response to hearing about the protests was, "If there has to be a bloodbath, let's get it over with." Another bloodbath had occurred at the nearby Altamont racetrack a few months earlier during a Rolling Stones concert when the Hell's Angels murdered a man. Jimi told journalist Keith Altham that Altamont made him feel as if "the whole of America is going to pot." With the increased racial tension, violence, and divisiveness caused by the Vietnam War, Jimi told friends he was considering moving back to London.

Jimi's Berkeley concerts were themselves plagued by a number of ugly incidents. Most of his shows on the 1970 tour were marred by clashes with protesters, who either demanded that admission be free or, as in Berkeley, tried to break into the venue when they were denied entry. Michael Jeffrey had hired a film crew to document the Berkeley concerts, and they shot footage of protesters attempting to break through the roof of the theater and throwing rocks at attendees. The filmmakers also captured a more comical scene down the street, where another group was boycotting a theater showing *Woodstock,* arguing that $3.50 was too high a price for a movie ticket and that "all music should be free."

Arriving in a stretch limousine with Devon Wilson and Colette Mimram, Jimi saw none of this as he entered through the back door. He had canceled shows the previous week because of the flu, and in Berkeley he looked ashen, with glazed eyes. But if the star appeared unwell, his two performances were extraordinary, and the film of the night represents some of the best Hendrix concert footage. It was a memorable show before it even began: During the sound check, Jimi played a seven-minute version of Carl Perkins's "Blue Suede Shoes," giving the empty seats a powerful reading of a song he had turned into a straight-ahead blues.

The first show saw Jimi transform another classic, Chuck Berry's "Johnny B. Goode," into a quick-tempo rave. In his usual crowd-pleasing pandering, Jimi played part of the solo with his teeth. No theatrics were needed for "Hear My Train A Comin'," which he introduced as being "about a cat running around town and his old lady, she don't want him around. And a whole lot of people from across the tracks are putting him down. And nobody don't want to face up to it, but the cat has *something,* only everybody's against him because the cat might be a little bit different. So he goes on the road to be a voodoo child, and comes back to be a magic boy. Right now he's waiting down at the train station, waiting for a train to come in." The introduction was, in essence, a recounting of Jimi's life story.

One of Jimi's unique gifts as a guitar player was an ability to play the lead and at the same time answer this with the part usually handled by a secondary rhythm guitarist. By using the wah-wah pedal, the fuzz-face effects box, extensive feedback, and sustain, he was able to create the illusion of additional guitars where there were none; he could also use his thumb to play echo-like riffs. He displayed all these skills on "Hear My Train A Comin'," creating a call-and-response between his own riffs and those put down by Cox and Mitchell. As with all his long improvisations, the version he played that night was unique, and only players with the deep intuitive skill of Cox and Mitchell could have followed him through the winding route of the song, which ended more than twelve minutes after it began. It was the kind of rousing power-house anthem that most performers would use to close a show—for Jimi, it was just the third song of a twelve-number set.

The night's second show was even better. An eleven-song set featured two newer numbers, "Straight Ahead" and "Hey Baby (Land of the New Rising Sun)," but also included fiery versions of chestnuts like "Voodoo Child" and "Hey Joe." Before "Machine Gun," Jimi gave a detailed introduction: "I'd like to dedicate this to all the soldiers fighting in Berkeley, you know what soldiers I'm talking about. And to the soldiers fighting in Vietnam, too." Before he played "The Star Spangled Banner," he said, "This is for everybody together, the American anthem the way it really is in the air." He called "Voodoo Child" "*our* anthem," and dedicated it to the People's Park and especially the Black Panthers. Nearby Oakland was the national headquarters for the Panthers, and Jimi's dedication was the strongest public statement he ever made in support of the organization.

Carlos Santana saw the Berkeley shows and thought they were artistic achievements on the level of John Coltrane: "Very few people play fast and deep," Santana recalled. "Most play fast and shallow. But Coltrane played fast and deep, so did Charlie Parker, and so did Jimi."

Backstage, Santana chatted with Jimi, but their conversation was less than intimate because of the presence of a bevy of groupies. "He was around with those ladies," Santana said. "I used to call them 'monitors' because they would go to bed with everybody, and tell you everything about everybody else."

The second Berkeley show was also notable for Jimi's costume, a blue dragonfly with fabric resembling wings hanging from his arms. It was designed by Emily "Rainbow" Touraine, who had begun sewing elaborate stage clothes for him. "He and I were about the same size," she recalled. "He had a size-28 waist so he could wear my clothes." Only Elvis Presley was wearing such outrageous stage clothes at the time, but while Elvis's jumpsuits were covered with sequins and were created to hide his weight, Jimi's were elflike, with African and Native American elements. His look by 1970 was so different from his 1967 image that it seemed a complete re-creation of his person: His pants were now always velvet tights or blue jeans; his witch hat had given way to headbands; and the antique military jacket had been replaced by kimono-like shirts and brightly colored scarves.

Emily Touraine was primarily a painter and her Los Angeles home was a working artist's studio. Jimi occasionally stayed at her house to escape the increasing chaos that followed him. "It was a zoo around him," she observed. When he visited, Jimi frequently used her supplies to create his own art, making hundreds of drawings and paintings. "He was very, very good," she said. Jimi told Touraine that if he hadn't made it in music, he would have tried to become a commercial artist.

∽∾∾

THE BERKELEY SHOWS were examples of what the band called "fly-outs," weekend concerts that required them to fly out at the last minute. Jimi spent most of the spring and summer of 1970 in the studio in what had become a Sisyphean effort to complete a new album. Back in December 1969, he was already telling reporters he had enough songs for another two albums, though he couldn't decide what to release and when. By the next summer, he had enough material for four albums, but still wasn't ready to let anything out, and given his obsessive nature, he spent entire days working on one overdub. "It was an expensive way of doing it," observed engineer Eddie Kramer, "but considering all the stuff that was happening, it seemed to be the only way." Few of Jimi's sessions began with any set plan, and he'd make use of players he'd met in a club earlier in the evening. In one case, he invited a cabdriver in for a session after the driver mentioned he played congas.

Things became slightly easier when his studio, Electric Lady, was near completion. Since Jimi and Michael Jeffrey owned the facility, costs were reduced. "He was very proud of that studio," Eddie Kramer recalled. "Being a black man of his stature, making a lot of money, and owning your own studio in New York City, that was the pinnacle of success for him. He had suffered a lot of slings and arrows, but here he was on top." There had been a time when Jimi was willing to sign away his rights simply to get inside a studio; now he owned the best facility in New York City. The studio became his home away from home, but it was also a contributing factor in his perfectionism. In a July 1 session, he cut nineteen different takes of "Dolly Dagger" before achieving a master. "He loved that studio, and he spent night after night there," recalled Deering Howe. "But he'd get hung up on a song, and one eight-bar thing would take three days to fuck with."

By the middle of June, Jimi had begun to whittle down the dozens of songs into a rough form for his next album. He considered several titles, including *First Rays of the New Rising Sun,* but he never settled on a final title or track list. He and Jeffrey were at odds over what length the release should be; Jeffrey said a single album would sell better than a double, while Jimi suggested it be a triple set titled *People, Hell, and Angels.* The closest Jimi came to a finished album was a list he wrote in June called "Songs for LP, *Strate Ahead,*" which included "Room Full of Mirrors," "Ezy Ryder," "Angel," "Cherokee Mist," "Dolly Dagger," and twenty others.

That summer the tour-that-never-seemed-to-end took Jimi to Dallas, Houston, Boston, and a few other stops. The only show that didn't require a "fly-out" was a July 17 date at Randalls Island in New York City, part of the New York Pop Festival. A number of radical groups—including the Yippies, the Young Lords, the Black Panthers, and the White Panthers—demanded that all proceeds be turned over or they would riot. Promoters made a donation to those groups, but thousands of protesters snuck in without paying anyway. Jimi didn't go on until 4 AM, and as he played, the public address system kept picking up radio transmissions. The malfunctions put Jimi in a foul mood, and he snapped at the crowd several times. When he dedicated "Voodoo Child" to Devon, Colette, Deering, and a few others, the crowd booed. "Fuck off," Jimi replied. "These are my friends."

The Randalls Island concert would be the last time Jimi ever appeared on a stage in New York City. He had starved in New York, he had struggled for acceptance uptown, and he had ultimately been discovered in the Village. In time, he had become one of the most successful musicians ever identified with the city. The concert was hardly a fitting farewell, and as the final song ended, the radio station interference drowned out Jimi's guitar. His last words to a New York crowd were ones of anger: "Fuck you, and good night."

ᔎᔐᔎ

TEN DAYS LATER, Jimi was flying west again for a show in Seattle. The tour had originally skipped the Northwest, but Jeffrey had arranged a last-minute booking, which Jimi agreed to, thinking it would help them keep up with their staggering bills. Jimi was a superstar worldwide, but his strongest markets remained New York, Los Angeles, London, Europe, and his hometown Seattle. The show was scheduled for Sick's Stadium, a twenty-six-thousand-seat ballpark in the Rainier Valley that had been the home of the Seattle Pilots before Bud Selig moved the team to Milwaukee in the spring of 1970. It was the first and only time that Jimi, as a star, performed in his old neighborhood. He had walked by Sick's Stadium countless times in his youth, perhaps fantasizing that one day he'd be the attraction inside—now he was.

Jimi took a morning flight to Seattle on Sunday, July 26. Though his stadium concert was scheduled to start at 2:30 PM, he wouldn't go on until the evening because of two opening acts and extraordinarily long set breaks. He had hoped to get a few hours of sleep in the afternoon, but that proved impossible when his family converged. "He was tied up from minute one," recalled promoter Dan Fiala. Jimi had initially asked that his family not be told his arrival time. "They'd be calling our office ten times a day saying they were going to pick him up," observed Fiala. "Meanwhile, management was telling us, 'We've got to isolate him because they are driving him nuts.'" Jimi appeared torn during each of his Seattle visits: While he enjoyed seeing his family, his visits only reinforced how different a world he now lived in. In Seattle, he was "Buster Hendrix," who still deferred to his father; everywhere else he was a self-made man, and a superstar.

Fiala had worked on other Experience shows but had never seen Jimi as exhausted as he appeared that day. Jimi complained he had been up all night. "Everyone thought it was drugs," Fiala observed, "but he was really beat; he was even beat-up looking. He had been working way too hard, going in the studio when he wasn't touring, and it was really getting him." Jimi repeated the tale of his exhaustion to several people, who urged him to take some time off. He was scheduled to fly to Hawaii the day after the Seattle show, but rather than a vacation, the trip was for a concert and to film a movie. Just a couple of days before, Jimi told a San Diego reporter, "I was like a slave, man. It was all work. In the beginning it was fun, and now it's time to get back to having it fun again. I'm retiring now. It's going to be pleasure *first*. No more work." The day after that interview, he was back on tour again.

Jimi spent most of the afternoon at Al's house, visiting with the many neighbors and relations who had come by. He had a few drinks, which soured his mood, and at one point he got into an argument with Al, which greatly upset both of them. Jimi also felt somewhat sad because his brother Leon had to miss his visit: Leon was in jail for larceny at the time, a turn of events that deeply disturbed Jimi. His spirits were boosted slightly later in the day when he learned that his cousin Eddy

Hall—Aunt Delores's youngest son—had taken up the guitar. Delores brought fifteen-year-old Eddy by, and his playing impressed Jimi. "Jimi asked my mom if he could take me on the road with him," Eddy recalled. Delores turned down the offer; though she loved Jimi dearly, she was afraid he would be a bad influence on her son.

At one point in the afternoon, there was an unexpected reminder of the Hendrix family's fractured history when an eighteen-year-old woman who lived down the street came by and asked for Jimi's autograph: She said she was his sister. Jimi went out and discovered it was Pamela Hendrix, who had been adopted by a family that didn't live far from Al. Jimi had not seen Pamela for almost seventeen years. He gave her an autograph and a hug. Perhaps the visit with his lost sister put him in a reflective mood, as not long after it he called up his old "Auntie" Dorothy Harding and invited her family to his show, arranging for a limousine to pick them up. One of the Hardings was sick with pneumonia and couldn't attend, so Jimi called her several times that day to inquire about her health.

Sometime that day, Jimi also sneaked away long enough to dial one number he still knew by heart: It was to his high school sweetheart Betty Jean Morgan. "It had been years since I'd heard from him," Betty Jean recalled. It had been, in fact, eight years; Jimi's last conversation with Betty Jean had occured when he'd gotten out of the army in 1962 and called off their engagement. Betty Jean had since married, but had split with her husband and was living back with her parents. A friend had informed Jimi that she was single. As for his motivation for the call, he never made it clear. Betty Jean was not a hipster, and though she knew he was a star, she hadn't followed his career. He had headlined Woodstock, played the Royal Albert Hall, had even met the Beatles; she had gotten married out of high school and never left Seattle. They shared almost nothing except a past history: walks home from school, hands held on a porch, kisses behind a tree. She was the one girl he loved so much he named his first guitar after her and had painted her name on it—now he hardly knew what to say to her. She asked if he stayed in touch with his schoolyard pals. He told her that Pernell

Alexander was around, but Jimmy Williams and Terry Johnson were both in Vietnam. She said she hoped they came back safe, a sentiment he echoed. And with that they ran out of things to talk about. "It was a short conversation," she recalled. Jimi ended the phone call telling her that on his next visit, he'd buy her the hamburger he'd promised her years before when he was destitute.

He then headed to Sick's Stadium, where an unseasonable downpour threatened to cause the cancellation of the concert. When Jimi came onstage at 7:15 PM, the rain briefly let up. Some of the equipment wasn't grounded, which was a concern to the promoters, who feared that their headliner might be electrocuted, but Jimi insisted on going on nonetheless. He began the show with what had become his standard introduction over the last two years, but the words had an added poignancy in his hometown: "I want you to forget about yesterday and tomorrow, and just make our own little world right here." Addressing the soggy crowd, he said, "You don't sound very happy, you don't look very happy, but we'll see if we can paint some faces around here." With that, the band launched into "Fire."

As the song ended, a pillow was thrown onstage. When Janis Joplin had played Sick's Stadium three weeks earlier, this same pillow was tossed onstage; Joplin autographed it and threw it back. Jimi knew nothing of this, but the idea of an object being hurled onstage upset him. "Oh, please don't throw anything up here," he said. "Please don't do that, because I feel like getting on somebody's head anyway." It was a rare acknowledgment of his foul mood, and it got worse: "Fuck you, whoever put up the pillow." He kicked the pillow off the stage and raised his middle finger to a crowd that included many of his friends and relations. He acknowledged that he'd had a few drinks of Scotch. During "Message to Love," he left the stage without explanation, forcing Mitch to improvise a drum solo on a song that had never before been given an extended instrumental break. Jimi returned two minutes later and the show continued.

The rain started again, and during "Purple Haze," Jimi switched the lyrics: "'Scuse me while I fuck the sky," he sang. After he played

"Red House," a song inspired by Betty Jean Morgan, he said, "The rain makes me feel like that." He ended the show with "Foxy Lady," one of only two times in 1970 he used that hit for the show closer. And then, like Elvis Presley—whom Jimi had seen play in this same stadium back in 1957—he left without an encore.

After the concert, Jimi headed to his father's house, where he entertained the throngs of friends and neighbors who had gathered and tried to forget about what he thought had been a horrible show. He had played four concerts in Seattle as a star, and not one had lived up to his expectations, which had probably been impossible to meet. He wanted more than anything to show his hometown how good he'd become, but that goal forever eluded him, or so he complained.

Jimi looked even more exhausted than usual after the concert, but he still managed to find time for an extended conversation with Freddie Mae Gautier. Gautier was another link with the past—her mother had cared for Jimi when he was an infant. She described Jimi as wistful and sad during their visit, and said it was "as if he were under a spell." Gautier had known Jimi his entire life, and she knew all the important characters in his early life. That night, he wanted to hear about his youth. Despite his argument that day with Al, Jimi spoke warmly of his father, saying he had come to understand the difficult life that Al had endured. "His dad had struggled to raise him and Leon," Gautier would later recall, "and Al would be up all night sometimes working. As Jimi got older, he realized how much his dad had given up for him and Leon."

At about midnight, Jimi decided to go out on the town with three young women: his cousin Dee Hall (Delores's daughter), Alice Harding (Dorothy's daughter), and Marsha Jinka (one of his new stepsisters). Jimi had grown up around Dee and Alice; they had turned into beautiful women, and he was pleased to be in their company. Dee hadn't seen him play before, and though she was more a jazz than a rock fan, that evening's show had impressed her. She asked Jimi if he had explored jazz much and he replied that he was tinkering with it. "He said he was ready to make some big changes in his life, and that his music would be changing, too," Dee recalled. Apart from his friendship with

Miles Davis, Jimi had discussed making an album with arranger Gil Evans. No recordings had yet taken place, but he had a meeting set with Evans for the end of September; it was one of many projects Jimi was discussing for that fall. He had also written a screenplay and had told friends he wanted to go back to school to learn how to compose music. None of this surprised Dee Hall—all his Seattle relations knew Jimi had forever been a dreamer.

At one point in the evening, Jimi pulled a bullet out of his pocket; the bullet twisted open and inside were several hits of LSD. "He called it Purple Haze," said Dee. Tripping on acid, Jimi then took the women on a circuit that mirrored his last trip to Seattle, when he had searched for his past, directing them to Garfield High School and to every house he'd ever lived in. At one point, they drove by a club where Jimi had once tried to get a job; he mentioned the names of the people who hadn't let him join their bands. Dee had known Jimi her entire life and she had never seen him so nostalgic, but she was also surprised at the strong resolve he showed toward the painful parts of his past. "They really treated you like dirt; they would laugh at you," she told him. Jimi's response startled her: "Oh, sometimes you have to go through that," he said without any hint of acrimony. They stopped by the Yesler Terrace Neighborhood House, which had been one of the first places he ever performed in public. The Neighborhood House was just two blocks away from Harborview Hospital, so they drove by there, too; Jimi had been born in the building, and his mother had died in it. Dee asked Jimi if he had seen his brother Joe. "Not for years," he said, "but I sure would like to." He even insisted they drive by the detention center where he had spent several days after getting arrested in a stolen car. He got out of the car and walked around the facility. "It was like he was trying to come to terms with his past," Dee recalled.

They drove for hours, going to all corners of Seattle. "He wanted to look at everything, every place," Alice Harding remembered. It would be Jimi's second night in a row without sleep, and the women suggested he go home and rest, but he refused. They drove by Betty Jean Morgan's house, though they didn't go in. They even drove around

Lake Washington on back roads, which took almost two hours. When they reached the south part of the lake, near Renton, Jimi insisted they visit his mother's grave—he had never seen it but knew the graveyard was in the Renton Highlands. "We drove around for an hour or so, looking for it," Dee Hall said. "It was dark, and it was a rural area without streetlights." They searched and searched but never found the graveyard, and finally drove back to Seattle.

At one point, back in Seattle, the car passed a house on Yesler Way where Jimi had lived with Al and Leon—the house was now vacant and run-down. Jimi was saddened by the home's condition, as some of the few carefree moments of his childhood had taken place there. A light rain was falling, and the women stayed in the car while Jimi approached the darkened structure alone. At the window to the room he had once slept in—where he had played countless hours of air guitar with a broomstick—he put his hands around his eyes, pressed his face against the glass, and peered into the shadows, as if he were searching for something he had lost.

# WILD BLUE ANGEL

MAUI, HAWAII

*July 1970–August 1970*

*"Call [me] the blue wild angel. The wild blue angel."*
—JIMI telling the emcee how to introduce him on the Isle of Wight, August 30, 1970

JIMI HENDRIX LEFT Seattle for Hawaii and arrived on Maui on July 28 for the filming of *Rainbow Bridge*. The movie was the brainstorm of director Chuck Wein, whose initial idea had been to collect renowned figures in several fields—surfing, yoga, art, and music—and film their interactions. Wein had previously made three films with Andy Warhol's Factory and had been the boyfriend of Edie Sedgwick. If the idea of gathering surfers, mystics, seers, and hippies along with Jimi Hendrix looked brilliant on paper, the additional element of psychedelic drugs shifted the paradigm. When *Rainbow Bridge* was released in 1972, *Rolling Stone* described the film as "acid trip memorabilia." Complete with Day-Glo special effects and bizarre audio manipulations—like making a drill sergeant talk with a dog's bark—it was one of the oddest films ever made.

Still, the film shoot proved restorative for Jimi, who lived in a dormitory for a week and ate vegetarian meals with the crew and cast. The laid-back Maui lifestyle gave him a much-needed respite. "He loved Maui so much," recalled Melinda Merryweather, who was part of the cast and befriended him. "He seemed really happy to be there." Jimi told her he wanted to retire to the island and grow grapes on the side of the volcano.

Jimi reveled in the chance to talk about religion and mysticism in a setting he called a "cosmic candy store." "It was a spiritual cleansing for Jimi," Chuck Wein observed. Many of the actors in the movie called Wein "The Wizard," because of his ability to speak on a myriad of topics. Wein gave Jimi several books, including *The Tibetan Book of the Dead* and *Secret Places of the Lion: Alien Influences on Earth's Destiny*. The latter was a book about space aliens' involvement in human culture for centuries, a theory Jimi believed. Jimi also had with him *The Book of Urantia,* an alternative Bible for UFO believers that mixed tales of Jesus with stories of alien visitations. Jimi carried this book with him everywhere—along with his Bob Dylan songbook—and told friends he had learned much from its pages.

The Hawaii trip was also a physical cleansing of sorts for Jimi. Though acid was abundant on Maui, potent Hawaiian pot plentiful, and cocaine also frequently present, heroin was not available. Jimi had become increasingly reliant on snorting narcotics, and in Hawaii, he broke a heroin dependency. In the four years he had been a star, drugs had moved from a celebratory ritual into a daily crutch necessary to bear the pressures of touring. On Maui, when one cast member suggested they fly Devon Wilson over to bring drugs, Jimi urged against it. "Devon would have brought heroin, one way or another," Chuck Wein observed. Jimi talked openly to Melinda about his codependent relationship with Devon and his efforts to extricate himself from it. "Devon knew how to hold on to him through the drug trip," Melinda said. "Devon had that black widow thing going on, and it was like he was the nectar she sought."

Devon never arrived on the island and Jimi's original elation at being in Hawaii was tempered by dramatic mood swings: One minute he'd be talking about how much he loved Maui and the next he was deeply depressed. He had made millions but had also spent millions, and he found himself without great wealth to show for his work, just one of several issues he was complaining about. The Ed Chalpin lawsuit had been somewhat resolved, but a paternity suit, brought against him by Diana Carpenter, loomed. By early 1970, Carpenter's lawyers had made several requests for a blood sample, which Jimi had resisted. Jimi never publicly registered his opinion on whether he thought Tamika Carpenter was his daughter, but in an unreleased song called "Red Velvet Room," he sang about his child "Tami." The song revealed affection for his daughter, though Jimi steadfastly maintained in public that he had no children. Perhaps, like many in an age where "free love" had become a mantra, he was unready for the responsibility children entailed; for someone whose own childhood had been truncated, parenting would have represented too great an emotional leap. It is also possible that any discussion of out-of-wedlock children stirred up painful memories for a man who had grown up in a family where paternity had forever been an issue, and where two sons and two daughters were taken away by welfare authorities. The brief line "How's Tami?" in "Red Velvet Room" was the only acknowledgment Jimi ever made about his daughter. He made no move to support Tamika or even to meet her.

In Maui, disturbed by these and other ghosts, and still haunted by the Moroccan fortune-teller, Jimi went so far as to threaten suicide. It was on a night when he was to shoot a scene for the film, and predictably he had been drinking. To director Chuck Wein and actress Pat Hartley, Jimi suggested, "Why don't we all just commit suicide, the three of us?" Wein didn't take Jimi seriously and within ten minutes Jimi's mood had changed. A few days later, Jimi surprised Melinda Merryweather when he announced that he would soon be "leaving" his body. "I won't be here anymore," he told her. When she asked him what he meant, he went mute. On another day, Wein asked Jimi if he'd be playing Seattle again soon. Jimi told Wein, "Next time I go to Seattle, it'll be in a pine box."

The despair behind those thoughts wasn't in evidence when Jimi was playing music. On his third day in Hawaii, he walked to the Maui Belle, a nightclub in Lahaina, where a jazz piano player was performing. Jimi was asked if he wanted to sit in; he did. For two hours, he and the pianist played jazz standards to a handful of astonished patrons.

His "real" concert came the next day when Jimi, Billy Cox, and Mitch Mitchell played a show billed as "The Rainbow Bridge Vibratory Color/Sound Experiment," for the filmmakers. Wein had constructed a tiny stage in the middle of a field on the side of the crater. A tepee had been put up as a dressing room and portable generators powered the sound system. The free concert had been publicized by posters on Lahaina's main street, and eight hundred fisherman, surfers, and native Hawaiians showed up. Wein seated the audience in sections based on their astrological signs. Before Jimi came onstage, a group of Hare Krishnas led the crowd in chanting "Om" for several minutes.

Jimi began in a good mood but the laid-back response of the crowd initially disturbed him. He played a ten-song first set, and then sat in his tepee for forty-five minutes smoking pot and drinking beer before retaking the stage. The second set was more energetic and he played like someone in love with the guitar again. The worst moment of the day came when a dog that had been dosed with LSD trotted on-stage and bit Jimi's leg. Thankfully, the bite barely broke the flesh.

Two days later, Jimi and the band flew to Honolulu, where they played the last show of their U.S. tour. Jimi appeared distracted, and had little of the ease he had displayed on Maui. The *Honolulu Advertiser* critic called him "a Madman Butterfly" because of his velour outfit, which was orange, hot pink, verdant green, and bright red. The day after the show, Mitch and Buddy flew home while Jimi returned to Maui.

Jimi spent the next two weeks as an extended vacation. The break was not planned, and in fact it had only been achieved by subterfuge: Jimi cut his foot on the beach, but pretended the injury was worse than it was to prolong his stay and put off his management. "We put on about twenty times the amount of bandages it needed and took pictures to make it look like he was seriously injured," Melinda Merryweather recalled. The deception was indicative of the degree of control Michael Jeffrey continued to exert over his client—Jimi was now faking illness to escape the demands of touring. Jimi rented a small house where he spent most days writing music and poems. He wrote a long song for Melinda titled "Scorpio Woman," her zodiac sign.

Melinda observed that the longer Jimi stayed in Hawaii, the clearer his mind became. In that clarity, she found him contemplative and sometimes sad. "He talked about his mother a lot, and her Native American roots," Melinda said. Jimi's feelings about Al were still conflicted because of their recent fight, but he told Melinda he felt no anger toward his father. Jimi struck Melinda as a man very much at a crossroads, and he kept vowing he was ready to make many major changes to his madcap lifestyle.

During his second vacation week in Maui, Jimi sat in his small house and wrote Al one of the most extraordinary letters he had ever composed. He had been drinking and was perhaps high on LSD before he put pen to paper; by the end of the letter, he was scribbling in the margins and crossing out much of what he'd written. The letter was rambling, and at times nonsensical, but it showed an emotional side Jimi rarely revealed. When he had been in the army, he had written his father almost every week—those letters stopped once he began the life of a touring musician. This Maui letter was remarkable both for what it said about Jimi's reflective state of mind and about his relationship with his family. It began:

> Dad, my love, what, or at *least most* of what I bring is riff-raff—but you know and I know that's where they seem they want to be. But who can (in many respects I'm riff-raff, you know, the one who talks all the JIVE). Just because you can't or don't have the patience for it, why even come to the gig? I know as much love [as] you have of even me and Leon (not necessarily clear), discuss in privately

(you and me) Mother Rock is there. Always living up on
this world of Blindness and so-called REALITY. But talking of the heaven-bound PATH—Angels, Holy spirits etc.,
Gods, etc., have a very difficult job to shoot to the word on
a soap box, or pumpkin, or cloud, to convince the world
without argument or debate or etc., of the subject dealing
whatever angels exist in conventional acceptance form or
not. You are what I happily accept as an angel, a gift from
God, etc.! Forget the opinions and gossiping existence of
the world.

Jimi then admits that he "drank a lot" before writing the letter, and asks
his father's forgiveness, at the same time begging Al to read "every
word of this instant but ageless wonderment of a letter." He continues
to write of angels, Sammy Davis Jr., heaven, "eternal light," but then
the letter takes an almost confrontational tone when he challenges his
father on his mother Lucille:

One day maybe I can get around to asking questions of
great importance and experience (back to normal) of unan-
swered history and lifestyle of my mother that bore me—
Mrs. Lucille. There are some things I *must* know about her
for my own strictly private reasons.

Jimi ends the letter apologizing for his fight with Al in Seattle, suggesting it was caused by "bad nerves," and asks that his cousin Dee Dee and
stepsister Marsha forgive him for his drunken, melancholy trip through
his Seattle past. He leaves his number in New York, asking for his
cousin Diane to call him, and he says "love forever" to his stepsister
Janie, whose name he misspells as "Jenny."

☙

ON AUGUST 14, two days after he sent the letter to his father, Jimi
flew back to New York. "He didn't want to leave Hawaii," Chuck Wein
recalled, "but there was a point where he had to go back to being Jimi
Hendrix." At the airport, Jimi had a tearful good-bye with Melinda
Merryweather and some of the surfers from Maui. "You people are so
lucky," he told them as he climbed the stairs onto the plane. "You get to
*stay* here."

∽∾

THE SAME DAY Jimi arrived in New York, he was back at Electric
Lady Studios working on overdubs. He spent a week in the studio prior
to an upcoming tour of European festivals that was to start at the end
of August. His friends in New York noticed that he seemed energized
after Maui. That week he met with the Aleems to talk about forming a
new publishing company, and with Ken Hagood, an African American
lawyer, about representing him in a legal battle with Michael Jeffrey.
"Jimi wanted to play his music his way, and he had several conflicts with
doing so," Hagood recalled. Jimi brought many of his contracts to his
meeting with Hagood but discovered he was missing key paperwork.
Jimi had dozens of ideas about where he wanted his career to go, including moving away from rock and more into R&B and jazz, but he
told Hagood his first priority was to get his business affairs in order,
and either fire Jeffrey or renegotiate his contract.

Like Chas Chandler before him, Michael Jeffrey had become
more than just Jimi's manager—he held Jimi's publishing contract and
they were partners in the new studio. Though Jeffrey had made numerous decisions Jimi objected to—starting with the Monkees tour and
stretching through the difficult tour routings—he did deserve credit for
making his client the biggest star in the world. "There were things that
Jimi did not like," Taharqa Aleem said, "but Michael was trying to talk
things through. Jimi had a temper, and he was reactionary. He was also
a difficult client for Michael." As Jimi and Michael increasingly clashed,
Bob Levine, Jeffrey's assistant, began to handle most interactions with

Jimi. "Jimi told me he would never leave Michael," Levine recalled. "He knew Michael was a heavy, and it was popular to make him a villain, but Jimi knew Michael would make him the most money." Life had become so complicated for Jimi: Owning a studio had been his dream, but he found that the studio debt gave him little choice but to continue with a career he felt trapped in.

A bigger problem than Jeffrey was Jimi's relationship both with his fans and with the body of work that had made him famous. He repeatedly told his friends that he felt bound by audience expectations and believed that if he didn't play "Purple Haze" and "Foxy Lady," his audience base would evaporate. "He didn't feel things were going well career-wise or monetarily," Deering Howe said. "All his audiences wanted to hear were the four big songs that they knew, and Jimi wanted to play other stuff. Artistically, it was like he was trapped back on the Chitlin' Circuit again, forced to play what someone else told him. He didn't feel he could break free of that."

On August 26, a day before he was scheduled to fly to London for the next tour, the Aleems and Jimi met near Central Park. "We drove up in a brand-new gold Cadillac and talked with him on the street while he looked at the car," Tunde-Ra said. Dressed in a flowing African robe, Jimi said he was going to play a festival on the Isle of Wight. "Isle of White?" Taharqa quipped. "Why can't you go play at the Isle of Blacks?" Jimi smiled at their joke, and for a moment it seemed as if the Aleems were back again with the fresh-scrubbed young man they had met when he didn't have a nickel to his name. The Aleems were Jimi's oldest friends in New York and they had seen him starve and soar. Jimi told them he wanted to name their new company West Kenya Publishing because Kenya was a part of Africa where "you could retreat and not be found." He joked that he'd meet them in Pago Pago if he could escape the tour. "It's beautiful, and you can get away there," Jimi said of a place he had never visited. As the Aleems climbed in their Cadillac and began to pull away from the curb, Jimi's parting words were, "I'll meet you in Pago Pago." He waved good-bye as the car left.

That night, Jimi attended the opening party for Electric Lady Studios. Though he had been working in his studio for almost nine months, it was only now opening to other artists. Yoko Ono, Johnny Winter, and Mick Fleetwood were a few of the attendees at the star-studded fete. Jimi ran into Noel Redding and told him, "We're going to Europe; I'll probably see you there." The party quickly turned into chaos when a few pranksters began throwing food. Jimi, who was upset at seeing his studio trashed, left early.

Later that evening, he met up with Colette Mimram and Devon Wilson—Colette had originally talked about accompanying Jimi on the upcoming European tour but had been unable to renew her passport. Devon begged Jimi to let her go in Colette's stead, but he rejected this idea. "Jimi really wanted to cut it off with Devon because of the drugs," Colette recalled. "She had a great rap—she could get blood out a stone—but she was a junkie and he didn't want anything to do with that." Devon's addiction had even begun to ruin her looks: Her eyelids now drooped, and she was no longer grooming herself. She had once been one of the most beautiful women in rock 'n' roll, but as her heroin addiction had spiraled out of control that summer, even Jimi—who hated to say no to anyone—found himself cutting off their friendship. He told her that night, "I want you to leave," and so she left.

The next morning he took a plane to London.

∽↷↶∾

JIMI HENDRIX ARRIVED in London on August 27 and had three days before his appearance at the Isle of Wight Festival. The show would be his first English concert in eighteen months, and media interest was extraordinarily high; over the next two days, he did almost a dozen interviews with the British press. He was staying in a penthouse suite at the Londonderry Hotel, and it was there he held court, with friends, musicians, and journalists queueing up in the hall, waiting for a reception with him.

In his interviews, Jimi talked about the possibility of ending his career. "I'm back right now to where I started," he told *Melody Maker*.

"I've given this era of music everything. I still sound the same, my music's still the same, and I can't think of anything new to add." He suggested he was ready for the large R&B ensemble band he had wanted since he first arrived in London in 1966. "A big band full of competent musicians that I can conduct and write for," he said. When he talked about his current band, he spoke in the past tense. "It was fun, it was the greatest fun. It was good, exciting, and I enjoyed it."

Though he talked mostly of music, Jimi was, as always, quizzed about politics, drugs, and fashion. His hair—which had grown long—was mentioned in most articles. Jimi had taken his hairdresser, James Finney, on tour to make sure his Afro looked right. He told the *London Times* that he felt "like a victim from public opinion. . . . I cut my hair. They say, 'Why'd you cut your hair?'" His explanation: "Maybe I grow it long because my daddy used to cut it like a skinned chicken."

Kathy Etchingham recalled that Jimi had spoken often of his fear of having his father grab him and cut his hair during his visits to Seattle. In London, he was probably more afraid of running into Etchingham and her new husband; she had married that year. Kathy and Jimi had remained friendly, and he phoned her occasionally, but she learned he was back in London, however, only when a friend called to say that he had gone "mad" and kicked two girls out of his suite. Etchingham came immediately and found the nearly naked girls outside the room, afraid to enter. Kathy went in and discovered Jimi in bed amid broken lamps and empty whiskey bottles. She thought he looked ill rather than crazed, as his complexion was pallid and he had a high fever. It was a summer day, yet he had switched the heat in the room to maximum. Etchingham later wondered whether Jimi's sickness might have been related to drug withdrawal. She turned the heat down, put a cool compress on his forehead, and he went to sleep peacefully.

On August 26, the day after Etchingham's visit, two other women came to the hotel and found him miraculously recovered. Karen Davies knew Jimi from New York; Kirsten Nefer, a twenty-four-year-old Danish model, was meeting him for the first time. Jimi was immediately besotted with Kirsten and spent the afternoon talking to her. "He was more or less interviewing me," Kirsten recalled. "I kept saying I had to leave and he kept saying, 'Don't go now.'" They talked for hours, though most of the conversation was Jimi, in his sly way, getting Kirsten to reveal herself. When she joked that at his upcoming show in Denmark he could visit her mother, Jimi suggested they call her mother then and there. Kirsten phoned, and Jimi and Mrs. Nefer chatted for an hour. Kirsten and he kept talking until three in the morning, while Karen fell asleep on the sofa. When the women finally got up to leave, Jimi said it would look bad for them to be exiting his room at that hour, so they slept in the room adjacent to his bedroom.

Kirsten finally left at ten in the morning, though an hour later Jimi appeared at her house, asking to take her to lunch. At lunch, he put his hand on her knee, but that was the extent of his flirting. He was leaving the next day for the Isle of Wight show, and he urged Kirsten to attend.

On Sunday, Jimi landed in a helicopter on the Isle of Wight for his evening show. The crowd of 600,000 had exceeded all expectations, making it even larger than Woodstock. As was typical with such a huge show, the logistics had created havoc: Hundreds of people were trying to break down the fences, equipment was malfunctioning, and the show was running behind schedule. To make matters worse, the trousers of Jimi's elaborate butterfly stage costume—which Germaine Greer later described as "a psychedelic minstrel clown's gear"—split at his crotch. Noel Redding's mother was backstage, and she helped mend the outfit for him.

Richie Havens ran into Jimi backstage and was shocked at how ill he looked. Havens had known Jimi since his early days in New York, yet had never before seen the mania that he exhibited that night. "I'm having a real bad time with my lawyers and my managers," Jimi complained. "They are *killing* me; everything is turned against me and I can't sleep or eat." Havens gave him a recommendation for a new attorney. He also told Jimi to call him when he got back to London and to get some rest. "He looked like he had been up for days," Havens recalled.

Kirsten Nefer had managed to rendezvous with Jimi at his hotel, and she accompanied him to a trailer at the festival site. From the trailer they could hear clashes outside between police and protesters who were demanding the concert be made free. "It was horrible," Nefer said. "It was not the loving and beautiful thing they had planned." As Jimi waited for his stage call, he became agitated. He told Nefer that he wanted her onstage, giving him encouragement. "Stay where I can see you," he said, "because it's you I'm playing for."

It was 2 AM before Jimi got his cue. Onstage, but still behind a wall of amps, the emcee inquired how Jimi wanted to be introduced. "Call [me] the blue wild angel," Jimi said. "What?" the announcer asked. "The wild blue angel," Jimi yelled. Instead, the emcee introduced him as "the man with the guitar." In truth, no introduction was needed in Britain, where Jimi's fan base was rabid; this was, of course, the nation that had made him a star. As a shout-out to those loyal British fans, Jimi began the show with a few bars of "God Save the Queen."

The show, however, was an exercise in frustration. Where Jimi's first concerts in Britain—playing to select audiences of musicians in clubs like the Scotch of St. James and the Bag O' Nails—had seemed blessed, this night he performed under what seemed to be a curse. There were problems with his guitar, which kept going out of tune; plus the sound system had many difficulties, the most obvious being that it picked up walkie-talkie communications in the midst of Jimi's music. Even Jimi's pants were uncooperative: He imagined he had split them again and spent a full sixty seconds behind an amp inspecting them. The very act of paying so much attention to his crotch made him look clownish rather than suave.

There were musical highlights among the aggravations. "All Along the Watchtower" and "Red House" were particularly well played and received, and the crazed walkie-talkie interference even sounded appropriate during a thirty-minute take of "Machine Gun." Though the crowd gave old favorites like "Hey Joe" and "Voodoo Child" the greatest applause, the stalwart English fans were also appreciative of new numbers like "Hey Baby" and "Freedom." Still, when Jimi inserted the line "my whole soul is tired and aching" into "Midnight Lightning," it seemed a fair review of his state of mind.

During "In from the Storm," Jimi's last song, protesters launched flares onto the wooden awning of the stage. The roof was some thirty feet above Jimi and he was never in danger, but no one knew this at the time. Security guards rushed onstage to stop the flames from spreading. "The show just fell apart at the end," observed Kirsten Nefer. To compound the injury, someone spread the rumor that it was the performer himself who set the fire to avoid doing an encore. Jimi had come to fame in Britain, and his gimmick of setting his guitar on fire had been at least partially responsible for his early press attention. The Isle of Wight performance would be Jimi's last official concert on British soil. Hours after he left the site, the festival stage roof still smoldered, a small reminder of a meteoric rise and incendiary career.

# CHAPTER TWENTY-SIX

# THE STORY
# OF LIFE

STOCKHOLM, SWEDEN

*August 1970—September 1970*

*"The story of life is quicker than the wink of an eye."*

—a line from the last song JIMI HENDRIX ever wrote

LESS THAN SIXTEEN hours after he walked offstage at the Isle of Wight, Jimi Hendrix was onstage in Stockholm. He went on an hour late and played an hour longer than scheduled, which made the promoter angry, since an amusement park next to the concert venue had to be shut down during the performance. It was a far better show than the one on the Isle of Wight, but it, too, ended on a distressing note: While Jimi was still performing, the announcer came on the PA to declare the show over—the amusement park needed to open again. Jimi had long thought that his life had turned into a circus; now he was an act in one.

Backstage, Jimi ran into Eva Sundquist, who had always been his favorite girlfriend in Sweden. This meeting was not so fond: Since his last visit, Eva had given birth to James Daniel Sundquist, Jimi's child. She had written Jimi several times about the baby, but he had not responded. Eva had left the baby home, but asked Jimi if he wanted to come meet his son. The question temporarily stunned him—perhaps he was considering the paternity suit he was already fighting with Diana Carpenter. The scene backstage was a madhouse, with journalists, groupies, and fans all tugging on Jimi's sleeve, and he was pulled away from Eva without ever giving her an answer. Jimi never met James Daniel Sundquist, his only known son.

If the backstage scene in Stockholm had been crazed, at the band's next tour stop Billy Cox was dosed with a psychedelic drug. Cox assumed someone slipped him a considerable quantity of LSD in a drink, but his bad reaction was exacerbated by fatigue. "The pace in Europe was both exhilarating and exhausting," Cox recalled. Billy was normally the most sober of the band members, but now he began to rant incoherently. In his wild state, the only one who could calm him was Jimi. Jimi frequently had to attend to Billy over the next several days.

As if Cox's problems weren't trouble enough, before a show in Århus, Denmark, Jimi took what witnesses described as an entire handful of sleeping pills in the early afternoon. He was suffering from what seemed to be a bad cold and had complained he'd been unable to sleep for three days. Why he took sleeping pills in the middle of the day, just a few hours before a show, is unexplained—they may have been an attempt to counteract the effects of another drug, as it was not uncommon for him to take both uppers and downers at the same time. Kirsten Nefer had flown in from London, and when she arrived at the hotel that afternoon, she ran into Mitch Mitchell in the lobby. "You better go up there because Jimi's in a very bad mood," Mitch said. "He's not having a good time." Kirsten was shocked at Jimi's condition. "He was talking about spaceships in the sky," she said. "He was staggering. There was no sense to what he was saying." As Jimi attempted to conduct interviews with several reporters, he insisted Kirsten sit next to him and hold his hand. She was embarrassed by his condition, but was afraid that if she left he'd be worse.

Kirsten and Jimi took a cab to the concert site, but she remained unconvinced he could play, as he was stumbling. He would alternately eject the large crowd from his dressing room and then instantly order them back in. At one point, he announced for all to hear, "I can't do this gig." Kirsten told him there were four thousand people in the hall, and many in the crowd had begun to stomp their feet. Jimi eventually walked onstage with help from a roadie. His first words to the audience were: "Are you feeling all right? Then welcome to the electric circus." He began to strum his guitar without bothering to chord it. Mitch started a drum solo, hoping Jimi would join in, but after only two songs Jimi dropped his guitar and collapsed. The show was canceled and the audience given refunds. Jimi was onstage for less than eight minutes, about the same span of time as his 1966 jam with Eric Clapton and Cream. Those eight minutes, on a small London stage, had positioned Jimi as a rising star; now, in an equally short period of time, he had at least temporarily derailed his career in one of his very best markets.

Kirsten and Jimi took a cab back to the hotel. When they entered Jimi's room, journalist Anne Bjørndal was waiting there. Jimi had been spouting wild adages all day and at one point had said, "I've been dead for a long time." Unwisely, he attempted to do his interview with Bjørndal despite his condition. He announced that he did not like LSD anymore "because it's naked. I need oxygen." He quoted from *Winnie-the-Pooh* and said he loved reading Hans Christian Andersen fairy tales. His playing, he said, took much out of him: "I sacrifice part of my soul every time I play." And he talked about his mortality, with the same visions of the Death tarot card still haunting him: "I'm not sure I will live to be 28 years old. I mean, the moment I feel I have nothing more to give musically, I will not be around on this planet anymore, unless I have a wife and children; otherwise, I've got nothing to live for." Jimi was stoned out of his mind at the time but there was truth in his confession—the life he had created as a star was as lonely and as isolating as his fractured childhood. As he said this, however, Jimi looked at Kirsten with an inviting, ardent stare. Kirsten then suggested the writer leave. Jimi, in a bizarre turn of events, announced he was afraid of Kirsten and asked *her* to leave, only to immediately beg her to ignore what he'd just said and stay. The confused journalist departed and Kirsten was finally alone with Jimi, who was still acting like a madman.

Despite telling numerous journalists that he desperately needed sleep, Jimi informed Kirsten he would die if he closed his eyes. "He was afraid something was going to happen because of all the drugs he'd taken," she recalled. Instead of resting, they talked for several hours. At one point, he leaned over, looked Kirsten in the eye, and asked: "Do you want to marry me?" Kirsten had known Jimi for less than a week and was surprised by the inquiry. Earlier in the night, he had said he didn't want to be alone with her; now he was asking her to marry him and have his children. She protested, but he pleaded nonetheless. "I'm so fed up with playing," he said. "They want me to do all these shows. I just want to move to the country. I'm so sick of burning my guitar." She was convinced that his proposal of marriage was little more than a desperate grab at an excuse to escape a career that was killing him. At six in the morning, Jimi finally fell asleep.

When he awoke at noon, his condition appeared improved, though he was still complaining of exhaustion. On the way to the airport, Kirsten sang a few bars of Donovan's "Wear Your Love Like Heaven." "Who did that song?" Jimi asked. He said he wanted to record the song. It was the first time he had spoken positively about music in several days, and Kirsten felt he was starting to snap out of his fog.

When they arrived in Copenhagen, Jimi's hotel was across from a loud construction site. He said he wouldn't be able to rest there, so Kirsten suggested they stay at her mother's house. They went to her family's simple home, and her mother made Jimi soup. It calmed him and he went into a bedroom and slept for several hours. Kirsten's brothers and sisters arrived by the time he woke, and he sat down for a meal of spaghetti with the family. One of Kirsten's sisters was pregnant and due in late November; Jimi joked that the baby might share his November 27 birthday. Reporters, who had gotten wind of the story that Jimi was dating a Danish model, came to the house and interrupted the meal. Kirsten suggested sending them away; Jimi, instead, invited them in, announcing that he wanted the world to know about his new love.

That night at the concert hall, Jimi was late because he was serenading Kirsten with his acoustic guitar. "You could hear the crowd screaming for him," she recalled, "yet here he was in his dressing room playing his acoustic for me." Then, suddenly, he announced he couldn't perform. Kirsten told him he had to go on because her mother was outside waiting to see him. With that plea, Jimi went onstage. In marked contrast to the night before, he put on a show that had critics raving. "The concert of the year!" one paper proclaimed. Afterward, Mitch came up to Kirsten and said, "What have you done to him? Jimi hasn't played this good in years." She attributed the transformation to her mother's soup. Jimi spent the night at the Nefer house, and slept like a log.

Jimi had asked Kirsten if she could attend his next few shows in Germany. She was in the middle of filming a movie, but the next morning she gleefully announced she had managed to get the time off. In what she found was becoming a pattern, Jimi flip-flopped and said he didn't want her coming after all. "No, you can't," he said, "because a woman's place is in the home." She later wondered if his erratic behavior was the result of drugs, though anything he used during this tour he skillfully hid from her. Soon after announcing his views on women and work, he said he was sorry, he didn't know what had come over him, and he begged her to come. But Kirsten told him she was done with his wavering affection and was going back to her film. They had frequently talked about their mutual love of Bob Dylan, and when she saw him off at the airport, Jimi quoted the songwriter: "Most likely you'll go your way," he said as he walked up the stairs to the plane. From the door, he turned and declared, "I'll go mine." It was a rare display of melodrama, and decidedly out of character.

The next day in Berlin, Jimi seemed ill again, most likely from drugs. "He plays as if he is drunk," one critic wrote. Another writer reported going backstage and witnessing Jimi sniffling. "Do you have a cold?" the journalist asked. "That's from snorting, man," was Jimi's curt reply. Guitarist Robin Trower visited backstage to announce that the concert was the greatest thing he'd ever seen. Jimi's response: "Uh, thank you, but, naw!" Even in his altered state, he knew when his playing was on or off, and this whole tour had, with the exception of one show in Copenhagen, been a disaster.

Jimi's next show was at the "Love and Peace Festival" on the German island of Fehmarn. On the train ride there, in an act of apparent psychosis, Jimi broke into a locked sleeping car. The conductor discovered him, and Jimi claimed he was just seeking rest; he avoided arrest only when a train official recognized him and intervened with police. Jimi was scheduled to play at Fehmarn on the night of September 5, but bad weather caused his set to be postponed until the afternoon of September 6. The Fehmarn concert was plagued by incidents of violence among gate-crashers, police, and the crowd inside. A large contingent of European Hell's Angels were in attendance, some armed with weapons. The crowd became restless because of the delays, and when Jimi finally came onstage, a few chanted "Go home." Some in the audience actually booed. Jimi's reply: "I don't give a fuck if you boo, if you boo in key." As he walked offstage, after a thirteen-song set, he said to one reporter, "I don't feel like playing anymore." While Jimi had been onstage, Hell's Angels had broken into the box office and made off with the festival's entire receipts. Jimi missed that part of the drama as he immediately caught a helicopter out and then a plane back to London. But once he was airborne, if Jimi had looked down on Fehmarn, he would again have seen a festival in flames: Moments after he left the "Love and Peace Festival" site, Hell's Angels burned the stage to the ground.

❧

IN LONDON, THE uncertainty surrounding the band's future continued as Billy Cox's condition worsened; whatever drugs he had been slipped seemed to stay in his system. Billy's breakdown put the band's upcoming tour into doubt. Jimi had checked into the Cumberland Hotel, and on Tuesday, September 8, Kirsten Nefer decided to swallow her pride and visit him there. When she went to his room, the door was ajar and she saw him prone on the bed; at first, she thought he might be dead. She checked his pulse and discovered that he was sleeping. She decided not to wake him, but the phone rang; it was someone calling about Billy. Kirsten and Jimi went and found Billy and took him out for tandoori chicken at a curry house on Fulham Road. "Billy was talking in tongues and making all these strange noises," Kirsten recalled. Afterward, they deposited Billy with a roadie, and Kirsten and Jimi went to a cinema and saw Michelangelo Antonioni's *Red Desert*. The movie improved Jimi's mood dramatically, and as he left the cinema he danced along the curb. "It was like he was in *Singin' in the Rain*," Kirsten recalled. "He was so happy, he was skipping." Just as quickly, though, his mood shifted and he became morose. He told Kirsten he wanted to take two years off. "I only want to play the acoustic guitar from now on," he announced.

That night, Billy's condition worsened and a doctor was summoned. The physician could find no organic cause to his illness and suggested Billy be sent home to America. Later, Kirsten and Jimi briefly went out to a disco. At the club, Jimi refused to dance, complaining that he wasn't a good enough dancer—this from a man whose stage moves had electrified a whole generation. Back at the hotel, they attempted to have a romantic evening together, but were continually interrupted by Billy. "Every time we were about to go to bed, he was there," Kirsten said. "Jimi was so good to him. He'd say, 'Remember when we were in the army together?' Billy kept saying, 'I'm going to *die!*'" The doctor came again and gave Billy an injection of a sedative. The next day Billy was put on a plane to the States, where he recovered.

Jimi had a show scheduled on September 13 in Rotterdam and he immediately began to dial around for a new bass player. He even considered Noel Redding, but eventually decided to cancel the remainder of the tour. On Thursday, September 10, Jimi attended a party hosted by Mike Nesmith, who had left the Monkees and was launching a new band. Jimi told Nesmith he intended on moving toward R&B, an idea that Nesmith tried to dissuade him from. It was one of many ideas Jimi was talking about that September; most of the people he spoke with felt he was overflowing with ideas and determined to change his career, but unsure as to what his next direction should be.

The next day Jimi did a long interview in his hotel suite with Keith Altham during which he offered a few contradictory clues. Altham had been an early supporter and was the man who originally suggested that Jimi set his guitar on fire: It was some small justice that Jimi's last interview would be with a longtime champion of his music. They talked for an hour, drifting from topic to topic. When asked if he wanted to be recognized as a songwriter, Jimi replied: "I wanted to just lay back and predominantly write songs when I can't go on a stage any more." When asked what he'd change in the world, he said "the color in the streets." When asked if he was a "psychedelic writer," he answered, "I think maybe it's more that than anything else. I'm trying to get more so into other things, you know, as of where reality is nothing but each individual's way of thinking." He sounded optimistic, but many of his answers were nonsensical. He drank wine as he talked and watched a comedy on television as the interview was conducted.

One of the few things Jimi was concrete about was that his next album would include "Valleys of Neptune," "Between Here and Horizon," and "Room Full of Mirrors." Speaking of the latter song, he explained, "That's more of a mental disarrangement that a person might be thinking. This says something, about broken glass used to be all in my brain, and so forth." Altham ended the interview by asking if Jimi had enough money for the rest of his life. "Not the way I'd like to live," he replied, "because I want to get up in the morning and just roll over in my bed into an indoor swimming pool, and then swim to the breakfast table, come up for air, and get maybe a drink of orange juice, or something like that. Then just flop over from the chair into the swimming pool, swim into the bathroom, and go shave and whatever." "Do you want to live just comfortably, or to live luxuriously?" Altham asked. "Is that luxurious?" Jimi answered. "I was thinking about a tent, maybe, overhanging a mountain stream!"

On Saturday, September 12, Jimi spent time with Kirsten again, but she felt discouraged after overhearing a long argument he had on the phone with Devon Wilson. Devon had read a report in a newspaper about Jimi being involved with a Danish model and had announced that she was coming to London to see him. "Devon, get off my fucking back, for Christsakes!" Jimi yelled into the phone. He hung up.

The next day Jimi's yelling was redirected at Kirsten. Kirsten was cast in a movie opposite George Lazenby, who had played James Bond in a previous movie, and Jimi was convinced she was sleeping with Lazenby; Jimi insisted she quit the film. When she refused, he protested. "He shook me until I had blue marks all over," Kirsten said. Angry at his jealousy, when she suspected he'd been unfaithful to her even in the short time they'd dated, she stormed out. She tried phoning him later that night, but he wasn't in. Kirsten left a number of messages over the next few days and even stopped by his hotel looking for him, but she would never see him again.

⌖

KIRSTEN NEFER WASN'T the only one looking for Jimi that week— Michael Jeffrey had come to London briefly and he, too, was unable to find his client. Jimi had contacted Chas Chandler that week and told his former manager that he wanted to fire Jeffrey and have Chas represent him. Jimi's lawyer was also looking for Jimi; meetings were planned that week in London to try to settle the overseas claims resulting from the Ed Chalpin PPX lawsuit. Jimi never showed for those appointments. Diana Carpenter's lawyers were also seeking Jimi, trying to force him to take a blood test in her paternity suit against him over daughter Tamika; they, too, were unable to find him.

If Jimi was a phantom to those seeking him for legal or professional reasons, several of the important women in his life found him easy to locate. Kathy Etchingham bumped into Jimi at Kensington Market. "He came up right behind me and grabbed me," she recalled. Jimi was shopping for antiques and he had a blond woman with him, whom he didn't introduce. He told Kathy to look him up at the Cumberland Hotel. Jimi's relationship with Kathy had been the longest, and perhaps most intimate, romance of his life. As they parted, she gave him a peck on the cheek.

That week, Jimi also ran into Linda Keith at the Speakeasy. Linda was leaving the club and he was entering, and they chatted for a few minutes in the foyer. Their exchange was awkward: Her relationship with Jimi in New York, back in 1966, had spelled the end of her romance with Keith Richards, but four years later, she was sporting an engagement ring and a new fiancé. Jimi was with a mysterious blonde himself. While their meeting appeared accidental, Jimi had, in fact, sought her out. Though they had not stayed close since the tumultuous New York period—and they had not managed to stay friends—Linda had recently been on his mind. At his Isle of Wight concert, he had changed a line in "Red House" to "because my Linda doesn't live here anymore." He had also recorded a studio track two months earlier titled "Send My Love to Linda," which was an ode to her. At the Speakeasy, Jimi handed Linda a guitar case and said, "This is for you." Inside was a new Stratocaster, his repayment for the instrument she had procured back when he was a backup player named Jimmy James with no guitar of his own. Jimi had never fully acknowledged what Linda had done for his career—dragging three producers to see him—but the guitar was a small confession of their past. "You don't owe me anything," Linda said as she attempted to give it back. She told him, in fact, that her fiancé had a tiny sports car and they had no way to transport a guitar. Still, Jimi insisted. "I owe you this," he said. He left Linda the guitar case, grabbed his blond date's hand, and walked away. Linda drove home with the guitar strapped to the roof of her fiancé's car. When she later opened the case, she found that in addition to the guitar, there were letters she had written to him during the summer of 1966. Jimi had apparently kept these during the entire four years since that time; now, like a lover forever spurned, he was returning them as if to remind her of their earlier feelings of romance.

The blond woman whom both Linda and Kathy saw with Jimi was Monika Dannemann, a twenty-five-year-old ice-skater from Düsseldorf whom Jimi had first met in 1969. On Tuesday, September 15, after his argument with Kirsten Nefer, Jimi had paired up with Dannemann, who had tracked him down at his hotel. According to Dannemann's version in her 1995 book, *The Inner World of Jimi Hendrix*, over the previous two years she had maintained a close, intimate relationship with Jimi, whom she visited in London on several occasions, and they had "kept in touch by letter and phone." During the last week of August 1970, he had "moved into" a room she was renting in a long-stay hotel. Much of Dannemann's story has been discredited over the years—some of it declared fraudulent by a court of law—but she was indisputably Jimi's London paramour for several days beginning on Tuesday, September 15. That night the pair showed up at Ronnie Scott's nightclub, where Eric Burdon and War were playing. Jimi had hoped to jam with his old friend Burdon but was turned away at the door because he was staggering, and obviously stoned. "For the first time I'd ever seen him, he didn't have his guitar," Eric Burdon recalled. "When I saw him without that guitar, I knew he was in trouble." In one of Burdon's two autobiographies, he described Jimi as having "a head full of something—heroin, Quaaludes." Whatever Jimi had taken, several people at the club recalled that his level of intoxication was embarrassing, as was watching him—the master of the jam—be turned away from a stage because of his condition.

Jimi spent at least part of the next day with Monika. In the late afternoon, they stopped by a party, where Monika introduced herself to anyone within earshot as "Jimi's fiancée." Though much of Monika's story was exaggerated, one can easily imagine Jimi rashly asking her to marry him; he had asked the same of Kirsten Nefer just a few days prior. Any proposal, however, would hardly have constituted a true intent to wed. Later that night, Jimi and Monika again went to Ronnie Scott's, where Jimi successfully jammed with Eric Burdon. "He looked better that night," Burdon recalled. They played "Tobacco Road" and "Mother Earth," and Jimi chose to go back to his old role as band guitarist rather than lead singer. After the jam, Jimi spent the night at Monika's hotel.

The next morning—Thursday, September 17—Jimi woke up late.

At around two PM, he had tea in a little garden outside Monika's room. Monika took twenty-nine photographs of him, some with him playing his black Stratocaster, which he called "the black beauty." During the afternoon, they went to a bank, a drugstore, and an antiques market. Jimi bought shirts and trousers. Monika maintained that he was never out of her sight, yet several people, including Mitch Mitchell and Gerry Stickells, reached him by phone at his hotel across town that day where he said he was alone. Mitch said Jimi made plans to meet him later that night to play with Sly Stone but Jimi failed to show at the appointed time. During that afternoon, Jimi and Monika ran into Devon Wilson, who was walking down King's Road. Devon had taken a quick flight over to London; she was surprised to find that Monika had already replaced Kirsten Nefer. Devon invited him to a party that night, and Jimi said he'd come. Monika said nothing, though the icy glare exchanged between she and Devon sucked any warmth out of the air.

Jimi and Monika then drove toward his hotel. While they were stopped in traffic, a man in a car next to Monika rolled his windows down and playfully invited Jimi to tea. Jimi said yes, and he agreed to follow the car, which held the man and two young women. Monika complained about this idea, though it was exactly the kind of spontaneity by which Jimi had lived his entire life.

The young man was Phillip Harvey, the son of an English lord. At around five thirty PM, they all arrived at Harvey's opulent home. The entry to the place led them through a thirty-foot-long hallway lined with mirrors—a true room full of mirrors—and into a large living room. The house was lavishly decorated in a Middle Eastern style, much like Jimi's New York apartment, and he immediately felt comfortable in the grandeur. The fivesome sat on pillows, smoked hash, and drank tea and wine. They chatted about their various careers, and when Harvey asked Jimi what lay ahead, he said he'd be moving to London again. At around 10 PM, Monika became agitated, thinking too little of the conversation had involved her. She stormed out of the house announcing, "I've had enough." Jimi went outside to fetch her. Harvey and the two women could hear her yelling loudly in the street. "You fucking pig" was one of her many angry shouts. In a later court deposition, Harvey testified that it was his impression Monika was jealous of the other women. He went out and requested they quiet down, fearful the police would come to break up the loud row. Jimi and Monika continued to argue for another thirty minutes, though their screaming seemed to subside. At 10:40 PM, Jimi came back in, apologized for Monika's behavior, and left.

Jimi returned to Monika's hotel and took a bath. Afterward, he sat down and wrote the lyrics to a song titled "The Story of Life." An hour later, Monika dropped him off at a party at Pete Kameron's home. She herself did not attend, most likely because the earlier argument had left a chill in her relationship with Jimi. Pete Kameron had helped start Track Records and Jimi complained to him about his many business problems. Also at the party were Devon Wilson, Stella Douglas, and Angie Burdon, Eric's estranged wife. Jimi ate Chinese food, took at least one amphetamine tablet, and, considering his reckless drug use that month, in all likelihood consumed several other drugs. After he had been at the party for thirty minutes, Monika rang the intercom and said she was there to pick him up; Stella Douglas told her to come back later. Monika soon came back. "[Jimi] got angry because she wouldn't leave him alone," Angie Burdon wrote in a letter she later sent Kathy Etchingham. "[Jimi] asked Stella again to put her off, Stella was rude to her and the chick asked to speak to Jimi." Jimi spoke to Monika, and then abruptly left the party with her around 3 AM Friday morning.

Only Monika witnessed Jimi's next few hours, and much of her later account can be considered an attempt to inflate her role as Jimi's alleged fiancée. She claimed to have made him a tuna-fish sandwich before he went to bed—Kathy Etchingham declared that Jimi hated tuna fish, and several witnesses testified that there was no food in the flat. Monika also asserted that at around four in the morning, after drinking some wine, Jimi asked for some sleeping pills. That part of her story is believable: Jimi often took sleeping pills, and after having used amphetamines earlier that night, he would have been wired. If the wisdom of mixing so many different drugs with alcohol was suspect, it was,

nonetheless, a common practice for Jimi, and several times in the previous two weeks he had used similar dangerous combinations. Monika
claimed she didn't give Jimi any sleeping pills, writing in her memoir, "I
persuaded him to wait a little longer, hoping he would fall asleep naturally." At around six in the morning, with Jimi still awake, Monika said
she secretly took a sleeping pill herself and had a short nap.

Monika Dannemann's prescription sleeping medication was a
powerful German brand of sedative called Vesparax. One was supposed
to split each tablet and take only half a tablet—taking an entire pill, as
Monika admitted to, would have put someone in a deep, long sleep;
this casts doubt upon her claim that it was six in the morning before she
took her Vesparax and that she awoke a few hours later. A more likely
scenario is that earlier that morning, around four, she took a pill and
slept through the next events.

With Monika asleep, Jimi was awake in the apartment. Despite
having complained of exhaustion for the prior two weeks—in fact, he'd
been pleading exhaustion for over two years—sleep still eluded Jimi.
Monika said her sleeping medication was on the other side of the room
from the bed; at some point early that morning, Jimi located the Vesparax. There were fifty pills in Monika's supply; he took nine of the
tablets. In all likelihood, he was under the impression that the pills were
weaker than American pharmaceuticals, and desperately needing rest,
he took a handful. If he had intended to kill himself, it was odd that he
left over forty pills in the cabinet, more than enough to have assured an
easy and virtually immediate death.

As it was, the nine pills he swallowed would have been almost
twenty times the recommended dose for a man of Jimi's frame and
weight and would have made him lose consciousness quickly. Sometime during the early morning hours, the combination of the Vesparax,
the alcohol in his system, and the other drugs he'd used that night
caused Jimi to heave up the contents of his stomach. What he spit up—
mostly wine and undigested food—was then aspirated into his lungs,
causing him to stop breathing. A person who was not inebriated would
have had a gag reflex and coughed out the material, but Jimi was well

beyond that. If Monika had been awake herself, and had heard him gasp, she might have cleared his airway. Jimi's reckless mixing of drugs and alcohol had become so commonplace the previous year that Carmen Borrero regularly woke up hearing him gasping and had to clear his windpipe on several occasions.

But there were to be no angelic rescues on the overcast morning of September 18, 1970, and the circumstances and choices that had led Jimi to this hotel room, and this fate, were solely of his making. Though a young woman was sleeping near him, she was a stranger really, and Jimi was, for all practical purposes, alone with his fate. Sometime during the early morning, around the time when the rest of London was waking up, he passed away. As he had predicted just two weeks before in an interview in Denmark, he did not live to see his twenty-eighth birthday. He was twenty-seven years old, and it was just five days short of the four-year anniversary of his first arrival in London.

# CHAPTER TWENTY-SEVEN

# MY TRAIN COMING

LONDON, ENGLAND

*September 1970–April 2004*

*"The express took them away and they lived happily, and funkily, ever after and, uh, excuse me, I think I hear my train coming."*

—JIMI's liner notes to a BUDDY MILES album read at JIMI's funeral

MONIKA DANNEMANN TOLD a number of different versions of what happened when she woke up on Friday, September 18, 1970, and found Jimi Hendrix dead next to her. One story was that Jimi was not in fact deceased, but simply looked ill; Monika dialed up an ambulance, she said, and Jimi passed away en route to the hospital as a result of the incompetence of the medical team. This story, along with several variants, was disproved by a 1994 Scotland Yard investigation. Monika stuck to the scenario even when every shred of evidence indicated her story was an outright lie.

What must have occurred was that Monika woke up groggy from her sleeping medication and found one of the most famous rock stars in the world dead next to her. She did what most twenty-five-year-olds would do in a similar circumstance: She panicked. She didn't know any of Jimi's friends closely but started desperately dialing for those people she'd heard him speak of. After a few phone calls, she finally reached Eric Burdon. Rather than state that Jimi was dead, Monika told Eric that Jimi was "sick, and couldn't wake up."

Burdon later recalled that he urged Monika to summon an ambulance, but how much time passed between their conversation and her call to authorities is unclear; official records indicate an ambulance was called at 11:18 AM. Sometime before the ambulance arrived at 11:27, Burdon showed up at the flat, and finding Jimi already dead, he became concerned about drugs in the room. The drug hysteria of 1970 in London cannot be underestimated; few stars at the time were as closely associated with the drug culture as Jimi—if he were found dead with a stash of drugs in a strange woman's apartment, a substantial witch hunt among his friends and associates would surely have followed.

As he began clearing all drugs and paraphernalia out of the flat, Burdon came upon "The Story of Life," which Jimi had written the previous evening. Reading the lyrics, he assumed Jimi had taken his own life. Though the song did mention Jesus, life, and death, it was not dissimilar to many songs Jimi had written—angelic themes were his most common motif. "At the moment that we die," one line read, "all we know is God is by our side." Many of Burdon's further actions this day would be based on his incorrect assumption that Jimi had killed himself, and this misinformation served only to shroud Jimi's death in more mystery. "I made false statements originally," Burdon admitted. "I simply didn't understand what the situation was. I misread the note: I thought for sure it was a suicide note, so I felt that I should try and help cover that up, and get it over with. Jimi had talked to me about suicide and death a lot, and I knew he was in a hole. I thought it was a goodbye note." Burdon added that he also misunderstood Jimi's relationship with Monika: "I didn't know that this supposed-girlfriend was a stalker-type." On the assumption that Jimi had taken his own life, Burdon cleaned the drugs out of the room with a roadie who had been summoned, and then they all left.

When the ambulance arrived, the emergency workers found Jimi alone in the room; neither Monika nor anyone else was present. Jimi's face was covered with vomit. "It was horrific," driver Reg Jones told writer Tony Brown. "The door was flung wide open, nobody about, just the body on the bed." Jones felt for a pulse but there was none. In one of her accounts, Monika claimed she rode to the hospital with the crew and that she and Jimi chatted during the drive; the two ambulance men denied this, as did two policemen who also arrived on the scene— all four testified that Jimi was alone, and very much dead, and that Monika was nowhere to be seen. Two physicians who were on duty that day at St. Mary Abbots Hospital confirmed that Jimi was dead upon arrival and put his time of death as several hours earlier. Tour manager Gerry Stickells came to the hospital around noon and identified the body. At 12:45 PM, on September 18, 1970, James Marshall Hendrix was officially pronounced dead.

ᗤᗠᗢ

THAT AFTERNOON, JIMI'S public relations agent in England, Les Perrin, issued a statement that Jimi had passed and that an inquest was planned. A hospital spokesperson, however, had already informed the newspapers that Jimi had "died of an overdose," which was then the story that appeared in most media outlets. Newspapers in London and New York trumpeted the death-from-accidental-overdose account with sensationalistic headlines, though some papers instead celebrated what Jimi had created in his short career. Michael Lydon, writing in the *New York Times,* called Jimi "a genius black musician, a guitarist, singer and composer of brilliantly dramatic power. He spoke in gestures as big as he could imagine and create."

In Seattle, Al Hendrix got a phone call that morning from management, and like everyone who loved Jimi, he was stunned to hear the news. Leon Hendrix was still in prison; he was summoned to the warden's office, told the grim news, and sent back to ponder his brother's death alone in his jail cell. When a friend called Noel Redding in his New York hotel room, Noel hung up, assuming it a prank. Mitch

Mitchell had been up most of the night at the Sly Stone jam, waiting all that time for Jimi to show—he'd been home only for an hour when a phone call came with the grim news. Kirsten Nefer was still leaving Jimi messages at the Cumberland Hotel when she found out he was dead.

On Monday, Eric Burdon appeared on a BBC television show, during which he stated, "[Jimi's] death was deliberate. He was happy dying. He died happily and he used the drug[s] to phase himself out of life and go someplace else." Burdon received death threats after this interview—he felt this one appearance forever destroyed his career in England because what he'd said was so shocking to people. Jimi's management and record company wished to discourage any idea of suicide since Warner Bros. Records had a million-dollar accidental-death insurance policy on Jimi.

The official inquest concluded that the cause of death was "inhalation of vomit due to barbiturate intoxication." Vesparax, amphetamine, and Seconal were detected in Jimi's blood, along with alcohol. There were no signs of needle marks on his arms; any narcotics he'd done in the two weeks before his death had not been injected. Surprisingly, the coroner failed to detect cannabis despite evidence that Jimi had smoked significant amounts of marijuana and hashish the day before. From the morgue, Jimi's corpse was sent to a funeral home. His vomit-and-wine-covered clothes were destroyed, and the undertaker dressed him in a flannel logger's shirt to ship his body back to Seattle. For a man who, as an adult, had been such a fashion maven, this was perhaps the greatest indignity of all.

The decision to bury Jimi in Seattle was Al Hendrix's, despite protests from Eric Burdon and others, who said that Jimi had often mentioned he wanted to be buried in London. No will was found, and therefore Al Hendrix became the sole executor of his son's estate and inherited everything Jimi owned. Al was overwhelmed with grief, so family friend Freddie Mae Gautier planned the arrangements.

∽∼∾

JIMI'S FUNERAL WAS held on Thursday, October 1, at Dunlap Baptist Church on Seattle's Rainier Avenue South. Both Noel Redding and Mitch Mitchell came to the service, and Mitch later wrote that the event was such a large-scale production that when Gerry Stickells knocked on his hotel door—to announce it was time to go—Mitch instinctively asked, "What time's the gig?" In fact, a superstar memorial jam was planned after the funeral.

Over two hundred people attended the funeral, and another hundred mourners and curious observers gathered outside the church behind barricades. Twenty-four limousines carried the collected family and friends, and dozens of police officers held up traffic for the procession. Michael Jeffrey had purchased a huge acoustic-guitar-shaped floral display, which dominated the many arrangements. Jeffrey was also at the funeral, as were most of the band's crew and associates, including Gerry Stickells, Eddie Kramer, Buddy Miles, Alan Douglas, Chuck Wein, and press agent Michael Goldstein, who had to keep dispelling rumors that the Beatles were in attendance. A number of New York musicians attended, including Johnny Winter, John Hammond Jr., and Tunde-Ra and Taharqa Aleem. Miles Davis came, and later said he hadn't even attended his own mother's funeral. Devon Wilson flew in from New York, and Melinda Merryweather from Hawaii. Seattle mayor Wes Uhlman attended, which itself was quite a turn of events. When Jimi had left Seattle in 1961 at eighteen, he was essentially run out of town by the police department; now the mayor of the city wore a black suit to honor its most famous "fallen son."

For pallbearers, Freddie Mae Gautier had picked James Thomas, Jimi's manager from his teenage band the Rocking Kings, and Eddie Rye, Donnie Howell, and Billy Burns from the old neighborhood. "Freddie Mae told us not to wear black," Burns recalled. "She said, 'Wear your bright colors, loud and proud.'" As it was, the funeral was a fashion mishmash, with many wearing black suits but others sporting purple jumpsuits or blue jeans and T-shirts.

Jimi's family was there in force, including Al, grandmother Nora, stepmother June, and her children. Leon got a special dispensation from prison officials but had to attend with an armed guard watching over him; he was in handcuffs until right before the ceremony began, when the guard felt sorry enough for him that he was temporarily unshackled. Aunt Delores Hall attended along with all her children, as did Jimi's "Auntie Doortee," Dorothy Harding, and her kids. It had been just over two months since Alice Harding and Dee Hall had stayed up all night with Jimi while he visited every Seattle house he'd ever lived in. Both Alice and Dee recalled sitting in the funeral and wondering if Jimi had indeed suspected his death was imminent, considering his nostalgic behavior that night and his prophetic comments.

Many friends and neighbors were also present, including Arthur and Urville Wheeler, who had been foster parents to Leon and had helped raise Jimi. Some of Jimi's London and New York friends were confused when they heard so many people referring to him as "Buster." Jimi had rarely mentioned this was his childhood nickname.

The ceremony featured an open casket, and Jimi was dressed in the same suit he'd worn at his Toronto drug trial. His beloved hairdresser, James Finney, had flown in for the service and he privately worked on Jimi's precious curls before the ceremony. The already somber mood became heartbreaking when Buddy Miles collapsed in front of the casket weeping, and five men had to drag him away. "Jimi looked so waxen in the coffin," Al Aronowitz recalled. "In life, he always looked like a buccaneer, like a swashbuckler." Almost everyone in the hall was moved to tears when Al Hendrix started rubbing Jimi's forehead and scalp with his knuckles, just as he had done when Jimi was a boy. Al moaned "my boy, my boy," and many in the crowd wept.

The Reverend Harold Blackburn led the service, which featured three gospel songs performed by Pat Wright: "His Eye is on the Sparrow," "Just a Closer Walk with Me," and "The Angels Keep Watch over Me." Leon read a short poem he composed about how Jimi and their mother Lucille now both watched over them all from heaven. The service had an angelic theme, as Freddie Mae Gautier also read the lyrics

to Jimi's song "Angel" and the short liner notes Jimi had contributed to
a Buddy Miles album. The liner notes read, in part: "The express had
made the bend, he is coming on down the tracks, shaking steady, shaking funk, shaking feeling, shaking life . . . the conductor says as we
climb aboard . . . 'We are going to the electric church.' The express took
them away and they lived happily, and funkily, ever after and, uh, excuse me, I think I hear my train coming." Freddie Mae also read a poem
a Garfield student had written: "So long, our Jimi," it read: "You answered the questions we never dared to ask, painted them in colorful
circles and threw them at the world . . . they never touched the ground
but soared up to the clouds."

Most of the assembled crowd went to a short graveside service
that followed at Greenwood Memorial Cemetery in Renton, Washington, but some hurried over to the Seattle Center House, where a musical wake was planned. Jimi had once told a reporter, "When I die, I'm
not going to have a funeral—I'm going to have a jam session. And
knowing me, I'll probably get busted at my own funeral." The jam session happened, though it was a less-than-celebratory event, and no
busts were reported, despite significant drug use among the mourning
musicians. Most of the songs that were played featured Johnny Winter
or Buddy Miles, though Noel and Mitch briefly performed together.
Both said something felt just wrong. "You just couldn't think of having
a jam without Jimi," Noel said.

Much of the attention at the wake was focused on Miles Davis,
who, it was speculated, might play a grand eulogy. *Seattle Times* writer
Patrick MacDonald sat at a table with Davis at the wake. Without being
asked, Miles offered an explanation of his relationship with Jimi: "We,
we both worked together." MacDonald remarked that Jimi and Miles
could have been a tremendous combination. "You could have brought
the jazz to rock, and he could have brought the rock to jazz," MacDonald suggested. "Exactly," Davis replied. Davis said he and Jimi had
planned a concert at Carnegie Hall, but it had never come together.
Someone brought Miles a horn, but he refused to play, saying even he
couldn't add a coda to the musical life Jimi had already created.

✁✁✁

THREE DAYS AFTER Jimi's funeral, Janis Joplin died in Hollywood of a heroin overdose. Nine months after that, Jim Morrison died of a heart attack in Paris. Like Jimi, both Joplin and Morrison were only twenty-seven years old.

Though Jimi's death ended any idea of the Experience reuniting, it only began the fighting over Jimi's estate: Band members and managers kept battling as the years passed. Though Al Hendrix inherited Jimi's assets, Michael Jeffrey informed him that there was little cash in Jimi's account. Al asked attorney Ken Hagood to administer what there was. "When they turned the estate over to us, it had twenty thousand dollars," Hagood recalled. "We had to go about renegotiating a lot of the recording-company relationships. Jeffrey had it all locked up and tied away. That led to a protracted two- or three-year negotiation with Jeffrey that we called 'the final settlement.'" That settlement was anything but final, and when Jeffrey died in a plane crash on March 5, 1973, the settling of the estate became even more complicated. The plane crash that killed Jimi's manager over Spain came after an air-traffic controllers' strike. Some, including Noel Redding, believed that Jeffrey faked his own death and escaped with millions to a deserted island. In those pre-DNA days, Jeffrey's remains were never identified, though some of his luggage was discovered.

With Jeffrey gone, Al Hendrix agreed to let a lawyer named Leo Branton assume control of the legacy. Branton had worked with civil rights pioneer Rosa Parks and also handled the estate of Nat King Cole, and these qualifications were enough for Al to give him near-total control. Branton brought in producer Alan Douglas, who took creative control of Jimi's posthumous releases. Douglas had done a small amount of work with Jimi previously; he would be in charge of Jimi's musical legacy for the next thirteen years.

In February 1971, Devon Wilson fell to her death through a window of New York's Chelsea Hotel. Her heroin addiction had worsened after Jimi's passing; the circumstances of her own death were never determined. Her fall may have been suicide, homicide, or a drug-induced accident. Devon knew as much about Jimi's darkness as anyone.

Not long after the death of Michael Jeffrey, Noel Redding agreed to a $100,000 buyout of all his future rights to royalties from the Experience catalog. Mitch Mitchell agreed to a similar buyout in 1973 for $300,000. At the time, neither man had any inkling of how lucrative compact-disc and DVD technology would later make the estate. None of the other musicians who played with Jimi, including Buddy Miles and Billy Cox, benefited financially from Jimi's record sales or from his estate. Billy Cox had played with Jimi, on and off, for almost a decade, and his friendship back in their army days had been crucial in boosting Jimi's self-confidence. Billy had cowritten a number of songs with Jimi, though he never received credit for them. "In the studio, I think they just put Jimi [on the credits], and we were going to take care of the paperwork later," Cox said. Cox was one of the few who did not become bitter in later years despite his failure to receive the wealth that he was due. "I probably would have played with Jimi for a dollar," he said. In 2004, Buddy Miles began legal action to seek royalties he said he was owed—he claimed that the Band of Gypsys had been a partnership, and thus he deserved royalties from album sales.

In 1972, Diana Carpenter lost her legal bid to have her daughter Tamika declared Jimi's heir. The New York court ruled that since no blood test had ever been taken during Jimi's lifetime, paternity could not be established—this was, of course, before DNA testing made such posthumous evidence a routine matter. In 2002, Carpenter resumed efforts to establish her daughter as an heir. She was not successful. Tamika Carpenter now lives in the Midwest and is the mother of three children of her own. She never met her famous father, but did visit Al Hendrix on at least two occasions.

In the early seventies, attorneys representing James Sundquist were successful in getting a Swedish court to recognize the young man as an heir to Jimi Hendrix—his physical resemblance to Jimi alone was so striking that it was hard for authorities to ignore his claim. That Swedish ruling had no binding power in the United States, however, and Sundquist and his mother filed at least two separate cases seeking a share of Jimi's wealth. As he grew older, Sundquist's kinky hair grew into a huge Afro, the size of which would have undoubtedly made his late father proud. In the late nineties, facing continued legal action, Al Hendrix settled with Sundquist, giving him a million-dollar payout. Sundquist lives in Stockholm and avoids the spotlight.

~~~

BY THE MID-SEVENTIES, attorney Leo Branton and producer Alan Douglas controlled the Jimi Hendrix estate for all practical purposes, and paid Al Hendrix fifty thousand dollars a year plus occasional lump sums. Douglas produced a number of posthumous Hendrix albums, including one release on which he recut instrumental tracks on Jimi's original studio tape and added studio musicians playing new background tracks. By the eighties, sales of the Hendrix back catalog grew dramatically, buoyed by compact-disc technology and renewed interest in Jimi's legend worldwide.

The next decade saw an extraordinary number of deaths among those who had known and loved Jimi. In September 1991, Miles Davis died in Santa Monica, California. In December 1992, Angie Burdon, Eric Burdon's ex-wife, who had been a lover of Jimi's and attended his final party in London, died in a knife fight; she had been addicted to heroin for many years and had been in and out of jail. In July 1996, Chas Chandler passed away as a result of heart problems. After Jimi's death, Chandler managed the rock group Slade for several years, but nothing he did ever equaled the records he had produced during his three years with Jimi. Randy Wolfe, who as a teenager had played in Jimi's early band the Blue Flames, died in 1997 in a swimming accident off Hawaii—for his entire career he had been known as "Randy California," the nickname Jimi had given him. In 1999, Curtis Knight died of prostate cancer. Knight had written one of the first Hendrix biographies, 1974's *Jimi,* which largely argued that Knight was the genius who had discovered Jimi. The handful of inferior recordings Knight made with Jimi were reissued hundreds of times, though Knight said he had not profited from them.

In one of the strangest chapters in the Jimi Hendrix saga, Monika Dannemann, the woman who had been with him on the night he died, took her own life on April 5, 1996. Dannemann had spent the two and a half decades since Jimi's death working as a painter, though her primary subject was Jimi, and many of her ghoulish paintings depicted the two of them in a supernatural embrace. She did many interviews over the years under the persona of Jimi's "widowed fiancée" and told a number of different versions of Jimi's final night, though she steadfastly maintained that he was alive when the ambulance arrived. In 1994, partially urged by Kathy Etchingham, British authorities reopened the case of Jimi's death because Dannemann's story had raised so many questions, including claims of incompetence by medical authorities. That investigation concluded that Jimi was most certainly dead when the ambulance men arrived, that the emergency workers and doctors had done all they could in attempting to revive a dead man, and that much of Dannemann's story was questionable, if not completely false. The next year, Dannemann first published her memoir, *The Inner World of Jimi Hendrix,* which repeated many of her fabrications about Jimi's death. Not long after the publication of the book, Kathy Etchingham filed a defamation complaint against Dannemann and won a judgment. When Dannemann continued to make claims, despite a court order barring her from such assertions, Etchingham took her back to court in April 1996. Etchingham won and Dannemann was declared in contempt, told to stop repeating her falsehoods, and ordered to pay all court costs. Two days later, Dannemann poisoned herself with carbon monoxide piped from the exhaust of her Mercedes. With Monika's death, the only witness to Jimi's demise also went to the grave without ever honestly recounting the events that preceded it.

Though Al Hendrix had hired Leo Branton to run the estate, he began to question that arrangement by the early nineties. On April 16, 1993, Al filed suit against Branton and Alan Douglas in Federal Court in Seattle, seeking to reclaim control of his son's legacy. He was able to fund the expensive litigation only because of a $4.1 million loan from Seattle billionaire Paul Allen, who as a boy had seen Hendrix play in Seattle and had become a huge fan. The protracted legal battle ended in June 1995 with a settlement in which Branton and Douglas gave up any future rights, though Al had to pay the defendants $9 million essentially to buy back control of what he had inherited twenty-five years before. "I am elated," Al said at the time. "Jimi would be happy to know we won this thing and got it all back."

In July 1995, Al created Experience Hendrix, LLC, as the family business and appointed his adopted stepdaughter, Janie Hendrix, to run it. Janie had only met Jimi on four brief occasions during his Seattle concerts, and she was a child then, but Al trusted her. Al also hired his nephew Bob Hendrix, who previously had been an executive at Costco, as a vice president—Bob was one of the only employees of Experience Hendrix, besides Al, who was related to Jimi by blood. Al retained the title of CEO, but Janie and Bob handled the company's daily business.

ᗢᔕᗢ

AL HENDRIX CONTINUED to work as a landscaper through the mid-eighties until heart problems limited his ability to mow lawns and trim bushes. He was a wealthy man by then, but had continued to work more out of habit than need. He seemed to enjoy his public role as Jimi's father, and he conducted many interviews with journalists and accepted numerous honors in the name of his famous son. Years after Jimi's death, he still seemed amazed that his son had created something that had meant so much to so many.

In the early eighties, Al and his second wife, Ayako "June" Jinka Hendrix, separated. They remained legally married until her death at seventy-nine in 1999 but did not live as man and wife again. Al instead had a series of relationships with younger women, several of whom, oddly, had been girlfriends or associates of Lucille. One was Loreen Lockett, Lucille's best friend in junior high. Gail Davis, another of Al's girlfriends, heard Al speak of his ex-wife so often that she accused him of still being in love with Lucille forty years after her death. "He denied it," Davis said, "but the way he denied it, it was clear it was true." In November 1994, when he was seventy-five years old, Al was arrested on charges of domestic violence for striking another girlfriend, who was then pregnant and twenty-five years old. The charges were later dropped; whether the child truly was Al's is still unclear.

Leon Hendrix initially seemed to straighten out his life after his brother's death. He worked for a time at Boeing as a draftsperson and later had a job with a mailing service. He married Christina Narancic in February 1974 and they had six children. One of Leon's sons was born on November 27, Jimi's birthday, and Leon named this child Jimi Jr., seeing the coincidence as a good omen. By the late eighties, Leon was struggling with drugs and alcohol and was convicted in 1989 of a hit-and-run and of telephone harassment. He separated from his wife in 1989 and developed a problem with crack cocaine a few years later. After several attempts, Leon eventually completed rehab successfully in the late nineties. In 2000, he began to play guitar professionally and formed the Leon Hendrix Band.

In 1999, Al self-published his autobiography, *My Son Jimi*. Co-writer Jas Obrecht said that he had no reason to doubt any of Al's stories with one exception: When it came to Al's assertion in his book that Leon Hendrix was not his son, Obrecht thought that story seemed unnatural. "Al just brought that up one day out of the blue," he recalled. "I almost had the impression he had had a meeting or something, and it was important for somebody—somewhere along the line—to get that established."

On April 17, 2002, Al Hendrix passed away of heart failure at the age of eighty-two. He had been in poor health for the last decade of his life, and his death was no surprise to those who had witnessed how frail his once-muscular body had become. Still, Al had managed to outlast his ex-wife Lucille by forty-four years and to outlive three of his children: Jimi, Alfred, and Pamela Hendrix. Alfred and Pamela had both died as adults at relatively young ages. Al's other daughter, Kathy, was still alive in 2005, but lived in a state facility for the blind, as she had all her life. Though she still carried the last name Hendrix, Kathy wanted nothing to do with the family that had abandoned her when she was an infant, born blind.

ᥴᥲᥰᥱ

PATERNITY, LINEAGE, AND family bloodline became a very public debate for the Hendrix family after Al's passing. His estate was valued at around $80 million—the vast majority of this wealth came from ownership of Jimi's copyrights, as Al himself owned little. He left the estate to eleven relations, the largest share going to Janie Hendrix, the stepdaughter he had adopted in 1968. Janie's four brothers and sisters, who were not related to Al by blood, were also included in the will, each receiving around 5 percent. Not a single person from Lucille's side of the family received anything in Al's will. This meant, in essence, that the majority of those who were related to Jimi Hendrix by blood did not, and would not, benefit from his album sales.

The most obvious omission in Al's will was Leon Hendrix, who received only a gold record of Janie's choosing. Leon had been included in all of Al's earlier wills, with a share comparable to that of Janie; only in Al's last will, signed in 1998, was Leon given nothing and Janie bequeathed 48 percent of the Hendrix estate.

Leon had no money of his own to challenge his father's will, but real estate developer Craig Dieffenbach put up several million dollars to contest the validity of the document. Four months after Al's death, Leon sued Janie Hendrix and cousin Bob Hendrix in King County Superior Court seeking to throw out Al's last will and to reinstate the previous will, which gave Leon a fourth of the estate. Leon's suit alleged fraud and "tortious interference," claiming that Janie exerted "undue influence" over their father by convincing Al that Leon wasn't his biological son. "We believe that this was not *Al's* will," argued Leon's attorney Bob Curran, "but that it was essentially *Janie's* will."

The case was already a complex one but was further muddled when Leon was joined in his suit by seven of the relatives who *were* ben-

eficiaries of Al's will—including Janie's own sister Linda Jinka. All argued in court that despite having multimillion-dollar trusts on paper—
Al had set these up back in 1997—they had never received a single
payment and they blamed Janie Hendrix, who oversaw the trusts.
David Osgood, the attorney for those beneficiaries, argued that Experience Hendrix was so poorly run, and Janie's salary was so large
($804,601 in 2001 alone), that the trusts might never pay anything.

Janie and Bob Hendrix steadfastly maintained that they had had
no involvement in setting up Al's wills or trusts and that Al's disinherit-
ing of Leon was as much a surprise to them as it had been to anyone
else. Janie and her attorneys said it was Leon's drug problems in the
nineties that had caused Al to change his will more than anything Janie
had said or done. She argued that Al's final will was valid, and he was, in
fact, videotaped signing it. As for the issue of the trusts, Janie argued
that the legal fees created by Leon's suit, along with company debt from
the original Branton litigation, had prevented the funding of the various trusts, but they would be funded in the future.

At the same time that Leon's case was in pretrial motions, Noel
Redding began his own separate legal action against Experience Hendrix. Noel charged that he had been improperly represented when he
had signed his rights away and that he had been promised a renegotia-
tion of his settlement after Al Hendrix won back the estate. Comment-
ing on his and Mitch's lack of any ongoing share of the Experience's
earnings, Noel said in April 2002, "If Jimi had eight arms he could have
done it without Mitchell and myself." A month later, as he was preparing to file his case, he died suddenly at age fifty-seven from liver disease.

❧

THE LEGAL BATTLE between Leon and Janie Hendrix was long,
complicated, and costly. After almost two years of depositions and motions, the trial began on June 28, 2004, before King County judge Jeffrey Ramsdell and with a packed courtroom. The proceedings were filled
with twists and turns but no surprise was bigger than the eleventh-hour

appearance of Joe Hendrix—the son Al had given up for adoption some fifty years before—asking to be given status in the case and included in his father's estate. Most of the family had not seen Joe for decades; he had spent years in and out of medical facilities and had been brought up by a foster mother. For over a decade, Joe had lived on disability. Once, in the late nineties, he ran into Al Hendrix in a local store. Though they had not seen each other in decades, their recognition was immediate—as both had grown older, the men looked so much alike that they could have been brothers. Al had embraced Joe and said, "My son, my son." That was the extent of their relationship, though Joe argued in court that as Al's offspring, he had as much right to his father's estate as anyone else.

Joe was ordered to undergo DNA testing by Judge Ramsdell; Joe's DNA was compared with a blood sample that Al had given several years earlier when Al suspected he might have impregnated a girlfriend. Joe tested negative, which meant that according to that blood sample from Al, Joe was not Al's child, and Judge Ramsdell denied his claim. Considering the remarkable physical resemblance between the two, many in the courtroom were shocked by the DNA results. "There's something wrong with that blood sample," Joe's friend James Pryor said. "This is just not right."

Leon Hendrix was also ordered to undergo DNA testing, again using Al's sample. When those results came back, Janie Hendrix's attorneys sought to present them to the court as part of the case. Judge Ramsdell ruled, however, that the results—whatever they might be—had no bearing since Leon was legally Al's son by Washington state law; he was, of course, also undeniably Jimi's brother as Lucille had given birth to both of them. The judge ordered the results of Leon's DNA tests sealed. At no time did any of the parties to the case, however, test Leon or Joe's DNA against each other—or against Jimi's, for that matter. Leon claimed that Jimi did not believe that Al was his biological father—whether that was just a suggestion raised by a teenage Jimi in a fit of anger, or some secret truth gleaned from Lucille, can't be known without further testing of the two dead men. Short of DNA results, the

only uncontested lineage in any family is through the maternal line—
and it is certain that Lucille was the mother of Jimi, Leon, Joe, Pamela,
Kathy, and Alfred Hendrix.

The legal battle between Leon and Janie went on for three months
and saw testimony from many of the principals in the family. Delores
Hall was the first witness. At eighty-four years old, it was no surprise
that she needed a walker to reach the witness stand. Delores testified
that Al had told her directly that he would take care of Leon in his will.
Delores, who had much to do with Jimi's upbringing, never benefited
financially from her famous nephew's success, and instead had lived off
of social security benefits. Judge Ramsdell's purview, however, was not
to determine whom Jimi would have supported—the trial was, instead,
to make sure that the wishes of Al Hendrix had been carried out. The
primary legal question was whether Al's will was valid, and whether Al
understood that he was leaving Leon out. As for whether Jimi would
have wanted his brother to benefit from the estate, on this point every
one of Jimi's childhood acquaintances, to a man or woman, was certain. "*Jimi* would have wanted Leon included and taken care of," said
Jimmy Williams, who also testified in the trial. "There's absolutely no
doubt about it."

Judge Ramsdell handed down his decision on September 24,
2004—a week after the thirty-fifth anniversary of Jimi's death. An over-
flow crowd heard the verdict in the King County Courthouse. What no
witness in the trial had mentioned was that this same building had been
the site of Lucille and Al's marriage vows, the place where they divorced, and the place where they gave four of their children away to the
state. It was also the place where Judge Ramsdell, in a complicated
thirty-five-page decision, upheld Al's will and denied Leon's claims.
While the judge agreed with some of Leon's charges—that to a degree
Janie had exerted influence over her father—he found that Leon's drug
struggles, and frequent demands for money, may have given Al reason
to leave Leon out of the will without influence from Janie. At the end
of the trial, Leon was left with nothing but the one gold record Janie

had selected and a huge legal bill. In early 2005, Leon began an appeal of Judge Ramsdell's decision.

In the separate matter of the beneficiaries who were in Al's will, Judge Ramsdell ruled that questions about financial impropriety were great enough that Janie Hendrix was to be removed as trustee for those trusts and a separate independent party appointed. Janie was also ordered to pay the beneficiaries' attorney fees for that portion of the case.

∽∾∾

THOUGH THE STRUGGLE between Leon and Janie revolved around money and the expectation of inheritance, there was at least one ancillary issue that arose during the proceedings that had nothing to do with money—it had to do with burial spots. Al had initially been buried in a grave next to Jimi in Greenwood Memorial Park. Several months later, on the eve of the sixtieth anniversary of Jimi's birth, the final remains of both Al and Jimi were moved to a new $1 million, thirty-foot-high granite memorial that was a hundred yards north of their original gravesites. Thirty-year-old caskets frequently fall apart when moved; in Jimi's case, a protective cement barrier—installed originally to prevent grave robbers—kept his remains intact. The exhumation occurred at night, when the cemetery was closed to the public. Because the remains were moved within the grounds of the cemetery—rather than taken outside it—Janie Hendrix did not need, or seek, approval from the rest of the family. When Leon found out about the exhumation of his brother from a reporter months later, his lawyers sent a letter of protest to Janie's attorneys, but once the bodies were moved and encased in the new granite structure, the point was moot. Leon objected to the fact that so much money had been spent on a new memorial when Lucille, his and Jimi's mother, was still in a pauper's grave without even a headstone.

Janie's attorneys wrote back and said that Al Hendrix had never made any dispensation for Lucille's headstone and that Al had not wanted Lucille included in the new memorial. This assertion seemed to be in contradiction to at least two pieces of evidence: When Al had signed the contract with the cemetery for the new memorial, he listed Lucille as one of those he wished included in the crypt; Delores Hall also testified that Al had told her he would make sure Lucille had a proper headstone. "All that money, and she doesn't even have a marker," Delores said. "That the mother of Jimi Hendrix doesn't even have a headstone is nothing less than a sin."

The only marker for the grave of Lucille Hendrix remains the single welfare brick reading MITCHELL, the name of her second husband whom she was only married to for a matter of days. There is no indication that the grave holds the mother of Jimi Hendrix, the same man who lies interred next to his father on the other side of the cemetery in a thirty-foot-tall memorial.

# LONG BLACK
# CADILLAC

*"Roy became rich and famous because of his broom guitar.*
*People would come from all over to hear him play. He became so*
*rich that he drove around in a long, black Cadillac."*
—one of SHIRLEY HARDING'S bedtime stories to a young JIMI HENDRIX

WHEN AL HENDRIX died in April 2002, his funeral service was held
at the Mt. Zion Baptist Church in Seattle's Central District. The ceremony featured a slide show of photos of Jimi, Al, Leon, and the rest of
the relations, though Jimi was by far the main focus of the slides—one
attendee commented that it felt more like Jimi's funeral than Al's. Shel-
don Reynolds, the former guitar player with Earth, Wind & Fire as well
as the husband of Al's adopted daughter, Janie, played a poignant version of "Angel," an appropriate song for the family history: The lyrics
to this tune had been read at Jimi's funeral, and Jimi had written the
song to describe the spiritual comfort he felt at knowing his mother was
looking down upon him from heaven. The funeral was particularly
tense because Leon and Janie Hendrix were already battling over Al's

estate. Both spoke to the crowd in the church, though they did not speak to each other. When Leon rose to address the crowd, he struggled to keep his composure. "It's been a long, hard road for the Hendrix family," he said. Those words were surely some of the few that no one in the larger fractured family could contest.

After the ceremony, a procession of two hundred cars, escorted by motorcycle police officers, left the church and headed toward Greenwood Memorial Cemetery fifteen miles south. Though it hadn't specifically been planned this way, the route of Al's procession was roughly the same journey that Jimi's hearse had taken thirty-two years earlier. The route cut through the heart of the Central District, Seattle's traditional African American community, which had grown tremendously in the sixty years since Jimi's birth, back when each family knew every other family, and when Buster Hendrix was a latchkey kid in the midst of it all. The winding journey, for both Al and Jimi's processions, traveled the length of a neighborhood that for the first eighteen years of Jimi's life represented his entire known universe.

It went past Washington Hall, the dance hall where back in 1941 a pretty sixteen-year-old girl named Lucille Jeter had met Al Hendrix at a Fats Waller concert and liked the way he danced. It went past the home where Delores Hall had once lived with Lucille, her brother-in-law Al, and the new baby that Delores nicknamed Buster. It went past several of the dozens of run-down apartments, boardinghouses, and cheap hotels where the young family had lived in their early days. It went close to the still-standing Rainier Vista Housing Project, where the Hendrixes had lived in a two-room apartment and where Jimi and Leon had watched their brother Joe leave the house for the last time. It went past the site of an old neighborhood movie theater where, as a ten-year-old, Jimi had watched *Flash Gordon* serials for a dime on weekends and dreamed of outer space. And when the route neared the Rainier Vista Housing Project, it was just a block away from the apartment of Dorothy Harding, where Jimi used to fall asleep to bedtime stories of Roy, Audrey, and Bonita, the fairy-tale characters who always did right and, eventually, found fame and wealth.

The cars passed directly in front of Garfield High School, a storied institution that a newspaper writer in 1970 actually suggested would have been a more apt location for Jimi's funeral than a church. Across from Garfield sat a fried chicken stand that forty years before had been a hamburger joint, and it was there that Jimi had begged for leftover burgers at the stroke of midnight when the stand closed. The hearses went right past two clubs where Jimi had played with early bands, finding in his guitar a pleasure that transported him beyond his circumstances, and that opened up a beauty he had only imagined. And those long black cars went right near a site that had once held Sick's Stadium, the baseball park that stood long enough to see both Elvis Presley and Jimi Hendrix perform on the same stage—the most famous white man in rock 'n' roll, followed, just fifteen years later, by the most famous African American to ever master the guitar. And though the route did not go near it, downtown Seattle now had its own Hendrix shrine as billionaire Paul Allen—who had seen Jimi's Seattle concerts as a boy—had spent over $280 million constructing the Experience Music Project, which opened in 2000 and featured an entire gallery of Hendrix artifacts.

Eventually, the journey of the funeral procession led out of Seattle proper and up a winding road to Renton and Greenwood Memorial Park. Upon Jimi's death, Al had picked this cemetery because on his landscaper's wages—and with Jimi's estate in disarray in 1970—it was cheaper than cemeteries in Seattle and all Al could afford. Yet Jimi wasn't the first member of his family to be interred at Greenwood: His mother had been buried there in 1958 in a pauper's grave. Jimi's funeral came only twelve years after that of his mother—though much had happened in that short span.

Over those twelve years grass had grown over Lucille's small welfare marker and her burial plot was lost to history. At Jimi's funeral, a few in the immediate family had gathered in a circle and said a prayer over where they suspected Lucille was buried. "We just stood over a patch of lawn near the cemetery gate where we thought she was," Leon recalled. That spot was off by two hundred yards, as Lucille's grave was to the north and west of the cemetery's front gate, among the vast acreage of tombstones in the center of the giant graveyard.

Lucille's final resting place was, remarkably, just forty paces east of where Jimi was buried between 1970 and 2002—his original, almost-final resting place. When Jimi's grave was moved in 2002, the new site was located in a previously undeveloped corner of the cemetery, away from all other gravesites. Jimi's original 1970 grave, however, was just a stone's throw from Lucille's, an unplanned and undiscovered twist of fate in the ten-acre cemetery. The nearness of mother and child was a strictly random happenstance, but one that Jimi Hendrix, with a sly and knowing smile, would have thought was preordained.

# SOURCE NOTES

Writing this book entailed conducting more than 325 interviews over the course of four years. To avoid fifty pages of source notes reading "from an interview with the author," each chapter notation lists my interview subjects for that particular section, with the year or years of my interviews noted on the first mention.

## PROLOGUE

Author interviews with Solomon Burke, 2002; Kathy Etchingham, 2001, 2002, 2003, 2004; Tony Garland, 2004; and Noel Redding, 2001, 2002, 2003. Noel Redding first told me the Liverpool story and others gave more insight into this specific day.

## CHAPTER ONE: BETTER THAN BEFORE

Author interviews with Joyce Craven, 2004; Delores Hall Hamm, 2002, 2003, 2004, 2005; Dorothy Harding, 2003, 2004; Al Hendrix, 1987, 1990, 1991; Diane Hendrix, 2002, 2003, 2004, 2005; Leon Hendrix, 2001, 2002, 2003, 2004, 2005; Loreen Lockett, 2003; Betty Jean Morgan, 2002, 2003, 2004; and James Pryor, 2002, 2003, 2004. For further background on Seattle's Jackson Street scene I'd recommend Esther Hall Mumford's *Calabash: A Guide to the History, Culture, and Art of African Americans in Seattle and King County* (Ananse Press, 1993); Quintard Taylor's *The Forging of a Black Community: Seattle's Central District from 1870 through the Civil Rights Era* (University of Washington Press,

1994); and Paul DeBarros's *Jackson Street After Hours: The Roots of Jazz in Seattle* (Sasquatch Books, 1993). For more on Jimi Hendrix's early days look to Al Hendrix's autobiography *My Son Jimi* (AliJas Enterprises, 1999) written with Jas Obrecht; and Mary Willix's *Voices From Home* (Creative Forces Publishing, 1990). Willix's book can be ordered from creativeforcespub@earthlink.net.

## CHAPTER TWO: BUCKET OF BLOOD

Author interviews with Delores Hall Hamm; Dorothy Harding; Al Hendrix; Diane Hendrix; Joe Hendrix, 2003, 2004; Leon Hendrix; Loreen Lockett; James Pryor; Jimmy Ogilvy, 2004; Bob Summerrise, 2003, 2004; and Chief Tom Vickers, 2004. In the text of Delores Hall's letter to Al Hendrix, page 23, she misspells Al's name as "Allan," which I've corrected in my text.

## CHAPTER THREE: OVER AVERAGE IN SMARTNESS

Author interviews with Kathy Etchingham; Delores Hall Hamm; Dorothy Harding; Al Hendrix; Diane Hendrix; Joe Hendrix; Leon Hendrix; Loreen Lockett; and James Pryor.

## CHAPTER FOUR: THE BLACK KNIGHT

Author interviews with Pernell Alexander, 2002, 2003, 2004, 2005; Booth Gardner, 2003, 2004; Delores Hall Hamm; Alice Harding, 2003; Dorothy Harding; Ebony Harding, 2003; Melvin Harding, 2003; Pat Harding, 2004; Frank Hatcher, 2004; Al Hendrix; Diane Hendrix; Joe Hendrix; Leon Hendrix; Terry Johnson, 2004; Loreen Lockett; James Pryor; Arthur Wheeler, 2003; Doug Wheeler, 2003, 2004; Urville Wheeler, 2003; and Jimmy Williams, 2002, 2003, 2004, 2005.

## CHAPTER FIVE: JOHNNY GUITAR

Author interviews with Pernell Alexander; Joe Allen, 2004; Cornell Benson, 2004; Ernestine Benson, 2003, 2004; Henry Brown, 2002; Diana Carpenter, 2003, 2004; Sammy Drain, 2002, 2003, 2004; Frank Fidler, 2003; Booth Gardner; Carmen Goudy, 2003, 2004; Delores Hall Hamm; Frank Hanawalt, 2004; Alice Harding; Dorothy Harding; Ebony Harding; Melvin Harding; Frank

Hatcher; Diane Hendrix; Leon Hendrix; Terry Johnson; James Pryor; Jimmy Williams; and Mary Willix, 2001, 2002, 2003, 2004, 2005.

## CHAPTER SIX: TALL COOL ONE

Author interviews with Pernell Alexander; Anthony Atherton, 2004; Cornell Benson; Ernestine Benson; Ernie Catlett, 2004; Sammy Drain; Bill Eisiminger, 2003; Lester Exkano, 2004; Frank Fidler; Carmen Goudy; Delores Hall Hamm; Frank Hanawalt; Alice Harding; Dorothy Harding; Ebony Harding; Melvin Harding; Frank Hatcher; Diane Hendrix; Leon Hendrix; John Horn, 2004; Terry Johnson; Jim Manolides, 2004; Betty Jean Morgan; Jimmy Ogilvy; James Pryor; Luther Rabb, 2003, 2004; Gordon Shoji, 2003; Bob Summerrise; Mike Tagawa, 2003; Jimmy Williams; and Mary Willix.

## CHAPTER SEVEN: SPANISH CASTLE MAGIC

Author interviews with Pernell Alexander; Anthony Atherton; Jamie Campbell, 2004; Larry Coryell, 2003; Rich Dangel, 2002; Sammy Drain; Lester Exkano; Carmen Goudy; Delores Hall Hamm; Leon Hendrix; Terry Johnson; Jerry Miller, 2004; Betty Jean Morgan; Pat O'Day, 2002, 2003, 2004, 2005; Jimmy Ogilvy; Buck Ormsby, 2004; Luther Rabb; Denny Rosencrantz, 2004; Jimmy Williams; and Mary Willix. Pat O'Day's own memoir is *It Was All Just Rock'-n'-Roll II* (Ballard Publishing, 2003).

## CHAPTER EIGHT: BROTHER WILD

Author interviews with Billy Cox, 2003; Dee Hall, 2003, 2004; Delores Hall Hamm; Dorothy Harding; Terry Johnson; and Betty Jean Morgan.

## CHAPTER NINE: HEADHUNTER

Author interviews with Solomon Burke; Billy Cox; Terry Johnson; Johnny Jones, 2004; Bobby Rush, 2003; James Pryor; and Alphonso Young, 2004;

## CHAPTER TEN: HARLEM WORLD

Author interviews with Taharqa Aleem, 2002, 2003, 2004; Tunde-Ra Aleem, 2002, 2003, 2004; Rosa Lee Brooks, 2003, 2004; Billy Cox; Steve Cropper,

2003; Terry Johnson; Johnny Jones; Martha Reeves, 2003; Glen Willings, 2003; and Alphonso Young. The quotes from Little Richard, pages 114 and 115, are from Charles White's *The Life and Times of Little Richard: The Quasar of Rock* (Da-Capo, 1994). For a further exploration of Jimi's blues influences I'd recommend Charles Shaar Murray's *Crosstown Traffic* (Faber and Faber, 1989).

## CHAPTER ELEVEN: DREAM IN TECHNICOLOR

Author interviews with Taharqa Aleem; Tunde-Ra Aleem; David Brigati, 2003; Rosa Lee Brooks; Diana Carpenter; Ed Chalpin, 2003, 2004, 2005; Billy Cox; Joey Dee, 2003; Johnny Jones; Mr. Wiggles, 2004; Bernard Purdie, 2003; Mike Quashie, 2003, 2004; Glen Willings; and Lonnie Youngblood, 2003.

## CHAPTER TWELVE: MY PROBLEM CHILD

Author interviews with Taharqa Aleem; Tunde-Ra Aleem; Diana Carpenter; Paul Caruso, 2002; Ed Chalpin; Billy Cox; Janice Hargrove, 2004; Richie Havens, 2004; Linda Keith, 2004; Mike Quashie; Bill Schweitzer, 2003; Danny Taylor, 2004; and Lonnie Youngblood.

## CHAPTER THIRTEEN: DYLAN BLACK

Author interviews with Taharqa Aleem; Tunde-Ra Aleem; Paul Caruso; Ed Chalpin; Bill Donovan, 2004; John Hammond, 2003; Janice Hargrove; Richie Havens; Kiernan Kane, 2004; Linda Keith; Buzzy Linhart, 2004; Ellen McIlwaine, 2004; Andrew Loog Oldham, 2003; Mike Quashie; Danny Taylor; and Lonnie Youngblood.

## CHAPTER FOURTEEN: WILD MAN OF BORNEO

Author interviews with Keith Altham, 2004; Brian Auger, 2003; Ernestine Benson; Vic Briggs, 2003, 2004; Eric Burdon, 2003; Kathy Etchingham; Kim Fowley, 2003; Tony Garland; Terry Johnson; Linda Keith; Andrew Loog Old-ham; Noel Redding; Mike Ross, 2002; and Trixie Sullivan, 2004. For further reading on London in the sixties I'd recommend Shawn Levy's *Ready, Steady, Go!* (Doubleday, 2002); Harriet Vyner's *Groovy Bob* (Faber and Faber, 1999); and Andrew Loog Oldham's *Stoned* (St. Martin's, 2002). There are several memoirs written by Hendrix's close associates including Kathy Etchingham's *Through Gypsy Eyes*

(Victor Gollancz, 1998); Noel Redding and Carol Appleby's *Are You Experienced?* (Fourth Estate, 1991); and Mitch Mitchell and John Platt's *Inside the Experience* (Pyramid Books, 1990). For more information on the Experience's concert tours see the excellent series of books by Ben Valkhoff, *Eyewitness* (Up From the Skies, 1997); or refer to back issues of *Univibes* magazine (www.Univibes.com).

## CHAPTER FIFTEEN: FREE FEELING

Author interviews with Lou Adler, 2002; Keith Altham; Brian Auger; Vic Briggs; Eric Burdon; Neville Chesters, 2004; Stanislas De Rola, 2004; Kathy Etchingham; Marianne Faithfull, 2002; Tony Garland; Linda Keith; Roger Mayer, 2002; Andrew Loog Oldham; Noel Redding; Terry Reid, 2004; Mike Ross; Trixie Sullivan; and Pete Townshend, 2004.

## CHAPTER SIXTEEN: RUMOR TO LEGEND

Author interviews with Lou Adler; Keith Altham; Brian Auger; Paul Body, 2003; Vic Briggs; Eric Burdon; Jack Casady, 2003; Neville Chesters; Steve Cropper; Stanislas De Rola; Pamela Des Barres, 2004; Kathy Etchingham; Tony Garland; Michael Goldstein, 2004; Richie Havens; Jorma Kaukonen, 2003; Howard Kaylan, 2003; Lee Kiefer, 2004; Al Kooper, 2002; Eddie Kramer, 2002, 2003; Roger Mayer; Buddy Miles, 2003; Jerry Miller; Andrew Loog Oldham; D.A. Pennebaker, 2002; Noel Redding; Terry Reid; Trixie Sullivan; Peter Tork, 2003; and Pete Townshend.

## CHAPTER SEVENTEEN: BLACK NOISE

Author interviews with Taharqa Aleem; Tunde-Ra Aleem; Eric Burdon; Paul Caruso; Ed Chalpin; Neville Chesters; Kathy Etchingham; Tony Garland; Michael Goldstein; Lee Kiefer; Al Kooper; Eddie Kramer; Buzzy Linhart; Roger Mayer; Noel Redding; Trixie Sullivan; Dallas Taylor, 2004; and Paul Williams, 2004.

## CHAPTER EIGHTEEN: NEW MUSIC SPACEQUAKE

Author interviews with Cynthia Albritton, 2003; Ernestine Benson; Eric Burdon; Jack Casady; Lester Chambers, 2003; Neville Chesters; Kathy Etchingham; Tony Garland; Michael Goldstein; Jess Hansen, 2002, 2003, 2004; Vickie Heater, 2002; Leon Hendrix; Jorma Kaukonen; Eddie Kramer; Buzzy Linhart; Patrick

MacDonald, 2002; Roger Mayer; Pat O'Day; Noel Redding; Peter Riches, 2003; Trixie Sullivan; and Paul Williams.

## CHAPTER NINETEEN: THE MOON FIRST

Author interviews with Taharqa Aleem; Tunde-Ra Aleem; Terry Bassett, 2003; Carmen Borrero, 2003, 2004; Eric Burdon; Paul Caruso; Kathy Etchingham; Tony Garland; Michael Goldstein; Boyd Grafmyre, 2004; Diane Hendrix; Leon Hendrix; Deering Howe, 2004; Eddie Kramer; Buzzy Linhart; Roger Mayer; Betsy Morgan, 2003; Pat O'Day; Roz Payne, 2004; Noel Redding; Trixie Sullivan; and Herbie Worthington, 2004

## CHAPTER TWENTY: ELECTRIC CHURCH MUSIC

Author interviews with Taharqa Aleem; Tunde-Ra Aleem; Carmen Borrero; Eric Burdon; Diana Carpenter; Paul Caruso; Kathy Etchingham; Tony Garland; Michael Goldstein; Leon Hendrix; Deering Howe; Eddie Kramer; Buck Munger, 2004; Pat O'Day; Noel Redding; and Trixie Sullivan.

## CHAPTER TWENTY-ONE: HAPPINESS AND SUCCESS

Author interviews with Taharqa Aleem; Tunde-Ra Aleem; Carmen Borrero; Eric Burdon; Kathy Etchingham; Michael Goldstein; Deering Howe; Colette Mimram, 2004, 2005; Pat O'Day; Noel Redding; Billy Rich, 2003; Trixie Sullivan; Juma Sultan, 2004; Johnny Winter, 2003; and Herbie Worthington.

## CHAPTER TWENTY-TWO: GYPSY, SUN, AND RAINBOWS

Author interviews with Taharqa Aleem; Tunde-Ra Aleem; Al Aronowitz, 2003, 2004; Carmen Borrero; Eric Burdon; Billy Cox; Michael Goldstein; Richie Havens; Deering Howe; Eddie Kramer; Colette Mimram; Pat O'Day; Roz Payne; Noel Redding; Billy Rich; Hank Ryan, 2004; Trixie Sullivan; Juma Sultan; Dallas Taylor; and Pete Townshend.

## CHAPTER TWENTY-THREE: KING IN THE GARDEN

Author interviews with Taharqa Aleem; Tunde-Ra Aleem; Al Aronowitz; Carmen Borrero; Eric Burdon; Billy Cox; Michael Goldstein; Ronnie Hammon, 2004; Deering Howe; Eddie Kramer; Buddy Miles; Colette Mimram; Pat O'Day;

Luther Rabb; Noel Redding; Terry Reid; Ronnie Spector, 2004; Trixie Sullivan; Juma Sultan; and Johnny Winter. Bill Graham's book is *Bill Graham Presents* (Doubleday, 1992) written by Graham and Robert Greenfield.

## CHAPTER TWENTY-FOUR: MAGIC BOY

Author interviews with Danny Fiala, 2002; Dee Hall; Delores Hall Hamm; Eddy Hall, 2004; Alice Harding; Dorothy Harding; Pat Harding; Deering Howe; Linda Jinka, 2003; Eddie Kramer; Betty Jean Morgan; Colette Mimram; Pat O'Day; Carlos Santana, 2002; Trixie Sullivan; Emily Touraine, 2004; and Juma Sultan.

## CHAPTER TWENTY-FIVE: WILD BLUE ANGEL

Author interviews with Taharqa Aleem; Tunde-Ra Aleem; Carmen Borrero; Diana Carpenter; Billy Cox; Kathy Etchingham; Ken Hagood, 2003, 2004; Richie Havens; Deering Howe; Eddie Kramer; Bob Levine, 2003, 2004; Melinda Merryweather, 2002, 2003, 2004; Colette Mimram; Kirsten Nefer, 2003; Pat O'Day; Les Potts, 2005; Noel Redding; Trixie Sullivan; Chuck Wein, 2004; Dindy Wilson, 2003; and Johnny Winter. Tony Brown's *Hendrix: The Final Days* (Rogan House, 1997) is an excellent source of more details on Jimi's last week.

## CHAPTER TWENTY-SIX: THE STORY OF LIFE

Author interviews with Keith Altham; Eric Burdon; Billy Cox; Kathy Etchingham; Deering Howe; Linda Keith; Bob Levine; Colette Mimram; Kirsten Nefer; Noel Redding; and Trixie Sullivan.

## CHAPTER TWENTY-SEVEN: MY TRAIN COMING

Author interviews with Taharqa Aleem; Tunde-Ra Aleem; Keith Altham; Al Aronowitz; Eric Burdon; Billy Burns, 2003; Diana Carpenter; Billy Cox; Bob Curran, 2002, 2003, 2004; Gail Davis, 2003; Craig Dieffenbach, 2002, 2003, 2004; Kathy Etchingham; Ken Hagood; Dee Hall; Delores Hall Hamm; John Hammond; Diane Hendrix; Joe Hendrix; Leon Hendrix; Deering Howe; Linda Jinka; Eddie Kramer; Bob Levine; Loreen Lockett; Lance Losey, 2002, 2003, 2004; Patrick MacDonald; Melinda Merryweather; Colette Mimram; Kirsten Nefer; Jas Obrecht, 2003, 2004; David Osgood, 2002, 2003, 2004; Noel Redding; Eddie Rye, 2003; Trixie Sullivan; Chuck Wein; Jimmy Williams; and Johnny Winter.

# ACKNOWLEDGMENTS

Writing *Room Full of Mirrors* was only possible because of the assistance of several hundred of Jimi Hendrix's friends, family, and associates who took time to sit for numerous interviews, and who trusted me to tell this story—you will find their names in the text and the source notes. Additionally there were dozens of people who provided interviews, documents, recordings, photographs, research assistance, a spare cabin, and, at times, just advice, and many of their names do not appear in the text. They include, in alphabetical order: Fred Accuardi, Gail Accuardi, Melissa Albin, Andy Aledort, Julian Alexander, Ken Anderson, Paula Balzer, Jim Barber, Joseph Barber, Jen Bergman, Harry Blaisure, Franklin Bruno, Peter Callaghan, Kanashibushan Carver, Bettie Cross, Cathy Cross, Herb Cross, Steve DeJarnett, Dave DePartee, David DeSantis, Don DeSantis, Craig Dieffenbach, Patrick Donovan, Melissa Duane, David Dubois, Sean Egan, Joe Ehrbar, Kim Emmons, the Experience Music Project, Lisa Farnham, Jason Fine, Erik Flannigan, Elmo Freidlander, Jim Fricke, Chris Fry, Gillian G. Gaar, Donna Gaines, Jeff Gelb, Danny Glatman, Kevin Goff, Fred Goodman, Nancy Guppy, Joe Hadlock, Manny Hadlock, Elaine Hayes, Kiera Hepford, Pete Howard, Louie Husted, Josh Jacobson, Larry Jacobson, Ted Johnson, Remi Kabaka, Susan Karlsen, Corey Kilgannon, Jeff Kitts, Ed Kosinski, Harvey Kubernick, Brenda Lane, Gretchen Lauber, Shawn

Levy, O. Yale Lewis, Alan Light, Patrick MacDonald, Geoff MacPherson, Maureen Mahon, Yazid Manou, Tracy Marander, Cindy May, Catherine Mayhew, Bob Mehr, Mike Mettler, Bob Miller, Curtis Minato, Damian Mulinix, Bill Murphy, Theo Nassar, Marshall Nelson, Eddie Noble, David Osgood, Doug Palmer, Peter Philbin, Chris Phillips, Marietta Phillips, Chloe Porter, Perry Porter, Ann Powers, Dominic Priore, Christine Ragasa, Dale Riveland, Patrick Robinson, Steven Roby, Evelyn Roehl, Jasmin Rogg, Phil Rose, James Rotondi, Robert Santelli, Seattle Public Schools, Deborah Semer, Gary Serkin, Christina Shinkle, Clint Shinkle, Eric Shinkle, Martha Shinkle, Neal Shinkle, Lisa Shively, Pete Sikov, Matt Smith, Megan Snyder-Camp, Sarah Sternau, Gene Stout, Denise Sullivan, Cid Summers, Alison Thorne, Eleanor Toews, Brad Tolinski, Jaan Uhelszki, Cara Valentine, Chief Tom Vickers, Abby Vinyard, Steve Vosburgh, Bill Vourvoulias, Bruce Wagman, Michele Wallace, Alice Wheeler, Tappy Wright, Jason Yoder, and Bob Zimmerman. I also wish to acknowledge Polly Friedlander and the Willard R. Espy Literary Foundation (www.espyfoundation.org), whose support allowed a significant portion of this book to be written in the natural beauty of Oysterville, Washington.

There is an active community of Jimi Hendrix fans around the world and many of them assisted in my effort including Ray Rae Goldman, whose commitment to the Hendrix family over the years, and skill in tracking down the characters in this story, is unmatched; Jess Hansen, one of the original Seattle fans from when he was a child shaking Jimi's hand backstage; Keith Dion, the steady guitar who powered Noel Redding's last band; Neal Skok, with the magical basement; and Jas Obrecht, who kindly shared material from his own research. Noel Redding and Kathy Etchingham were particularly important for their early support of this book—Noel's death brought a dark sadness to many, including this author. Leon Hendrix, Delores Hall Hamm, and several other Hendrix and Jeter family members assisted me with photographs, leads, and contacts. Many of Jimi's Seattle friends and schoolmates also provided extensive help, particularly Jimmy Williams—who has shown five decades of loyalty to his friend Jimi Hendrix—and Mary Willix, a good friend of mine and a diehard Garfield bulldog for all time.

My e-mail contact for any sources with additional information for future updates is charlesrcross@aol.com. Any addendum to this manuscript will be posted on www.charlesrcross.com, where you can also view a schedule of readings and lectures, and learn more about my other books.

My literary agent Sarah Lazin was an indispensable advocate for this project, as were Hyperion editor Peternelle Van Arsdale, Hodder editors Rowena Webb and Helen Coyle, and the supportive staffs at both Hyperion and Hodder. Several people read my manuscript in progress and for that I owe special thanks to Peter Blecha, Carla De-Santis, Joe Guppy, John Keister, Carl Miller, Matt Smith, and my son Ashland Cross, who even at his youthful age has a keen appreciation for the power of Hendrix's "All Along the Watchtower" to shake, rattle, and roll both a dad at the steering wheel, and a little boy in the backseat. "Louder, Dad," he says. "Louder."

*—Charles R. Cross*
*April 2005*

# INDEX

Mh

9-105